In the Beginning

By the same author

No, I'm not Afraid
Pencil Letter
Grey is the Colour of Hope

IRINA RATUSHINSKAYA
In the Beginning

Translated by Alyona Kojevnikov

ALFRED A. KNOPF NEW YORK

1991

THIS IS A BORZOI BOOK
PUBLISHED BY ALFRED A. KNOPF, INC.

Copyright © 1990 by Alyona Kojevnikov
Poetry translations copyright © 1990 by David McDuff
All rights reserved under International and Pan-American Copyright
Conventions. Published in the United States by Alfred A. Knopf, Inc.,
New York. Distributed by Random House, Inc., New York.
Translation from an unpublished Russian-language manuscript by Irina
Ratushinskaya. Copyright by Seahorse, Inc. All rights reserved.
This translation originally published in Great Britain by Hodder and
Stoughton Limited, London, in 1990.

Library of Congress Cataloging-in-Publication Data
Ratushinskaia, Irina.
In the beginning / by Irina Ratushinskaya: translated by Alyona
Kojevnikov.—1st American ed.
p. cm.
Translated from Russian
ISBN 0-394-57141-X
1. Ratushinskaia, Irina—Biography.   2. Poets. Russian—20th
century—Biography.   3. Women prisoners—Soviet Union—Biography
4. Political prisoners—Soviet Union—Biography.   I. Title.
PG3485.5.A875Z468   1991
891.71'44—dc20
[B]   90-52867
                                                                         CIP

Manufactured in the United States of America
FIRST AMERICAN EDITION

Poems

In the
Beginning

Chapter One

"Granny, have I been alive for a thousand days?"

Grandmother looks at me long and attentively, and I begin to feel uneasy. Have I asked something I shouldn't have? Now, why didn't I just keep my mouth shut? I wasn't meaning to say anything out of turn, and I have none of that precocious wisdom which Grandmother suspects because of my question. The thing is, I heard the word 'thousand' for the first time today, and understood that it meant an awful lot. Not that I can really visualise up to ten, even, but that's beside the point. All I want to know is whether I have existed for an awfully long time, or not. In the meantime, Grandmother engages in mental arithmetic, and finally comes up with the results: "No, you're not a thousand days old yet. Now, when such and such comes to pass . . ."

But that's beyond my comprehension. The future doesn't exist: tomorrow, or the day after – all that is so far, far away. But I've always been, haven't I? Or . . . ? Grandmother says . . . but no, no! I don't believe her! Always, always, always!

That's why I remember both the question and the answer, even though I don't remember anything before that. After that there's a blank space for some time.

Bars and Murzik are incredibly mighty and kind creatures. Bars is a German shepherd and Murzik an amazingly fluffy, sand-coloured cat. They are clearly keeping a benign, protective watch over two silly human children, my cousin Valentin ('Valka') and me. Bars is huge, much bigger than we are. If you want to give him a hug, you have to stretch right up as high as you can, and he will condescend to lower his head. It's hard for me to gauge the difference between Murzik's size and mine, because that depends on whether I am down on all fours, or standing up. But Murzik is able to jump up onto the table or even the piano, and he can pace along the forbidden shelf with the painted clay ornaments without knocking over a single one. Not a day passes without Murzik opening our eyes to new and awesome possibilities. Apart from that, Bars and Murzik are much better than we are: we fight occasionally, and then they are pointed out to us as an example. They are the best of friends, they never fight, and it's impossible to imagine them apart. Their favourite pastime is to trot around both rooms and the kitchen: Bars holds Murzik in his teeth by the scruff of the neck, Murzik hangs there with his legs drawn up, and the expression on their faces is one of unalloyed bliss. When we try to get Bars to do the same for us, he just licks our noses dismissively.

'Bars' was the first word both Valka and I spoke, which annoyed our parents and amused Grandmother and Grandfather. Later, when we were older, Bars ran out into the yard and never came back. We were upset, but came to accept it: Murzik, however, was desolate, and several days later he, too, disappeared forever. And that is how they have remained in my memory: huge, gentle beasts, wise and loving and loyal. Once, at school, during a lesson with a moral, the teacher asked us: "What is the main difference between humans and animals?"

And I blurted out: "Animals never hurt children!"

As a result of my 'silly' answer, the whole class had to suffer a lengthy homily to the effect that labour elevates man above beasts, and it is a pity that not all of us have yet understood that.

My parents have a 'communal' apartment. Two rooms in it are ours: one occupied by 'old Granny' Alexandra Kuzminichna, my father's mother, the other shared by Mother and Father, and occasionally by me. Our 'communal neighbour', known to us as 'Auntie' Lena, is the kindest soul imaginable. She has a very strange face: during the war she was a radio operator on the front, and a fragment of a shell pierced one of her cheeks and exited from the other, smashing her teeth and jaws. To the end of her days she was doomed to attend sessions at the Institute of Jaw and Facial Surgery, suffer periodic inflammations, and have yet another operation of some kind. Auntie Lena has a sort of obsessive love for me: she always tries to pinch me, or give me a kiss, or shower me with a spate of endearments uttered in one breath. I hate being kissed, affection confuses me, so I tend to snort and pull away.

Father noticed this once and, taking my hand without a word, led me into another room. The omens weren't good – it looked as though I was in for a hiding.

But to my surprise, Father's voice lacked its usual thunderous intonations, and he said very quietly: "Auntie Lena's husband and son were killed in the war. Her son was little, just like you are now. She loves you because she doesn't have anyone left. Do you understand?"

"Yes," I said, wanting to cry. But crying in front of Father was out of the question. I went over to my toys, and aimlessly started scraping a silver strip off a rubber ball.

We live on the third floor, so that means extra prohibitions for me: I mustn't jump, stamp my feet or overturn any chairs. The floors and walls separating the flats are more symbol than substance: our floor is the ceiling of the people below, and they have enough to worry about without my noise overhead. Not a situation conducive to a little jumping around! My parents either have to pull me up all the time, or spend their time apologising to the neighbours. Apologies must be made in any case: we have to wash out of basins in the communal kitchen because there is no bathroom. If you spill so much as half a cup of water on the plank floor, there is an immediate outcry from the people below – their ceiling is leaking. Like all children, it takes me a while to realise my parents' difficulties. There is a tap in the kitchen, but water is available from it only rarely. Father has to bring water in buckets from the yard, and when there's no water to be had from that tap, either, he has to trudge several blocks, looking for a working tap in other yards. Dirty water is poured into a bucket and disposed of down the outside lavatory, a latrine surmounted by two wooden cubicles. These are the only toilet facilities for everyone in the building, and the people have to go there be it winter or summer. It's not too bad for those on the ground floor, but we have to chase up and down an iron stairway, with the words '1906, Zhorno Factory, Odessa' moulded on each step. It is said that once upon a time there were flush toilets and bathrooms in the house, but then came the devastation of the Revolution, after which several families had to share each apartment: the baths and toilets were torn out to make more room.

Rubbish collection is carried out by a special van: the rubbish collector comes into the yard, rings a bell, and all the tenants come flying out to empty their rubbish pails. Such moments are to be cherished, because the van doesn't call every day, and until it does, buckets of refuse have to stay in your rooms whether you like it or not. Every so often the rubbish collector gives us children a special treat, by letting us run about and ring the bell for him. But the competition is fierce, and usually only the older children manage to have a turn with the bell. When by some miracle Valka and I once managed to get hold of that bell and ring it, we were so overjoyed that that evening we told the adults we had made up our minds about our future career: Valka would be a 'rubbish collector' and I would be a 'rubbish collectoress'. Our ambition amused the grown-ups greatly, and they spent a considerable amount of time discussing the details of our future occupation with us. Actually, when we became a little bit older and were saddled with the chore of taking the rubbish out to the van, the romance of this line of work palled very quickly.

At present I am the most useless creature in the house because of my age: I can neither carry water, nor take my place in a shop queue to buy something, nor light the stove. All my activities seem to come up against an implacable 'don't do that!', which, admittedly, is not without reason considering I am always up to something. Still, the very number of prohibitions is galling, and I much prefer to stay with 'young Granny' and Grandfather, who share accommodation with Valka and his parents. So, more often than not, that is where I am: the parents are at work, Grandmother and Grandfather allow us much more scope for activity, the apartment is a separate one on the ground floor, and there is lots of jolly company out in the yard. By evening we have pretty much exhausted our energy reserves, so when the parents come home we are suitably subdued and well behaved. Grandmother sets the table, and the adults hold their own conversations and laugh to the rattle of dishes and clinking of spoons. Valka's parents and mine are still young, there have been no deaths in the family, the light bulb under its old-fashioned shade throws a gentle light on the tablecloth, and we – the younger generation – sit under Grandfather's desk and try to guess whether I'll have to go home today or will be able to stay here. About two hours ago Valka and I fell out forever over the brush which Grandfather gave to us to polish the parquet floor. But then we realised that the brush was just the thing to use for pretending we were racing skaters, and we made up our quarrel in order to exploit these new possibilities. Grandmother barely had time to clean the polishing wax off us before my parents turned up for me. Valka and I have no desire to be parted because we have had the brilliant idea of building a house by draping blankets over Grandfather's desk, and then retreating behind them, into Stygian darkness, with a torch. Bars and Murzik will be the wild beasts of prey roaming about outside – but no, they will be our wolf and lion, who will accompany our hunting. Grandfather's walking-stick makes an excellent rifle, the cushions on the sofa are hostile savages, and they had better watch out! But if the adults tell me to get ready to go home, there will be no hope of changing their minds. So we strain our ears, trying to catch the drift of the adults' conversation. No, they're talking about Mother's school, and something about the state farm on which Uncle Jan, Valka's father, works. Then comes the inevitable question: "Well, how have they behaved themselves today?"

Grandmother and Grandfather don't usually tell tales about our misdeeds, but we hold our breath all the same. The usual reply is that we have been 'good', but occasionally, when we have really surpassed ourselves, come the dreaded words: "Let them tell you themselves!" And then we have to emerge from under the table and account for out misdemeanours.

"They've been good," says Grandfather. Our sigh of relief must have been a little too loud, because all the adults burst out laughing.

"They polished the floor all by themselves today," adds Grandmother. "They're growing up into real little helpers. Look what a good job they did!"

The shine on the parquet elicits due admiration, but then I hear my father's voice saying that it's time we were off.

"Maybe you'll leave Irusya here for the night?" suggests Grandmother. "It's raining outside."

Hurriedly, I scramble out from under the table to say good night to my parents before they can change their minds.

Grandfather enters fully into our construction project, suggests that we add a chimney made out of rolled-up newspapers, and dignifies our building with the grand-sounding name of *khalabuda*, or shack. Then he helps us equip ourselves for the hunt by pulling out an enormous pair of felt boots: we have to stand on tip-toes just to reach their soles, and walking around in them is an adventure in itself. By bedtime we are so overwhelmed by the day's events that we retire without protest. Heavy rain spatters against the dark window, and Grandmother tells us a story about a mother rabbit who lived in a burrow with her three baby rabbits. One of these little rabbits was very disobedient and went off in search of adventure. In the end, despite all the hair-raising things that happened to him, he returned safe and sound to his overjoyed mother.

"But the two obedient ones didn't have any fun at all," I think as I fall asleep. "They didn't get to meet up with the fox, or the hunter, or anything. They just sat around in their boring old burrow . . ."

Chapter Two

Igor was born with deformed feet, and his mother burst out crying when he was handed to her for the first time. In medical terminology this is known as *pes equinovares*. It meant in practice that the boy would either spend his entire life in a wheelchair, or, at best, get around somehow with a walking-stick. My future mother-in-law, a young geologist, had no useful connections, and could not expect to obtain the services of any prominent specialists. Nor did the family have enough money to pay some medical luminary to treat Igor privately. By that time, the real nature of 'free medicine' in the USSR was well and truly established, and enshrined in the pithy saying: 'treatment for nothing – is treatment of nothing!' But maternal determination is a formidable force, and help was found against all odds.

This came in the shape of a young woman surgeon who was just embarking on her career. The two women looked each other in the eye, and understood without words that they were both prepared to risk everything. Refusing to have anything else to do with other doctors, Igor's mother took him to this surgeon when he was a year old for an operation which involved cleaving the shin-bones, working on the muscles and tendons below the knee, ninety-two centimetres of sutures on the baby's legs, and then encasing in plaster.

Igor's first childhood memories are of having the plaster changed: shiny, fascinating instruments, his mother's serious, concentrated face, the knife to cut through the plaster, and fear that his legs would be cut off. Then there was the sight of those legs: white as milk and transversed by the sharp red lines of scars. He didn't cry, and everyone was surprised, because the procedure was a painful one. He must have realised, somehow, that if he were to start crying because of the pain, he could spend the rest of his life in tears. Until the age of two he was kept in special plaster boots which laced up to the knees. Twenty-five years later, when he was redecorating the flat, we found these tiny, shrivelled husks at the back of a cupboard, and I realised then how terrible all those months of uncertainty must have been for Auntie Larisa (that's how I called her then), wondering whether her son would ever walk. She breast-fed him until he was two years old. At that age, screwing up his little face in pain, Igor took his first, faltering four steps.

He began to talk very early and without the usual childish babble, but most of all he liked to sit in the corner behind a cupboard and think. Grandmother's bed stood behind that cupboard, because Igor's parents, grandmother and older sister all had to live in one room. A nursemaid shared that room for a while, too, but then she robbed the family and disappeared. The children had few toys, so Igor's sister Lalya initiated an original game in which he was 'King Cheat' and she was 'Alice the Fox'; as all kings, this one had to grant favours, so he would have to give the fox all the toys, one by one.

Every so often they would be visited by an old lady who was very fond of Igor. She would make a fuss of him, kiss him, and sometimes cry over him. Her son had been a contemporary and close friend of Igor's father, they were together in Kiev when it was under German occupation, and together they survived and studied as best they could. In 1944, shortly after the Soviet army liberated Kiev, this young man was gunned down by a drunken Soviet soldier: those who had been in Kiev under the Germans – even if they were civilian adolescents – were given short shrift. There was nobody to complain to, and in any case, confusion was total. So this lad – whom the soldier blasted in the stomach with his machine-gun – died long and agonisingly. Igor was named after him.

To Igor, the most fascinating creatures on earth were beetles. There were many of them in the empty lot behind the house, shiny bluish-black ones, which looked like miniature motorcars. He would hobble out there in his orthopaedic boots to play with them, certain that they talked with their feelers and loved to chat about this and that. One day we were taken on a rare outing to an ice-cream parlour, and Igor, in a burst of childish trust, pulled a box from his pocket and shook a green caterpillar out onto the tablecloth with the proud words: "Look! Isn't she a beauty!"

My mother, who has a horror of caterpillars, frogs, mice, rats, and all the other things which are supposed to terrify women, stared at the green, hairy, wriggling monstrosity on the tablecloth and agreed in hollow tones that yes, here was a beauty indeed. Igor has retained a quiet fascination with all living creatures to this day.

When Igor was five, the family moved to Koenigsberg, which became a Soviet possession after World War Two and was renamed Kaliningrad. Kant's grave is there, and Igor was taken to see it, so that he would 'remember it in future'. There were still many traces of the war, and the soil was full of weaponry of all kinds. Any self-respecting boy had at least a pistol, and Igor, too, acquired a rusty but still serviceable parabellum. While his father was working in the Stechkin engine laboratory and his mother was getting herself a job in a kindergarten, Igor and his new friends went out exploring. They found an aerial bomb in a swamp, its tempting, rusty metal sides half-buried in mud. They spent several days trying to pull it out of the mire, but, luckily for them, did not succeed. At night he could not sleep from pain, and his mother applied hot compresses made with herbal extracts to his legs. Too ashamed to cry, he learned to bite his lips in silence until they bled.

When he was six years old and I was five, his family came to visit mine in Odessa. That was when we met for the first time. He impressed me by his passionate interest in Greek mythology, a subject on which we came to an immediate tacit understanding. We spent a great deal of time discussing whether Ulysses was a good or bad person. I liked Igor's name, his freckles, and the way his eyes changed from grey to green when he was angry. But I was not the only girl he knew. There was a little girl called Marina in the kindergarten. She was always prettily dressed, and she and Igor were teasingly called 'the bride and groom' until the time when the five-year-olds decided to make something out of sunflower seeds secretly. The seeds were shelled and piled up, but before anything could be done with them, Marina succumbed to temptation and gobbled the whole lot down. This traitorous act replaced Igor's love with contempt, he swore off women, and decided to confine himself to masculine company. But in male company one must assert oneself, and Igor turned out to be an incurable fighter. His mother was constantly receiving complaints about his aggressive behaviour. Especially memorable was the occasion when the director's son, a sturdy seven-year-old schoolboy, paid a visit to the kindergarten. He called Igor a name, Igor punched him on the nose and put him to flight after a short but intense battle. Once his opponent had been vanquished and ran off shouting defiant insults, Igor could not chase after him and catch him because of those damned orthopaedic boots . . . He has never forgotten how he had to stand there, swallowing tears of rage because his legs would not do what he wanted them to do. Blast it, they're his legs! They are supposed to obey him! Well, he'll make them. To hell with any pain, those legs would obey him in future. At the age of twelve, he finally shed the orthopaedic boots for ordinary shoes. At fifteen, he took up boxing and made his legs jump and move on command, even though this meant fainting from pain after training bouts.

Chapter Three

Evenings in Odessa are blue or brown. This one is blue. Blue evenings are always somehow unsettling and not at all cosy, but something invariably happens on them, whether good or bad. My parents and I are walking home to our communal apartment. At five years of age it is impossible to walk sedately hand in hand with adults: it's too confining, and your hands get damp. So Mother and Father walk along like normal people, and I weave around them in circles, first running ahead, then falling behind. However, I am not allowed to cross the road alone, so every time I reach a kerb, I have to stop and wait for them to catch up. Finally, we have crossed the last road in the approved manner, and I can run all the way home by myself. If I put on an extra burst of speed, I may have time to get up to our floor, and then slide right down again on the banister before they're inside: this is something I'm not allowed to do in case I fall off and plunge head-first down the stairwell. With luck, I can whizz down, and be waiting for them at the foot of the stairs, looking angelic, and nobody any the wiser. They think, for some reason, that I am afraid of going up and down the dark stairs by myself (the lights hardly ever work), and I make the most of this delusion: it would never enter their heads that I would slide down the banister in the dark. At the age of five I already have a considerable arsenal of tricks up my sleeve. I had to learn to tell fibs between three and four years of age, and I remember my first excursion into falsehood very vividly. My parents' friends had the stupid adult habit of asking: "Whom do you love best, Mummy or Daddy?"

The first time this question was put to me, I was sincerely indignant. "None of your business!"

Naturally, I received a severe telling-off for being rude to grown-ups, and a promise that if I did so again, I would get a beating I wouldn't forget in a hurry. Actually, I couldn't word my reply in a more polite way, because neither my vocabulary nor my knowledge of social niceties was adequate at the time. Later, when this inevitable question was asked by others, I would mutter something to the effect that I loved them equally.

Maybe this form of interrogation was the adults' way of testing my quick-wittedness, but for me it was the first time I had to tell a lie. Before long I felt no qualms of conscience: you forced me, so you can bear the consequences! As for my quick-wittedness – well, if you set so much store by it, I'll show it to you, have no doubts about that . . . It was some ten years later that I realised, once and for all, that it is wrong to tell lies, especially successful ones. But realisation isn't everything: it took a further ten years of conscious effort to cast off falsehood altogether.

But right now I am far from all such knowledge, and I tear along towards those forbidden banisters: here's our drive, smelling as always of cats and refuse pails, and I shout "Ah!" as usual as I run through, listening for a muted echo. Into the yard, with its stone pathway and acacias . . . but then – what's that I see? Waddling towards me, a dark patch against the indigo evening, is a huge creature with waving arms and square shoulders, and without any legs. It seems to walk on its sides. It makes a mooing sound, then it shouts, then it roars: "We are all h-u-u-u-uman!!!" I stand there, paralysed with fear, and it comes to me that there are ordinary, day-time people: men, women and children. But there are also terrible 'people' belonging to the hours of darkness, and if you fall into their grasping hands, that's it. Curtains! I cannot cry out or do anything to get away from those awful hands which are getting closer and closer. It's just like those ghastly dreams when one cannot move, let alone run, but this is no dream. The thing comes right up to me and scoops me up, I feel the scrape of bristles. The smell of the creature is terrifying, nauseating, unfamiliar. Its mouth moves towards me, and I cannot say how I managed to get away, whether I squirmed out of its embrace, or whether it let me go. I fly into the darkness of the house, huddling against the stairs. Surely it can't see me here? Or will it find me by smell? If it should touch me, will I become a 'h-u-u-u-uman' like it, and walk around on my sides catching children?

Downstairs, from the lobby, I hear my parents' calm, cheerful voices. I rush down to them, but, catching their hands in a vice-like grip, I have no certainty of defence: the roaring of the creature outside can still be heard, but they seem to find nothing amiss. Back in our apartment, in the light, I look myself over apprehensively: my legs are covered in scratches, but they're still there: splash of green paint, dusty sandals, mosquito bites . . . Whew! I haven't turned into a 'h-u-u-u-uman' after all. Of course, I don't say a word to my parents:

they wouldn't believe me if I did. After all, they didn't hear the creature, even though they walked right past it!

If only somebody had told me, then, that the creature was simply Kolya, the husband of the caretaker, 'Auntie' Zhenya! That he had lost his legs in the war, after which he did not return to Odessa but was sent to Siberia, like so many, and had come home to his wife only now. That he doesn't walk on his sides, but gets around on special leather cushions attached to his hip-bones. That he was yelling and waving his arms around simply because he'd got drunk, and that was why he smelled like that. And that all he wanted was to give me a kiss. He saw this little girl in a white dress, and wanted to make an affectionate gesture, nothing more. My parents avoided talking about a misfortune which they were powerless to help alleviate, and even if they had seen him scoop me up, it would not have worried them unduly, because no harm was done.

It was quite by chance that later that same evening the horror was revived. "We want to bring you up to be a decent h-u-u-man," said Father in minatory accents as he ticked me off for some small misdemeanour. A barely suppressed cry of fear resounded through my entire being: No, no, no! I won't let them! I won't let anyone make me into anything! I'm not going to be something I don't want to be! I want to be myself, even if I am disobedient and have scabs and cuts on my knees!

Chapter Four

Most parents are very pleased if their offspring learn to read before the age of four. Firstly, it means that the small but destructive tornado in their midst quietens down from time to time, and sits poring over a book without – oh, joy! – ripping it apart. Secondly, all the parents' friends 'ooh' and 'aah' over such a wonderful achievement, while the parents say, modestly, that really, it's nothing special, and no, they didn't make any particular effort to teach the little one to read, it somehow just happened. And thirdly, the young reader is a source of considerable amusement to his elders, because he tends to repeat things that he has read in wildly unsuitable contexts.

"What are you up to, you wretched child!?"

Father's cigarettes have been shredded, and the pride and joy of the family sits there carefully scooping up the tobacco into the palm of her hand.

"I'm taking snuff!"

"What on earth put that into your head?"

"I want to be a famous beauty and have people write poems about me . . ."

"And what have Daddy's cigarettes got to do with it?"

"But look, Mama, it's written down here: 'To the beauty who took snuff.' Pushkin himself wrote that!"

Mother, of course, expresses the opinion that the best way to become a beauty is to go and wash my hands immediately – and my face, for that matter.

Children's books – with the exception of folk stories and fairy tales – are usually rendered odious by their insufferable, smug moralising. So there's no pleasure greater than hunting through bookcases filled with 'grown-up' books. The parents don't object, so long as I put everything neatly back into place. They have a quiet laugh about my attempts to master the contents of my father's technical dictionaries (they are the most accessible to me, because they are ranged on the open lower shelf). In order to prolong the enjoyment, Father answers all my questions in great detail, from integrals to differential equations. And then, looking at my puzzled face, he allows me to keep my pride by adding: "But I think you had better read about that later, when you start school."

"I don't want to go to school! I want to go to a *lycée*!"

"What? Oh, of course, I forgot: you've been reading Pushkin. Well, there are no more *lycées* these days, only schools."

What a blow! I've read books about schools, too, and I don't like the sound of them. All the characters in those schools seem to be constantly battling against someone to avoid low marks, or to get full marks. And if someone doesn't do well, then the whole class has to 're-educate' that person. Occasionally, even the whole school, until the culprit comes up to scratch. What if I don't do well at school? How do I know whether I'll be any good? Now a *lycée* is a different matter altogether:

The same are we. For us – the world is alien,
Our homeland's here, in Tsarskoye Selo . . .

The Decembrists were *lycée* students. Lenin – great man that he was (this is something taught from kindergarten days) – went to a 'gymnasium'. As for schools – what can they boast about?

"If you do well at school, you'll go to university later," says Father comfortingly.

I breathe a sigh of relief. University is fine. University is synonymous with 1st May demonstrations, when fantastically handsome athletes march along in brown and yellow uniform, accompanied by young girls holding hoops. Inside each hoop is a letter, and all those letters taken together form a mysterious and fascinating word: UNIVER-SITY. And the people say to each other: "Here comes the University!" When I'm there they will give me a fluffy yellow jacket and I'll join them in singing an incredibly incomprehensible song, *Gaudeamus igitur.* Maybe it's worth making the effort to do well at school just for that.

Sooner or later, the hour strikes, and school days begin. Brown uniform dress, white pinafore, new yellow shoes which pinch unbear-ably. Mother, fussing over my white hair ribbons, produces a news-flash: "Your Igor is in the second grade now."

What a slick operator! He's only eight months older, yet he managed to start school a year ahead of me. And anyway, what's this 'your Igor' business? For their information, Victor Zolotov from Grandmother-Grandfather's yard has got a lot more to recommend him: he's an absolute wizard at making explosions. Of course, I was underestimating my green-eyed friend badly here, because he went to great pains to enliven the first dull years of school with explosions. Naturally, he started off with relatively straightforward tricks; for instance, smearing the school stairs with nitrogen triodide, and waiting for the fun to start: as soon as the solution dried, any step on it would produce a harmless but loud bang. The culprits would be ordered to wash the stairs, a punishment they carried out very willingly, imagining gleefully how the floorcloth would give out bangs any time it was touched after it dried. By the time he was ten years old, Igor was tired of trivial bombs made out of aluminium filings and potassium permanganate, and he decided that bigger and better explosions could be achieved with magnesium. He had to be taken to hospital by his father, suffering from temporary loss of hearing, to have splinters removed from his eyes. While the doctors fussed over him, Igor was astounded to see, through tears and blood, that his father's face was whiter than the doctors' coats. To his amazement he was not given the hiding of his life when they returned home, but his father handed him a thick volume by Nekrasov on inorganic chemistry with the strict instruction: "If, next time, you can't explain the chemical reaction to me and what precautions should be taken in that specific case, I'll have your hide!"

The next explosion – three days later – brought an uninjured Igor running to his father to explain (though not without a few inward qualms!) the chemical nature of the experiment. Igor's father shot him a keen sideways glance, but, true to his word, muttered, "Well done."

Chemistry was to remain Igor's main interest throughout his youth, somewhat eclipsing the wonders of biology, although the six-volume biological reference work by Bram, which Igor knew off by heart, was always close at hand, right up until the day we finally left Kiev.

In the meantime, here I am in my agonising new shoes, sizing up the crowd of my new and as yet unknown classmates. The teacher takes us around the school, explaining what's what: "This is the girls' toilet, and this is the boys'. This is the headmaster's study. I hope that none of you will ever have to be sent there. This is the gym hall, but in the first grade you will be having your gym lessons in your classroom. None of you are allowed to go to the third and fourth floors: that's where the older children's classrooms are. This is your floor. Now, have you all got that? And now, everybody look over here! Do you know whose picture that is?"

"Lenin!" we shout in unison. That would be one for the books, not to recognise Lenin!

"Very good! And who's that?"

"Marx!" respond some, and not with the same volume or degree of certainty. Portraits of Marx are carried around at demonstrations, too, but we have only a very vague idea as to who he is. Still, it's a memorable face, all that fluffy grey hair and luxuriant beard.

"Right, that's the great Karl Marx. And now, who knows who this is?"

This question produces confusion in our ranks. The 'uncle' on the portrait isn't bald, and his moustache and beard aren't as eye-catching as Marx's. Who can it be?

"Stalin?" a girl with fair, curly hair ventures timidly. The teacher pulls a face at such a *faux pas*.

"For goodness' sake! . . . Stalin . . . !"

It is unnecessary – indeed, it is highly undesirable – for us, first-graders in 1961, to know what Stalin looked like. The last monuments to this 'genius of all times and nations' were demolished several years ago. There was one such monument on the Cathedral Square where I was taken for walks. It was a bronze statue of Lenin and Stalin sitting with their arms around each other's shoulders, and at their feet there was a miniature Black Sea, with real water, on whose shores our Odessa was marked with a red star. The whole ensemble was surrounded by flower-beds.

"Who's that, Grandfather?"

"Lenin and Stalin."

"But why is this square called 'Cathedral Square'?"

"Because there was a cathedral here once. They blew it up later."

The monument is gone now, and has been replaced by a fountain, surrounded by the same flower-beds of pansies and daisies. Maybe the fair-haired girl had also been taken for walks there, and she remembered the statue, but made a mistake in identifying the picture in the school. And mistakes like that – as we were to learn later – are not encouraged.

"Come, children," persists the teacher. "Who can tell us who this is?"

"Engels," says a tall, fair boy who bears himself with adult dignity. But he keeps his voice low.

"Good boy! Engels it is! What's your name?"

"Seryozha Schissel."

How about that, Seryozha! We are all stunned by his erudition.

"And now, class, we will go to our room. Form up in pairs! Hold hands! What do you mean, you don't want to stand with her? You can leave your whims at home, this is school, and you'll do as you're told! That's right!"

The experienced Evgenia Mikhailovna directs us to our places. At first we sit three to a desk: there are more than forty pupils in our class. In the middle of the school year there was a reshuffle, and the two first grades were split up into three classes, A, B and C, after which we were able to sit two to a desk. Naturally, the teachers of 1A and 1B tried to get rid of their more troublesome pupils by relegating them to the newly formed 1C, which meant I lost a new friend, the dark-haired and reckless Misha Kharasandzhants. I remain in 1A, probably because I read and write; I get full marks very easily until my total inability to learn English is revealed. At first, this puzzles the teachers: how can it be? She does so well in all the other subjects, but can't cope with English? The answer is much simpler than any of them imagine, because the fact is that I am not learning anything at school (and didn't, for the first four years at least). All that they're teaching I already know, all I have to do is adapt the entries in my exercise books to suit their rules. Things got off to a bad start with the English teacher from the word go. She ordered us to start building up our own dictionaries, and to find and paste in pictures to illustrate every new word. And where were we to get such pictures? Out of magazines and books at home, of course. Drawings were unacceptable, presumably because our artistic abilities were considered inadequate: the teacher intended to show our home-made 'English dictionaries' to the school inspectors as an example of innovation in language study. Things went very badly for me. As soon as my parents realised that I had designs on their books, they expressed horror at such barbarity, and forbade me to cut out anything at all. They also refused the 'compromise solution' offered by the teacher – that they buy special books which I could cut up. No need to have the child become accustomed to mutilating books. All I got was a pile of old magazines, but how much would they yield? The pictures in them weren't even in colour. Flicking listlessly through a copy of the journal *Yunost* (*Youth*) I could hear Father's rising voice from the kitchen: "It's an outrage! We're supposed to connive at teaching our daughter to cut up books! I'm going to go and have a word with that teacher . . ."

"Borya, I beg of you, stay out of it! I'm a teacher myself, and I can't bear these mothers and fathers who keep turning up with endless objections to this or that! You know that nothing good will come of it if you go storming down to that teacher! You'll only lose your temper . . ."

"Look, I managed to keep my temper when your wonderful Evgenia

Mikhailovna said at the first parents' meeting: 'Parents, I would like to ask those of you who are *hengineers* to help us install power points in the classroom.'"

"But you said then that you were never going to come to the school again!"

"Yes, I did, and I won't!"

"So don't go. Let her hack up those wretched copies of *Yunost*. And, in any case, you draw so well – why don't you do her some drawings in her book?"

"How can I, when that idiot woman refuses to accept drawings?"

"Borya, keep your voice down! Irka will hear! I'll have a word with the teacher myself, maybe she'll allow drawings . . ."

Drawings were allowed, but only received a maximum mark of three out of five. Father wouldn't believe that this was through no fault of mine, and was very cross. As for me – I accepted my inability to learn English with a child's fatalism, and, after asking Grandfather about a number of letters, learned to read Ukrainian and a little Polish. There were plenty of books in both these languages in the house.

Chapter Five

God doesn't exist. Only silly, ignorant old women believe in Him. We third-graders sit in the school auditorium; this 'truth' has been drummed into us for the past hour. This is atheist instruction, and attendance is compulsory. It's snowing outside – such a rare occurrence in Odessa! Usually there's not enough snow even to get up a decent snowball fight. The boys scrape it carefully off window-sills, parked cars and off the road with reddened fingers until they get a smooth, lovingly fashioned snowball. It's hard to part with such a beauty. Now, where should one throw it? But today, you can bet your life that all the snow will be gone by the time we're dismissed! If God exists, then surely (oh, mad hope!) He will keep the snow falling until we can get away! After all, it's because of Him that we're sitting here instead of being outside among the falling snowflakes.

Atheist instruction was quite fun at the start: the Pioneers from the seventh grade sang and acted out funny ditties about priests and fools. But now it's plain boring: talk, talk, talk . . . Why do grown-ups spend so much time talking about something that doesn't exist? You can't help feeling suspicious. Now they're on about a Baptist woman who, they say, roasted her child alive in an oven. That's terrible, of course, but very strange, too: because 'Auntie' Vera, the janitor at Grandmother and Grandfather's place, is a Baptist, and her two children, Petya and Sasha, are alive and well. She drops around to have a cup of tea with the grandparents from time to time. She's very quiet and kind, and never bangs her head against the floor, the way the Pioneers showed. And my 'young granny', for that matter, is a Catholic, she's no ignorant old woman! And my grandfather! Of course, they don't talk to me about God, because my parents have forbidden it, reasoning that people of the grandparents' generation are still victims of 'outdated prejudices', which must not be passed on to me.

Yet one can't help feeling sorry for God: He's going to be left completely alone and friendless when all the believers die. He's all by Himself, and everybody's ranged against Him – the Pioneers, our teachers, even the headmaster, the speakers on the radio, the whole country . . . And I know full well – from the ethics of our street games – that it's not fair for everyone to gang up against one person. At times like that you have to take the side of the underdog, and then sort out the rights and wrongs of the situation. On the other hand, nobody is actually assaulting God physically, are they? They just don't believe in Him, so they go around shooting off their mouths. Hang on, though, they've just said something about 'unrelenting war' . . . Do they mean making war on Someone who doesn't exist? Oh I see, against the clergy, not Him . . . I look out of the window without much hope . . . It's still snowing, thank God! Thank whom?! Well, nobody really, it's just a figure of speech. Everyone uses it, even non-believers, so why can't I think it? Because it's dishonest, that's why! It's all right to tell lies to adults when necessary, but it's always wrong to think dishonestly. But what if I were to think that He does exist? Even if He doesn't – it could be like a game, and I wouldn't tell anyone about it – anyone at all. I won't beat my head against the floor, of course, or do anything so silly, but I'll talk to Him. He must feel very hurt that everyone laughs at Him. And I'm sad, too, because it's going to stop snowing any minute now, and I won't be able to catch so much as a single snowflake, and look at how beautiful it is.

When we finally burst out into the yard in a noisy throng, the snow was still falling, and it was an evening to remember. It even snowed the next day.

And I had a secret, just as well concealed and as burning as my poetry. I regularly amused my classmates with ditties, parodies of the poems we had to learn in class and with the serial adventures of Seryozha Diamant, but I kept it a close secret that I wrote other things, too, things that got me out of bed in the night, or, from time to time, made me oblivious of my surroundings in class. And now, just as secretly, I talk to God. At first I only ask endless questions. On His side, God makes no attempt to appear to me personally in a blaze of light, or anything like that, or even answer my questions audibly. Yet the answers come, all the same: either a book with the answer turns up the next day, or I suddenly feel an inward certainty about the right reply to this or that question. The way I conduct my conversations with God has evolved into a form quite far removed from what is commonly described as prayer. There is no feeling of remoteness, no sense that He is God, an exalted being, and I am just one of His lesser creations, nor do I address Him with the kind of politeness demanded by adults. The questions I fire at Him are demanding and unceremonious. Is He kind, or not? – that is what I need to determine in the first place. If He's not, then I don't want to have anything to do with Him, even if He's all-powerful. So if He starts punishing me for undue familiarity or failure to observe some formalities of which I know nothing, then I don't want to know Him. But He never punishes me. Naturally, I have my misfortunes, my childish disappointments, but I never feel that He has brought them down on my head, even though it is well within His power to give a hint of displeasure now and again. On my own side, I consider it improper to ask Him for anything. After all, what have I ever done for Him, that I should expect any favours? Why should He intercede in our earthly life if we, the people, have decided that we can manage without Him? After all, here I am living in an atheistic country and doing nothing about it, so how can I start demanding that God do this or that, or prevent something I don't want from happening? For this very reason, the atheist's favourite argument that if God existed, He would not let children die in wars, and suchlike, cuts no ice with me. If we the people start wars knowing full well that innocents will perish in them, what right have we to reproach God for granting us free will? If I am robbed and get my throat cut tomorrow, is it God's fault? No, if He's really kind and all-powerful, He'll take me to Him, and I'll be much better off than in school or on the streets. In fact, if I do have a complaint, it's that I don't know what He wants from me. This is through no fault of mine, when all is said and done; I had no choice about where to be born. As it is, seeing He set me in this place and time, He could at least give me a clue about His view of things! Yet the moment I thought this, an answer came from within: don't worry, you will find out what you need to know when the time comes. There was always a response of some kind.

Years later when I was a student I realised that all that happened to me had a definite pattern. And, indeed, that the circumstances of every person's life are a sort of training, like the training devised for an athlete by a strict and demanding coach, who knows what is best for the athlete to attain his full potential. So you want to stop running and catch your breath? No you don't! Come on, keep it up! I'll decide when it's time for you to take a break! So you think you're about to drop? Don't worry, you won't, you'll be all the stronger! You say you can't go on? Nonsense, of course you can, you simply don't realise how much you've still got in you! You're my pride and joy, so don't expect me to give an inch!

But for the time being, none of us ten-year-olds give a great deal of thought to such matters. Later, this same generation was to turn to God, to the consternation of the Soviet authorities. Some of us became Christians, some turned to Judaism or to the teachings of the Hare Krishnas – yes, there are Hare Krishnas in the Soviet Union! But in the meantime we join the Pioneers, take part in gathering scrap iron, fight, and play truant from school. My secret night-time talks to God have little discernible effect on my daily conduct.

In the autumn I was accepted into the Pioneers, and soon experienced at first-hand what is called 'the political process', albeit in the milder form applicable to children. There were not enough English textbooks to go round the class, but despite this we had that blasted 'special programme' to cope with. For a while, those who didn't have a textbook were lucky – they had a legitimate reason not to submit English homework. However, our 'Englishwoman' Zinaida Iosifovna soon put a stop to that: those with textbooks had to submit their homework ahead of schedule, and then give the textbooks to the formerly 'lucky' ones. As we don't have English lessons every day, this system is workable. So, according to this scheme, I have to bring my textbook in on Thursdays and give it to Vitka Molodtsov. On one occasion, I didn't bring the book: our apartment was being redecorated, so on Wednesday night I was packed off to stay with Grandmother and Grandfather – and forgot the wretched English textbook at home. I explained the situation to Vitka, and suggested that we both come to school half an hour early the next day. Then he could either do the homework himself, or copy mine. Vitka, of course, failed to turn up – only an idiot would willingly come to school a moment before it was absolutely necessary, especially to do a dreary English exercise! Fate caught up with us on Friday.

"Get out your homework books! Molodtsov, where's yours?"

"I didn't have a textbook!"

"Why didn't you get one from someone else?"

"Ira Ratushinskaya didn't bring hers back on Thursday!"

"Aha!" cried Zinaida Iosifovna. "You're a Pioneer, Ratushinskaya, yet you grudged your classmate a textbook?"

And so it went on and on, about the moral duties of a Pioneer, about mutual assistance, about the valiant behaviour of Pioneers during the war, when they delivered ammunition to the soldiers, let alone a pathetic textbook. She gives me no opportunity to say a word in my own defence: she is riding high on a wave of righteous indignation. Now, at the age of thirty-four, I do not really blame her: the best years of her life had passed in Stalin's time, when public denunciation was an essential aspect of social activity – in schools, institutes, offices, factories . . . You either had students denouncing their professors or vice versa. The idea was that all and sundry –

today's accusers and tomorrow's accused – should repent of their misdeeds, whether real or imaginary, but nobody had the right to try to justify themselves. And indeed, why should they? Is not 'the collective' always right, and an individual always wrong? From Zinaida Iosifovna's point of view this was all very right and proper, and she had no intention of sacrificing such a useful pedagogical method in order to listen to my justifications and explanations. Moreover, it would do 'the collective' a world of good, too: we third-graders had not yet really been exposed to the joys of unpunished, officially sanctioned denunciation, when no holds are barred, any lie is permissible, in order to bring an accusation. At the time, Zinaida Iosifovna's accusation seemed ridiculous beyond all imagining: after all, who in their right mind would want to hold on to that hated English textbook? It's not as if it were something really worthwhile . . . In fact, it is a safe bet that anyone having it would gladly get it off their hands even if they had to give up some treasured possession like a lens, an old coin or a bullet to do so!

So, while Zinaida Iosifovna gleefully gives me the lowest mark (one out of five) as she continues to rail at me, my classmates look at me with sympathy, and Vitka wriggles uncomfortably.

"Don't think you've heard the last of this!" Zinaida Iosifovna warns me in conclusion.

At home, I fling myself at my parents, pouring out my tale of woe: I've got into trouble over nothing, and the teacher says that they're going to do something else to me! Mummy and Daddy – help me! Send me to another school! Or get me transferred to another class! Anything to get away from that Zinaida, she'll always be after me now! But my parents show no inclination to become embroiled in my conflicts with my teachers; you made your bed, you lie on it, is their attitude. The whole thing is obviously a storm in a teacup, anyway: I must have simply botched up my explanation of what had happened, or spoken rudely. I'm being rude even now, by referring to my teacher as just 'Zinaida'. Teachers must be addressed and spoken of by their name and patronymic, and if you have annoyed your teacher, then you should apologise, and all will be well.

So who is there left to turn to for help? It's no use appealing to Grandmother and Grandfather, there's nothing they can do, and it will only upset them. Maybe the headmaster, Pavlo Mikolayevich, who is the kindest soul imaginable, the only person in Odessa I heard speak in pure Ukrainian, an ardent admirer of Shevchenko, and who melted at the sight of a tear-stained childish face? But we have been conditioned to be afraid of the headmaster and the senior teacher, no matter what they are like. To us they are synonymous with punishment. For instance, if a monitor catches you running in the corridors or on the stairs during break (all the classes except the junior ones take turns at monitoring) you get hauled off to the headmaster's study forthwith. Horror of horrors! Heaven forbid! And wasn't it Pavlo Mikolayevich who took that tearaway Sashka right round the school after some misdemeanour or other, and made him apologise to every class for 'offending against the honour of the school'? Poor Sashka had to apologise to our class in the middle of an arithmetic lesson, even though none of us had the faintest idea what it was that he had done. He was only nine years old, and finally burst into tears, after which Pavlo Mikolayevich couldn't bring himself to continue with the punishment.

It was clear that I could expect no support, and I set off for school each day in dread, waiting for the promised unspecified retribution to catch up with me. But Zinaida Iosifovna is in no hurry. Five days go by, a week . . . I begin to permit myself the hope that the matter will end there, that everything is back to normal, Zinaida Iosifovna simply lost her temper, and she has forgotten all about it. Or maybe she feels that she went a bit too far, and is pretending that nothing has happened: she's an adult, after all, and is hardly likely to apologise to me, a mere schoolgirl. I comfort myself with such hopes and wishful thinking. And, naturally, the blow comes when I least expect it. It was at an English lesson with a difference: apart from our class, all the school's teachers of English were in the room, as well as our form teacher Evgenia Mikhailovna (who taught us other subjects), the senior teacher . . . It was obvious that something unusual was in the offing. For a start, Zinaida Iosifovna launched into a homily, in Russian, about the honour symbolised by a Pioneer's neck scarf. Then she dragged Marik Kegulikhes into the middle of the room, took up the ends of his ink-stained scarf in her hand, and asked us in English: "Look at this Pioneer's scarf. Is it clean and neat?"

To tell the truth, none of us knows enough English, let alone all the other reasons (Marik is a nice kid) really to understand the question or give a grammatically correct reply. But the top student, a girl called Tanya, raised her hand: "No, Kegulikhes' scarf is not clean and neat."

To my horror, I see that Tanya is reading her answer off a piece of paper on her desk: that means that the scenario has been worked out and rehearsed in advance, that's why she speaks so readily and confidently. She doesn't give a hoot about Marik – this is going to earn her full marks. I guess the nature of Marik's 'crime' not because

I understand what Zinaida Iosifovna is saying, but because she points an accusing finger at the purple ink stain on his red Pioneer's scarf. But Marik isn't pilloried for long, and is sent back to his desk in disgrace. After that, they set about me. Zinaida Iosifovna's well-manicured fingers reach towards my scarf.

"Is this scarf clean and neat? Diamant, what do you say?"

"Yes!" retorts my friend Seryozha, and flops back on the bench in relief.

"I didn't tell you to sit down!" says Zinaida Iosifovna sternly. "So you say that Ira's scarf is clean and neat. Now, children, do you think that Ira is a good friend?" She has switched to Russian, making allowances for the paucity of our English vocabulary.

My classmates respond in Russian: "Yes, she's a good friend!"

I must confess that I am pinning all my hopes on them. Among children, the worst offenders are those who tell tales and are cowardly or greedy. I don't think I am any of these, and my relations with the others in the class are good. So, of course, my Pioneer organisation will defend me, a Pioneer too, especially if I am finally given a chance to explain myself. But, alas! The question is repeated in English: "Is Ira a good friend?"

And the same Tanya responds smartly in English: "No, Ira is not a good friend. She did not want to give her classmate Vitya Molodtsov the English textbook!"

I try to protest, to explain . . . no chance! I haven't been given permission to speak, so how dare I open my mouth? I am told to keep quiet, and Zinaida Iosifovna, alternately pulling my scarf and then relaxing her hold, starts discoursing, in a mixture of English and Russian, whether this sacred fragment of the Red Banner should be removed from around my neck immediately, or whether I should be given another chance to redeem myself with the assistance of 'the collective'. I don't remember much of what happened next, or how long it lasted: when I found myself back at my desk, I could not stop myself from bursting into tears, and sat there crying, my face buried in my folded arms. This proved to be too much for our silent 'collective': I was never a cry-baby, and this was the first time any of my classmates had seen me in tears. A murmur went round the room, and someone from the back called out in Russian: "Zinaida Iosifovna, Ira's crying!"

"Never mind, let her cry!" replied Zinaida Iosifovna regally, and in Russian so that everyone would understand. I don't know what force it was that catapulted me out to the front of the class and made me declare that I would never attend any of Zinaida Iosifovna's lessons again, that she was despicable, despicable, despicable! Thank you very much, true Soviet citizen Zinaida Iosifovna (who, as I learned by chance, now lives in New York), that with that single sentence you taught me never to cry again, no matter what. It was you who showed me that there is neither sympathy nor pity for those who weep, that a sadist can experience no greater pleasure than seeing the tears of his victim, that once I had succumbed to weeping, it was for me to bear, and for you to enjoy! Who knows, had it not been for you, would I have been able, later, never to show a tear to anyone again: not to the KGB, not under interrogation, not to my gaolers? Since that day, only those who love me have seen my tears: God, from whom I never asked for anything, and later those people who were closest of all to me. Very few. Three, in fact.

But on that day, as I shot frantically out of the school into the street, I realised that my situation was not good. How could I not attend Zinaida Iosifovna's lessons if there was no chance of transferring to another school, or even another class? How could I go if she . . . In other words, it was impossible to attend, and equally impossible to stay away. Had my parents really been aware of what happened, had I been able to explain the extent of my misery to them properly, they would certainly have settled the matter without too much trouble. There were plenty of schools in Odessa. But, snotty-nosed know-all that I was, I no longer expected their help or understanding: they had refused me earlier, so why bother trying again? That winter there was, luckily, more snow than usual, and I ate it by the handful, hoping for tonsilitis, for pneumonia – anything! Injections and medicines were a much more desirable prospect than going back to that school to HER. I lay in bed sick at Grandmother and Grandfather's place, running a temperature. My parents were kind and loving, they brought me books, kissed me . . . I felt no resentment towards them, but having lost faith in their omnipotence and fairness, I made no attempt to discuss my troubles with them. But the tonsilitis passed, and the time came to go back to school. It was a Thursday, when we had arithmetic, Russian, Ukrainian, craft and physical education, but no English. But the next day – Friday – meant English, so what was I to do? Luck was with me again: sharp abdominal pains! I tottered over to my grandparents' place, and my parents came round in the evening. The adults were rather suspicious about my pains, because it was quite clear that I had great hopes that they would allow me to stay away from school. But by evening my temperature had shot up, and I had to be rushed to hospital in an ambulance with acute appendicitis, which called for an immediate operation. Hurrah! I looked so radiant on my way to the operating theatre, that the experienced nurses shook their heads: "A bad sign . . ."

I came round from the anaesthetic and called out feebly, but nobody responded: it was the middle of the night, parents aren't allowed into the surgical wards, and the nurses are taking a nap. A heavy bag lies over my fresh scar, and sand trickles out of it on to the sheet. In the morning they tell me that this is standard procedure for such an operation, that I will be able to get up in five days' time, and, if everything goes well, I'll be going home on the seventh day. As for the sand leaking out of the bag – well, that doesn't matter, because the bag will be taken off in twenty-four hours' time. There's no sense in complaining about the rudeness of the nurses, either, or that they make the 'mobile' patients sweep and polish the floor in the ward – they'll be out soon. There are twenty-five girls in the ward, aged between five and twelve, and we manage to amuse ourselves very well: the ward is a 'light' one, for appendectomies. Larisa, who has the bed next to mine, is the quietest of all: she's from an orphanage, and she'll be going back there, not to her parents. The nurses are sorry for Larisa, so they don't yell at her. She's happier here than at the orphanage, but she will soon have to go back there in any case. Their supervisor at the orphanage has a novel way of punishing the children: beating them is forbidden, so she either smears their tongues with soap, or makes them stand on one spot, holding a stool in their outstretched hands. And there's nothing they can do but submit. Larisa doesn't believe that her parents abandoned her: they must have died performing some act of heroism. Or maybe her father works in counter-intelligence and is on some assignment abroad; that would be a state secret, and that's why nobody can tell her about it. But one day he will come back, get a medal, take her home, and she won't be an orphan any longer, but a general's daughter. As for the orphanage supervisor who smeared Larisa's tongue with soap – well, he'd simply draw his gun and shoot her, and nothing would happen to him because she's a fascist. That's what the children call her among themselves. I am two years older than Larisa, and the experience of my extra years makes me doubt such a simple and easy resolution of all her troubles. But I don't dare voice my misgivings – anyway, what if she's right? We spend our time planning for that marvellous possibility, and also how, when we are both grown up and beautiful, she will come over in a general's car to visit me, and we will go driving together. Of course, there is also the possibility that she will be adopted by some really nice people, but her father will eventually turn up anyway . . . Neither of us knew, at that time, that in order to adopt a child in the

Soviet Union, the adopting family must prove that they have thirteen square metres of living space for every member of the family, and who in Odessa has anything even close to that? Generals, perhaps, but not lesser mortals. We hope and believe with all our hearts that maybe, maybe ... Larisa draws better than anyone in the ward, and the nurses keep asking her for pictures, which she obligingly draws for them. She draws pictures of ballerinas, nothing else. Because there is nothing more beautiful than ballerinas in the whole wide world. She knows that because the orphanage once went on an outing to the Opera Theatre to see the ballet *Cinderella*. When Larisa grows up, she is going to be a ballerina, she's already started teaching herself to dance: it's a pity she can't get up for another two days, or she'd show us. Of course, she will be the best ballerina ever, and when she finishes a performance, her father will throw her a bouquet of white roses from the audience ...

My English lessons and the despicable Zinaida Iosifovna are a bagatelle by comparison with all this. It looks as though I am a very lucky girl: I have a mother and father, a grandfather and a whole two grandmothers! And to think that only last year I had contemplated running away from home and asking to be taken into a children's home after I had been told off for something or other! In books, everything is always fine in children's homes and orphanages, everyone is wonderfully kind and understanding, and the inmates have a happy childhood thanks to the care of the Soviet state. What a fool I had been to believe that!

Larisa, however, is much more practical than I. She doesn't want to go back to the orphanage, I can't face the prospect of going back to the 'Englishwoman'. So, as soon as we are allowed out of bed, we spend as much time as possible in the infectious diseases ward in the hope of catching something that will prolong our stay in the hospital. The children in the infectious diseases ward have all sorts of things: measles, scarlet fever, yellow jaundice, and all in acute form, otherwise they would not have been admitted into the hospital. We enjoyed the risk (what if we should catch something?), we made a host of new friends, we indulged our childish hopes. . . .

They came for us on the same day: my parents for me, someone from the orphanage for Larisa. Putting on my street clothes, I discover a forgotten piece of catapult elastic in the pocket of my jacket. How about that? Nobody has taken it away, and I had been certain that all my clothes would have been searched, because they're very strict here. But the elastic doesn't please me as much as it should. It looks as though I have matured considerably over the past week. That evening, hissing through their teeth with annoyance, my parents tried to comb out my hair – my thick, luxuriant braid – which had turned into something akin to a roll of felt during my stay in hospital. In the end they had to give up: there had been nobody to comb my hair in the hospital, and in this instance I could not be blamed, either, because I wasn't allowed to get up for five days. So they had to cut off the braid completely, an outcome which pleased me inordinately, because I hated the bother of combing and braiding. I don't know about Larisa, but I was lucky enough to pick up any number of things in the 'infectious' ward, with the exception of yellow jaundice. So I managed to stay away from school until mid-April, and after that, restored to health, I simply played truant from school and went down to the sea. By that time of the year the beaches are empty except for ownerless dogs – my friends – for whom I always tried to bring something to eat. It wasn't much, but they came to know me, and we ran around the slopes and the edge of the water playing games: will the wave catch your feet, or not? My satchel lay abandoned behind a shed, and nobody at school wondered what had become of me, because by now they were accustomed to the thought of me being constantly ill. I felt no pangs of conscience either then or later, trundling along home in the tram after school hours. My head was full of thoughts about spring, and the sea, and poetry – so who wants to think about English lessons? Strangely enough, nobody ever caught me out on these escapades, I got excellent results in the May exams (easy as falling off a log), and I managed to go up into the fourth grade. All that summer, however, I worried about doing English again. On 1st September I learned, to my great relief, that we had a new English teacher, who was young and very nice. I thanked God, though I swear I had not asked Him for any help in this matter!

Chapter Six

In the meantime, Igor was leading a lively existence at school: chemistry, explosions – in short, male pursuits. Girls were of no interest, but the boys engaged in periodic fights for no reason, just to establish the pecking order. The teachers managed, somehow, to keep some degree of control over him, punishing him occasionally as a cautionary measure. The punishment usually took the form of a comment in his report book: every pupil in the Soviet Union has such a book, in which one's marks for the week are entered, with a space for remarks by the teacher. They must be signed by the parents every week and sometimes the teacher asks the parents to 'take steps'. This means the pupil gets a hiding. There are parents who don't beat their children, but in cases of school conflict, many teachers reproach parents at face-to-face meetings for not taking the appropriate action: "If it were my son," they say, "I'd skin him alive for misbehaving like that!" And so on, to the effect that we all have the same aim – to make a decent human being out of your son/daughter.

So it came to pass that Igor and his chum Sashka had pulled off some stunt that they would have got away with if the best student in the class, fat little Yura, had not tattled to the teacher. Telling tales is encouraged in Soviet schools, and we are always being reminded of the best example of an informer – the legendary Pioneer Pavlik Morozov, whom we are all supposed to emulate. In the 1930s, Pavlik Morozov's father helped people with documents which would enable them to flee to the city from the starvation of the state collective farm. For this, they needed special permission, and Morozov senior, as chairman of that doomed collective farm, signed releases for the workers. It is said that he also distributed state-owned grain to the starving, and that is a terrible offence in itself – you can't go around giving away state property, even to people dying of hunger. Pavlik informed against his father, who was shot immediately in accordance with the laws of the time. After that, Pavlik himself was axed to death by the infuriated workers of the collective farm, because they knew that they and their families were doomed, anyway. But in the cities and villages of the Soviet Union they exhorted us, schoolchildren in the 1960s, to be like Pavlik! If you're an informer, you're to be commended, if you're not – then you're a coward, and have no sense of civic duty! So tattle-mongering there was, but not by the majority: some feeling of inner protest rose against it. Some refrained out of a feeling of solidarity with other children, others because it went against what they were taught at home. I well remember how my father charged me before I started school: "Whatever happens, don't be a tell-tale!" Igor was taught the same. But in Yura's family, clearly, they took a different view.

So Yura informed, the other boys found out, and the next thing that happened – predictably – was a fight. Man to man, as is only right. First the guilty Igor had a go, then his partner in crime Sashka. It wasn't a really serious fight, either, as school fights go, they just wanted to show Yura that they despised him. Indeed, it was not uncommon for school fights to end with broken teeth and other injuries, and no great fuss was made over them. And in this case, it was a matter of a tell-tale getting his just deserts, almost a 'political' case, you might say!

Igor and Sashka were banished from school for a week after a huge scandal. Igor fully expected that his father would be furious, and would give him a belting: his father never hesitated to 'take steps' if he thought Igor was in the wrong. But in this instance, he obviously did not feel that Igor had earned a hiding. He didn't say anything to encourage him to fight, but he did not lay a finger on him, either. The week's expulsion from school turned out to be a holiday: the ten-year-old miscreants spent their days chasing pleasurably around Kiev in the warm autumn sunshine. Sashka's father was an archery instructor, so they took themselves off to the target range to look for discarded arrow-heads! But it was a bitter disappointment to discover that none of them were anything like the ancient, sharpened, saw-toothed Scythian arrow which was hidden away at home. Civilisation was clearly going to the dogs: judging by that arrow-head and today's pathetic offerings, people back in antiquity were much better at making weapons!

Needless to say, this led to dreams about fleeing to Africa, information about which was gleaned from books. Now there, people go hunting lions with only a spear; when they bend a bow, their aim is true, and their arrows are everything an arrow ought to be, instead of some feeble toy! Three fearless voyagers were involved in the plan, and occasionally they would be joined by a fourth, Lenchik, who was, however, a bit of a coward. They wouldn't have admitted him into their circle normally, but Lenchik's father had an air-rifle on which the intrepid adventurers had definite designs. While Lenchik was torn by doubts and hesitations, the others were busily engaged in gathering suitable pieces of wood to make a raft. Their plan was brilliant in its simplicity: they'd sail the raft down the Dnieper river as far as the Black Sea, then through the Bosphorus and the Dardanelles: after all, Ulysses had followed that route, and he didn't even have an air-rifle, just some wax to block out the voices of the Sirens. And from there – straight on to Africa, to prove their manhood by catching a lion by the tail and not letting go until the beast was dead. At last, the great day came, and they were off! By evening, their alarmed parents had half of the city on its feet, the adventurers were caught and returned to face the music. Igor, who worships his father despite the latter's strictness, remembers only those occasions in their relationship when he *wasn't* given a hiding. And this is one such occasion.

None of us knew that in those days there was a fierce struggle going on for our naïve hearts and minds: the social stirrings of the turbulent sixties did not reach as far as our school desks. Alexander Solzhenitsyn was already working on his *Gulag Archipelago*, Anna Akhmatova was still alive, and hurrying to put down on paper all that had had to remain locked in her head during the terrible years, a new young literature was abroad in Moscow, the literary heritage of those who had perished was being painstakingly reassembled, scrap by scrap: every singed bit of paper, every line . . . All this suppressed heritage was being scrupulously gathered and hidden away from the danger of house-searches; it was carefully typed and retyped on manual typewriters, with four carbon copies at a time . . .

We, in the meantime, stood in lengthy queues for bread (we were old enough by now to count the change properly), and were amazed by the number of debts we seemed to owe the state. When had we managed to become so heavily indebted? From birth, they told us at school. We get free schooling, free medical treatment, and each one of us costs the state such and such an amount per year. We even had problems in arithmetic exams where we had to work out how much the state spends on us. This was very offensive: it seemed as though the state grudged us everything. But why should it? Our parents work for the state, and they give us the money to buy the bread for which we're queuing; we bring home coppers of change, and they don't count them, because they trust us, even though we're only ten years old! As for free education – what an argument! We're forced to go to school: just try to avoid it: they'll make you go, even if they have to bring the militia into it! The free medical care, too, boils down to an annual visit by the class to a dental clinic, and being stranded among hungry cannibals is preferable to that! It would be better if they just left us alone.

"Aaah!!!"

"Stop jerking! It hurts? Rubbish! It can't hurt yet!"

The drill bores into a nerve (no injections are available to make this a painless exercise) and seems to go right through the back of your head. The dentists are tired and irritable: they have three schools to do today, so there's no time for any messing around. Quickly, quickly; "You can cry when you go home to your mother! Come on, open your mouth! Do you hear me? Open up!"

The class teacher sits like a sentinel to make sure that nobody escapes. Oh, when will they let me spit the blood out of my mouth? Everything appears in a red haze, and Vitka in the neighbouring chair is already bawling his head off . . .

And for this we're supposed to be grateful? It makes my blood freeze to remember it now, so many years later. Nor are we inspired by continual lectures on the subject of the Motherland: mothers don't count every crumb that goes into your mouth or the nights they have spent sitting up with you. We know nothing yet about that other Motherland, the one which sows corn for us on instructions from above, puts shoes on our feet and treasures charred bits of paper with immortal poetry and prose for us to read later. But the compulsory Motherland which is pushed down our throats at school strikes us as being more like the wicked stepmother in fairy-tales. But maybe it's only like that towards children? Maybe things will change when we grow up?

"Igoresha, son, shall we go and visit Auntie Shura?"

Auntie Shura is eighty years old, has nobody in the world, and lives in an old people's home. She's not even a relative, properly speaking: she lived once with Grandmother's nephew, that's all. She managed to get through secondary school before the Revolution, then she worked, then she got old . . . Igor and his mother put together a parcel of goodies, apples, a bunch of flowers . . . The old people's home is on the outskirts of Kiev. Inside, it reeks strongly of urine, but apart from that, it has ordinary-looking stairs and wards. There are six beds in each – just as in a Pioneers' camp or in a hospital. But once here, you are here for life. The old women are all still capable of getting around, Auntie Shura is still on her feet, too. But the smell . . . ! Dry voices, like rustling leaves, express gratitude for the treats in the parcel, then attention focuses on Igor.

"What a lovely lad!"

"What a handsome boy!"

There's a superstition that one shouldn't praise children to their face. But these old women can do what they like. They are impartial, almost as though they are already half-way into the next world. Maybe they will never see another little boy again? And he's so polite, he's brought them some apples . . .

Igor sits in stunned silence all the way home. His mother, too, is silent and withdrawn. The sun shines over the Dnieper, the terrible stench of urine and imminent death has been left behind. But never, never will Igor let his mother be put into such a place!

Chapter Seven

From the fifth grade life becomes a bit more interesting: there are separate teachers for every subject, and there are more subjects, too. Among such a number of teachers there are some wonderful people. The reserved and very correct mathematics teacher fills me with deferential admiration. She never raises her voice, let alone says anything nasty or hurtful. I don't know how she manages to handle us, but we all pull ourselves up in her presence, and for some reason I always feel as though my hair is a mess when I am in her class. Yet she always seems to look somehow through us and never favours anyone above another, she doesn't divide us up into 'good' and 'bad' pupils. She addresses pupils and other teachers in exactly the same way and keeps everyone at a slight distance with her unfailing courtesy. Mathematics cease to be nothing more than problems followed by dreaded exams, and become a world of ideal order. Everything, it emerges, is so logical, you can't argue against the incontrovertible, it's the same for everyone, small schoolchildren like ourselves and the greatest scientific minds. Geometry problems 'to be proved' were to become my specialty a year later. How about that? I can prove something to somebody – anybody! And how satisfying it is to see one result following from another, and then – hey presto! A sudden quirk, almost a party trick: let's divide both parts of a fraction by minus three, throw in a power, and everything can be successfully reduced, cancelled out, and all the enormous lines of calculations will taper down to a fantastically compact result, which calls forth a burst of laughter, like a successfully performed conjuring trick.

Our handicrafts teacher is a bit of a rough diamond, a very witty, streetwise former fitter and turner. He enriches our vocabulary with all sorts of racy words and sayings, which we store away and repeat at any opportunity. At the same time, he doesn't let us get away with sloppy work, or holding a file wrongly, and speaks about metal with such love, that he makes us feel that turning out a bad part is tantamount to sacrilege. He measures the angles of our creations with good-natured disdain, and snorts despairingly: "You could see half of Europe through that clearance! And what have you drilled here, you unsung hero?"

"A hole."

"I can see it's a hole. Now, if you had drilled an opening, it would be properly centred, wouldn't it? Take this to a kindergarten exhibition, that's all it's good for!"

He won my heart by the simplest of tricks: by taking a thin metal rod, placing it casually on an even surface, and holding the top end against the palm of his hand. Looking off into the middle distance, he challenged us: "It's vertical. Come and check!"

We surged forward with our metal measures and checked from all angles: he was right – it was dead vertical! The full glory of this achievement strikes us only when we try to do it ourselves, and find it to be virtually impossible. Before that, a group of us saw the film *Daki* and practically cut our fingers to shreds trying to stab a knife down between the spread fingers of our hands with our eyes shut. Now we had something else to strive for. Standing a pencil on our desks, we would declare: "Vertical!"

"You call *that* vertical?! Ha!"

"Well, how about now?"

"Stop jiggling your hand around, or I can't measure!"

"Will you stop pushing my hand around while you measure, you unsung hero!"

Amusing myself in this manner, I found that I was damaging my father's instruments much less than before, when I made wooden buttons and toys for myself. I was always wanting to make things, within the limits of my childish abilities, of course: either a tiger-cub out of peach-stones, or a tiny dagger the size of my little finger, or a key-ring. I would go to the table with all of Father's instruments more and more often, and he would only grunt resignedly when I broke yet another fine drill: they were always harder to replace than anything else. And in order not to break them, the hand-drill must be held vertically, and the wheel turned smoothly, without forcing or jerking. To escape criticism at home, I tried to engage in my hobbies away from the eyes of the adults. Now how could I explain to them why I wanted to burn through a solid plastic ball with a hot needle until I reached the colour bands inside it? Of course, this serves no useful purpose, but it's interesting! One strip shrivels, the other one melts, but the third – fabulous! – peels off like the branches of a fir-tree, which is just what I need for the key-ring I'm making, and give immediately as a present to my friend Tanya.

Father once spotted my tiny dagger: "Show me that! What on earth do you need that for?"

"Just to play with."

"And where did you get it?"

"I found it . . ."

"Hmmm . . . Are you telling me the truth? This was made by silly hands like yours, only more skilled."

That was music to my ears indeed!

The young teacher of Russian enjoys setting us short essays, about ten minutes long, at just about every lesson: humour is encouraged, so is poetry. It's like a game, which she enjoys as much as we do. I relish this almost as much as swimming in the sea – right out to the underwater reef, which you can only reach if you know the shore landmarks to watch for, and then you can stand waist-high in green water.

Nelly, the Russian teacher, soon found time to meet and have a talk with my mother: "Your daughter has considerable talent. Don't make a big thing of it, but try to nourish it."

I learned about this many years later, as a student, from a chance remark of Mother's. Even so, I didn't get all the details. It seems that Nelly, with her youthful enthusiasm, praised me so much that my parents took fright, and deemed it better not to give me any inkling about any talent I might have. Still, I know the name of my first adult reader and literary critic: Nelly Faddeyevna Snigur, who would shout at us until she was red in the face as we took advantage of her inexperience to get up to all sorts of larks in class. She was amazingly demanding towards me: no superficially 'acceptable' essay written just to get it over and done with would get past her critical eye. She would describe such occasions as 'Ratushinskaya being below par today'. And all this time my Odessa swirled and eddied around me, fish was roasted in its little courtyards, people jostled around water taps, and ordinary squabbles in trams turned into contests of wit. Towards autumn, the wild grapes growing along the fences would run through a whole gamut of colours, we would stuff our pockets full of new horse-chestnuts, which were royally useless and therefore much treasured. Actually you could make little horses out of them by sticking in matches, or simply throw them at each other. One particular horse-chestnut was to become to me one of those objects which change the course of one's life. Unfortunately, it disappeared without a trace, or I would carry it in my pocket to this day.

It was thrown at the end of the last, dreariest lesson of the day, when the history teacher had already floated out of the room. I didn't do the throwing, even though it could have been me just as easily, out of sheer joy that school was over for the day. The chestnut splashed into an inkwell, which fell to the floor and smashed, spattering a nearby wall and making it look as though someone had emptied a machine-gun into it. Half of the class made haste to leave, but I couldn't disappear because it was Seryozha's and my turn to clean the classroom. And then, as if out of nowhere, the history teacher reappeared.

"Who broke the inkwell?"

Silence.

"What, you don't have enough courage to say?"

Silence again. Some courage that would be, to tell on a friend!

"Well, as you're such cowards, you can stay here, and wait for the senior teacher. Then we'll get to the bottom of it!"

When the senior teacher came, he summoned all the remaining pupils into the corridor, one by one, and questioned them. Seryozha and I were summoned last, together.

"You're on duty today, and responsible for order in the classroom. If you are not the guilty ones, tell me who is?"

I began to pour out the customary lies: that I don't know, I didn't see anything, when it happened I was searching for something in my satchel (a detail to increase credibility), that I'd say if I knew who did it, but as I saw nothing, I can shed no light on what occurred.

But Seryozha, who occasionally annoyed the rest of us with his knowledge and markedly adult manner, answered briefly and to the point: "I'm not going to tell you."

Oh, how ashamed I felt! How much more to my liking was his answer than mine! And it hadn't even entered my head to say that, for all that I was in the fifth grade.

Fear of authority and a readiness to lie had become so ingrained in my heart, that my first instinct had been – even while telling a lie – to create the impression that I was full of goodwill, and it took Seryozha's action to make me aware of the humiliating nature of my own reaction. But aren't there different ways of not informing on someone . . . ? The senior teacher, Efim Kharitonovich, took a long look at Seryozha, then switched his attention back to me: was I sure that I had nothing more to add?

Our class was rostered for study in the second shift on that day, and I made my way home in the dark, lingering for some reason around the street lights as though I had lost something. I had to have time to think things through: could it be that I was becoming what THEY wanted me to be – a cowardly, spineless creature, with no concept of honour, but ever obedient? One who considers a glib lie to be an act of heroism, and the result the cardinal issue? Could it be that for me, the means were now justified by the end? Maybe in several more years' time I'll become a tell-tale, and will find reasons to justify that, too? I castigated myself in this vein until I got home, and then made my decision: right, that's it, never again! I shall never, ever lower myself like that again before anybody. If I must disobey in order to preserve my self-respect, then I shall do so openly. Even if I'm beaten, or expelled from school. I'm still a juvenile, I have no rights, and who can say if I'll ever have any? But I will not let those who are stronger make me do anything of which I would be ashamed. I have always found it difficult to endure conflicts, shouting and even raised voices, so am I going to let this be a means by which I can be controlled? No, better learn to handle conflict. I've had more than enough instruction on how to be obedient, and look where it's got me! I'll learn how to behave decently from books, and also I'll think a lot and talk to God more. Then my soul will remain my own: nobody will be able to manipulate me to suit themselves.

Every night after that, when I went to bed, I would go over the events of the day: should I have behaved differently on any particular occasion, and if so – how? Should I have said something differently, or kept my mouth shut altogether? These post mortems were not particularly painful: I knew that I had years of real life ahead, and that I would have time for everything, if I wanted to. For don't I have sufficient enthusiasm to play 'hangers' – that's when we want to hide from adults, and accomplish this by hanging with one hand off the roof of our three-storey building, holding on to some rusty piece of metal or protrusion? Don't I swim out so far from shore that only boats go there? Don't I have enough brains to solve mathematical problems? And I haven't had time to do anything really bad yet, something that's irreversible, so that means that I can still straighten out my life.

Of course, I was an extremely self-confident child, I had no idea that things were not as simple as I thought. But luckily, I had not yet learned to lie to myself, for there is nothing more terrible than feeling ashamed of yourself in solitude.

The enormous number of books which I read voraciously blended countries and epochs into one in my mind, leaving a general picture of Man, and the situations into which life places him. The situations were almost invariably inauspicious, but the human values of 'good' and 'evil' did not change. Korczak went knowingly to his death because he refused to desert the orphans who were his responsibility. In some other time and place, when Jewish children were not being annihilated, he would not have had to do so, but he would have remained the same man as the one who sacrificed his life. The Decembrist Lunin was one of the few who refused to give any evidence during the tsarist investigation of that ill-fated revolt. How would he have acted during the Civil War? Or in Stalin's time, when they knew how to extract confessions even from the dying? Would he have informed on his friends under a Soviet interrogation? Or what would have been the outcome if such a Lunin were to be approached for co-operation by the Spanish Inquisition, or the Gestapo, or the KGB?

These were Khrushchev's times, the Stalin cult was being criticised, there was mention of numerous innocent victims. But reading about the trials of Nazi war criminals and their henchmen, I could not see any difference between their attempts to justify themselves by claiming that they were 'merely following orders', or that they had acted under duress, or out of ignorance, and the excuses advanced by adults of the Stalin generation. What kinds of times will I live in when I grow up? What kind of orders will be issued to me, and what will I, perhaps, prefer not to know? The newspapers promise that we shall have attained communism by 1980: universal well-being, general plenty and the Golden Age. I'll be twenty-six then – almost into old age. And honour, as the saying goes, must be cherished from one's youth: in case I should forget that, Pushkin made it an epigraph to a novella about a seventeen-year-old lad in Pugachev's time. Of course, he was a lad from Pushkin's point of view: to me, though, he was big, a whole six years older than I.

Chapter Eight

I'm going on for twelve, it's a Sunday, and Father takes me into town for a walk. Such times, like swimming together in the sea, are the happiest moments of our relationship. He strides along, and I try to match my steps to his. From time to time he points out his favourite places to me: that house over there is known as the 'three-cornered' one, here's a double-passaged yard, and this street used to be called 'Preobrazhenskaya', the Street of the Transfiguration, in the old days ... Like most residents of Odessa, I pay no attention to the names on street signs: who cares what new names were given to these streets after the Revolution? They were renamed after Lenin, or Klara Tsetkin, or Dzerzhinsky, just as in other towns, but who gives a hoot about that? It's for 'them' to put up new street signs, and for us to keep the old names alive.

But today Father seems to be going out of his way to be particularly attentive to me. So far he hasn't said a word about the fact that I still haven't finished reading the radio manual (amateur radios are his particular hobby, and he's tried to interest me in it despite my barely concealed lack of enthusiasm), nor has the subject of my getting only four out of five for maths – disgrace! – been raised. He even puts his arm around my shoulders and gives me a squeeze as he steers me into a souvenir shop. Why on earth has he brought me here? I have been taught from my earliest days not to pester my parents to buy me toys: they only just manage to make ends meet, proudly, but with great difficulty, determined not to get into debt. They detest children who are always making whining demands on their parents to buy them this or that, and I never, never do so. From time to time they buy me things of their own accord, but how can they possibly know what I really want?

"Let's buy Mama a toy," suggests Father, steering me into the shop.

What a brilliant idea! Of course, Mama is grown up, but for sure she must have a secret desire to play, one which she can't admit because she's a school teacher. After all, she has a much-prized creature of some kind made out of green glass: it's very fragile, especially its tail, and I'm only allowed to hold it in my hands when I'm ill. Still, I'm almost big now, and I try to conceal my interest in toys. We choose a clay figure of a smoker with an assortment of cigarettes: you light one of them, and it sends out smoke rings. Father explains that bits of film have been inserted in the cigarettes at regular intervals, but this does not detract from the magic of the moment; let's get it to Mama as quickly as possible! I bet she's never seen anything like this in her whole life! However, along with the excitement, I feel stirrings of apprehension: the toy is obviously for me, even though, ostensibly, it's a present for Mama . . . There must be something wrong. Why else go in for such elaborate diplomacy?

Still, I have no choice but to go along with it and ask no questions, especially as outwardly, at least, there's no cause for them; we've had a nice walk, I've received an unexpected treat, but this has happened before. Well, maybe not quite like this: there's some hidden motive behind today's events . . . I am torn in half all the way home. But surely that's silly? All that will happen is that we'll come home, Mama will have a lovely surprise, I'll explain to her about the bits of film in the cigarettes, and will laugh at my own stupid fears . . . But . . . Heavens! Maybe my parents have decided to get divorced? No, that's nonsense, utterly impossible! Maybe they're going to tell me that Mama has some fatal illness? Or Father? Or something just as terrible?!

Mama is waiting for us, wearing her best green dress. After some beating about the bush (if only they'd get it over and done with, whatever it is!) they tell me that I'm going to have a baby brother or sister. Whew! Is that all?! But I realise now why they've gone to all this trouble in breaking the news to me: they want me to know that they won't love me any less after the baby is born. Really, Mama and Papa, you're so funny! What book put this idea into your heads? Have you really been worrying yourselves sick thinking that I would be jealous, and for that reason scared me half to death? Do you really think I don't know why you haven't had another baby for so long, the son you've dreamed about? How can anything be a secret when you have so many people sharing just two rooms?

I know full well that Mama's blood group is Rhesus negative, while mine is positive. Nobody thought anything about this when I was born, the problem only came to light when I was very ill once, and the doctors attempted to give me a blood transfusion from Mama, which almost ended in death . . . I knew that because of me Mama had antibodies which meant she should have no more children. Still, twelve years later it seemed worth the risk. Hurray! Forget your fears that I'll suffer from any lack of your attention. You're both up to your ears in work all the time, Mama even brings books home to mark in the evenings, and Papa sits over a drawing board. And that has no adverse effect on me, does it? On top of that, whenever you have a spare moment, you try to correct all my shortcomings in one go, and I would happily do without such concentrated 'attention' – there's easily enough of it for two children!

There's also the pleasant thought that when my new brother gets older, I'll be able to play with him. My joy is not overshadowed by any misgivings until it becomes clear that it is still very dangerous for Mama to have a second baby, and all because of those blasted antibodies. She might die, or the baby may be handicapped ... But then, everything could turn out all right, after all! Who knows? A woman doctor who's a friend of Mama's is going to be in charge of the birth when Mama goes into hospital. Time passes. Occasionally, Mama succumbs to nerves, Papa too, but for the first time ever, I don't feel hurt or angry with them: what if they should lose each other, they, whose love is so complete that I never remember a single cross word between them? What if the worse comes to the worst, and Mama dies, leaving Father with just Grandmother and myself . . . ? I don't remember anything of school, or my lessons at that time – only a constant fear for them, whose love for each other was always more important to both than anything else in the world.

The day came for Mama to be admitted to hospital, and I remained at home alone, going through old photographs. My hands were unsteady and terribly cold, the shiny surface of the photos seemed as smooth and cold as glass. There was one photo that Father had taken of Mama: young, her hair in braids around her head, long before I was born. I took this photo and hid it under my pillow. After several days of suspense, Papa told me over someone's phone (we didn't have a telephone) that I had a baby sister, and that she and Mama were both doing well.

We picked them up from the hospital with bouquets of flowers, but before that Papa and I worked out our nervous energy by completely re-upholstering the parents' divan-bed and tightening its springs. From reading everything I could lay my hands on I knew that a younger child is invariably a disappointment to the older one. But I had my doubts about this book-culled wisdom. It seemed unlikely. When all is said and done, here would be this tiny living creature, with little fingers, with eyes, with its own desires and needs ... It would have to have its nappies changed, it would need to be cuddled and amused with rattles and toys. What could be bad about that?

I loved my sister Helen (so named after the doctor who brought about her successful birth) from the moment I saw her: she seemed so precious, so clever, such a fascinating being. I was convinced that even at ten days from birth she could understand absolutely everything that was said to her, and that she cried only because we were too stupid to understand her. June that year was insufferably hot, the baby's nappies had to be boiled in a large saucepan on the gas stove and then ironed on both sides. Water still had to be brought up in buckets from the tap in the yard . . . Mama had very little milk, and I remember Father cooking up some kind of gruel for the baby out of pearl barley and cow's milk. My sister, meanwhile, had started to smile, and babble . . . then at eight months she lay in the shadow of death from pneumonia.

Mama and the baby were rushed to hospital, where they were placed in a separate cubicle, which meant that the doctors did not think she had much chance. They even warned Papa to expect the worst. Father seemed somehow to shrink into himself, and for the first time I saw how lost and helpless men become in times of grief. I did not know how to help him, so I brewed endless cups of strong tea for him, swept the floor, and made clumsy efforts to pitch in and help with everything. He bore it all with great patience and took me with him to the hospital to talk to Mama through the glass of her cubicle. Mama looked back at us with huge, pain-filled eyes, while the baby lay there, barely moving her head on its small, thin neck.

Grandmother Alexandra Kuzminichna (Papa's mother), a dyed-in-the-wool atheist and by this time barely able to move from her chair, sat there repeating, over and over, like a litany: "She'll live, she'll live, she'll live . . ."

All maternal care, taken away so abruptly, seemed frighteningly gone forever. It was February, and through vitamin deficiency, I became covered in boils. Where had Mama always managed to get hold of vitamin pills? As for the family wash – which had to be done a bit at a time in a small basin – it seemed to take us both all day. But my stye-swollen eyes saw everything in a different light when it was borne in on me that, myself apart, there was nobody to see that Papa had an ironed shirt, or that his ashtray was emptied and washed. I don't think he noticed my doing these things for him, and I think I was glad that he didn't.

My sister pulled through, and when she and Mama came home at last everything returned to normal. My little sister sat in my lap, emaciated to the point where I could feel her little bones pressing against my knees. I carried her from room to room, and she would point at things with her tiny finger, and ask: "That?"

"That's a window. See that tree outside? There'll be leaves on it soon."

"That?"

"That's a book. Let's look at the pretty pictures. See? That's an elephant, and that's a cat. And here's a cr-r-r-ocodile!"

All the adults were amazed that the baby had started to talk before she was a year old, and in hospital, of all places! Mama told us laughingly how the doctors were completely nonplussed when Alya (as we call her) saw someone in a white coat bending over her, and pointing her small finger at him said sternly: "Go 'way!"

As for me, I could see no reason for their surprise. It's only silly adults who set time limits on when a child should be able to do what, because children can do everything. Do they think they could do better learning an unknown language from scratch while the baby learns Russian? Children are more talented than adults, but out of pedagogical considerations nobody admits this to them. And later, as children grow older, their brains become less lively, but set – rather like honey, which thickens and hardens after a while – and their talents decline through insufficient encouragement to develop. There are the lucky few whose development doesn't become arrested: they are deemed to be gifted, geniuses, everyone fusses around them, envies them, and sometimes – just in case! – they get killed. After that, in posthumous eulogies, they are hailed as the pride and joy of the nation. Yet when one reads their bigraphies, the fact emerges that not more than one in perhaps a hundred had an enviable lot in life. Still, they would have had a greater share of joys, for they were courageous and set themselves no limits. They could achieve whatever they wanted in their chosen field, they were not afflicted by doubts such as 'I won't be able to manage that', or 'Maybe this will prove beyond me'. That is to say, they had their doubts, that's no secret and much is written on this, but they were able to overcome these misgivings when necessary. Nor did they pay any heed to doubting Thomases as they worked.

As for us lesser mortals – we're pretty much formed by the time we reach twenty years of age: there are few major discoveries awaiting us, we know our limits, and if we don't, we'll learn them soon enough through bitter experience. All we can do is push our limits back as far as possible while there's still time. For a start – plough through as many books on psychology as possible. A plague on children's libraries with their Pioneers' adventure stories and books about spy-catching! It's a whole four years before I'll be allowed to join an adults' library ... However, there's no need to ruin my day by seething over something I can't change, especially when the chestnut trees are about to burst into bloom and my parents have given me fifty kopecks to go to a movie and buy an ice cream!

Chapter Nine

Life seems hardly worth living if you don't own a dog. Especially when you're thirteen years old and have been nagging your parents to get you a dog for the past year.

"I want a dog! The biggest dog possible! A big, black, clever dog! I'll do everything myself: I'll feed it, I'll walk it, I'll clean up after it! If you like, I'll even promise to get top marks in everything at school if you'll let me have a dog! And the dog will win shows, too!"

Igor dreams about such a dog constantly, and in his dreams he throws his arms around its shaggy neck. And the dog's nose – is there anything in the world more expressive than a dog's nose? – pokes trustingly against his ear.

In principle, Igor's parents don't object. Of course, it will be a bit of a nuisance getting meat for the animal, and it will be a miracle if even half of the fervent promises being made are kept . . . On the other hand, the lad is far from robust, and his legs below the knee are like sticks ending in deformed feet. He finds it painful to walk, but if he were to be given a puppy it would be a distraction, which would encourage him to walk around more. If he wants a big, black dog, that probably means they'll have to try to get a Newfoundland. Igor's father set enquiries afoot, only to learn that Newfoundlands are available through the kennel club in Tallinn, nowhere else, and even that's virtually impossible. Extracting a solemn promise from Igor to excel in his studies (Who knows? It might work!) Igor's father took him to Moscow. He had to go there on a business trip anyway, and something just might turn up in the capital.

The state kennels have remained in Igor's memory as a cheerless, dirty place. In one room, which had been barricaded by an office desk, they saw an enormous, grey Great Dane, with the sad eyes of every unwanted dog. No pup was available, and Igor's father was against taking a grown animal. However, from that moment on, Igor no longer wanted a Newfoundland, but a Great Dane. Quite by chance, they discovered that there was a Great Dane fancier in Kiev. He bred them, and considered all other breeds an accident of nature. "They're gods!" he enthused about his beloved Great Danes. The breeder, Rabinovich, had two bitches – Nora, the older of the two, and Vesta. He regaled Igor and his father with incredible tales of the intelligence and capabilities of Great Danes. For instance, he recounted, a friend of his would gather seven of his cronies in one room, pull out seven different newspapers, and then order his Great Dane: "Give *Trud* to Misha, *Pravda* – to Kolya, *Evening Kiev* – to Alex . . ." and so on. Naturally, the dog carried out these commands without a single error.

Igor lapped up this story, but on the way home, his father poured cold water over it: "I wonder what would happen if that dog's owner were to be given a bunch of foreign newspapers, whose titles he didn't know, and told the dog to take them to this or that particular person? Now *that* I'd like to see! If he were as talented as his dog, he'd go a long way . . ."

All further negotiations were left to Igor: his father had heard enough about the brilliance of Great Danes. He would pay the bill, but it was for Igor to effect the purchase and train the dog to the required level of intelligence, and – who knows? – maybe even improve his own in the process.

At last, the great day dawned. Igor and his mother set off to Rabinovich's place to choose a pup. One out of seven – and, of course, the best of the lot! Nora, the proud mother, lay surrounded by all her medals and awards. She was weighed down by swollen teats, and did not seem particularly pleased with her visitors. Igor took her growl to mean: "Blasted nuisances, coming in and out, because of them I have to wear all these decorations, and that's the last thing I need, right now! I've got a family to feed! Gr-r-r-r!"

Rabinovich brought the pups out in a box, and a fluffy, four-day-old black bundle, which gave no clue as to its future size, fitted snugly, tail and all, into Igor's hand. Its tiny nose sniffed the fingers of its future master, and Igor was in seventh heaven.

A month later Igor took his new friend home by tram, cradling him under his jacket. The puppy's name would be 'Small' and together they would share a new and magnificent life. Igor would ensure that Small would be the luckiest dog in the world. He had already done the groundwork by reading everything he could find about dogs. Not for nothing had he coaxed their neighbour, Elizaveta Samoylovna, into lending him the first volume of Bram, and learnt it off by heart. This neighbour was an elderly, well-educated lady, and she was touched that the boy showed an interest in books printed in the old, pre-Revolutionary orthography: for that reason, she was quite willing to lend him the book, even though he had a questionable reputation

for staging explosions. When he returned the book and quoted copiously from it, even indicating chapters and page numbers, she melted
completely, and allowed him unrestricted access to her other literary
treasures. What a wonderful, mysterious smell they had, these old
books! They were big, and heavy, and you had to use both hands to
get them down from the top shelves. And every book – older than his
grandfather! – spoke to Igor as to an equal, as though he were not a
twentieth-century tearaway, but a serious young man in a frock-coat,
or whatever it was they wore in those days.

Soon Igor was to receive a fantastic present – all six volumes
of Bram, beautifully bound and with gold-lettering on the covers,
published between 1869 and 1874. With a theoretical basis like that,
Small's childhood was secure.

Small turned out to be a very placid puppy. He didn't even cry for
his mother, even though Igor was all set to comfort him. Some three
months later, when they were on a visit to the country, Small barked
for the first time in an 'adult' voice. In fact, he had such a deep bark
that everyone around was amazed: a pup with the vocal might of the
Hound of the Baskervilles, no less! Igor kept his promises better than
his parents had expected. He would walk Small for a total of five
hours each day: never mind the pains in his legs, the dog's welfare
had to come first. He spent hours in queues at the market to buy
calves' heads and ox spleens for Small's dinner. The prices for offal
kept rising, but by that time Igor's father was already the head of a
laboratory and a rising academic, so money for the dog's food was
not a problem. Igor acquired plenty of experience in market-place
haggling, and, at the same time, got to know all the local dog-fanciers,
among whom there were many very colourful characters. At home he
would hack up the calves' heads with an axe, and cook them in a large
green saucepan.

Then, suddenly, tragedy! It became apparent that the set of Small's
jaws was not quite right: despite his pedigree, despite all the care that
had been lavished on him, Small would never win the gold medal
everyone had confidently expected awaited him.

It's a well-known fact that dogs are very sensitive to distinctions of
this nature: it's enough to go to a dog show to see how proudly they
receive their prizes. But apart from that, if there was a distortion of
the pup's jaws, shouldn't he be treated for it? Our families lived in
different cities, but Igor and I used to meet when our parents went
on shared vacations. Igor knew that I had an 'incorrect bite', too – my
lower jaw is set too far back. This was an inherited characteristic among
all the women in our family; I knew that from the old daguerreotypes

Grandmother had in an album. My mother went to enormous lengths to have this corrected in me, and at the age of eleven I was fitted with braces. The doctor who fitted the braces made life even more miserable by tightening them each week. So if this defect can be remedied in people, surely it can be corrected in a dog?

In Kiev, such braces were fitted in an orthodontal clinic on Zoolog-icheskaya Street. When Dr Bratus, who worked there, first saw Igor – who had absolutely nothing wrong with his jaws – he couldn't understand what the kid was after. By the time he knew, it was too late. From his mother, Igor inherited an ability to move mountains for the sake of someone he loved. Bratus could not bring himself to send this thin, stubborn stripling packing. He could not explain why, nor could Igor. Bratus rose to the challenge: he had never worked on a dog before – nor, indeed, could any of his colleagues boast about something like that. He made special plates for Small, with crowns and anchorings. Small was still growing, and his braces were as much of a nuisance to him as mine were to me. Only I held out for two and a half years at the persuasion of my mother, but Igor's father found it all too much to take. He thought that the experiment was question-able, at best, and there was no doubt about the dog's discomfort.

"The upshot will be that the dog will be left without teeth!" he declared. Then, despite Igor's frantic pleas, he removed the braces from the dog's mouth with a pair of pliers. Though Small lost his chance of ever taking the first prize at a dog show, he more than made up for it in obedience competitions at the kennel club. Admittedly, he didn't learn to read newspapers, but he mastered everything else he was taught from the word go.

In the beginning, Igor had no hesitation in clouting Small for any perceived misdemeanours, and the puppy took his punishment without complaint or, it seemed to Igor, offence. But once, at some function at the kennel club, Igor hit the dog (as he now admits) without adequate reason. Small broke away from him and ran off. Catching a healthy young dog is a virtual impossibility. While he scoured the city for Small, Igor had ample opportunity to think about what he'd done. And the stark truth seemed to be that he was just a cruel boy who was trying to establish his supremacy by being unfair to another 'boy' of the same age – the only difference was that Small was a dog, not a two-legged human.

He came home alone and in despair, to find Small was already there. Igor apologised, they made up, and had no conflicts again for many, many years.

Shortly afterwards Small became ill with a skin disease, which itched abominably. Igor's father approached a friend who worked in the Institute of Physiology, and Small was given intravenous treatment, which resulted in his marking the environs with dark blue urine for the next few days. As for Igor – the visit to the institute put paid to all his ambitions to become a biologist. It was here that he saw laboratory rabbits and other animals, including Ukrainian sheep-dogs, a breed which has almost become extinct since the war. Here, they disappeared for ever: big white dogs, with incredibly long hair. Igor saw animals which had already been 'cut' – heads shaved, electrodes attached, and an almost human resignation in their eyes. Exactly like the old women he had seen in the old folks' home . . . He was fourteen years old, inseparable from the year-old Small, and he understood once and for all that this branch of science was not for him. He knew that the work done at the institute was necessary, that the biologists working there were not sadists, and did not perform operations on animals without reason, but he knew that he would never be able to do so. He would just have to find a new profession. Go into chemistry, maybe? The future would show.

Small completed his obedience training, and took the gold medal. Of course, the medal was really made out of aluminium covered with gilt, but master and dog were equally thrilled. Igor took Small out without a leash, and one word – 'heel!' – was enough to ensure that Small would pace unswervingly beside his master for the full length of Kiev's main street, the Kreschatik, to the delight of all Igor's pals. In those days, Igor and Small both had a tendency to show off.

Chapter Ten

An old person always evokes pity. Not because he is close to death: once he dies, he will go to God, unless he is extremely evil, and all will be well for him, and he'll be reunited with his loved ones. But while he is still alive, he is terribly vulnerable. The old are so easily hurt. Naturally, anyone can be hurt: but if someone hurts me, will that trouble me for long? I can always go down to the sea, or climb up on the roof, or fly up a long stairway so fast that my heart will feel as if it's bursting, feeling nothing but breathlessness and a shivering in my knees – and all is well again.

If anyone upsets our teacher Nina Nikolayevna, she takes it out on us, and really does feel better for it. She's not unique – there are lots like her, be they adults, or children, or dogs. When Natasha the janitor has walloped her dog Belka for some reason or other, it's better not to venture into the yard for a while, because Belka will do her utmost to give you a nip, at the very least. There are other reactions, too. For instance, the great Russian poet and writer Lermontov was slighted once at a New Year's ball, and the next day he sat down and wrote a work that will still be learned off by heart in centuries to come. I suppose it's easier for sculptors – they can vent their anger on a chunk of stone. Trainers have been known to goad sportsmen deliberately, just to get the adrenalin flowing and urge them on to greater feats. When I played volley-ball, our trainer Vasili Alexeyevich used to pull that trick with me whenever I wasn't doing as well as I might . . .

Generally speaking, we all have some means of letting off steam when we've been hurt. But what can an elderly person do? Someone offends him, and all he can do is go off into a corner and brood about it. Most of his friends will have died, and he can't get his troubles off his chest by talking to those who are much younger. In fact, there's nothing he can do but sit there, nursing his hurt, and maybe not even bother to switch on the light when it grows dark. Not because he can't make the effort physically, but because he thinks: why bother? I can't think about this coherently any further, all I feel is a lump in my throat. Maybe this is due to some innate instinct, or, perhaps, something that is there despite 're-education'. What is the attitude of the government institutions responsible for my upbringing towards old age? It starts with the frenetic Mayakovsky (who was an institution in himself) and ends with school, where if there is an anti-religious poster on the wall, it will invariably depict an old woman down on her knees in front of an icon, with a superciliously facetious slogan of some kind superimposed. In other words, the attitude toward old age is that it is something to be brushed aside and undeserving of sympathy. However, we are taught respect for certain 'deserving' old people. For instance, those who fought against the White Guard in their time, or happened to meet Lenin personally. But pity is not to be extended even to them, because pity is considered demeaning. This, too, is something I find hard to understand: whom does it demean? If Pushkin's contemporaries had pitied him instead of subjecting him to constant pin-pricks, would that have demeaned him? All the humiliations he had to suffer were the work of those who had no scrap of pity for him! If someone has no pity for you, they will definitely demean you: that is a lesson we all learn by the time we're ten years old.

So what is this that they are trying to din into our heads? And with a persistence that borders on the absurd, at that? Here we are, sitting through a literature lesson. I'm big now, fourteen years old. Old enough, one would think, to be able to work it out, it's not so hard! And to have a point of view on the question, too. But no: I am totally at a loss. We're 'doing' Gogol's story about two old landowners, an elderly couple. They are sweet, not terribly bright, but endlessly kind and unworldly. They love each other dearly. Death means separation. There is some slight comfort in that the separation will not be for long. Intense grief is never for long. They both die, and Gogol weeps. So do I, every time I re-read the *Old-World Landowners*. Crying in class, naturally, is out of the question, especially for us terribly grown-up eighth-graders. Luckily, we don't actually read the story in class; reading has to be done at home. At school we analyse. We are told how we should understand the work in question. To my amazement I hear that Gogol is indicting this elderly couple. That far from pitying them, I should despise them and anyone like them. In this instance, we are informed, Gogol's humour is satirical: and I know the difference between humour and satire – humour is kind, satire is cruel. For this reason, every institution and workplace has a 'window of satire' with unfunny caricatures of those who are deemed to have erred in some way. I have never seen a complementary 'window of humour', though. Satire, we are told, is a socially useful phenomenon which facilitates progress. So come on, stupid, use your brains and realise in which direction this progress is supposed to go! You know all the components – all you have to do is piece them together!

Instead of that, I sit there like a dummy at my scratched green desk, gaping at Antonina Alexeyevna, our Russian Literature teacher. And she continues to pontificate. She's not a bad person, really, a rotund, rather jolly woman. I know that intellectually she is as thick as two short planks, and that the ideas she is propounding are not her own. In fact, she never voices any original thoughts, so there is no reason to think that what she says differs in any way from the 'official' viewpoint. I have not looked at the textbook yet, but I am certain that she is repeating, practically verbatim, what it says. Gogol's work has been read and studied by erudite persons, real specialists in literature, and they have written textbooks on it. It's only fourteen-year-olds like us who imagine that we're above the dictates of authority. How self-sufficient, how independent we feel! I have sufficient nous not to take Antonina Alexeyevna seriously, but can I dismiss the views of a professor of literature just as easily? So I sit there, gaping like a landed fish, my thoughts in complete disarray. Do the elderly couple who are the central characters in Gogol's story have any useful contribution to make to society? No. Such a question had never occurred to me before, but facts are facts: what use are these old people to society? Are they landowners? Yes, they are. In that case, they're a pernicious element, aren't they?

"In what way does Gogol stress their soullessness?" asks Antonina Alexeyevna.

We sit in silence. None of us had thought, until now, that Gogol was stressing their spiritual poverty. On the contrary, he seemed positively sympathetic towards them . . . Especially when the old lady in the story worries, before dying, about how her husband will manage without her, and does everything she can think of to lessen the blow. What if he, left alone, should die from lost love and grief? Is that an example of 'lack of soul'?

"And what about their gluttony?" presses Antonina Alexeyevna triumphantly.

Hold it, hold it! True, they're always eating or feeding somebody else in the story. I suppose, in a way, that could be classed as gluttony. But why didn't it seem so until now? Of course, eating to excess can indicate a lack of soul, everyone knows that. Certainly, it deserves censure. Unarguably. My poor, bewildered brain is left with no alternative but to agree. Yet it won't – it just won't! Some instinct rebels against such a conclusion. Antonina Alexeyevna, in the meantime, has passed on to the difference between cultured and uncultured readers, and the importance of detail in the correct interpretation of a literary work.

I went home depressed by my seeming lack of culture, and settled down to reread the story. It's a fact – there they go, eating and eating! But hold on a moment! They don't eat out of greed or self-gratification; their preoccupation is to feed others! Nobody around them goes hungry: neither the servants, nor the estate manager, nor their guests. This is their way of expressing their care for each other and for all the people with whom they come into contact. It's their way of expressing love. The husband, Afanasi Ivanovich, has a dozen snacks a day not because he's greedy, but because his wife wants to give him a treat, and he doesn't want to hurt her feelings. When she dies, all his interest in food vanishes; the only time it reappears is when someone comes to visit him.

I shed secret tears over the story again, but this time they were also tears of relief. Nobody will confuse me like that again! They almost had me fooled for a while! But maybe they weren't deliberately trying to fool me, maybe that's what they really think? They may be professors, but it's quite clear that they're devoid of love and pity. Not like Gogol, who saw no shame in either emotion. No, now I understand, and I'll never believe them again!

Little did I think, then, how often I was to believe them in the years to come . . .

Chapter Eleven

I gor never did manage to become a star pupil: he was always a few 'fives' short of an all-round perfect score. However, he didn't let this upset him unduly, because he was not particularly interested in school, and he found his own contemporaries rather uninspiring: he made new friends and acquaintances much older than himself.

One such was Seryozha Domnin, a champion weight-lifter. He used to walk his boxer, Gin, in the same park where Igor exercised Small. The friendship began with an exchange of compliments about each other's dog. In half an hour, each knew the concise life history of the other one's animal: its age, its main characteristics, and the most outstanding evidence of the dog's exceptional intelligence. Only after all this data had been aired did Seryozha ask Igor how old he was.

"Thirteen?" he exclaimed unbelievingly. "Don't get me wrong, lad, but you look positively weedy! Come on, get over to the bars over there! Can you pull yourself up on them at least once? No, I thought not! Do you get sick often, or what? Legs? Never mind the legs, they're nothing: head, heart and lungs are what's important in a man!"

At that time, Seryozha was studying at the Medical Institute, having already graduated from the Institute of Physical Education. It went against a sporting man's grain to see an adolescent who was in less than perfect physical condition. The medical instincts of a future doctor found it even less acceptable. He dragged Igor off to his home and checked out his heart: everything was in order.

The upshot was that a year later, after Seryozha had taken him in hand, people recognised Igor only because he was accompanied by Small. Seryozha and Igor met every morning at six o'clock in the Pavlovsky park, where the dogs were released to run around while Seryozha had Igor doing push-ups, press-ups, squatting, running . . . Seryozha decreed it imperative to buy weights: he's a specialist, he will ensure that Igor's use of them will be correct and supervised. He had a word with Igor's parents, and then set about Igor in earnest.

The half-overgrown park was empty and damp in the early morning, and wrapped Igor in its chilly embrace. The old trees looked down, knowing that in five minutes' time the lad would be panting and sweating. Igor drove himself to the point of exhaustion, but didn't give up: he knew how lucky he was. Those who showed no initial promise were not encouraged to join sports clubs. If the trainers didn't see a potential champion in you, you needn't waste your time attending. That's why I gave up volley-ball: I didn't have sufficient combat instinct, and my strike lacked the necessary power. As for Igor – what chance did he stand? Whereas now he had a personal trainer, a mighty weight-lifter who promised to make a new person out of him in a year.

Seryozha used to get so carried away during the training sessions with Igor, that occasionally he would forget to keep an eye on Gin. That was a big mistake. By nature, Gin was a hunter, a troublemaker and a habitual winner of all dog fights. Igor, who never had the slightest problem with dogs, was somewhat wary of Gin. Every movement of this heavy beast spoke of cold lack of mercy. The only creature for whom Gin had any affection was Seryozha, and he was devoid of any canine sense of humour or fun. Only a lunatic would have dared to try to give Gin a pat; indeed, nobody ever tried.

Once after they had finished working out, Seryozha and Igor jogged to the top of a rise over which the dogs had disappeared once their owners stopped paying attention to them. As they crested the hillock, they stopped in horror. A little girl of about three stood holding Gin by the collar with one chubby hand, and was doing her best to catch him by the tongue with the other. Gin stood there turning his head from side to side, but made no move to get away or harm the tot. Standing beside them was the child's father, beaming benignly at child and dog. Obviously, he had not the slightest idea of the potential danger to his child: he was the epitome of an unworldly bookworm, the kind one sees depicted in comedy films, right down to his spectacles, his hat, and clumsy movements. Seryozha, for all that he was an avowed atheist, crossed himself, carefully extricated Gin from the little girl, and then kept hissing through his teeth: "What the hell brought them here at this time of the morning? I wouldn't trust a cockroach into that idiot's care, let alone a child!"

The magnificent Seryozha was something of a mystery to Igor. Why did he suffer from insomnia, why was his mother so openly hostile towards all his friends, including young Igor?

Once Seryozha asked whether Igor's father could obtain some Nembutal. The name meant nothing to Igor, and all that Igor's father knew was that it is a strong remedy for insomnia. Why not help out? he reasoned, and went to considerable lengths to acquire some

Nembutal tablets with the help of an aunt who worked in the Central Committee clinic. There's no shortage of medicines there.

Igor went running to Seryozha's place, but he was out, and Seryozha's mother sent him packing without any further ado. Igor did not feel it right to ask Seryozha any personal questions: if a man wants to tell you something about himself, he will, if not – then not. Once, in a moment of candour, Seryozha told Igor that from time to time he contemplated committing suicide. This seemed so out of character that Igor simply let it pass.

He had no way of knowing that Seryozha, who seemed so content with his lot outwardly, who had money, a beautiful wife and excellent prospects for the future, was even then a hopeless drug addict. Igor was not quite fifteen when Seryozha died. The first to go was Gin: Seryozha asserted that someone had poisoned him, but even then it seemed strange that he took the death of his beloved dog so calmly. Straight after that he went off on holiday to the south, and – experienced swimmer that he was – drowned in the sea. He was twenty-nine years old.

When Igor heard about this, he went rushing around to Seryozha's house. The wake had just finished, and Igor was not even able to find out where Seryozha was buried, because his mother slammed the door in his face. This was the first time that Igor experienced the death of a friend. Seryozha had put so much time and effort into him, the best he had to offer. Possibly he had wanted to make Igor into what he himself would have wanted to be. As for Igor, he blamed himself for not seeing that his first adult friend had a problem. Of course, Seryozha never offered Igor any drugs in any form, but could he not have guessed? Oh, if he had only known then what he knew now, how differently he would have acted! Maybe he would have tagged along with Seryozha on that fateful holiday, maybe he could have distracted him somehow from that lengthy horror . . . But it was too late.

At the same time, Igor had to continue going to school, take Small for walks to the same park, where the autumn leaves now rustled underfoot, carry on with his workouts – if only in deference to Seryozha's memory, to grow. It's not an easy thing, after all, to become an adult. What a lot they must contend with, the grown-ups, what strange fates they have!

Vitali Andreyevich, another member of the Kiev dog-lovers' fraternity, met Igor when their respective dogs were sniffing around each other in a city square. And what a picture they made: the black, enormous Small, and the pocket-sized reddish Malysh with a funny, squashed-up face. Igor asked about the breed because he had never seen a dog like that before.

"He's a Pekingese, an ancient Chinese breed!" answered Vitali Andreyevich proudly. "He's smart as a whip: understands everything you say to him in Russian or Chinese."

"Do you speak Chinese?"

"I certainly do: I worked there as a military translator for five years after 1945. You're probably wondering why I got a small dog like this instead of something like that tank of yours? All you youngsters are the same – if you want a dog, then it's got to be something huge. What none of you understands is that times can change. None of you knows the meaning of hunger. Just think, if history were to repeat itself, I could still keep Malysh fed – a little nipper like that doesn't need much. But what would you do with that monster of yours?"

"Well, I'd get by somehow . . ."

"That's what you think! All you kids are optimists. As for me – I've had enough of that 'somehow' business to last a lifetime!"

To the considerable surprise of their masters, Small and Malysh became fast friends; people used to laugh, seeing them together: little Malysh would trot proudly in front and Small would follow, adapting his pace, and holding the Pekingese's leash in his mouth. Malysh was secure in the conviction that with Small as an ally, no larger dog would dare challenge him, and did not even bother to glance around to make sure that his master was nearby. Once Igor and Small were away from Kiev for a few days, and Malysh was trounced by a nasty fox-terrier. The little dog nursed his grudge, and managed to complain to Small when his friend and protector returned. Igor and Vitali Andreyevich sat on a park bench and watched Small and Malysh in what was, clearly, an exchange of confidences, after which Small took off like a rocket towards the offending fox-terrier, grabbed him by the scruff of his neck, and began to shake him mercilessly. Igor leapt up, shouting at Small to let go. Small obeyed, but with a toss of his head that sent his victim hurtling through the air. The avenged Malysh licked Small's nose in gratitude (Small had to lower his head practically to the ground to receive his thanks) and the two dogs continued their interrupted stroll as if nothing had happened.

While the dogs ran around, Igor would listen to Vitali Andreyevich reminisce about the past: the old man had many interesting stories to tell. He had gone through the war, and, like most of those who had fought, spoke about it without bitterness. There was an enemy, the enemy had to be destroyed, and that was right and proper. It's not an easy thing, to be at the front, and foaming at the mouth with hatred only makes things harder; leave the histrionics to those who stay securely in the rear. A soldier can't afford to give way to anger: it only makes your hands shake, and you need a steady hand to hold a rifle.

He talked a great deal about China: how houses are heated by ducts under the floor instead of stoves, how the vegetable gardens have no paths, but are laid out with stepping-stones. He talked about the endless, back-breaking labour of the peasants and the strange custom of eating dogs. It's a sin to kill a dog, but the sin is evenly distributed: a noose is placed around the animal's neck, and all those who will eat its meat pull on the rope, so no one person bears more guilt than another.

Vitali Andreyevich described how he once had to translate in a brothel: a group of lecturers had come from the Soviet Union with the aim of inspiring the prostitutes to turn to 'an honest way of life'. Prostitution, insisted one lecturer earnestly, runs counter to the socialist lifestyle; it's a negative hangover from the feudal past. He cited copiously from Marx and Lenin, talked of historical inevitability and numerous standard 'isms'. For about an hour, Vitali Andreyevich sweated through the translation of these uplifting strictures. Finally, it was over, and the women were asked if they had any questions.

"Yes!"

"Ask away, women-comrades, feel free!"

"Well, we understood everything that the speaker said, except which one of us he wants to sleep with tonight?"

Despite all the inevitable misunderstandings produced by the collision of two totally different cultures, Vitali Andreyevich developed a deep respect for the honesty and hardworking nature of the Chinese. He spoke with unconcealed admiration about their unhurried way of doing things: nobody seems to rush around, yet every inch of arable land is tended, and what a father has left unfinished will be completed by his sons or grandsons. The death of an individual does not bring everything to a standstill.

At the same time, Vitali Andreyevich was a committed Ukrainian nationalist. He had been a Party member since the war years, and spoke with deep sorrow about the way that same Party was destroying Ukrainian culture. It was from Vitali Andreyevich that Igor first learned about the terrible famine of 1933, when Ukrainian peasants were herded into collective farms and those who resisted were mercilessly stripped of everything, down to their last grain, and thus condemned to death by starvation with their families. He talked about the bloated corpses of children in the gutters, the dead bodies of those who had come to Kiev in a desperate bid to find something to eat, lying in the city streets ... six million, all told – 15 per cent of the population of the Ukraine – died in one year, the terrible price of 'voluntary collectivisation'. That four million Russians died the same death in that year Igor was to learn only some ten years later, from reading *samizdat*. But for the time being he was avidly soaking up the unknown history of his own nation: he's a Ukrainian himself, and his mother's traditional Ukrainian embroidery is renowned locally. Oh, the pain of national problems! Is it not possible to enjoy two heritages – Ukrainian and Russian – in equal measure? Can he, Igor, help it if he loves the poetry of both Pushkin and Shevchenko?

"A nationalist is someone who remembers and loves his own heritage," explained Vitali Andreyevich, "and a chauvinist is someone who hates another's. It's the same difference that exists between a wise man and a fool. And because the communists have no discrimination, the result is that even though they seem to be combatting the fools, it's the wise men's heads which roll."

Two years later Igor attended a lecture at his institute wearing a shirt embroidered by his mother with traditional Ukrainian designs: that was enough for the powers-that-be to mark him out as a Ukrainian nationalist. The deputy dean gave him a friendly warning: manifestations of Ukrainian nationalism could cause Igor a lot of trouble in the future, and there was already one black mark on his record. In May every year, students were stringently warned not even to think about attending any memorial rallies near Shevchenko's monument. In other words, they were effectively forbidden to honour the old Ukrainian tradition of gathering at the monument on the anniversary of the day Shevchenko's remains were brought back home, and to read his poems. Why? Because it is unthinkable to permit uncontrolled public meetings, that's why. What if the students and schoolchildren should suddenly recall that they are not just Soviet children, but children of their own nation, too? For that reason – no mass meetings! They will be broken up by the militia, anyway, and put paid to any hopes of higher education for the participants. Similar policies have been practised for years with regard to Estonians, Armenians, Georgians – all ethnic groups, and it would be a mistake to think that the Russians are exempt: it applies to them as well.

Many participants of the now famous meetings by Mayakovsky's monument in Moscow lost their chances of tertiary education for that reason. Some, like Vladimir Bukovsky, found themselves imprisoned. On that particular occasion, those who had gathered were reading from the works of Russian poets ... Forget your nationality, even though it is stated in every Soviet citizen's passport! That information is there for the benefit of the authorities, not for yours! You are Soviet, and only Soviet ... And your state language is not the language of Pushkin and Dostoyevsky, but the language of the Soviet Party bureaucracy, debased and distorted by semi-literate 'leaders'.

Igor had sufficient analytical ability to avoid becoming a chauvinist: he realised that all the nationalities in the Soviet Union shared the same misfortune. He was ready to respect every nationality, while honouring his own. He continued to wear the shirts made by his mother: she did not spend so many hours of loving toil over them only for him to thrust them into a bottom drawer.

Many, many years later, when we were leaving our country, the greatest treasures in the small suitcase which contained all our worldly goods were a shirt and a blouse, made by Igor's mother out of a sheet: an exquisitely embroidered maternal blessing in traditional cross and satin stitch.

Chapter Twelve

I am still fourteen years old, and it feels as though this state will drag on forever; in fact I am growing at an enormously fast rate at the moment. At puberty most girls are as trying to others as they are confused themselves. I had read about puberty and its attendant difficulties in books, but I had no idea that it could be as bad as this. My former happy childhood dreams of flying blithely above the sea now changed to nightmares of plunging down helplessly towards the cliffs, and I would wake up gasping in terror. At school I was dull and sleepy, understanding nothing, incapable of remembering anything, even though a short time before, I had never had any trouble with my lessons. My parents were alarmed and bewildered: six months before, their daughter had been a normal, happy adolescent, whose success at school they were secretly very proud of: now they found themselves looking at an apathetic, lazy creature whose marks at school threatened to fall below average. My marks for maths had slipped to three out of five, and I could hardly expect the teacher (my favourite, as it happened) to bump them up artificially. My parents panicked and resorted to punishment, even though they knew that, with my nature, that was the course least likely to give positive results. I was forbidden to read anything except school textbooks until I should get 'fives' in a row for maths. Five 'fives'! But that would take two to three months at least! I held out for about four days, and then seized a book, like a drowning man clutching at a straw. Father caught me, and flung the book across the room. He began to shout at me – something that had not happened for a long, long time: it was most unusual for him to raise his voice, let alone yell. Of course, he did this out of a feeling of helplessness and desperation, but I was too self-absorbed and, at that time, totally incapable of understanding or forgiving anyone else, so I glared at him with hatred. Matters had come to a pretty pass, no mistake! Hatred – in our family? After all that we had gone through together?

But there was no halting me then; laughing wildly, I taunted my parents that books were suppressed first by the Inquisition, and then by the fascists . . . Heaven knows what other denunciations I flung at them. I was carried away on a tide of what seemed to me to be scintillating wit, and had no idea of the meaning of hysteria. To me, hysterics meant uncontrolled weeping, but I wasn't shedding so much as a tear – I was laughing, and in control of myself . . . Then I saw two pairs of eyes – Father's brown ones, and Mother's grey ones – staring at me with an identical expression of wounded grief. I broke off in mid-sentence, and realised that I was shaking from head to foot. They saw it, too – I couldn't stop myself. This was no time for any more recriminations about poor marks: what if the child had gone off her head? From that evening, they were patient and loving, the ban on reading was lifted, and as for my schooling – they decided, fatalistically, to let things run their own course.

As for me – I was tortured by pangs of conscience: what a monster I am, to be sure! Not only am I an absolute dunce at school, not only have I become a gangling, spotty-faced gargoyle, but I've even lost the ability to love my own parents! And if that is the case, how can I possibly hope to be able to love anyone else? For that matter, who could ever love a clumsy Plain Jane like me? It hurts just to look in the mirror: my bust thrusts out so much that no amount of stooping can hide it any longer, and my eyes look like those of a caged beast. God, what's happening to me?

There are complications with God, too. I had always been certain with a child's unquestioning faith of His love for me. But now it occurs to me that He might find it impossible to love such an unlovable creature as me, and might turn away from me. What if He has already done so, and the traumas through which I am passing are the direct result of this? Going to church to consult a priest is impossible: in the first place, I have no idea to what faith I belong. There are a lot of religions, and they all appear to be at odds among themselves. So the chances are that they'll make me even more confused than I am already. Naturally, I have never held a Bible in my hands: where would I get it? And just imagine what a fury would ensue if I were to go to an Orthodox church, or a Catholic one, or to the Baptists? My life would not be worth living at school, and my parents would be in even greater trouble, because I'm a minor and they're responsible for me. Up until now, I had always found relief in books, but nowadays I begin to notice that even the Russian classics tend to have conflicting views. According to Pushkin the truth lies in Russian Orthodoxy, beyond dispute; but Tolstoy's theories amount to a virtual assault on the spirit . . . Maybe I'm not a Christian at all? That could well be: after all, I know so little about Christ, just a few quotes here and there, picked up from various books, not enough to form a complete picture of Him. There's nobody trustworthy to ask, either. For that matter, I know by now that books can lie, too.

I mull over these unhappy possibilities and see no way out, short of putting an end to my existence. And then I suddenly feel self-loathing wash over me: what a pathetic creature I am, sitting here and feeling sorry for myself! You can plague yourself with doubts for ever and ever, but there are two things which I know for sure: God exists, and God is kind. And that means that He wants me to be kind, first and foremost, and anything else He deems necessary He will give me in His own time, if I try very hard. Admittedly, my brains aren't functioning as well as they used to, but perhaps this will pass?

That night I crept out into the communal kitchen and switched on a small lamp. I was gripped by a familiar feverishness which I knew, by that time, meant a poem coming on, even though I would have no idea what it would be about. I scribbled quickly, abbreviating words in my haste:

> How the road to Him to find?
> With what the hope and pain to measure?
> People seek a God who's kind.
> God grant they find, and trust, and treasure.

Years later I was to see the verbal rhymes and the childish lack of accomplishment, but that night I wrote, without pausing to correct or think. Why bother? Nobody but me would ever see it, it was just for me. I was filled with joy, for I could feel a benevolent eye looking over my shoulder at my pencilled scribblings. No, it was nobody in the house – they were all fast asleep in their beds. I shivered despite a delicious warmth, for I knew whose glance it was. He had not abandoned me, He was with me. And He didn't mind that I couldn't pray properly.

At the end of that school year I managed to gain my parents' consent to transfer to another school. So what if they teach English in my present one? It's not as though I have acquired any knowledge of that language over the past seven years, and the teaching is not all that good. The school I have picked out has an excellent record for teaching maths and physics, and this is the line I want to follow. After some initial hesitation, my parents agreed. Enquiries reveal that Seryozha Diamant's mother teaches at that school, and wants to transfer him there, too. The chances are that Seryozha and I will be able to transfer into the same class. This will mark a new beginning, and nobody there will know how hopeless I've been at my work this year. Maybe I'll even make some new friends: I've become a real loner lately, shunning all contacts because I'm embarrassed by my ugliness. It's not as though I'm an oil painting now, either, but at least I'm closer to average in appearance, I've lost some weight and have devised a new hair-style for myself. My clothes aren't much to look at, but I now have a new red sweater as well as my old blue one. The only skirt I have is the green one from my old school uniform, but my shoes are new, and I've so outgrown my hated old coat that my parents have agreed to throw it out. They've also bought me a proper adult bag for my books, spent a fortune on textbooks and suchlike, so it would be a bit much to expect them to lay out any more money for a second skirt. In any case, I'm shooting up at such a rate that it's likely that all my clothes will have to be changed in another six months' time. Most of the other girls are not dressed any better than I am, apart from those whose parents have additional income on the side, or hold senior Party posts. In our family, too, there's Alya for whom provision has to be made. Father buys himself the cheapest shoes possible, even makes a joke out of it: "Never mind! When I was a student, I had to keep my shoes together with wire when they fell apart!"

Seryozha and I found ourselves faced with an unexpected condition: "Since you both consider yourselves old enough to choose which school to go to," said our parents, "you must realise that we originally sent you to the 'English' school so that you would learn that language. There is a three-year English course for adults – it must be paid for, incidentally! – and you will both attend it in the evenings. The entrance exam is in August, and you must both pass at least well enough to be admitted to the first term. Surely you've mastered the English alphabet, if nothing else? We'll get you the books, but you'll have to prepare for the exam by yourselves. While we're feeding and housing you, we have the right to a say in your education."

There was no moving either set of parents from this ultimatum. Madness! They want to pay good money for us to attend this English course! That's thirty-seven roubles per term, and the course consists of six terms! They're going to have to pay even if we don't pass the first term, but we can see that their minds are made up. And we had been nurturing the hope that we could forget all about that detested 'inglish', being certain that we would never need it in our lives. For pity's sake, who goes abroad? Famous actors, high-ranking communists, but that's about it! Neither Seryozha nor I are likely to find ourselves in their situation, so we're not likely to have any opportunity of socialising with foreigners. Just look at our two families: nobody among our relatives has ever been able to go abroad, if you don't count my two grandfathers and Seryozha's father going off to war. So why bother?

But the parents have a ready answer for that, too: "You both claim that you want to be physicists, don't you? Well, at least half the world literature on physics is written in English. And the most up-to-date journals. Without a knowledge of English, you'll not be able to make head or tail of them, will you?"

We knew when we were beaten, and surrendered without further ado. All right, give us those blasted textbooks, let's see what they've got set down for the first term: we'll master it, or die in the attempt. That wipes out the whole of our summer vacation for sure.

We received unexpected assistance from my Aunt Victoria. Strictly speaking, she wasn't really my aunt. She was transported to Germany during the occupation, but the rest of her family perished. In Germany she did forced labour on some farm or other, and when she returned to the Soviet Union she had a stroke of luck: as she was so young, she wasn't exiled to Siberia, as were most former POWs. The few distant relatives she had, however, repudiated her 'just in case'. There is nothing to justify such behaviour, but it is understandable: the fact that someone had been in Germany was considered a worse stigma than having been in the occupied territories, and that in itself was bad enough, as Igor's and my father learned through bitter experience. Being admitted to higher education was a boon even if you were a child during the war, and even so, you could not hope for a career equal to that of those with a 'clean' background, especially in Stalin's times.

Lucky Victoria, though, managed to enroll in an educational institute: not as a full-time student, of course, but for evening classes. During the day she had to work: she was nineteen years old, and had neither friends nor relatives in Odessa. In such circumstances, one quickly learns to stand on one's own feet. Victoria and my mother met in a library, and the friendship that sprang up between them was as firm and intense as friendships made by girls at that age usually are. But Victoria's luck did not hold out: another wave of purges directed at 'internal enemies' was launched, and her captivity in Germany came to light. The authorities did not blame themselves for leaving her, a young girl, undefended, as the Soviet army retreated and the Germans advanced. They blamed her. It began to look as though Victoria would be expelled from the institute, and even – if worse came to worst – imprisoned. She tried to commit suicide by swallowing a handful of sleeping tablets, but, luckily, she had no idea of how many constituted a lethal dose, so all that happened was that she was temporarily paralysed. My mother's parents took her in and nursed her, and my grandfather, who had joined the Party when he was at the front, set about getting permission for Victoria to continue her studies. My grandparents liked Victoria very much: she could be a sister to their daughter and a second daughter to them. They would have two grown-up daughters and a grown-up son – what a lovely family! And become a family they did. From my earliest childhood I knew I had an Aunt Vicky. She stood on no ceremony with me, either, whenever she came to stay (she taught in village schools): she made me wash my feet twice every evening, would give me a clip round the ear when she considered it necessary, and from time to time spoiled me rotten with ice-creams and trips to the cinema, compensating for the deprivations of her own childhood.

At the time in question, she was working by the sea, in a nursing-home for children with tuberculosis. When she heard that Seryozha and I had taken up the gauntlet and intended to spend our entire summer vacation swotting, she declared that she would take us to stay with her. She had a room measuring nine square metres, which would not be enough for the three of us, but the dormitories were unoccupied during the summer, and she would make arrangements for us to be housed there. Mattresses and beds were available, she would supply us with blankets, and as for food – we could eat in the kitchen for the summer residents, because she supplemented her income by working there as housekeeper.

"When you feel your head bursting from English verbs, you can run down for a dip in the sea. Only you have to promise faithfully that you'll be careful crossing the railway tracks: a train needs one hundred and twenty metres to brake, remember that once and for all!"

Oh, the sea, our beloved, untamed sea! There's nothing dull and adult about it, it is ready to play with us, whatever the weather, so long as we come to it. It will hurl you out on to the shore with one of its stormy waves, and you hear it hissing "English? Rubbish!" as it retreats.

The grown-ups worried about our progress, but left us to our own devices, trusting us. How often we would promise ourselves, as we settled down on the institutional mattresses, that the moment we knew this or that conjugation, we would nip down to the beach! Alas, we realised all too soon that we did not even have the basics of English, that we couldn't even read properly, and that the language has a grammar of which we knew absolutely nothing. But, as a matter of honour, we mastered what was necessary for the first term, passed the entrance exam, and were enrolled. However, the course yielded little: we sat faithfully through every evening class, but we were half-asleep by the time they finished at 11 p.m. We managed to retain the barest minimum needed to pass the term exams, and then it would fly out of our heads forever. A year later, there was a string of illnesses and deaths in our family, and studying was the last thing on my mind. Seventeen years after that, sitting in a plane bound from Moscow to London, I gave my first interview in English: almost immediately I realised, to my horror, that I could barely understand the questions being asked by the correspondent of the *Observer*, and that he wasn't able to make much sense out of my replies. We did the only thing possible under the circumstances: gave up trying to communicate verbally, and drew little pictures for each other instead. It is my great fortune that Andrew was such a conscientious reporter, and came the next day to check out the article he had written with the help of the bilingual friends with whom we were staying. As it turned out, our questions-and-answers-in-pictures had not been quite as successful as we had imagined, and we all spent a good deal of time laughing ourselves into stitches over the results. It must be my lot in life to learn English, after all, and after this pitiful performance, I finally understood why.

Chapter Thirteen

After the ninth grade, Igor decided to take up boxing in earnest. There were pragmatic reasons for this decision: it was unwise to trifle with the Kiev riff-raff, and there was a well-known crook called 'Duke' who made a habit of terrorising the children from school No. 106, which Igor attended. Occasionally alone, or in the company of his cronies, Duke would catch the children after school, and force them to give him any money they had on them to keep himself supplied with drink. There was a temporary reprieve when Duke was called up to do military service, but everyone knew that he would be back. Moreover, he was not alone in going for such easy pickings.

So Igor and a classmate, also an Igor, turned up to see boxing trainer Karimov, who, despite their worst fears, agreed to take both of them on. He did cast a glance at Igor's legs which showed that he did not think much of this kid's chances, but he didn't argue. Karimov never turned anyone away as a matter of principle, figuring that the chaff would sort itself from the wheat soon enough, after the first few training bouts.

Igor was determined not to fall by the wayside, and he had become accustomed to pains in his legs since his training days with the weight-lifter Seryozha Domnin. Pain or no pain, the most important thing is not to show it. This attitude served him well, because all the difficulties of training were nothing compared with the agonies shooting through his ankles. Karimov watched approvingly how the lad 'rode blows' as though he didn't feel them, and soon began to pay Igor as much attention as he did his future stars, even though it was quite clear that Igor would never reach top form.

For some reason, Duke served in the army for only one year. Soon after his return, he approached Igor with his customary demand: "Come on, kid, cough up!"

Igor looked at him with a friendly smile, and retorted: "What if I push your face in, instead?"

"How's that!?"

"Why, first a left, then a right . . ."

It was not even necessary to accompany words with actions: like all bullies, Duke was a coward, and preferred to keep his face intact. He hurried to say, very politely, that he had only been joking, and that was the last time he was seen anywhere near school No. 106.

That year, Igor made a final decision as to his future profession: he would follow in his father's footsteps and become a thermal physicist. From his school holidays he was accustomed to pottering around in his father's laboratory, and felt that there could be no more interesting job in the whole world. This meant that he would have to study at the Polytechnic Institute, which in turn meant preparing for entrance exams. So Igor buckled down to physics and mathematics. Seeing such enthusiasm, Igor's father arranged for a tutor to give Igor private lessons, as a result of which his knowledge of mathematics forged way ahead of the school syllabus. Despite good reports from teachers, Igor's father could not help worrying about Igor's chances of admission into the institute. The deputy dean of Igor's future faculty had been a colleague of his in the past, but had not advanced as far as Igor's father. In fact, he had not even succeeded in gaining a doctorate yet, and was obviously jealous of Igor's father, who had one. But surely he would not take it out on Igor? Surely he could not be so petty?

Igor returned totally drained from his verbal entrance exam in mathematics: it had lasted two and a half hours, and he was marked three out of five. This made it highly unlikely that he would be admitted to the faculty. Igor's father was furious: if Igor had been subjected to such intensive and long testing, it seemed obvious that the examiners were intent on failing him. He didn't absolve Igor entirely, either: why had he let himself get caught out? Why didn't he just plough ahead and solve all the problems, no matter how many of them there were, and how difficult?

The written exam yielded the same result – a three. This was distinctly fishy, because Igor had had no trouble solving much more complex problems than the ones set for the entrance exam.

After some thought, Igor's father came to the reluctant conclusion that he would have to do something that he had been determined not to do: that is, go to the institute to plead. Seemingly, this was what had been expected, because after that, everything resolved itself without the slightest trouble. Igor was given his student card with a welcoming smile: "We hope that you will get at least satisfactory results in your studies!"

Father and son returned home in silence. Finally, Igor's father said:

"Because of you, I had to go and beg, to lower the family honour. The only way you can justify this is by coming top of your group."

He never reminded Igor of this again, only grunting with satisfaction at the end of every term: Igor took top place, and held on to it. But even this was not quite enough for Oleg Arkadyevich Geraschenko: doing well in theory is one thing, but what kind of an engineer would his son be in practice? An experimental physicist should be able to do everything with his hands: and that meant that Igor was to spend his summer holidays learning experimental production in the Institute of Thermal Physics, helping the toolmakers. He wasn't paid for this, naturally. The toolmakers didn't mind: they respected Oleg Arkadyevich for his skill with his hands, for all that he was a boffin. The craftsmen taught Igor with pleasure, for it's not every rising head of department who puts his son to work at a lathe. By his second year, Igor heard no more complaints from Khaptyar, the senior toolmaker: and the other craftsmen stopped calling him 'Daddy's boy' and made it simply 'boy'.

Igor took no lecture notes as a matter of principle, but would pay attention to the lecture, and then head for the library. He felt that he would learn better that way. The scourge of the second-year students, lecturer Khilchevsky, once noticed that Igor was not writing anything down: "Why aren't you taking notes?"

"I remember it better by just listening."

"In that case, step up to the board!"

A murmur ran around the lecture theatre: everyone knew that Khilchevsky was a real terror during exams. He was quite capable of failing a whole group with the exception of one or two students, because he would form an opinion of every student during the course of a term.

While Igor sweated over a problem which Khilchevsky had set with the aim of showing him up, the lecturer went through his papers without a backward glance at the blackboard.

"Finished!"

Khilchevsky threw a brief look over his shoulder: "Wrong!"

"Why?"

"It's wrong, I tell you. I can see."

Igor took a deep breath. "We're not dealing with humanities here, but exact sciences, precise solutions. Show me where I've made a mistake!"

"With pleasure. Just a moment. No, young man ... what's your name?"

"Geraschenko."

"Aha ... Actually, Geraschenko, you have solved the problem correctly. I didn't realise for a moment that your solution would not be reached by the standard process. I agree that in this instance your method is shorter, but it can only be applied to a very narrow spectrum of problems. Let's take a look at the longer method, the one that's more widely applicable."

And so they did, with mutual enjoyment. From that day forward Khilchevsky amused himself by setting Igor particularly difficult supplementary problems, which Igor enjoyed solving. Because of this, Khilchevsky would overlook Igor's missing the occasional lecture, and gave him 'fives' in exams without bothering to check.

At the beginning of each term, Igor's father would go through the syllabus with him.

"You'll need to know about this in greater depth," he would indicate. "Get hold of such and such a book and read up about it. As for that – you can just pass it at the exam, and not bother going to any greater lengths with it."

"What about the History of the Communist Party, and Scientific Communism?" asked Igor once, provocatively.

His father only snorted, and changed the subject. The following summer holidays, Igor's father packed him off as a collector with an expedition from the Geological Institute. The institute was studying the warm currents off Kamchatka at the time, and the expedition was to the Valley of Geysers on the Kamchatka Peninsula. It consisted of three geologists, and Igor as their assistant. Igor's father was pleased: let the lad trek around for three months with a rucksack through the wilderness, learn to sleep in the rain, how to measure currents, and put up with mosquito bites. Igor was overjoyed: Kamchatka! The end of the earth! He would come back with a beard, brown as a berry, a full-grown man! After all, he's turned eighteen, but it seems to him that his father doubts, from time to time, that he is an adult. Sitting by the campfire out in the wilds, Igor finally purged his heart of his first, unlucky love: the fencer Katya, who had dumped him in favour of some master sportsman. How right was that old cynic, Vitali Andreyevich, who was wont to remark: "Dames deserve attention sometimes, but love – never!"

Against all expectations, Igor's mother took the idea of his going to Kamchatka very calmly. She was a geologist herself, and thought it would do 'the child' a world of good to spend a season in the field.

"Only do be careful to keep your feet dry, dearest!"

"Yes, Mum, I will. I promise!"

The expedition set off, first by plane, then by boat, then by helicopter, then finally on foot with their rucksacks on their backs. They pitched two tents – one for sleeping, one for stores. Mosquitoes turned out to be a lesser nuisance than bears, who saw the campsite as their stamping ground. At first, while the members of the expedition were studying individual geysers and deciding where to set up their instruments, the bears didn't show much interest. But pretty soon the bruins realised that there was food to be had, and turned aggressive. The most forward one made his way right up to the tent in which Igor, making the most of a free morning, was sitting and charting the measurements taken. The bear let out a roar, and marched towards Igor. Caught unawares, Igor leapt to his feet, empty-handed, and took a few paces towards the intruder. Luckily, instead of swatting him down like a fly, the bear was equally surprised and, growling angrily, retreated back into the forest.

During the night, however, he came back, slashed open the stores tent, and ate all the food it contained. So what was to be done? The next helicopter drop would be in three weeks' time, and it was impossible to reach the nearest settlement on foot. Dying of hunger was not an attractive prospect. The expedition decided that it would only be fair to capture and eat the beast who had left them without so much as a crumb. They had no rifles, only shotguns, but they figured that if you load a shotgun with a lead ball, there's a fair chance of making a kill – if you get a good, direct hit . . . and it must be a good hit because a wounded bear is something to make even the bravest quail. It would have to be killed outright.

One of the expedition refused to take part in the hunt, saying he had a wife and children to consider. Igor, who was not similarly encumbered, coaxed the others into letting him take the first shot. There was no need to go looking: they took up their stations around the tent, and waited. It was not a long wait. The first shot did the trick – it got the bear right through the heart.

Hacking up the bear's carcass, Igor felt a wave of some strange euphoria, with undertones of savagery: and for a moment, he was a savage. He stopped what he was doing, pulled himself together, and resumed work in a calm and collected way. But this incident convinced him that cutting up raw meat awakens a usually dormant, atavistic savagery in people, and since the day we got married he has never let me so much as carve up a chicken.

"One savage in the family is enough!" he says. "Don't start waking those instincts in yourself!"

For the next three weeks, the expedition ate bear meat. They returned considerably thinner than they had been when they left, and

Igor felt very proud of himself: the geologists were pleased with him, he had grown the beard of which he had dreamed, and he brought back heaps of slides, including a 'portrait' of each geyser. He was certain that he had now mastered thermometrics from A to Z, from making measuring instruments in his father's laboratory, through to calculations and deployment in the field. He did not expect to hear any words of praise from his father: firstly, it was not Oleg Arkadyevich's way, and secondly, he thought Igor had a high enough opinion of himself already.

However, when Igor clumped into the house in boots and toting a rucksack, his father rose to meet him: "Greetings, my cossack!" And gave him a hug.

As for Small – there was no sign that he intended to forgive Igor for deserting him for three months, even though he was the centre of the family's attention during Igor's absence. He had fretted terribly all this time, but even though he sensed his beloved master coming up the stairs, he showed his disapproval by coming forward to acknowledge Igor's arrival in a very formal manner, and went straight back to his corner. There was no jumping, no yelps of joy, no wildly licking tongue ... Igor apologised, explained, and Small finally relented: their relations returned almost to what they had been – but that 'almost' remained as a barrier between them for a long time. Only when he was dying did Small look at Igor with his earlier adoration.

Igor completed his studies at the institute, and at the same time became proficient at toolmaking, fitting and turning, glass-blowing, carpentry, and a host of other crafts so useful to a physicist.

As he graduated at the top of his group, he had the right to choose where to work. Not surprisingly, he chose his father's institute. Only after he laid down his honours diploma on the table before his father did he return to a conversation that took place five and a half years earlier.

"Have I justified myself?"

"Yes."

There is no need for more words between men. At that time, they thought they would be working together, shoulder to shoulder: the director of the Institute of Technical Thermodynamics, Oleg Arkadyevich Geraschenko, and his son. After a while Igor would write a thesis, become a fully-fledged scientist and his father's right-hand man. Why is it possible for a carpenter or a steelworker to pass on his trade to his son and leave him to carry on after him, and not possible for a scientist to do the same? Yet, through no fault of their own, it did prove impossible.

Chapter Fourteen

Nothing seems to change over the years in Grandmother and Grandfather's apartment on Podbelsky Street: the same shelves with painted ornaments, the same neatly darned white tablecloth, the same gentle lamplight. And they're still just as we remember them from childhood: Grandfather, handsome and imposing with his head of thick, grey hair and firm chin, and Grandmother, dark-eyed and always trim and neat. They still switch to Polish when Grandmother thinks that Grandfather is spoiling us too much (because it's not right to argue in front of the children!). As ever, we pretend we don't understand a word of Polish, and sit there looking as innocent as new-born babes, as if we don't know that Grandmother is referring to us when she talks about '*lajdaks*' or what she means when she says "Irusya has a rabbit in her head".

My cousin Valentin's parents have been divorced for a long time now, and he prefers to live with his father – that is, sharing the grandparents' apartment. His father spends most of his time at the collective farm, where he is awaiting the ripening of some special kind of tomato from seeds obtained by an incredible stroke of luck. I still share my time between home and Podbelsky Street – they're only three blocks apart. Valentin and I are at the end of our eighth year of school, sitting at the big table and doing our homework.

His algebra over and done with, Valentin casts aside his books, and gets up: "Grand-dad, time for a sweet!"

This is an old ritual, going back to when we were very small. In a drawer in his desk, Grandfather keeps a metal box with the cheapest caramels you can get. Occasionally, he gives us one each. And, just as ten years ago, we feel that these caramels out of Grandfather's tin box are the most delicious in the world. Long ago he used to tease us, saying that these caramels became magic, but only if given to very, very good children. In Grandfather's eyes we are still children, despite our fifteen years, but we don't object one bit.

"Irusya, go and put on the kettle!"

Any minute now, Grandmother will open the dresser, with its

dark-red glass panels, and pull out a paper bag full of miniature bagels. These will have to be put out on the big dish with the chip on the edge, because Grandmother maintains that only ruffians eat out of paper bags. Grandfather presides over the tea-brewing: of course, we could brew the tea just as easily ourselves, but it's somehow special when he does it. The four of us sit around the table, listening to the rustlings of creepers and other plants in the tiny garden tended by Grandmother. This apartment is the safest, most secure place in the world – quiet, bright, welcoming to children, never overcast by the slightest shadow of unpleasantness.

The next morning, even before we got up from our narrow divan-beds, we heard a strange moaning sound. As one, Valentin and I leapt up, and rushed over to the grandparents' bed.

"Granny, what's the matter?"

"Help me get up."

We grabbed hold of her with a will, supporting her shoulders.

"No, let me go! It hurts!"

Grandfather, who had got up earlier and was pottering around some household task or other, came hurrying in, alarmed: "Annie, dearest, what's wrong?"

"I've got pains everywhere."

Grandmother was never to get up again. The doctors said that she was suffering from paleoarthritis, and at her age – well, you understand . . . What nonsense! What's all this talk about 'age' in connection with our 'young grandmother'? This can't be! But why does she look at us in that odd way, as though she is seeing us from a long, long distance?

"Irusya . . . don't tell anyone . . . I had you christened when you were a baby."

It was easier for Valentin and me to miss school than for our parents to get time off from work. The only times Grandfather left Grandmother's bedside was when he went to make her 'something nice', even though she could barely eat at all. In several weeks' time she became so thin that we could lift her up like a small child to change the bedclothes. In the last few days, she hardly spoke at all, just looked at the world with austere, dark eyes.

Grandfather couldn't believe that she was dying until the very last moments. Afterwards, he was like a lost, bewildered child, and made no demur when my parents insisted that he come to stay with us for a while. He had never been tall, but now he suddenly seemed very small and old. He ate, obediently, the food put before him, just as obediently he went for walks with Valentin and me. We were very worried about him, but after a few months he insisted on going back home. Naturally, Valentin and I were there all the time. Every so often he would pull out the tin box of caramels, but seeing his forced smile, Valentin and I would feel like bursting into tears. That winter he suffered a severe heart-attack, and had to be taken to hospital. He was not allowed any movement, and a family conference took place, at which everyone agreed that somebody had to be with Grandfather in the hospital day and night: we knew only too well what the care there was like! Mother had a word with the hospital administration.

"Yes," she was told, "that will be all right, even if it is against the rules. Generally speaking, family can visit the patients only for three hours every day, but we're short of nurses, so your looking after him will be to everyone's advantage. But you'll have to get hold of some white coats, just in case an inspection committee should descend without warning . . . It will be harder with the children, though – they wouldn't even pass as students. Still, that's your risk: if they manage to get in, then we won't oppose them in this section."

Getting into the hospital outside visiting hours was as simple as falling off a log: Valentin and I quickly learned to slip fifty kopecks to the duty receptionist. It would have been impossible to manage without us, for our parents simply couldn't miss every third day at work. It didn't take us long to learn all that was necessary to care for an immobilised patient. At first, Grandfather felt rather embarrassed, but came around after a while: nobody in our family was short of a sense of humour. Valentin and I were cheerful tearaways, despite all the troubles of the past year, and managed to blend easily into hospital life. It wasn't long before we made friends with other heart patients: they seemed to enjoy our jokes and stories about school, and, when the need arose, did not hesitate to ask us to help with small, intimate needs. During his illness, Grandfather seemed somehow more like his old self, he smiled at us the way he used to before, he was calm and cheerful, and we only knew when he was in pain when he half-closed his eyes.

It was spring, exams were almost upon us, and we brought as many bunches of spring flowers as we could to the hospital. The nurses, who had become quite fond of us by that time, supplied us with various strange containers for the bouquets. The amount of lilac Valentin managed to pick was enough for the ward, for the nurses' office, and for the duty sister's desk in the corridor. Knowing that we were preparing for exams, they adjusted the blue night light so that it would fall directly on to our opened books, and we had no trouble reading. We rather enjoyed 'night-shift study'; if Grandfather was feeling reasonably well, he would sleep, the hospital would be quiet and peaceful, and the morning would begin with the ringing of tram bells out in the street. Our heads heavy from swotting geography or mathematics, we would go into the corridor and do a few exercises to loosen up. The duty sister would be there, either sleeping with her head on her arms, or knitting. A poster hanging on the wall above her desk proclaimed: 'Socialist obligation undertaken by the junior medical personnel of hospital No. 9: to lower the death rate in the hospital by such and such per cent in honour of the forthcoming 24th Congress of the Communist Party.' We simply couldn't stomach the cynicism of this piece of cardboard, and hurried back to the ward: to hell with their congresses and percentages, our grandfather wasn't going to become part of the 'permissable' percentage of deaths!

Nor did he: by the time we came to tell him that we had passed this or that exam, he was sitting up and could give us a hug, or tug us affectionately by the ear. Then he was allowed to get up, and was finally discharged from the hospital. Our parents had become thin and drawn from lack of sleep, but we were none the worse: we had managed to complete ninth grade quite creditably, had learnt to sleep in short bursts while sitting up, and were inordinately proud of our newly acquired medical knowledge. Valentin even became quite proficient at giving injections. The parents had come to acknowledge that we were no longer children but independent teenagers, and I found it hard to believe that we had had such terrible quarrels about my school marks just eighteen months ago. Grandfather was alive and well, and a blissful summer stretched before us: freedom, the sea, and three months of doing practically nothing. Alya had grown, and I took her for walks to the same places Grandfather had taken me years ago. What fun it was to push this little four-year-old creature on a swing, or teach her to swim! She would hang on to my shoulders with total trust, and kick her little legs up and down in the water.

But she didn't manage to learn to swim independently that summer. An epidemic of cholera broke out in Odessa. The city was cordoned off, and the beaches were closed. Swimming was forbidden because the water was found to contain cholera bacteria. Actually, this was only to be expected because several years earlier our thick-headed city authorities had the idea of turning Odessa into a money-making resort, and ordered a reconstruction of the whole sea-front. The natural cliffs and bays with their pebble beaches were deemed unsuitable, things had to be made 'civilised': that is, they wanted to make a large, sandy beach, put up ice-cream kiosks, restaurants, a life-saving club, loudspeakers to blast music ... There were already several beaches like that, but all self-respecting locals avoided them, preferring to stay away from the noise and tat, and 'go native' in little bays and coves, where there were neither marker buoys, nor fines for swimming out too far. Tastes like this, naturally, do nothing to swell the state's coffers. So the cliffs were dynamited, and to guard against landslides a breakwater out of huge rocks was built about fifty metres from the foreshore. The existing beaches were covered with imported sand, banners proclaiming 'We shall turn Odessa into an exemplary resort town' were strung up, and the city fathers sat back, waiting for the money to come rolling in.

Not surprisingly, the long breakwater caused the water between it and the shore to stagnate, and become an ideal breeding ground for all sorts of bacteria. First there was an epidemic of gastro-enteritis, then came the cholera. There was no official warning about the cholera outbreak: the radio carried vague announcements about 'stomach and intestinal ailments', and advised people to wash their hands as often as possible. Though it's a mystery how they hoped to keep the epidemic a secret when the whole city was in quarantine and surrounded by machine-gun-toting brigades. As was to be expected, there was a shortage of medical supplies needed to treat cholera. Odessa, as usual, turned even this into a joke. A popular ditty of the time ran:

> Though here we sit without our vaccine
> There is one thought that keeps us sweet:
> The latest method dreamt by medicine –
> Just wash your hands before you eat.

Every doorknob, every trolley-bus and tram railing in the city was swathed in damp cloth saturated with carbolic. All sorts of rumours flew around the city about the number of deaths, but we schoolchildren paid little attention to them. In fact, we enjoyed ourselves hugely: all the holidaymakers had fled, the city seemed half-empty, every day brought new jokes about the cholera – it all seemed like an exciting adventure rather than an emergency. Moreover, we all succumbed to a kind of malicious glee: we felt that it served the authorities right. Did it occur to them to ask whether the people of Odessa wanted to have their beloved small bays and cliffs levelled? Did they ask the hundreds of artists who came here from all over the country to paint these cliffs and slopes? Did they wonder what it would be like for us to lose that pebbly beach where Grandfather used to take us when we were small, and the sea-horses, and the underwater rock which we reached so proudly for the first time without our feet touching the bottom even once? You wanted millions of roubles? You made losses running into millions instead: you don't give a hoot about people, but you can't get away with treating the sea in a similarly cavalier manner! The sea is not to be trifled with!

In fact, the sea is exacting revenge to this day: as I write, the beaches in Odessa have been closed yet again, and tap water has to be boiled for at least an hour to avoid the risk of picking up yet another bug. The huge breakwater is still standing, the idea of the exemplary resort proved a resounding failure and the locals say with a grim smile that before there were food shortages, whereas now there's no drinkable water, either.

But that summer, the cholera epidemic proved to our advantage, because schools reopened three weeks later than usual, on 21st September.

Delirious with joy at such an extension of freedom, we chased around our favourite yards, filled with wild grapevines, messed around in Grandmother's little garden to keep the flowers she had planted alive, and questioned Grandfather about our family history.

He would pull out the ancient crystal family seal with its crest, and explain all the complex heraldic symbols engraved on it.

When school resumed, I persuaded Grandfather to start teaching me French: this was my way of rebelling against the hated compulsory English lessons which I had to attend two evenings a week. Alas, I had left it too late: there were only ten English lessons to go to the end of the course.

Early one November morning, Valentin and I were awakened by a strange shout. Grandfather was moving his hands about in a disoriented fashion, trying to say something but without success. His eyes were filled with tears, he could understand everything we asked him, but couldn't answer. He couldn't even write, because when we frantically stuck a pencil into his hand, only an unintelligible scrawl appeared on the piece of paper.

The doctors diagnosed a heart-attack and said that the case was hopeless. They offered to have him admitted into a special hospital: he could not be left alone, he could not be cured and, they added, he wouldn't know the difference because he must be unable to understand anything. The parents hesitated: after all, who could be in constant attendance on Grandfather? Hiring a full-time nurse was out of the question for financial reasons; they would be able to pay for one to come for a few hours a day at the most. What about the rest of the time? Maybe he really would be better off in hospital? But when an ambulance came for him, Grandfather began to cry, and clutched at his bed – the same bed in which Grandmother had died, and the one in which he wanted to die, too. Valentin and I threw ourselves forward to shield him: it's not true that he doesn't understand anything, we insisted frantically. It would be the basest kind of betrayal to take him away, he wants to stay here! If the grown-ups even *dared* contemplate such a thing, we'd make them sorry . . . ! At that moment, we were ready to hate them: how could anyone dare to take Grandfather away from home by force?

However, it proved unnecessary for us even to open our mouths.

"You can leave," said my mother to the ambulance-men. "We'll look after him ourselves."

A nurse was hired for three hours a day, and the family worked out a rota so that there was always someone with Grandfather the rest of the time. O Lord, why must Grandfather suffer so? Why should he – the kindest, wisest person in the whole world – have to spend the last months of his life in such a state? We spoon-fed him, changed his bedding and talked to him just as we had before. Sometimes he would understand everything and nod, at other times he looked at us blankly and pushed away the cup of broth, spilling it over himself and us.

Why did he have to go through this? Surely it could not have been in order that Valentin and I should finally shake off the remnants of our semi-childish selfishness? So that I would give up all thought of completing high school with a gold medal, gaining admission to the Moscow physics faculty – indeed, embarking on a career of any sort – in order not to betray the most dearly beloved one who struggled so painfully towards his death? Somehow, sometimes, we kept going to school, missing out days in a row, which caused a lot of minor and major problems with our teachers: I don't really remember it very well, nor do I want to. At that time, I wanted sleep more than anything else.

Grandfather died one night in mid-May. I was not the one attending him at the time. My mother came home very early in the morning, and it was she who broke the news to me. Then there was the funeral, on a blindingly sunny spring day. And finally – the moment when we had to go away, leaving Grandfather alone under a mound of fresh but rapidly drying clay which was heaped with flowers. They were jonquils, I seem to recall.

Valentin and I managed to graduate against all odds. He was accepted into an Institute of Refrigeration Technology, and I entered the physics faculty of Odessa University. We went to the cemetery often that summer: first to Grandmother's grave, then to Grandfather's. It had been impossible to have them buried side by side: the cemetery planning did not allow for it.

Chapter Fifteen

My parents were in seventh heaven: their daughter had gained entrance into university, even if it was only Odessa University, and not Moscow. The money for extra mathematics tutorials (shared with Seryozha Diamant) had not been wasted after all, and it was just as well they had made no attempt to interfere with her chaotic system of studying – either sitting up all night swotting, or lying around on the couch for half a day reading Tyutchev's poetry. They are so delighted, their faces radiate so much joy, that I find it impossible to share my disappointment with them, and do my best to appear cheerful and content.

Inside, however, I feel so bitter, I could cry: I won't be eligible for a student grant! And it's my own fault, too: if only I had graduated with a complete set of 'fives', I would have been able to bring home forty roubles a month. Instead of that, here I am, seventeen years old and still totally dependent on my parents for support. Oh, the shame of it! And why? I got full marks for mathematics and physics, but only a 'four' for my Russian Literature essay. And that was enough to put paid to any hopes of getting a grant. There was no way of finding out why, or appealing against the grading: the essays are marked by a panel of examiners whose decision is final, and who cannot be approached. So I had no chance of finding out what error it was that cost me the opportunity of becoming independent for at least another six months. By a curious quirk of fate, I was to see that essay many years later, when I was under interrogation in a KGB prison. It was in the hands of KGB officer Lukyanenko, who had it extracted from the university archives for a graphological analysis: I had flatly refused to provide them with a specimen of my handwriting, so they used this 'document' instead.

"Thought you had us stumped, eh, Irina Borisovna?" he jeered. "But I bet you forgot all about this essay, didn't you? Our state doesn't throw anything away! Would you care to take a glance through it, just to refresh your memory?"

I did, because I was keen to find out, at last, what it was that stopped me from getting full marks. But there was not so much as a single red mark on it, not a stroke, not a word. Just the mark '4' at the end. At the age of twenty-eight I found this rather amusing.

But back in that year when I was seventeen, I had to swallow my first bitter student pill: grants were paid out to some who had not achieved all-round full marks, too, but only when the monthly family income was below fifty roubles per head. And in our family, with the combined wages of both parents, it came to sixty-five. I even entertained a secret thought of giving up university and going out to work – tomorrow, if need be! When all is said and done, physics is not the centre of my existence. What is, come to that? Probably, just roaming around Odessa, composing poems, and keeping my steps in rhythm with them. And that is hardly likely to be relevant to my future occupation, whatever it turns out to be.

Naturally, I did not breathe a word of this to anyone: it would have been downright stupid to throw away the chance of a university education and deal the parents such a blow. They'd had enough troubles to put up with, and it would have been too brutal to rob them of at least this one joy. It's not as though they grudge me anything. Mama, her eyes shining with pleasure, said to me: "Life is like a sailor's jersey: one white stripe, one dark stripe. It looks as though we have finally emerged out of a dark stripe!"

So – let's enjoy ourselves! We went off to a cake shop, and bought a cake with the candied fruit Alya liked so much. Then there was another treat: Oleg Arkadyevich and Igor were to come to visit! Igor and I had not seen each other for several years: family affairs had got in the way, and it just didn't work out. It would be interesting to see what Igor was like now that he was an adult. What fun we would have reminiscing about our childhood escapades: the Pioneers' camp, where we both used to sneak out to watch the sun rise at dawn, the hikes to Pavlovskaya Hill, where we might – who knows? – find treasure. How we made boiled sweets out of sugar, and how we argued endlessly about the relative merits of Kiev and Odessa.

Igor turned out to be a handsome young man with an elaborately curled new moustache. From the exalted heights of a second-year student he spoke casually about the way he sailed through his studies, about the pike he had caught with an ordinary bait, and about his success with girls . . . I didn't like him at all. Who does he think he is, I thought resentfully, Don Juan? And in any case, why on earth all this talk about girls to me? If you're an adult, I reasoned, why do you show off so much? And if you're a man, then why talk about your amatory exploits to a Plain Jane barely out of school? But just as in childhood, when we argued until we were hoarse, it didn't come to a fight, for all that we were both hot-headed and had a fearful reputation for scrapping in our respective neighbourhoods. And now, too, it didn't get as far as an irrevocable quarrel – we just couldn't, and that was that. Finally we got to talking about poetry, for which we both had a youthful passion. Other people's poetry, of course. Neither one admitted to writing poetry in secret. Then the subject of dogs came up, and in a flash the old Igor was back, full of reverence for every living creature. When physics was mentioned, he seemed to light up like a torch, and this made me realise that being top of the class was not an aim in itself for him, but the means to an end. It was not mercenary ambition, it was just that he knew exactly what he wanted to do, and for research of that kind, his father's institute was the only place. His only hope of getting in there was to come top of his year, otherwise he would be relocated to spending the last three years studying subjects in which he did not have the same interest, and life would become meaningless.

At this point, I wordlessly acknowledged his seniority and superiority: unlike myself, he already knows the meaning of his life. As for the fact that everything is working out so well for him – he's not boasting about it, just stating facts, and that's normal when someone devotes himself entirely to his chosen field. I already suspected, deep in my heart, that I would never devote myself to physics to such an extent. But what? That I didn't know, either. So let's talk about dogs, instead!

During our student years, Igor and I saw each other quite often: either he would come to Odessa, or I would go to Kiev. With great pleasure, he would demonstrate his skill with his hands: for instance, as I watched, he made a beautiful, intricate ring out of a Manchurian nut kernel, adjusted it to fit my finger, put it on and closed my fingers around it: "Here, wear it! It suits you!"

When he mastered glass-blowing, he gave me an exquisite tulip, and I shed many a tear when my clumsy cat, Keshka, knocked it over and it shattered.

As old and close friends, we were able to talk easily to each other about our respective affairs of the heart: we were close enough for complete trust, yet there was sufficient distance between us for neither to suspect that there might ever be any romantic feeling between the two of us. He had got over his first love long ago, and I had yet to encounter mine: as for infatuation – well, we both knew that that wasn't really love. I told him how, at the age of fourteen, I became enamoured of my Uncle Jan's friend and blood-brother. He was a tall, blue-eyed svan (an ethnic minority) and his name was Vazha.

Grandmother and Grandfather's home was full of beautiful chased metal objects made by him. Vazha and my Uncle Jan were both keen hunters, and had met somewhere in Georgia. Later, Uncle Jan saved Vazha's life when they were hunting wild boar (or maybe it was the other way round), and they became blood-brothers according to svan custom. So every time Vazha came to visit, it was a major family event. The thirty-six-year-old Vazha paid scant attention to me, a rather unsociable and withdrawn thirteen-year-old: he would give me an absent-minded pat on the head, say a few conventional words, and that was all. I would stare at the floor – as is customary at that age – terrified lest anyone should notice that I . . . Horror of horrors! Never! But what could I do to . . . to what?! I have no idea myself, I'm just holding my breath in anticipation, and then succumbing to wild imaginings, which, it seems to me, are quite plausible. Vazha is an artist, after all, one day he will notice my drawings and be so impressed that he will start giving me lessons . . .

All these romantic fancies came to an end that same year. I could barely contain my impatience, waiting for Vazha's next visit, totally convinced that he would be bowled over by my portrait of our cat and my illustrations to Kipling's *Jungle Book*. And then, as bad luck would have it, two-year-old Alya caught chicken pox. For some reason my parents decided that I was too old to catch the infection, and let me look after her. However, catch chicken pox I did, and in a particularly virulent form. Running a fever and covered from head to foot with red blotches, I was isolated in the little box-room in Grandmother and Grandfather's apartment. My parents were terribly worried and explained to me that I must lie as quietly as possible, and not scratch the pustules, or I would be pitted with pock-marks for the rest of my life. To keep my mind off the incessant itching, they brought me a pile of new books, and I dutifully proceeded to 'distract myself'. Alya was up and about, but my illness dragged on and on.

Right then, Vazha came to visit. I lay in bed, listening to his laughter and slightly accented speech. Of course, he would not come in to see me: I'm infectious, and they say that chicken pox is more dangerous to adults than to children. So he wouldn't see my drawings. Or me . . . All the time I had been sick, I had not looked into the mirror even once, but now I got up and did so. Lord, what a nightmare! My whole face was a mass of dry, ugly scabs! I cried, and was too frightened to wipe away the tears in case one of those ghastly scabs should come off and leave a scar. My infatuation evaporated along with my tears, all that was left was the love of drawing. What poor, funny creatures we are at the age of fourteen – so funny, and so afraid of seeming funny. When I recounted this story to Igor, I, too, found my adolescent woe amusing.

"Well, every cloud has a silver lining, as they say," commented Igor philosophically. "You draw very well. Incidentally, I want to make Lily – remember, I told you about her? – a silver pendant for her birthday. Would you do me a drawing of a small dragon? And do you think it would be better for me to set it in a circle, or an oval?"

We put our heads together to draw a suitable little dragon, with clawed paws, horns and wings, put it in a circular frame, and Igor was to swear later that this pendant was the best thing he had ever made out of old silver coins.

Student life followed its course; Igor studied seriously, I coasted along from term to term. I was in a light-hearted, young crowd; we sang songs to the accompaniment of a guitar, went hiking and camping along the wild shores of the sea . . . I was getting a grant by this time, and was honestly surprised how I somehow managed to pass exams. I was much more interested in the semi-finals and finals of the KVN* competitions than my studies. The KVN was a competition of wit and humour, and one of the favourite pastimes in Odessa. It was considered just as important for the university to have a strong KVN team as to have a good football team. I was no longer too shy to admit to writing poetry, and my friends copied it out, passed it around, and set it to music. My contemporaries considered me a poet, and I was secretly very proud of this. I knew by now that I would not make much of a physicist: it was enough to compare myself with Igor or his father to see that. I accepted that after university I would be assigned as a teacher to some school. So what? I like children, and I would have enough education to earn my living, come what may. I was already supplementing my student grant by private tuition: that's where my interest in psychology paid dividends! As for the main thing in my life – perhaps it would be poetry? I don't mind if my poems never appear in official Soviet publications! As Pushkin said, "a poet should never have to drag his sword around office reception-rooms".

I had already heard from one professional how a young poet should go about beginning his career: "First, go to the local newspaper with three or four of your poems. One or two of those should be ideological: about Lenin, say, or the Communist Party . . . you know the sort of thing. Then, when they're published, you take that paper and a few more poems to another publishing body. Of course, this second set of poems should also contain something ideological on topical issues

* *Klub Veselykh i Nakhodchivykh*

. . . Once you've had work published in about ten papers, you can start trying to get your poems included in a young poets' collection . . ."

Thanks, but no thanks! That's not for me. I will not debase poetry to the level of official lies. I know what that Party and its policies are worth, and it's better to steer clear of it and all that ideological claptrap which has been forced down our throats from birth! Luckily, physics is far removed from that sort of thing: it offers an ideal escape from political problems which are decided for us, anyway, and which we have to applaud, whether we agree or not!

To me, poetry is the greatest and highest expression of freedom, and I want it to remain beyond the greedy grasp of 'caring' state hands, which touch every aspect of the start-to-finish censored existence of a Soviet citizen. But if anyone else likes my poems, then they can copy them out with pleasure: I would never refuse one of my readers. And here, yet another link was forged in Igor's and my interwoven lives: looking at him, I realised that I would never make my mark as a physicist, and he – reading my poems – gave up writing poetry once and for all. We were moving away from our youthful fancies, bidding them farewell while retaining affection and understanding. Many years later, Igor would wake me in the middle of the night to give an opinion about some brilliant technical idea he'd just had, and I could share his enthusiasm: how simple, yet how ingenious! As for him – he was able to understand the thought behind any incomplete line of mine at a glance, and to this day he is the only person to whom I will show an unfinished poem and ask: is it better this way, or that?

Chapter Sixteen

I only realised how lucky I was to be a student at Odessa University years later, when I had the opportunity of comparing it with universities in other cities. To be more exact, it was my luck to be a student in the physics faculty, a little kingdom in itself among the large sprawl of buildings in this 'institute of higher education'. The lecturers and the faculty administration were wise enough not to force the issue of ideology with their young, sharp-tongued student body. The inevitable lectures on 'social sciences' were presented without undue emphasis, and nobody demanded that we treat them seriously: examinations were conducted in a normal atmosphere, and the lectures were presented in a palatable way. There was one nasty clash when one of our lecturers on atheism, or scientific communism, or something of the kind, fell ill, and was temporarily replaced by some high-flyer from the law faculty. For some unfathomable reason, he decided to convince us – students of electron physics – that Lenin, genius that he was, was no laggard in our chosen field: indeed, with philosophical insight, he realised at the very beginning of the twentieth century that 'an electron is just as infinite as an atom'.

With malicious glee, we began to pelt the unfortunate lecturer with unanswerable questions, such as where could we get hold of any of Lenin's published works on the structure of electrons? What experimental basis did the great leader have? pressed someone else: no, please tell us, after all, you're talking about a phenomenal discovery, one about which we have never heard! Does this mean that an electron has a nucleus? Or did Lenin discover some other constituent elements of this fascinating particle? If so, what are they? Ah, he only *assumed* that it was so! But in that case, why did he not qualify the immortal phrase just quoted to us with the customary scientific formulation that this is an assumption, not a proven fact? Oh, how we made him sweat before we were satisfied! There was no way we were going to give him the easy ride he would have had with budding KGB agents and public prosecutors. We are taught to think logically, and irresponsible formulae are unacceptable: every word must have a precise meaning. We never saw that particular lecturer again. Our dean was against any clashes on treacherous 'ideological grounds', and did his best to enable us to by-pass them as much as possible. In all my years there, not a single student was expelled from the physics faculty for political reasons, nor was there a single collective vilification – none of those things which were the bane of most students' lives. The only expulsions were for poor academic achievement, but we accepted this as fair. Our lecturers, who gave us no quarter when it came to exams, joined our KVN team wholeheartedly, and shared the fun of our 'phys. fac. days'. In the summer months, any one of us could afford to go to the university's sports camp, where those who wished could also attend supplementary seminars on physics and mathematics. After lectures we would stay behind in the empty auditorium to prepare the latest issue of a daily broadsheet, knowing that not one of our lecturers would demean himself to the role of a censor. Unlike students in Armenia, we never had to stage sit-ins on the university steps to protest against the ban on the wearing of trousers by female students, nor did we have to see ideological danger-signals in the wearing of embroidered shirts and blouses. Kalustyan, our university 'Party organiser', gained fame in the student body for managing to get rid of the bed-bugs in one of the blocks of student living-quarters, and having the price of student canteen breakfasts reduced to twenty kopecks – an unheard-of bargain. Maybe he did play the role of an ideological Cerberus in other fields, but if he did we never felt the effects in our lecture theatres. We were given no cause to enter into conflict with the authorities, and we were quite happy to fill our heads with problems totally unconnected with politics.

Blithely, we sang the songs of Alexander Galich – who was already in official disfavour – without realising that these songs were 'forbidden'. They seemed a natural and integral part of our youth and freedom, on which, it appeared, nobody had any designs. Just like our lecturers, we accepted the mandatory autumn work on collective farms with humorous resignation. If we have to put in a month pulling up beets or picking tomatoes, so be it, since that is the way our omniscient authorities run the agricultural economy. Even members of the Academy of Sciences – ha, ha! – have had to go out into the fields to dig up potatoes. At that time, we were much more interested in passing an exam in quantum mechanics, or swimming out further than anyone else at the beach.

I was nineteen years old when, one day, I caught a chance glimpse of my reflection in a shop window: what I saw was a long-legged, tanned young woman in a red T-shirt and with a thick mane of hair. For a moment it didn't sink in that I was seeing myself. And then

came the stunning revelation that I was not hideously ugly, after all. At
home I studied myself attentively in the mirror: not the way one looks at
oneself in the morning, combing one's hair, but the way we look at
people when we meet them for the first time. I was no great beauty, to
be sure, but I wasn't too bad, either: merry eyes, a flattering tan ...
What I need to go with this red T-shirt, I thought, is a very pale pink
skirt! With a will, I set about sifting through assorted old clothes stored
away in the fold-up divan. Now here's something that could be altered!
I don't know anything about sewing, but Grandmother's trusty old
Singer is still here somewhere, on top of a cupboard. Down it comes,
and let's see if I can figure out how to put in the thread! My closest
friends at that time, Inna and Anna, entered into this new hobby with
great enthusiasm. There's a shop, Loskut, where they sell fabric remnants: it doesn't take much material to make a mini-skirt, does it? And
long skirts can be made by sewing contrasting pieces of fabric together.
Very soon we were flaunting our new finery, and making presents of
tote-bags with numerous pockets to the boys in our crowd. And, come
to think of it, it's high time that I learned how to dance properly. Piles
of textbooks and table are pushed against the wall, and Inna, graceful
and light on her feet, instructs me in the intricacies of the waltz and the
tango. Her parents are always pleased to let us use their one room and
kitchen for our noisy student dos and are keen and welcome participants. Inna's mother, Roxanna Markovna, dances every bit as well as
her daughter, with inherited German flair and precision, and her father,
Yuri Davidovich, teaches us the student songs of his time. They become
the heart and soul of our noisy crowd, older friends with whom one can
have fun and talk about serious matters as well.

Not long afterwards, I came running to Roxanna Markovna for advice
about a totally unexpected problem. I received an official summons
to present myself at a specified time to a specified office at the city
headquarters of the Communist Youth League, the Komsomol. There
was nothing to indicate why I was being summoned: I could only guess.
I was not unduly alarmed: most likely it would be something to do
with the KVN session we were planning to conduct with students from
Yerevan, in Armenia. Televised KVN competitions between teams
from different cities were very popular throughout the whole of the
USSR, but by that time they had been forbidden for a number of years:
somebody at the top had decided that some of the jokes on these shows
were 'politically tactless'. Our effort with the Yerevan students was not
going to be televised but it would be on stage, so I figured that even this
would not be permitted, and the potential participants were being called
before the Komsomol to be informed of that fact. It did seem a bit odd,

though, that nobody else from our team, not even the captain, had received a similar summons yet. Why were they starting with me? Oh, well, it will all become clear soon enough.

So I duly presented myself at the huge, grey building which, apart from the city Komsomol, housed the city Party executive and a number of other similar bodies. Notices in gold lettering hung all over the place. The man in the room to which I reported was quite clearly well past Komsomol age. Nothing surprising in that, though: all the leaders of Komsomol 'organs' are pretty high-ranking communists.

"Can you guess why we've invited you here, Irina Borisovna?"

"No."

"But what do you think?"

"That you will probably explain in a moment."

"Irina . . . you don't mind if I call you that? . . . this meeting today was preceded by our getting to know you by proxy, so to speak. And we heard very positive things about you. You're studying at the university, you've completed an English language course . . ."

What on earth has English to do with all this? I thought, bewildered. Are they thinking of sending me abroad, or what?

"Actually, my English isn't all that good . . ."

"Never mind," he smiled understandingly, "if need be – we'll help you polish it up. But tell me, do you read the papers? Could you say, for instance, what the situation is in Angola at the moment?"

Heavens, that's torn it! I never even look at the papers: what do I need with all that political stuff if I'm never going to be able to influence it one way or another? But this, too, does not rattle my interlocutor, who continues to smile encouragingly: "Not to worry, if you don't read the press. No harm done! After all, you're in the Komsomol, aren't you?"

"Yes . . ."

That is a fact. I joined the Komsomol with the rest of my class when I was fourteen years old – this is standard procedure. It made no difference to my life apart from mandatory attendance at dreary Komsomol meetings after school hours, where the main topics of discussion were who had not yet subscribed to the compulsory paper or had forgotten to pay their two kopecks membership dues. And at university, I continued to pay my membership fee, thinking nothing of that membership – I was just one of the crowd.

"What would you say if you were given the opportunity of joining a special Komsomol brigade?"

Lord, that's about the last thing I need! I have absolutely no desire for that kind of nonsense. But I must be careful with my answers:

"Well, I would want to know what sort of a brigade it is, and what I would have to do."

He began to explain at length, and in a strangely roundabout way: that what was being offered to me was a great honour, a task of some importance to the state . . . After beating about the bush like this for a while, he became more businesslike and got down to the real issue: the proposition was that I should scrape up acquaintances with foreigners in Odessa, become very friendly with them and have a good time. I'm young, sociable – just what's needed. Then I would carefully and unobtrusively find out their political leanings, their attitudes to our Communist Party, the names of the people they know in Odessa and elsewhere in the Soviet Union, how well they know them . . . It would also be useful to get the addresses of their relatives and friends, or at least their names. After every such 'friendship' it would be my job to forward the information I had gleaned to the relevant state 'organs'. Naturally, all this would be strictly secret, nobody must know what I'm doing.

What?! Can they really mean that they want me, a nineteen-year-old girl, to become a prostitute-informer? Are they lunatics? How dare they!

"No, I won't do it."

"Irina, I can hardly believe my ears! This is a Komsomol obligation, so how can you refuse? Are you tired of being in the Komsomol, of studying at university? No, no, you're speaking without thinking! I'm going to pretend I didn't hear what you said!"

Then he started on my family: my mother is a senior teacher, isn't she, and loves her work, my father is an outstanding engineer who, incidentally, works in an institute which deals with secret projects (they don't take just anybody there, you know!), as for my sister, why, she is old enough to go to school by herself now, and cross the street alone . . . Heavens, they even know that!

Of course, they resorted to such open and primitive blackmail only because I was young, frightened and inexperienced. In my later dealings with the KGB, when I was already an acknowledged dissident, they were much more subtle, because they knew full well that I would publicise everything they said to me, and that I no longer believed in the omnipotence of the KGB anyway. But on that first occasion they didn't pull their punches.

I sat there, scared stiff and on the brink of tears, unable to do anything but reiterate 'no' until they lost patience with me.

"Irina, we have interviewed two hundred girls before you" (He's lying! I thought immediately, and this cheered me up) "and not a single one of them refused. Still, if that's your attitude, we'll have to act differently."

We were joined by two other men: one was elderly, the other aged about forty. And it began: the older of the two, shaking his luxuriant mane of grey hair, averred that if he were nineteen and had his life over again, he would still deem it the highest honour to work in the 'organs'. I realised, at last, that by 'organs' he meant the KGB, and became really scared. This was the first person I had ever encountered who openly admitted to being a KGB officer. Then he and the other one (who, for some reason, stood behind me all the time as I sat on a chair in the middle of the room) began to alternate threats with promises of brilliant career prospects in the 'organs'.

"I've got to go now . . ."

"Sit down! Nobody leaves here without permission! We haven't finished with you yet."

In my panic, the only thing I realised clearly was that I must not, under any circumstances, agree to anything, or, God forbid, sign anything. They kept me there for another hour.

"Well, off you go now, and think things over," they said to me in parting. "And don't think we'll forget about you. When you make up your mind, ring this telephone number and ask for Sasha. No, don't write down the number, memorise it. You've got an excellent memory! And not a word to anyone about anything that's been said here today! We'll be watching you, and if you blab, we'll take the necessary measures against you, and against anyone you tell. Do your parents know that you were summoned here today?"

"Yes."

"Tell them you were asked to work as a Pioneer leader in the Sputnik children's camp. That's all. You can go now."

The first thought in my mind when I shot out into the street was to rush down to the sea and throw myself over a cliff. Not only will I never get out of their clutches (to hell with university!) but my family, too . . . I simply can't bring myself, physically, to work for them, but I'm frightened to death of them, too. Never again – not when I was arrested, nor when I was in solitary confinement in the KGB prison, did I experience even a shadow of that terrible, choking fear: it must have burnt itself out on that occasion. I also understood that they could not possibly kill everyone who refused to work for them, and their families to boot! The overabundance of petty details, reminiscent of spy stories, was quite clearly a ploy for effect. But what am I to say at home? Should I lie, as I have been ordered? If I do that, it will be the beginning of collaboration. So should I tell the truth? But then they might . . . I spent the next few days mooching about in silence, and my parents became quite concerned when I wouldn't answer their questions. Finally I went off to Roxanna Markovna for advice: I decided that I would tell everyone about what had happened, reasoning that the KGB could hardly kill off dozens of people. At worst, I would be the one to suffer, but then everyone would know the reason. "Am I right?" I asked Roxanna Markovna.

"You were right to refuse," she smiled approvingly. "Otherwise, you would have started with foreigners, and ended up informing against your friends. But you must tell your parents: they should know what happened. You haven't phoned that number you were given?"

"No."

"Good! And don't worry about university: chances are, they were only trying to frighten you. Of course, if they really put their minds to it, they could make difficulties for you, but everyone will know why."

Her wise and calm reasoning reassured me. My mother was immensely relieved: it turned out that she was worried that I was pregnant, and too scared to admit it.

"Really, Mama!" I protested. "How could you?" You know me, and you know that I don't have anyone . . ."

"Well, what was I supposed to think, when you seemed to be half-demented for so many days?"

"Pregnant in the line of Komsomol duty?"

We both burst out laughing, and then shed a few tears.

My parents, naturally, approved my refusal. Nevertheless, I couldn't resist asking my father: "But if they really began to take measures against me now, what would you do?"

"What could I do?" was his reply.

It was bitter to hear such an answer, but it was an honest one: what could he do against the KGB? It was a good lesson, too, for me to be aware that I was living in a country where a father could not come to his daughter's defence. So here it was, the penalty for my thoughtless entry into the Komsomol. And the outcome of my English lessons. Had I lost my head (as I could have, they did offer a less revolting alternative) and signed an agreement to collaborate with them, what kind of a person would I be now? No matter how hard you may try to get away from these politics and these authorities, they will catch up with you, and when they do, they will never let go.

At that time they retreated, for quite a few years. I was not expelled from university, but a note must have been made in my records that I was 'unreliable': at the end of our third year, our group was supposed to go to Poland for field work in some Physics Institute, and I was not allowed to make the trip. I was offered no reason, nor did I try to determine what it was: I was glad that I had got off so easily.

Chapter Seventeen

"Irka, are you in love with Alec Timofeyev?"

Ten-year-old Alya, clad in a nightgown, clambers over from her bed into mine. This is the traditional prelude for a serious heart-to-heart talk.

"Heavens, no! He's a friend, that's all, just like Alyosha Kozdoba, or Valentin."

"Well, from the way you were dancing with him yesterday, I thought . . . And then the earth shook straight afterwards, just like it's supposed to happen when two people fall in love."

Yesterday was my twenty-third birthday. All our crowd was there, including Ilyusha and Roxanna Markovna and her husband. Mama had baked a fabulous cake, and we were having the time of our lives, after apologising in advance to the people living downstairs for all the racket. Then suddenly the lamp started swaying, and bits of plaster showered down from the ceiling. This was too much for our neighbours: they began to bang on their ceiling in protest. But in fact, the cause turned out to be an earth tremor, something very unusual in our parts. We rushed out into the yard where most of the other inhabitants of the house were already milling around.

"The Ratushinskys danced one dance too many!" they joked.

"Seeing as there's a full moon," I joked back, "just thank your lucky stars that we didn't cause a tidal wave!"

However, my secretive little sister somehow linked the earth tremor with love. No, little one, your guess is miles out.

"Truly, Allykins, I've not so much as laid an eye on Alec Timofeyev!"

To 'lay an eye' on someone is how we describe that strange and fleeting something which can spring up between those who were just friends yesterday and will be just friends again tomorrow, but for a brief instant become the only 'you and I' in the world. Alya sighs with relief: "So that means I can go ahead and fall in love with him?"

"Of course!"

My sweet little moppet! Does that mean that you were afraid of ruining your older sister's chances?

"Are you going to tell him?"

"No."

"Then what do you mean to do?"

"Nothing at all," replies Alya, loftily. "Why should a woman do anything? Let him realise for himself."

"But what if he doesn't?"

"In that case –" (deep sigh) "I'll have to fall in love with somebody else!"

"With Oleg Rossiin, maybe?"

"No, he's too good-looking, and I'm afraid to look at him. He's like Dorian Grey. Maybe I should fall in love with 'The Count'?"

"But he's very handsome, too."

"That's the trouble, all the guys in your crowd are so good-looking, that I envy them. Will I be good-looking when I grow up, d'you think?"

"Better than anybody else!"

"And then I'll marry a very old man, like Marina marrying Mazeppa! How old will Alec be then?"

"When you're seventeen, he'll be thirty-two."

"Well, that's not really *very* old, but better than nothing, I suppose. But Irka, are you in love with anyone?"

"I'm not sure. Maybe I'm not in love at all, or maybe not quite. I feel very strange."

"Who is he?"

"Ilyusha."

"But he's married!"

"He's divorced."

"Oh, poor thing! But he's not even one of your crowd! Won't they be upset?"

"No. But even if they are – well, that's just too bad!"

"Are you going to tell him?"

"No."

"But, listen, he's definitely laid an eye on you. I didn't understand before, but now . . . Remember how he read your poems?"

"Yes, and said that half of them were junk."

"But he said that the other half were really good!"

"Come, on, Button, how do you know that?"

"You needn't think you're the only witch in the family! Full moon, my foot! Take that, for your full moon!"

Pillows scatter in all directions, and, weak with laughter, we finally settle down in our respective beds. In the morning we tell each other our dreams. Both dreamt of the sea, but in Alya's dream it was green, and in mine – grey – almost mottled. With lots of waves.

A few months later Alya, clad in the same nightgown, would scuttle out into the kitchen and whisper, conspiratorially: "Irka! Ilyusha's whistling outside!"

I'd drop a quick kiss on her little pink ear, and race out into the yard, under the acacias and large, twinkling stars.

In the evenings, Ilyusha conducts clandestine English lessons for people who are preparing to emigrate. He comes around at eleven o'clock in the evening, when Alya should be long asleep, and I would be sitting over my textbooks and waiting to hear his signal. My parents are not too keen on Ilyusha, but I am always made welcome in his home. Even an hour before midnight. Ilyusha's mother, Raisa Ilyinichna, smiles upon me benignly: "Irochka, would you like a cup of coffee?"

"Mum, I'll make it."

"In that case, you can make some tea for Papa and me. He's got to get up early tomorrow. Irochka, there are some biscuits on the top shelf of that cupboard. Do you know what they're called? Haman's ears!"

Ilyusha's father, Mikhail Nisanovich, tells me about the Hebrew festival of Purim, and about Esther, who saved her people from genocide. Afterwards Ilyusha and I drink coffee in his tiny room, trying not to make any noise. A candle stands on a small table, and our hands cast strange shadows on the walls and bookshelves. Joined hands – but for how long?

I know that Ilyusha and his parents have applied for permission to emigrate from the Soviet Union. I also know that only Jews are allowed to emigrate, and even then not all of them. I know that even if we were to marry, my parents would never give the necessary permission for me to go with him. Which would mean that Ilyusha and his parents, who are so fond of me, would have to remain here forever. All because of me. So I must not let myself think about it; my first, difficult, mad love can have no happy ending. From the very beginning, that love has been overshadowed by the railway station at which I shall see him off, and remain behind. But for now, for today, this evening belongs to us: to our youthful arguments, to sorrow, to poetry.

At the very beginning of our acquaintance, Ilyusha was stunned by my ignorance. He found it incredible that I knew nothing about the 'Silver Epoch' of Russian poetry, that the names of the 'great four' – Pasternak, Mandelstam, Akhmatova and Tsvetayeva – meant nothing to me. Of course I knew nothing of them: there was nothing like that on our shelves at home, and in our literature lessons in school there was only mention of the 'decadent period' during which poets, instead of helping the Revolution, wasted their time exalting classless blossoms and sunsets. Nor had I ever seen any works by these authors in the bookshops . . . Admittedly, I had read some Gumilev in *samizdat*.

In one week I was buried under an avalanche of all that which had been carefully concealed from our generation: Akhmatova's 'Requiem', Tsvetayeva's poems, and a blue-bound volume of Mandelstam, published in a tiny print-run. And they were now mine, painfully close, Russian! How could it be that I had not known about them? Who had dared deprive me of my legitimate heritage, and for what reason? I was old enough to realise who and why. So that I would not dream of emulating them, Mandelstam perished in the camps, Gumilev was shot, Tsvetayeva was driven to suicide, Akhmatova's son was imprisoned, and she was blackmailed into praising that murderer, Stalin . . . When Pasternak was being hounded out of the Union of Soviet Writers, the bravest of his colleagues avoided voting by discovering a sudden and urgent need to go to the toilet . . . The shock of it all sent my temperature soaring, and I became delirious: I saw myself stretching my hands towards them, but they stood as though on the other side of a river, and couldn't see me. Is it only the bullet or the rope which can make it possible to join them? And how feeble, how derivative are the poems of my youth! Without realising it, without having read them, I had subconsciously striven to imitate their greatness. Our apartment had central heating by that time, but the old fuel stove still remained. I got a fire going, and flung all my manuscripts into it: all my unknowingly stolen black horses, weeping accordions, white swans and gypsies . . . I would start afresh, even if I must pay the penalty of camps, and solitary death. The only crumb of comfort is that I had tried to write in their style, and not in the 'menopausal lyrics' and contrived militarism of 'famous Soviet poetesses', the sole exception to this dreary line-up being, in my opinion, the poet Bella Akhmadulina:

> Then to our friends let us be partial,
> Let us suppose they're wonderful!
> To lose them terrible: God forbid.

These lines, too, I heard first from Ilyusha, after I had rallied a bit. As well as his beloved Samoylov, another delightful discovery:

> There Anna sang – from morning on.
> Embroidering something. Or else sewing.
> And her song, from outside flown,
> His heart in spite of him set going.

The candle flickers, we sit cheek to cheek, dark heads together, his Jewish eyes looking into my half-Polish, half-Russian ones.

I don't think I cried at the station. Later, I was taken away from there by cousin Valentin and the faithful Alyosha Kozdoba, who never aspired to anything more than my friendship. We exchanged love letters. And tried to fool ourselves by pretending that maybe, some-day, somehow, we would meet again. Some of our letters got through, others disappeared, depending on the caprices of Soviet censorship.

> The thievish brand of the customs –
> On the shoulder of love that is leaving.
> Thank God: he's survived, what's left over
> The letter-box is receiving.
> Even this they'll rake up from in there
> And bury it without honours.
> The doorbell aches for a miracle:
> Hush, hush, on his throne the King governs!
> In the bedroom the Queen is not crying,
> The door there is closed – not a murmur.
> From her dolls and her ball withdrawing,
> Going away into grown-up suffering –
> At the same speed as the flame does
> The Queen turns the letters' pages:
> Do you see, there is smoke on the bridges?
> Since yesterday, smoke on the bridges.

Before he left, Ilyusha made me a present of an eighteenth-century Bible, printed in Old Church Slavonic, the Old and the New Testa-ments. I spent one and a half months learning to read that ancient, intricate alphabet, and then, finally, read the Bible. After that, all the revelations I had either guessed or read about elsewhere fell into place, like the pieces of a jigsaw puzzle. I realised that yes, I am a Christian, and my loving God confirms that it is so, and not otherwise! Russian literature, which had earlier saved my young soul from rejection and pride, confirms the same. But I did not experience the typical zeal of a neophyte: there is one God for all, for all faiths except paganism. Is it for us, humans, to try to carve Him up amongst ourselves? He will show the way, He will instruct: for we are all His children.

Many years later, Igor and I went to visit Ilyusha in Saint Louis, where he lives and works. By that time they already knew each other – not just from my words, but from frantic transatlantic telephone calls exchanged after my arrest. We became fast friends with his wife, Jane, and enjoyed ourselves immensely playing with their three children. Ilyusha's mother, pale and drawn after her husband's death, embraced us as though we were her nearest and dearest. Igor and I exchanged warm memories of Ilyusha's father, a gentle and kind doctor who treated the poor in San Francisco free of charge. He had lived like a man, and died like a man, despite a liver transplant, remaining calm and wise in the face of imminent death. We saw him one week before he died.

My cousin Valentin joined the Communist Party and I never had a single letter from him, either during my years in the camps or after I left the Soviet Union for the West. However, he refused to give evidence against me when he was pulled in for interrogation concerning my 'anti-Soviet activities'. Alyosha Kozdoba died of cancer, but we met once after my release: despite his illness, he came rushing down to Chernobyl-poisoned Kiev. He and Igor met like brothers; while I was in the camps, Alyosha had done everything he could to help Igor. As for Ilyusha, Jane, and the two of us – we are four friends who have learned much and passed through much, each in his own way.

Chapter Eighteen

In the autumn of 1977, Igor came to Odessa to attend a conference on thermal physics. Naturally, he came round to see us.

"Irka, it's good to see you! I'm here for a whole week! Well, let me look at you . . . I say, you'll be breaking a few hearts!"

"Make fun of me, will you? Someone's going to get their whiskers tweaked if they're not careful!"

We dodge around the room, laughing.

"Watch out that you don't tread on the cat! She's a strict lady, and will take offence!"

"Strict lady? Keshka? Who smashed the glass tulip, eh Whiskers? Pretending you don't know what I'm talking about, aren't you? All right, come here!"

To my surprise Keshka, who is usually so aloof, settles down comfortably on his lap. This is an honour she accords to very few people, and my friends usually have to cajole their way into her good graces. Igor starts to scratch her belly, another familiarity which is permitted to a favoured few.

"Well, how have you been keeping? Not married yet?"

"I told you I'd invite you to my wedding when the time came."

I don't want to discuss Ilyusha with him, or with anybody else. Know-all Alya is enough to be getting on with. And even she has maintained a tactful silence recently, understanding that I am going through a rough patch.

"What about you, though? Still single, too?"

"Yes. It all fell apart with Lily. I still can't figure out why: she was the best."

I feel it prudent to avoid sensitive subjects.

"Tell me, are you free now? Let's go out somewhere – no sense sitting around here! I'll just give you something to eat first."

"What's on offer?"

"Truffles, caviar and rare tropical fruits!"

We take ourselves off to the kitchen and make sandwiches with processed cheese, washing them down with tea.

"How are things at your school?"

"I've left."

"You're kidding! I thought you really liked it there . . . Yaroslavsky got you down, or what?"

Tolya Yaroslavsky, an eleven-year-old boy in my class, was notorious throughout the whole school: a nervous, difficult child who had set his face firmly against receiving any schooling. All his misdemeanours had particularly nasty overtones: he would drive needles into those sitting in front of him, fight like one possessed without noticing blood or injury, burn textbooks. The teachers loathed him, his father used to beat him within an inch of his life, and the child's conflict with the rest of the world grew increasingly acute. When I, a new teacher, was assigned to the class including this 'treasure', I was shocked by what I saw in that child's eyes: he looked like a caged wild animal . . . I patted him on the head, and he suddenly burst into tears. Heavens, I thought, when was the last time anyone showed you any kindness?

I went off to speak to his father, who rounded on me as though ready to throw me bodily out of the room: "I don't want to have anything more to do with that school! I belt him for every poor mark, what else do you want from me? What do you expect from the kid when he was the only one in the class not to be accepted into the Pioneers? Why is he any worse than the rest? Well, now he knows that he's worse, and you can cope with it as you see fit!"

"Wait a minute, that was before I came to the school – I've only been there just over a week!"

"Yes, you're all the same, you teachers, aren't you? You bring a kid to this state, and then wash your hands of him. At least my heart aches for him, but all you care about is your class averages . . ."

This was too much; forgetting all the rules of proper teacher conduct, I yelled back at him: "Then why the hell do you think I'm here, if I don't care? It's nine o'clock in the evening, and according to your logic, I ought to be enjoying myself at a dance! Don't you realise that half of Tolya's problems stem from your constant beatings?"

For some reason, this seemed to have an effect, and he subsided visibly: "But I was only doing what I was asked! Not by you personally, of course, but I've become used to the fact that after every visit by a teacher, I have to . . ."

"Well, since you're so keen on following teachers' orders, then bear in mind that I'm Tolya's teacher now! And I absolutely forbid you to belt him again! Do you want to turn him into a psychopath?"

"Listen, girlie, how old are you?"

"Twenty-three. So what?!"

"You don't know life yet . . ."

"And you do, I suppose? You ought to be ashamed of yourself! A head full of grey hair, and such things . . ."

"Look, what are you going on at me for? I'm not my son's enemy. But if he's not belted, there's no reasoning with him . . ."

"We'll manage!"

"Well, we'll see . . ."

From then onwards, placing no dependence on the co-operation of the older teachers, I simply left no space in his report book for their comments, filling all the available space with commendations such as 'Did an excellent job of cleaning the classroom after lessons', 'Helped the teacher during lessons', 'Gathered more scrap metal than anyone else in the class' and so on. Of course, there was a fair degree of exaggeration in all this, an investment in a better future, so to speak. I just seized on any positive manifestation and embellished his achievements without a single qualm of conscience. At first I gave him higher marks than he earned, but after receiving a completely undeserved four, my hopeless Yaroslavsky manfully (if not very ably) submitted his first-ever piece of maths homework. The other teachers, influenced by my glowing testimonials in Yaroslavsky's report book, began to hope that the little horror had turned over a new leaf. In fact, he had not the slightest intention of doing any such thing, but found himself facing a *fait accompli*: first the adults had given him a bad reputation, and now they were doing just the opposite. All children are fatalists, and Tolya accepted that he was now a good boy, deserving of affection. He remained a handful and a poor scholar, of course: no miracle had occurred to change that. However, he lost much of his aggression, and stopped having nightmares. This I learned from his mother a year later, who came to shower me with tears and kisses, much to my discomfiture.

Igor knew all about Yaroslavsky, because we liked discussing our work. Hence his dismay.

"No, everything is fine with Yaroslavsky. I have yet to meet a kid who'll get the better of me. The thing is, the children believe me! It's not too bad with the younger ones, but I have to teach in the older classes, too. Well, tell me: who invented the electric light bulb?"

"Edison."

"Right. But according to the school syllabus, light bulbs are called 'Lenin's lamp'! 'Communism is the Soviet government plus electrification of the whole country.' Or you get cases when they take something out for 'ideological reasons', which means that you have to enter into debates with the administration, and lie to your pupils!"

"Even in physics and mathematics?"

"And how! Do you know how you have to set out a plan for a lesson? They check to make sure that there's an 'ideological aim' in each one. For instance, I could be taken to task for making no mention of the Bratsk hydro-electric scheme when demonstrating the solution of a problem based on Ohm's Law . . . after all, the Bratsk project was a 'Komsomol construction' one!"

"But they had prisoners building that!"

"So do I tell the kids that? Or do I lie, the way I'm expected to? You should see their faces, when they look at me – they believe every word I say . . . I just can't do it! I'll give you another example. Say I'm taking the fourth grade for maths: it's the second half of the day, the kids have already sat through four subjects, so how much are they likely to take in? And my lesson is supposed to be on Roman numerals: I've got forty-five minutes to teach them the lot. So I line them up and take them out into the street. You know how all the old houses in Odessa have *Anno Domini* and the Latin numerals on them? The houses are pleasant to look at, the children get a breath of air to clear their heads, and then they can go home and boast to their parents that they know in which year this or that house was built. Sure, there was a lot of yelling and horseplay, but they learned everything I wanted to teach them! You should have seen them chalking Roman numbers onto the footpath! I said to them, 'Write down your year of birth, and those of the other members of your family'; and what do you think? One of those idiots wrote down the Roman numbers for this year. Well, I knew that he had no new-born brother or sister, and thought he'd made a mistake. But he looked at me in all seriousness and said: 'This is the year my dog was born!' and drew a picture of his dog, there and then."

"So what's wrong with that? I'd hang on to a teacher like that with all my might!"

"That's you. You lunatic, what are you doing to that cat? Put her down at once! Ham-handed oaf!"

"As your highness orders . . ."

"Do you know how much trouble I had because of that lesson? For taking the children out of school, and without the senior teacher's permission, at that? And in lesson time?"

"Is the senior teacher some kind of idiot, or what?"

"They all have nothing but rules and regulations in their heads for all eventualities. Did I tell you that they tried to talk me into joining the Party? Saying that they need young, promising people? They even said they'd make me the senior teacher when the current one retires. In order to get on – join the Party, then you'll have prospects."

"The previous generation did that, and I don't see any great sin in it. My father . . ."

"I know. And my mother."

"But there's a difference between ordinary Party members and Party functionaries!"

"Yes. And just think what the functionaries did in the name of the ordinary members. Our parents' generation may not have understood fully, but ours? The more you know, the greater the responsibility. And everyone knows everything now: this is not Stalin's time."

"So you left? But what about your three years' service?"

"They were glad to let me off with only one and a half. They want me as little as I want them."

"So what are you doing now?"

"Looking for a job. In engineering, or laboratory work. I applied to the Food Plant Industry, and they almost took me on, but then the personnel department vetoed my appointment. Never mind, I'll manage somehow. Come on, let's go out and get a bit of sun!"

The sun outside is lovely – typical for Odessa in September. The chestnuts are ripening on the trees, and we pelt each other with them in memory of the good old days. It's really very warm, I'm wearing my thin, newest jumper, but Igor drapes his jacket around my shoulders just in case. It feels warm and cosy, and has a pleasant male smell of tobacco and salt, and something else – after-shave lotion, perhaps, or is it the legacy of someone's kisses?

"What about you, O Bearded One?"

"Hanging on for the time being."

"What do you mean, for the time being?"

"I had a job last summer with aqualung divers. The subject matter is actually the province of the Institute of Physiology – the divers' lungs – but there's some overlap with us. It was all to do with loss of heat when an organism is in cold conditions for long periods of time. We produced some flexible gauges which could be worn under the diving suits, and I went to Novorossiysk, where the experiment was carried out."

There was no trace in my old friend of his earlier enthusiasm, and I probed as carefully as I could: "So you did some swimming?"

"Yes. Those divers are terrific guys. We got along like a house on fire. But do you know what all the measurements we took were for? There are different categories of work: light, medium, heavy, and debilitatingly heavy. In the case of the latter, the people doing it are eligible for high salaries, two months' annual leave, admission into a sanatorium, pension rights from the age of fifty. Well, the Institute of Physiology was seeking to determine into which category the aqualung divers' work falls. With the help of our gauges."

"And so?"

"The results showed that their work belonged in the heaviest category. And then there was a directive from the VTsSPS to amend the results of the tests, and rate the job in a lower category."

"VTsSPS? Enlighten my ignorance! I can never get to grips with their ghastly acronyms."

"The Supreme something or other of Soviet Trade Unions. It's their job to make sure that there is no 'excessive spending'."

"So you downgraded the job?"

"No, that had nothing to do with me, I was only small fry. The downgrading was done by the Institute of Physiology, I only found out about it by chance. And then I was told that I was kicking up a fuss over nothing: I'd done my job, handed in correct results, and it's none of my business what was done with those results later. But the divers were robbed. Guys I'd sat around a campfire with, drunk vodka . . ."

"But what happened isn't your fault!"

"Maybe not. But – I know about it."

"But then, this is not something you're going to be doing as a regular job, is it?"

"Do you really think it's easy to find a good field, which won't be affected by this kind of chicanery? I was offered a job recently, involving work with 'secret' matters: making gauges for study of the cerebral cortex."

"What's secret about that?"

"Don't you see? That means the studies are either for the military, or for the KGB. Now think, in what way is study of the cerebral cortex applicable to national defence? 'Secret' work is very well funded, they don't stint on that the way they do on ordinary research. You can go for your Master's and your PhD, get all the equipment you want. But if I were to get into that, how do I know to what use they'll put the results of my work? What they'll pump into someone's brains?"

"Yes, it's rather frightening. So you refused?"

"Of course."

"And now what?"

"Well, they can hardly label all scientific research top secret! For the time being I'm doing various things in my father's institute – on ordinary projects, that is. I want to improve my qualifications, and then I'll probably go in for electro-slag smelting."

He lights up with all his old zeal, and begins to explain to me how fantastically interesting this is. I feel rather sad: what kind of a career do you envisage for yourself, my mad physicist? One in which everything will be clean and honest? Oh, but you're in for some nasty surprises! Or will you also join the Party, so that you can work without impediment, and then find yourself making compromises great and small? And anyway, what right do I have to judge you, for didn't I stay on in the Komsomol after that effort by the KGB to recruit me? I was afraid of being kicked out of university if I left . . . Now, having quit my teaching job, I had my name taken off the Komsomol list, and will not be part of it in whatever new job I find. It's a way out, but there's no valour involved: you don't have to be particularly brave to make a quiet exit. I have not yet mustered up the courage to go to the local Komsomol headquarters and throw my membership ticket in their faces. The pennies paid in membership fees – is that a little, or a lot? Then again, a bullet in the name of 'fraternal assistance to a friendly regime' in Angola doesn't cost all that much to manufacture . . . If Igor is concerned about the use to which his work might be put, then surely I should give some thought to the Komsomol dues coming out of my former employment.

When Jadvyga Bieliauskiene reproached me, years later in labour camp, for my one-time Komsomol membership, all I could do was hang my head in silence: what she said was just. I was afraid to leave, even though I felt ashamed of staying. The fact that I was fourteen years old when I joined is no excuse: yes, I was a young fool, even felt upset about being the last of my class to be accepted into the Komsomol. But after that, right up until the age of twenty-four? The fact that 'everyone does it' is no justification for an adult: there's a difference between that, and strangling dogs in China!

I was soon to meet Kolya Danilov, who was already over forty by that time. He graduated in law in the early 1960s and went to work for the KGB. With a great deal of youthful zeal. That was the time of the Khrushchev thaw, when many former prisoners had been released and exonerated. Kolya hoped to find the name of his father, who had disappeared without trace during the war. He found nothing in the archives, but he made another discovery: he learned that "we release them with one hand, and put them away with the other," as he put it. First he went to the local Party headquarters, and flung down his Party ticket: "I'm no longer a communist!" After that, he went to the KGB: "I'm not a *chekist* any longer!"

He was forcibly interned in a psychiatric hospital, where he spent eight years. Here, he was injected with the strong depressant aminazin, and sulfazin, which causes racking pains in the whole body and raging fever. Psychiatric institutions are much more terrible than any labour camp: here, they not only beat you, they can inject you with anything they wish. It is a mystery to me how anyone manages to emerge sane from these ghastly places, but Kolya was one such. Later he worked at the '*Kisllorodmash*' as a fine craftsman with wood, but had no right to sell his own creations.

Over a cup of tea in their kitchen-living-room-workshop he once squinted at me and said: "You know, Ira, it wouldn't be bad for you to spend a year or eighteen months in a labour camp! You're a poet, it would do you good! Broaden your horizons!"

"Kolya, what on earth are you saying?" cried his wife, Mary, in dismay.

I can't say I felt too happy hearing those words, either: me – in a camp? I can't bear enclosed spaces, I've suffered from claustrophobia all my life! I wouldn't last a day in prison!

But a small, inner voice whispered: "Did they ask those who went before? Didn't Mandelstam suffer from claustrophobia?"

As it happened, it fell to my lot to spend not eighteen months, but more than four years in imprisonment. Kolya came galloping over to see me as soon as he heard about my release: "Greetings, god-daughter!"

"And to you, godfather!"

By that time I already knew that not only did he remember that conversation in the kitchen, but that after my arrest, he was one of the thirteen people in all the Soviet Union to sign a protest about it. My grandmother, who christened me, most likely not in a church but before God, as I lay at death's door from some childhood disease ("In the name of the Father, the Son, and the Holy Ghost, I baptise God's handmaiden, Irina"), would not grudge, looking down on us, that Kolya 'baptised' me again – to walk the terrible path which he himself had walked, in certainty that I, too, would come through.

Chapter Nineteen

I lyusha's departure left me feeling empty and numb inside. I watched, almost indifferently, how most of Odessa seemed to be on the move: quickly, quickly, emigrate quickly, before the doors are slammed shut again! Some received permission, others were refused, someone's son got drafted into the army: then he was classified as having had access to secret matters, effectively rendering his family ineligible for emigration, unless they left him behind. Someone's eighty-year-old grandmother was reduced to a heart-attack at a Party meeting: the old lady had to relinquish her membership prior to emigrating with her children and grandchildren. Time after time I went to the station to see off Ilyusha's and my old friends. And I stayed behind. And stayed. And stayed. Enough, this way lies madness! I saw the anxiety in Valentin's and Alyosha's eyes when they looked at me. I know, I thought, I'll take a week off and go to Kiev to sort myself out. Staying at Igor's place always has an invigorating effect on me: it's such a warm, friendly house with strong family traditions. One of these traditions is to make things with your own hands whenever possible. And they seem to manage this with just about everything, starting with the excellent bookshelves made by Igor's father to exquisite wall-hangings made by Igor's mother. With considerable pride, Igor showed off his latest creation to me: a Swedish style dresser made of oak.

"You think this is only what it seems at first glance?" he asked. He pulled it out of its fixtures, reversed it, and inserted a pair of legs on rubber rests:

"Not a bad table, eh? We managed to cram twenty-five people around it for my birthday. You could climb up and dance a jig on it! It's built to hold an elephant!"

"Thanks for the compliment! You do have a way with subtle flattery, don't you?"

"Come on, stop splitting hairs, you know what I mean! What do you think of the surface? It took me a full week to get the polish just right!"

The household is ruled by Grandmother. She is small and bent, and has a will of iron. Granny is held in universal esteem, and nobody argues with her. They all know me, and see me as the same little Irka who used to come to Kiev for summer vacations. Just like Igor and his sister Lyalya, I was accustomed to kissing the adults good night before going to bed. Lyalya's already married, and has a daughter, Anusia, a fascinating little being with a high forehead and serious mien, who has only just started to walk.

"I'm going through a bad time," I told Igor straight away, "so don't ask me any questions, okay?"

He nodded. We have a marvellous way of pulling each other out of the dumps without any lengthy discussions on painful subjects.

"Want to go to the Water Park?"

"Let's! Can we go swimming there?"

"You're out of your mind, girl! The water's still freezing cold!"

"Oh, well, if I drown, have me buried with full military honours!"

"Come on, cut that out! Drown, indeed! If you do that, I'll be stuck for a secretary once I become an academician!"

"So that's what you've set out to be?"

"Joking aside, it doesn't really look like it. D'you mind if I cry on your shoulder for a bit? Have you any idea of what the academic system is like? Here in the Ukraine, anyway? Well, I'll tell you: for every ten people who are really worth anything, there are at least a hundred parasites. Bribery, bureaucracy, Party bosses . . . It's like an impenetrable jungle. Intrigues, anonymous denunciations . . ."

"How does your father manage to hang on?"

"He's the goose that lays the golden eggs. Real workers are needed, too, to carry all the dross. It's a toss-up whether he'll be elected an academician, though, for all that. Have you ever heard of Bakul?"

"It rings a vague bell, but . . ."

"He was the first in the Soviet Union to make synthetic diamonds. Created a whole institute. Their hard currency fund is bigger than that of the entire Academy, the economic benefits run into billions. He manufactured industrial diamonds for the whole country. But once he had everything set up and running – he wasn't a young man – a Central Committee group descended on him out of the blue. Bakul was moved aside, and some moron of a Party boss was appointed director of the institute in his place. Do you think that Bakul made it into the Academy, at least? The greatest scientist in a non-secret field, a technical genius? No way: his candidacy was blocked at primary level."

"But the voting's supposed to be by secret ballot . . . ?"

"The important thing was that people like Bakul are the last thing they want. Just think how others would appear by comparison with him! I tell you, it's just like the Mafia . . ."

"But you said yourself that they need real scientists, too! So lay your golden eggs, and let them play their games without taking part in them yourself!"

"The times are different now. It was easier when Dad was starting out, because the system was a bit more flexible than it is now. It was like concrete that hadn't set yet. He started out working under Stechkin."

"But you've started out working under him!"

"D'you imagine that there aren't already whispers and insinuations about that? Family ties, favouritism, and suchlike? They don't know how he keeps me jumping through hoops: he makes me do the work of three people, at least! If I weren't his son, I would have had my Master's long ago!"

"Have you joined the Party yet?"

"Look, I don't like this 'yet' business!"

"Sorry! My mistake! Won't happen again!"

"It's not that they haven't offered, for your information!"

"Come on, I've already said I'm sorry!"

"Irka, don't get me wrong, it's just that I feel so lousy from time to time! You wouldn't believe how I'm fed up with hearing myself described knowingly as 'Daddy's boy' and a careerist! Have you encountered any of the so-called 'golden youth' generation? The children of big Party bosses?"

"No, luckily I've been spared that."

"Well, I was eligible to be one of them because of my father's status. Central Committee nomenclature and all that, the 'new nobility' as they like to call themselves. Their main pastimes are drink and sex, after which they are chauffeured home in black Volgas by their fathers' personal bodyguards. God knows I'm no plaster saint, but I couldn't help being revolted by what they get up to. They're drug-addicts and perverts. Just their 'daisies' are enough to make you sick!"

"What does that mean, 'daisies'?"

"The girls strip down naked, then stand in a circle, faces down, while some drunken swine . . . Oh, to hell with it! I'm damned if you'll hear such filth from me! Tell me, how's your work in the lab going? Is it all right to ask about that?"

"Sure. It's not too bad, actually. They pay me seventy roubles a month, but I make a bit extra by private tutoring."

"Still writing?"

"Yes. I've already had a warning from the KGB about that. A nice, cosy chat."

"Because of your poetry?"

"As a matter of fact, the poetry was incidental. They just issued a general warning to keep me in line. The main figure in this instance was Dolly Yanishevskaya, not me."

"First I've heard about any of this."

I told him how we young participants of the KVN decided to set up our own theatrical studio upon graduation from university. The actors were to be students, the comedy scenarios would be written by Seryozha, Alyosha and myself . . . oh, and Igor Shevchenko, of course! We met Dolly, our prospective director, down at the beach. We had managed to get a studio in the Odessa Conservatoire, and there was no holding us back! First we decided to stage a musical, setting it in the Middle Ages to avoid any 'dangerous topics'. Ah, the age-old problem of art versus bureaucracy! Our main character, a careerist called Immortali, did not try to be a Party member, all he wanted was to be a court violinist. He disposed of his talented rival with poison, not with newspaper articles. However, we did have him writing anonymous letters, too. We managed to stage one performance, after which the studio was immediately dissolved by command from higher up, and the Conservatoire's Party organiser, who had been careless enough to let us loose on the stage of the Ukrainian theatre, was dismissed from his job in disgrace. We were not quite sure in which way we had offended until every single person involved in the production had been hauled over the coals by the KGB.

"Don't you know that Yanishevskaya has applied to emigrate to Israel?" they demanded. "She's a Zionist, she's gathered students at her home, and they sang Jewish songs! It's your duty to give evidence about the unrest she caused among you!"

Dolly? Unrest? Directed at me, a Russian Pole? Or at Ukrainians Seryozha and Igor? Or perhaps at Alyosha, a real rag-bag of nationalities? No, nationalist differences were something that we had never encountered in Odessa to date. So – she's Jewish. So – she wants to emigrate. Good luck to her! But what has that got to do with us? As for singing Jewish songs, that's no big deal, either: we had sung Armenian songs with Armenian students, and Russian songs with students from Leningrad. Odessa has been a melting-pot from its very beginnings: Greeks, Italians, Ukrainians, Jews – you name it, we've had them in Odessa. The Duc de Ribasse, the first city father of Odessa, at the foot of whose monument students meet by tradition on the last day of school, was a Frenchman, and Count Vorontsov, who made the city a present of his library, was Russian.

"Never mind playing dumb! This is a political matter! And your scenario was anti-Soviet, come to that! We want you to surrender all copies of the script!"

We handed in the scripts, but it is to the honour of our disbanded studio that nobody gave a shred of evidence against Dolly. The fabrication of a political case fell through, and within forty-eight hours Dolly was on her way to Tel Aviv, accompanied by an article from the *Evening Odessa*, which contained a savage denunciation of her Zionism and anti-Sovietism. She wrapped her shoes in it to get it through Customs. The KGB brought up the subject of my poetry as an extra lever to scare me: they knew about my poetry by that time. However, I wasn't in the least frightened – it's not as though I was in their hands for the first time. And – probably – not for the last.

I told the story to Igor as a joke, not deserving of any serious consideration.

"Irka, read me something!"

> If your frightened ones are not guilty
> Why don't your nightingales sing?
> Why to the profaned crosses
> Do your tears, congealing, cling?
> How I dream of those you have crucified!
> How soon along their path –
> After you, my own, my accursed –
> I must go to a similar death!
> By that road of yours most terrible:
> On the border of hatred and love
> Dishonoured, wretched,
> Mother-stepmother,
> Your blessing give!

"You know, Irka, for some reason, I fear for you – yet at the same time, I don't . . ."

"Have you read Solzhenitsyn's *Living Without Lies*?"

"Yes, of course, it's going around in *samizdat*. There were some fine people in that generation, though, weren't there?"

"And what will we do, once we are all married with children, and the children ask us: 'Why were you cowards?'"

"We won't be cowards!"

"In that case, sooner or later they'll be after our heads."

"There's got to be some other way."

"So? Let's find it, then!"

"We'll just have a different set of values. Have you ever heard about academician Kilchevsky? He was a real man of science, and very widely respected. But do you know how he died? He expected to be awarded an Order of Lenin on his seventieth birthday – that's standard procedure. But they took one look at his biographical data, and all he got was a 'Red Banner'."

"Was he a Jew?"

"No, he was from the old nobility. So all they did was telephone him to congratulate him. The old boy had a heart-attack then and there, he was so upset, and died clutching the receiver."

"What a shame. It's a sin to laugh about something like that."

"Irka, I've come to believe in God."

"When?"

"From the time I was doing my pre-diploma practice. At that time, I was also looking into the second law of thermodynamics. You must have encountered it, surely?"

"Yes, of course. But what connection is there with God?"

"You mean you don't see it? That's because you studied it as part of your university syllabus, and I did it by myself. I'd read for two hours, then spend two hours digesting what I'd read. Do you know how many single formulae there are to that law? More than ten! And there's no law in physics that's more fundamental than that one: you have to think and think about it. Did you know that books published about it in the West can only be received with special permission? My father has sufficient status to order them through the library, but I don't. I'm not sound enough ideologically, by the looks of it!"

"How about that! So – you came to faith in God?"

"Well, there had to be a beginning of some kind for our world, that stands to reason. An impulse and meaning."

We went on to discuss this meaning, and couldn't help wondering how two people, who had come to God along such totally different paths, had yet reached an identical understanding. We both believed what we read in books with reservations: books, after all, are written by people, and people can distort the truth. But our understanding of the fine line that distinguishes 'good' from 'bad', between 'honour' and 'dishonour' was exactly the same. Could this be a sign? We were not accustomed, then, to trusting such signs; that was to come later. Right then, what we needed was to talk and talk: neither of us had talked about this to anyone, ever.

"Has it happened to you that the answer to some problem has come as if out of nowhere? As if you have been guided by an invisible hand on your shoulder?"

"Yes!"

"And it was always the right solution, one which you have never had to regret?"

"Why, yes. Do you mean to say it's happened to you, too?"

"Yes, it has. And I know what's behind it."

"Irka, are you cold? Here, take my jacket!"

"No, it's nothing, really. Look, there's Venus rising in the sky!"

We rattle home in the bus. It's after midnight, and we creep in, so as not to wake anyone.

"Do you know how to work the shower?"

"Forget about showers, it's after midnight!"

"So what?"

"Don't they switch your water off after midnight?"

"Oh, you people from Odessa!" he laughs. "Kiev stands on the Dnieper, just in case that little detail escaped your attention! Whatever else we may lack, it's not water! You can shower all night if you like. Here, grab this towel! I'll brew up some tea in the meantime. D'you want yours with lemon?"

"Yep. And if you've got any other rare goodies lying around, you might like to pull them out and give a country girl a treat!"

Chapter Twenty

A postcard lands in the letter-box: "Irka, why not come here for New Year? I'll feed you full of snow. Phone 44-33-95 in any case. Igor."

Going to Kiev doesn't really fit in with my plans: firstly, there's little chance of getting a ticket, and secondly, I had intended staying at home with my parents, and then sitting down to write to Ilyusha after everyone else had gone to bed. I was going to slip a needle off the tree into the envelope, and whisper a few secret words over it. So I set off for the post office to phone Igor to say that I can't make it. A lengthy queue stretches outside the phone booth, but finally it's my turn, and I drop the coins into the slot.

"Hi, Igor!"

"Hello, Irka! Hold on, I'll get Igor for you."

"Oh, Uncle Oleg, it's you! Sorry, I didn't recognise your voice: you and Igor sound exactly the same over the phone."

"Yes, everyone says that. Kisses to you, my pretty one! Hold on a moment."

"Igor, I'm going to run out of coins in a moment . . ."

"Irka, please come."

"I've . . ."

"Oh, do come! Do you want me to dangle a carrot in front of you? There's a surprise waiting for you here. So will you come?"

There's a note in his voice that prompts me to agree to come, after all. There's something afoot, definitely: it looks as though my friend is in some kind of trouble. That means I must drop everything and go to him: that's only right and proper. Didn't Alyosha Kozdoba spend two days comforting me when my Uncle Jan died after being stabbed in the back by a deranged mugger? Didn't Inna and Valentin – who were already planning to marry by that time – take me home with them after seeing Ilyusha off, so that I wouldn't be alone? And didn't they share as much of my grief as they could, and help me regain my equilibrium? So what's wrong with Igor? With luck, I managed to get a return ticket to Kiev.

He met me at the station.

"Irka! Great that you've come! Here, wrap Lyalya's sheepskin around you, it's minus twenty, and they say it will get even colder!"

I don't ask any questions, knowing that when the time comes, he will tell me everything without any prompting. And here we all are in the Geraschenkos' familiar kitchen, drinking hot tea, exchanging hugs and kisses: "Irka's here!" Only Small is missing: he has died of old age after an exemplary canine life. His only transgression was snatching butter off the table whenever the opportunity offered: this was his most valued, forbidden treat. Before he died, he forgave Igor everything, and since that time Igor has been unable to bring himself to acquire another dog. This is something I fully understand.

The promised carrot turns out to be a cow's head carved out of red wood, with a brass ring in the nose – to hang kitchen towels on. You silly fool, do you think I wouldn't have come without some kind of inducement, under the circumstances? The head, actually, is not bad: we both do carving, and know what's what.

"So what's our programme?" I ask.

"Well, I thought we'd go to Marik's place first, then spend a little while with the parents, and after that dance the night away at Elephant's place. You remember Elephant, don't you? He lives here, in our house."

I remember both Marik – a photographer and a friend of Igor's turbulent youth – and Elephant, who's just starting out as a dentist, and whose real name is Victor Ostapovsky. He lives next door, and swops instruments with Igor – a mutually beneficial friendship. I had taken to Marik straight away, but found Elephant harder to like. Still, what does it matter at whose place you dance to the sounds of a record-player? I'm twenty-four years old, and when I look into the mirror I see a dark-eyed, curly-headed, snub-nosed and very self-assured young woman. Enough of tragedy! Let's have ourselves a ball!

Igor still hadn't said anything, but at Marik's place we suddenly found ourselves alone under the Christmas tree, and our arms closed around each other. I felt a great urge to burst into tears on his shoulder. It was so strong, so masculine, that shoulder – so dependable, that it seemed to promise protection against all past and future troubles. What is this – some kind of New Year's madness? After all, we are not in love, I'm in love with somebody else! We'll come to our senses tomorrow, and this will all be highly embarrassing, for all that we are old friends! But why do his lips move across my cheek, and why do I cling to his hands as though they are my only hope and salvation? Is it a spell of some kind? If so, it goes on and on – across the table laden with Marik and Nina's culinary efforts, and later, in the last December snow, and all that New Year's night. The clock strikes three, it's time for everyone to be off to their homes. We return to a dark, sleeping house.

"Irka, there's something I want to give you."

He hands me an ancient seal, made out of topaz in a silver setting. It's their family seal, and I remember how he told me, once, that he was keeping it to give to his future wife. Is he out of his mind? I refuse to take it, and he doesn't insist. The next day I have to go back to Odessa. Igor escorts me to the station. Not a word about the future. About the past – we are subdued but businesslike. It turns out that Igor had had to resign from his father's institute. An anonymous complaint was sent to the city Party organisation, alleging that Oleg Geraschenko had 'lost his judgement through excessive power' and was using his position to advance his son's scientific career. Not that there was much in this complaint about Igor himself, the main thrust was against his father: that he was abusing his position as the director of the institute by indulging in nepotism. Anonymous complaints are treated very seriously by our academic system, and are investigated by special committees. And Igor's father is a candidate for election to the Academy in the near future! So that's the reason for the 'report' . . .

Igor brought his letter of resignation to his father, who, as the director of the institute, had to sign it.

They looked at each other in silence, then Igor's father picked up a pen and signed. That was the best way out: at least one of them retained the opportunity to continue research – the meaning of his life, his joy and his master. The other had to venture into the unknown: still, he was young, and a good specialist: to hell with the Master's dissertation, it's not the be-all and end-all of existence. He got a job as an engineer in the Steel Foundry Institute, forever forsaking thermal physics, and the youth he had dedicated to it.

I knew that the KGB was already aware of my poetry, and that I would not be able to maintain a low profile for much longer. I had no illusions: I knew that there were only two possible outcomes for me in the near future – arrest or emigration. Not being Jewish, I could not apply for an exit visa. Arrest? Then how could I dare even think about love? Arrest would be tantamount to the grave. Wasn't it enough that I wore Ilyusha's nerves to a frazzle? Could I do the same to Igor? No. Enough.

"Goodbye, my dear."

Kisses are so cold on frosty days. And perhaps it is better so: it will cool down our hot heads.
"Write!"
"I will!"

> Who has the gift to grasp leavetaking,
> Divorce of railway station shores,
> And who can tell why in night's quaking
> The silence of despair lies aching
> On the White Guard of the snows?
> And why a name on love impose?
> Better that name had no making.

The Odessa winter passes, marked by unusual snowfalls. The days pass in dreary laboratory work, and in earning extra cash by giving private tutorials in the evenings. My parents are pleased: I'm in a new job, I don't have any conflicts with anyone, and it looks as though I've come to my senses at last. Alya, ever sensitive, watches me with big, round eyes, but doesn't ask any questions. What a precious, rare gift it is – to be able to ask nothing, until the other person speaks first! This small, snub-nosed replica of myself who came into the world twelve years after me has this gift in plenty. I could entrust Keshka to her care without any qualms, should something happen. What nonsense! Why should I be thinking about someone having to look after my cat?

My twenty-fifth birthday comes around, but I have no intention of celebrating. My heart is heavy, and I want neither guests nor noise. Wearing an old dress, I settle down on the couch with a book of Tyutchev:

> As though fair Hebe, light of leaven,
> Feeding Zeus' eagle soared,
> And laughing, down to earth from heaven
> A thunder-seething chalice poured.

The doorbell rings. A telegram, maybe? I open the door to find Igor, soaked and tousle-headed, standing on the doorstep.
"Happy birthday, Irka!"
And he hands me a dark red, almost black rose, barely unfurled, a bud rather than a flower.
"Thank you! I'm glad you're here: I'm really down in the dumps."
My parents come in to hug and kiss him.

"Look, Borya!" exclaims my mother. "He's grown even more – he's taller than you, now!"

"No, Auntie Ira, I've stopped growing! Any chance of a wayfarer getting a cup of coffee around here?"

Alya is thrilled by Igor's arrival, and the cake, and by my more cheerful demeanour. After coffee, she vanishes on some allegedly urgent business of her own. We remain alone, even Keshka beats a tactful retreat.

"Irka, I want you to come to Kiev and be my wife."

"What?!"

Later, Igor was to swear that this was the only time he has ever seen me totally at a loss.

"You don't have to answer straight away. Think about it. But I've already decided, and I know that this is what will happen, sooner or later."

How do you like that? He's decided! And overlooked the little detail of asking me . . . Talk about categorical imperatives! Yet why is it that I, who had already refused others without batting an eyelid, suddenly find myself bereft of words? His eyes are green and blazing, just as they were when we were children. I was not to know that, specially for this trip, he had managed to get a pair of jeans on the black market for some phenomenal price, that someone or other had made him a knitted jacket to order, and that his mother and sister had sewn metal buttons onto this jacket so that he could come a-wooing dressed to the nines. His family knew before he set out what his intentions were. They were all a bit bowled over, except for his mother, who maintained that she had guessed ages ago. He leaves me no room for manoeuvre, declaring that I should quit my job and pack my bags.

The lunatic! Does he know . . . Of course, he knows everything: about my first love, about my poetry, about the KGB . . . In that moment he has a much greater understanding than I of my painful vulnerability, my pride, my feelings of alienation. He is older and wiser, and as for my silly doubts – well, he has a lot of patience.

"Let's go out and walk around for a bit."

This releases some of the tension: like children, we set off hand in hand, and like students, share the same jacket. We wander aimlessly around familiar streets, then go into some stupid restaurant: Igor has been saving up for this trip. Neither of us likes this restaurant: it smacks of something mercenary, crass, slimily servile. We're not used to this kind of thing. It's much better out in the fresh air!

"Irka, my little one, I'll never let you go, no matter how hard you may try to escape. We're a pair. That's all there is to it. No, don't say anything!"

We agree that it's too early to be talking about marriage: even if it were not, where would we live? Oh, with the parents? And if things don't work out, blame it on them? No, let's try to be independent, just the two of us. Then we'll see how it goes. He is willing to agree to anything.

"I'll rent us a place. But I won't leave you in Odessa: I'm afraid for you. You'll be under my wing, you'll be my wife . . . Okay, okay, have a bit of a last fling, you're an untamed little beastie, it's your right."

Soon I got a letter:

Irka, I've managed to rent a place for two months. It's only a bedsit, and there's nothing in it except a bearskin rug. The moths have devoured half of it. You'll like it here. Phone me as soon as you get this. Have you left your job yet? I'm waiting for you.

Your 'I'.

Just like that. 'The words of a man, and not a boy', as they say. After shedding a few tears by the sea for some reason not clear to myself, I packed my bag: jeans, a sweater, the two hundred roubles earned giving private lessons. My parents accepted my mumbled explanations that Igor and I were "going to give things a try, and see what happens" with a surprising lack of fuss. My father even found a moment to make a rather awkward offer of some money; clearly he doubted that his stroppy daughter would agree to accept help, but still . . . maybe, for initial expenses in a new place . . .

"Come on, Father! You know what a stack of money I made this summer! I had five pupils!"

I still feel ashamed of myself for refusing. Alas, at that time I had not yet learned to accept gracefully something offered from the heart, as well as giving myself. This was something I was to learn only a year later, from Natasha Lesnichenko, a penniless Leningrad dissident, on whose doorstep I arrived, soaked with rain.

"You're Ira Ratushinskaya? I've read your work. How lovely to meet you! Tell me, what size shoes do you wear?"

She turned away from me calmly, and began to search around in a cupboard. Finally, she extracted a pair of rubber half-shoes, half-galoshes.

"Here! Put these on! No, wait a moment, I'll get you a pair of dry socks!"

Lena, the friend who brought me, watched in open amazement as I made no objection, but meekly took off my saturated velveteen pumps, and left them in Natasha's house 'for those who come'. This is right, this is as it ought to be, and there is no room or reason for silly pride. When someone shares their last possessions with you, you must accept the honour and not strike stupid poses: everyone is a pauper, and everyone, just like you, should follow Christ's commandment about giving the shirt off your back to those in need. Literally. And it is something to be proud of that this has fallen to the lot of Christians of your generation, in Russia, in the seventh decade of the twentieth century. In 1985, the non-believer Tanya Osipova and I were to share one skimpy prison smock in a freezing cold camp punishment cell. Much later we tried to recall which one of us was supposed to have it for himself, and why the other one was supposed to do without. Actually, we never did work it out – it had seemed so immaterial at the time.

Igor met me at the station – calm, self-assured, tall. He slung my bag over his shoulder.

"Let's drop around to my folks' place first and say hello. They're expecting us."

Lord, how embarrassing! What am I? A fiancée? A wife? In what guise am I to face these people, who have known me since I was a baby? We must be out of our minds!

"Irka's here!"

Hugs and kisses are exchanged, we sit down, tea is poured all round. Everything is just the way it used to be. Only Aunt Larisa hugs me harder than usual, and whispers: "Irka, every morning he has to have a cup of hot water with lemon and honey. I'll show you how to make it . . ."

They give us an inflatable mattress and a couple of blankets.

"Can we come around later to see how you've settled in?"

"Mama, I'll phone!"

Finally, we are together, just the two of us, and all my doubts seem so trivial when I huddle up, encircled by a strong arm. Can this really be forever? Can it really be that we shall be man and wife? It's so frightening to take such vows before God: after that, divorce is unthinkable, yet life is so long! Difficult, too: we do not labour under any illusions. But right now it's April, and apple trees all over Kiev are in full bloom. Later on, in May, the chestnuts will burst into flower, like great, ornate candles.

"Irka, let's go out and buy you a canvas and brushes!"

An easel given by one of Igor's friends when he left for the army stands in a corner. I have never drawn and painted as rapturously as I did that summer. Igor spread out on the bare floor and carved yet another fantastic beast with curling horns out of red wood. Maybe there's a chance that someone will buy it? We can't sell anything through the arts and crafts studio, because that calls for a special permit. But maybe through friends? You can't get very far on a monthly income of one hundred and twenty roubles, out of which sixty goes to pay the rent.

Aunt Larisa brings glad tidings: "Children! One of my friends, an artist, will buy it for seventy roubles! She wants it for her new apartment!"

Gullible simpletons that we were, we didn't see through her little maternal deception, and handed the carving over gladly. Two years later, when we were cleaning her apartment before she returned from a visit to Leningrad, we found that carving hidden under a divan. Only then did we realise the truth about 'her friend, the artist'.

"Mama," asked Igor with affectionate exasperation, "Why did you put on that act? You could have said that *you* liked it, and . . ."

"And you would have made me a present of it, there and then, just as Irka did with her coral beads. Leaving you to go hungry, just because you have this bee in your bonnets about independence, right? Now, I don't want to hear another word! My nerves have taken more than enough already. Well, I suppose I can hang that carving on the wall at last, instead of hiding it away. You silly idiots! My children! Don't you know how much I love you both? How I pray for you every day?"

Chapter Twenty-one

I t was a funny place, that first abode of ours, rented from a pair of travelling circus artistes. The sole item of furniture was the inflatable mattress on the floor, which made sweeping up no problem at all. One whole wall was covered by a gouache creation of mine, painted directly onto the wallpaper: a road overgrown with grass, and in the distance a deserted pond, surrounded by half-ruined columns and fantastic plants. Two enormous playing-dice lay in the middle of the road, and the inverted perspective was full of rather ominous violet shadows. I got tired of this opus fairly quickly, but Igor liked it, and wouldn't let me dispose of it.

While Igor is at work, I try my hand at various culinary experiments in the tiny kitchen. There is no point in my even looking for a job, because my passport states quite clearly that I'm registered for residence in Odessa. That means no personnel department in Kiev will consider hiring me. Still, in the autumn, I'll be able to make a bit of money by giving private lessons: physics and maths tutors are always in great demand, and I should have no problems. Of course, this kind of work is highly illegal, but the authorities turn a blind eye to it: after all, their children have to pass exams, too, like everyone else.

Apart from the mattress we now have two stools, and pull them out to offer our visitors a royal welcome: Marik and his wife, Lena from Leningrad, Elephant, and, naturally, Igor's relatives. At such times I tend to get a bit flustered about the quality of my housekeeping. Igor chews my rock-hard rissoles and half-cooked potatoes manfully, and even utters a few words of praise, even though I honestly wonder why he hasn't dotted me one by now with the washing-up brush for serving up such dubious delicacies. But what will his parents think? I do my utmost, but feel far from confident. No, they eat everything, and even ask for second helpings. How tactful can you be?

Our unorthodox experiment of living together does not seem to upset them unduly, in fact, they even appear to approve: the children want to try things out before tying themselves down, so as not to have any regrets later? Fine! They want to be independent from the very beginning? That's good, too – they'll be better for it. Igor's parents are not particularly concerned that there is no entry in our passports that we are man and wife – their generation is used to civil marriages. A stamp in a document is no big deal from their point of view. All our qualms and doubts mean nothing to them: they don't even suspect that if we do decide to link our lives then we shall do so before God, and this is a responsibility we still find a little frightening . . . Such a step is not to be undertaken lightly: once you've said "I do" before God, there's no going back, ever, come what may. Igor made his decision a long time ago, but I'm still torn by conflicting emotions: I love him – but will I love him always? How well do I know my own heart? Have I not already betrayed my first love, and can't muster up the courage to send him a letter about it to St Louis?

Igor's parents begin to reminisce about how they started out. Aunt Larisa was a geologist, in a team made up equally of 'free citizens' and prisoners. She was given a very wilful stallion, and had a terrible time getting him used to the bridle. She had an unmistakable air of purity about her, one that was obvious even to the most hardened, bearded criminals, who would not have dreamed of laying a hand on 'our Larisa'. However, they had no compunction about stealing the embroidery work she did in her free time. They would wait patiently until she had set the last stitch into some runner or mat, and it would disappear before you could blink. She found this amusing rather than annoying: heaven knows, there are few joys in the prisoners' bleak lives, so who would grudge them any pleasure they might derive from some red and black roosters embroidered on a piece of linen by the hands of a young girl?

Uncle Oleg snatched her 'straight from the field', when he turned up and issued a single command: "Get your things together, and let's go!" She did, and never regretted it. Certainly their life was not without its ups and downs, but they managed to raise two children, and raise them well. They told me how Uncle Oleg and my father became friends in their young days. Oleg was a foreman, and my father, Boris, had only recently qualified as an engineer. Oleg was already married, but my father was still courting his Irina (I was named after my mother). My father had a step-brother, Leonid, whom he idolised with youthful fervour and looked up to more than anyone else in the world. In 1950 Leonid was imprisoned for no reason at all, in the best traditions of Stalinism. My father came to see Oleg and Larisa, not certain whether he would be allowed across the threshold. It was sadly characteristic of those times that many people, after reading the papers, avoided the rest of the victim's family like the plague. Leonid, a promising young man who already had a doctorate, had 'admitted' to being a spy for the Japanese. He held out while they beat and tortured him, but broke down and signed all the trumped-up charges against him when the KGB threatened to exact vengeance on his younger brothers. Under the circumstances, he would have admitted spying for the Martians.

Oleg and Larisa knew the worth of these show trials, and offered every support and sympathy to the prisoner's young brother. Aunt Larisa suddenly burst out laughing at an old memory: "Oleg, do you remember that New Year's party? How Borya whirled and twirled me around, not realising that I was seven months pregnant with Lyalya?!"

Igor and I have heard all these stories many times, but don't mind hearing them again. We know how, after Leonid's trial, my father made a firm decision to stay away from any kind of research work and avoid high-ranking positions. He would never be anyone's boss, or assume any responsibility for this shameful system. Oleg made a different choice: who would undertake the advancement of science in the country? Even if it involved compromises, he felt it unacceptable to leave all decisions in the hands of scoundrels and bribe-takers. The more decent people there are at the top, he reasoned, the better! Yet despite their differing views, they remained friends: both excellent engineers, valuing each other's ability. But Oleg, who joined the Party, rose to be the director of an institute, while my father steadfastly turned his back on any career advancement, and remained determined to answer to nobody but himself, and keep to himself . . .

Igor and I steal a look at each other: how shall we, their children, work out this unvoiced conflict of opinions between ourselves? And will they, the parents, be able to accept *our* decision, and understand us? Only time will tell.

All that summer went by in a frenzy of reading *samizdat*: a three-volume edition of Mandelstam, his wife Nadezhda's memoirs, Solzhenitsyn's *Cancer Ward*, A. Fedoseyev's *Collected Articles*, the life of Saint Seraphim of Sarov, and Avtorkhanov's *The Riddle of Stalin's Death*. I had had access to *samizdat* circles for some time now: my own poetry circulates in *samizdat*, and I'm known as 'Rhymesmith Irka' in Moscow, Leningrad and Odessa. I'm trusted. Very soon, similar contacts appear in Kiev. How strange it must look to an uninitiated observer: either you are loaned a typewritten manuscript for twenty-four hours, or there could be a gathering of about twenty people in one room, all silently reading the one work, a sheet at a time; you read one page, pass it on, and wait for the next from your neighbour. The smoke-filled room is in a silence broken only by the rustle of papers going from hand to hand. Somewhere my work is being read just like this, and we both understand fully what it means. Soon, soon, we shall come up against that bloody meat-grinder, and the more we know about who set it in motion and why, the better our chances of standing fast and surrendering nothing: not our fledgling faith, nor our convictions, nor our future freedom. For surely our homeland will not be enslaved and paralysed by fear forever? Can emigration really be the only solution? At present it does seem to be the only way, or they'll wring our necks the moment we dare utter a peep. And we want to live – oh, how we want to live! This system will last for centuries, is the gloomy prediction of our new friends, the Mishins. Never mind what people think: totalitarianism endures not through force of intellect, but by force of tanks. And there's no shortage of those!

Igor, annoyed by the poor technical quality of *samizdat* production, turns to devising improvements: he and Marik begin to print Solzhenitsyn with the help of a camera. A book published in the West lies flat on a table, a sheet of transparent plastic covering its pages. Every page is painstakingly photographed. The films don't take up any storage space to speak of, but then every page must be developed and printed on photographic paper, then dried, then the whole thing has to be bound into book form: the whole operation takes twenty-four hours. It did not take them long to find a qualified binder, an elderly man called Sasha Kozin. He has been dealing with *samizdat* since the 1960s, and he is jokingly referred to as 'our reproductive organ'. After a bit of arguing for form's sake with these two young greenhorns, Sasha enters into the spirit of things with great enthusiasm, and comes up with some excellent ideas of his own: there are very good, hard-cover editions with titles embossed in gold leaf in the 'Politbook' shops, and they cost next to nothing. The 'immortal' works of Lenin, Brezhnev and other leaders have to be sold at prices considerably below their cost of production. So why shouldn't we bind our *samizdat* into such ready-made covers? Firstly, it will keep better, and secondly, it would never enter anyone's head to look between the covers of a book by Brezhnev during a house-search.

So that is just what we did with your *Gulag Archipelago*, Alexander Isayevich! We bound it between covers obligingly supplied by Politbook, and in this guise it went all around the Ukraine and Russia. We established contact with other cities, and our library grew – never all in one place, but forever in the hands of night-time readers, circulating constantly. You fulfilled the paternal duty of the older generation: you called upon us to live without lies, and we could never again retreat into servile indifference. Although you were not there in the flesh, we argued with you over your now-famous letter to the Soviet leadership; we did not agree blindly with everything you said, but after reading your *Gulag Archipelago* we were afraid, and we understood, and everything became clear: if need be, we, too, would pass through that infernal circle, and would not commit any of the errors against which you warned us. Maybe we would make other errors: if so, and we survived, we should also write about them as honestly as you did, and they would serve as a warning to the next generation of young people in our unfortunate, beloved and shamed country.

Nevertheless, it's disquieting to think that we might both be arrested. My chances of arrest are greater, because, after all, I'm a *samizdat* poet. My change of address might slow things down a bit, but the long hand of the bureaucracy, even if it moves slowly, must still reach out for me sooner or later.

"Irka, we've got to leave. If they put me away – well, that's not so bad, I'm a man, after all. But what if they get you? I can't bear to let that happen: they'd torture you!"

We swear a silly, youthful oath to each other: even if the KGB were to torture each one of us under the other's eyes, we would not give in. I say 'silly' because it was not this promise that sustained us later; no promise can be kept if you do not feel a protecting hand on your shoulder. A hand which both of us had felt by that time, and knew what it meant, yet still – we feared what was to come.

We married in autumn, after we had gone on a trip to the Baltic states as a foursome with Alyosha Kozdoba and Lara Vilenkina. We travelled through Lithuania, Latvia and Estonia, staying in cheap hotels or rented rooms in private dwellings. Four old friends, finally with a bit of leave, free – what could be better than going on a trip? We were warned that Russian-speakers are not popular in the Baltics: symbols of occupation! Nobody will even give a Russian street directions, Russians are hated because they remind the people of the advance of Soviet tanks over their territory. However, we encountered none of this: our smiles elicited smiles, nobody refused to show us the way, and our Russian speech was forgiven. And in any case, what other language could we possibly speak, we, the heirs of so many different cultures? Lara is Jewish, Igor – Ukrainian, Alyosha – a mixture of just about everything, and as for me – I don't really know. Polish by blood, Russian by literature ... And we do not turn away from the Russian language: we speak it between ourselves, and use it to communicate with the rightful owners of these ancient cities of unusual beauty – Vilnius, Riga, Tartu ... Nobody said a cross word to us: we behaved like visitors: we were courteous, we asked, and we respected our hosts. And they saw us not as enemies, but young friends: so they answered all our questions, and advised us what to see and do to make our trip a memorable one.

Later, we stayed in a small, tumbledown holiday shack belonging to some friends not far from Leningrad. And it was here that all doubts about marriage were finally put to rest. The circumstances were strongly reminiscent of a Gothic novel: the local scum heard that there was a new young woman in the neighbourhood, and decided to pay a call. They arrived at night, and began hammering on the door, making no secret of their intention towards me: "C'mon, you sodding intellectuals! Open the door! It'll be worse for you if you don't!"

Igor shot out onto the verandah, gripping an axe in his hands: "Well, boys? Who's first? You? Come on, don't be shy!"

I crouched inside, shuddering, clutching a useless kitchen knife, and listening to the ripe epithets my protector showered on the thugs, and how they finally retreated.

"Steady on, fella!" said one of them, an unmistakable note of respect in his voice. "Why'd you go straight for an axe? No need for that! We were only having a joke, see? We thought you were city folks, and we'd have a bit of fun, like . . ."

When Igor came striding back into the house, sweating, his shirt askew, I burst into tears: "Igor, I love you! I was such a fool! Say you forgive me!"

"Well, so you've finally said it! Sweetheart, what's the matter? It didn't even get as far as a fight!"

"But what if you'd been killed?"

"By that lot? Come on, it wasn't as bad as you think, they were just messing about. Can you honestly say that I look like an intellectual?"

"With that axe in your hands? I should think not! More like a highwayman!"

"Just a spot of camouflage . . . I was ninety per cent certain they wouldn't really try anything."

"What about the remaining ten per cent?"

"Well, in that case I'd have hacked them down like mad dogs. Let them hurt you? Never! Come on, stop shaking! I'm here with you. Repeat what you said before."

"I love you."

"Will you marry me?"

"Yes!"

"Say that again."

"Yes!"

"And again!"

"Yes! My dearest one, my beloved, my one and only one! Oh, God, if anything had happened to you . . . ! Let's go back to Kiev, I'll stay with you – I'll probably make a lousy wife . . ."

"You'll be as you'll be. Come on, give me a kiss!"

I sit on his knee, and he rocks me to and fro, as if I were a baby: "Some day, we'll go to some lovely, warm country. I'll build you a big house. With a real fireplace and a chimney."

"And a tower?"

"With four towers. And we'll have four children, all of them madcaps like us. The first one will be a snub-nosed little girl. And we'll get ourselves a dog, a Newfoundland. And nobody will ever be able to hurt you. I won't let them. You'll write poems, and I'll gather them all together. There won't even be any need to hide them anymore."

"And will you take up physics again there?"

"Yes."

"And take me on as your secretary?"

"That will depend on how well you behave yourself! Come, my little one, go to sleep. Rock-a-bye baby! Here, let me put this blanket over you."

Chapter Twenty-two

It's not possible for us to go into just any church: Russian Orthodoxy has been under the vigilant eye of the authorities for so long, has had to make such concessions in order to ensure the physical existence of the Church, that we have no way of knowing which priest serves God honestly, and which one is a KGB informer. And there are priests with Party membership tickets in their pockets, just as there are church hierarchs who have not scrupled to lie to the world at large that the Communist Party of the Soviet Union has never persecuted believers. Yes, alas, there is no shortage of such clergy. But there must be some honest priests left, they could not have all been consigned to the camps! As we are determined to marry in church, we must first attend Confession and partake of Communion.

Unfortunately, we do not know anyone from these circles: all we have done is to go into a church in Kiev occasionally, to put up a candle and cross ourselves. Having come to God by ourselves, neither of us had experienced the need for an intermediary and counsellor, nor had we sought one. But in a case of such a serious step as marriage, an intermediary is essential. Lara Vilenkina, who is from an academic family in Moscow, comes to our rescue. She herself is not a Christian, preferring to adhere to the Jewish faith of her ancestors. However, there are many Russian Orthodox Christians among the young intelligentsia in Moscow, and Lara attends their numerous unofficial lectures (in private homes), about Russian icon-painting, the history of Russian churches, about the old Byzantine roots of Russia. One of her friends, Volodya, is a young deacon at the headquarters of the mission of the Antiochean diocese in Moscow. Lara has an unfailing 'feel' for people, and assures us that he is trustworthy. She had also heard about the mission's priest, Father Alexander, who seemed to be just the man we were looking for.

"Folks, come to Moscow!" invited Lara. "I've decided to try for a bit of independence, so I've rented a room. You can stay with me for a few days, and we'll arrange everything. I've already had a word with Volodya about you. By the way, Irka, he's read your poetry and would like to meet you."

Our obligatory civil marriage in the registry office turned out to be a hilarious affair. The female official whose task it was to put the relevant stamps in our documents, congratulate us ('a new young Soviet family') and read us a suitable brief valedictory lecture, turned out to be a former classmate of Igor's from childhood.

At first, she adopted an officially ceremonial attitude: "Dear newly-weds! I congratulate you on behalf of the registry office of the Radyansky district of the city of Kiev . . ."

After which she could not stop herself from giggling at the absurdity of it all. Marik and his wife, who attended as witnesses, were already snorting with laughter, whereas she, poor woman, was obliged to instruct us about the role of the family in the construction of a socialist society, about the moral code of true builders of communism, and similar vital ingredients for a successful marriage.

By this time, we were all laughing openly, and our poor 'official' lost the thread of the standard discourse completely. Who on earth thought up such a travesty of this particular rite of passage? After we had all laughed to our hearts' content, she changed to a normal manner of speech: "Igor – congratulations! Irochka, make sure you keep this firebrand on a tight leash! Truly – my very best wishes for your future happiness!"

Having received our attestation of marriage (you cannot marry in church without one), we caught the Moscow train that very day. Lara had solved the furniture problem in her new home with a simplicity as admirable as it was ingenious. Some friends had given her lots of thick sheets of plastic, and these could be piled up to serve as beds, couches or armchairs, as the occasion demanded. Volodya came around, and we sat, Oriental style, on mounds of these plastic sheets to discuss all the necessary details concerning our wedding in church on the following day. Unlike us, Volodya knows all the details of Orthodox church services, and instructs us on what we must do. A suitable dress and veil? Oh – oh, all I have with me is a pair of jeans, a sweater and a jacket! As Igor and I had led such a nomadic existence, constantly moving from one place to another, I had tried to keep my possessions down to a minimum. As a result, I don't have a single dress!

"Well, Ira, getting married in a pair of jeans is out of the question. And you must have a head-covering of some sort. Lara, you wouldn't have a suitable light-coloured dress, would you?" asks Volodya.

"No, I've only got a black one! Hold on, though! Will Masha be at the church tomorrow? She definitely has a pale dress."

"Brilliant! That's one problem solved."

"She'll think up something for Ira to wear on her head, and I can lend a pair of shoes that should do nicely. There must be some place near the church where Ira can change, or she'll freeze to death by the time we get there if she leaves home in that dress. We won't be going in a taxi, after all!"

"Don't worry about that, I'll organise something. As for Igor – it doesn't really matter how he's dressed. I suppose the groomsmen are already lined up?"

"No problem – there were offers galore for that duty."

"Fine. Now, remember – don't eat anything at all after you get up tomorrow morning, because you'll be taking Communion later. Father Alexander is a wonderful man. He'll hear your confessions, and look after the spiritual side of things. You'll like him; and don't be discouraged if there's something you don't know . . . Well, that's about it. I'll be waiting for you outside the church at nine o'clock tomorrow morning."

There were not many people at the Antiochean church the next morning. The church was half-empty: Father Alexander, Volodya, and a small group of friends who had come to be present at our wedding. There were also about a dozen regular parishioners, quietly putting up candles before the icons. It was a working day, so most of them were women. When they saw me in my hastily assembled borrowed finery, a whisper ran around among them: a wedding!

Igor and I hold hands, helping each other to remain calm. Father Alexander comes out, looking very serious – even rather forbidding. He wants to talk to us before beginning the marriage service. Far from going through an ordeal, we found it incredibly easy to talk to him, and we both trusted him instantly, the moment our eyes met his. So it was without fear that we unclasped hands to go to Confession. Standing beside each other again prior to Communion, our eyes meet. A shiver of pure happiness and a sensation of light. The church is quiet, but we feel friendly eyes upon us from all sides. More people have arrived: it's not every day that there is a wedding in the church. Volodya appears from somewhere off to the side of the church.

"Give me the rings. Father Alexander will bless them now."

Rings! Oh, heavens, we don't have any! Gold wedding rings are way beyond our budget, and anyway, why bother? We hadn't intended wearing any, because we were bound to lose them one way or another. For instance, when you're arrested, rings are confiscated. In our ignorance, we had thought that wedding rings were optional.

"Volodya, why didn't you say anything about this yesterday?"

"It didn't enter my head that you might not know! Never mind proper rings, though; in a situation like this, any rings will do!"

"But we don't have any at all!"

Of course, the wedding could be postponed until tomorrow, and today we could rush out and buy a couple of rings of some kind for about three roubles each. But what about the spiritual joy of today – would we feel it tomorrow? It's our own fault entirely, but must we really leave the church now? No, that's impossible, and we already feel the beginnings of something which transcends human understanding. Some of the women parishioners, hearing our agonised whispers, start whispering among themselves. And then, as if in response to some unknown force, they all begin taking off their own rings, and offering them to us:

"Here, children! Take them! Don't be shy, girlie, I'm a widow, I can do without my ring now."

A gnarled hand offers me a thin gold wedding band, another is extended to Igor. Seeing this, Father Alexander waves resignedly: "Never mind, take your rings back. I'll perform the ceremony without them: God will understand and forgive."

And God must have forgiven, indeed. Not only Igor and I felt His presence beside us in the church at that moment, it was felt equally by Father Alexander, and by deacon Volodya, and those kind strangers who reacted so generously to our plight. Everyone in that church felt that He was there, and the joyousness of the knowledge was echoed in the marriage service. Happily and with singing hearts we pledged ourselves to each other, happily we left the church. When we turned around for a last look, we saw that one of the old women who had been in the church stood there, making the sign of the cross at us and whispering something as she did so, although we could not hear her words.

I stayed on at Lara's, and Igor went straight to Kiev to find us somewhere to live. Our absentee landlords from the circus had come back, and finding alternative accommodation was a mammoth task. This kind of subletting is illegal, and the number of newly-weds always exceeds the number of people willing to run the risk of being caught letting rooms. Living with Igor's family was totally out of the question: not only because there was absolutely no space, but also because of our *samizdat* activity. If our 'production' were to be found during a house search, the whole family would be in danger of reprisals.

Finally, I got a long-awaited phone call: "Irka, success! I've found a place for a month, maybe even longer! And after that, something else is bound to turn up."

Marvellous, everything is resolved. I run around giving private lessons, and Igor has already gained a measure of recognition as a project engineer. In the evenings, we swap notes about the day's events.

"Well, how are you getting along with your little monsters?"

"I feel a bit knackered. It's the amount of time I have to spend travelling that gets me. By the time I get from Lena's house to Sasha's – well, you can imagine . . . The lessons themselves are no problem, though. They know about as much trigonometry as primeval man: they can barely distinguish a sine from a cosine, especially Lena. Still, they're trying, so I think they'll eventually come up to scratch. I set them a couple of problems out of Naum Yakovlevich's textbook today."

"Dragon!"

"Thanks for the kind words, O lord and master! And how did my lord and master fare today?"

"Irka, you wouldn't believe the performance they laid on for us today! Our whole department had to go and listen to a lecture on civil defence, and I didn't have a thing with me to read while they droned on. But I ended up enjoying myself hugely."

"Why, did they suggest that in case of a full-scale alert everybody wrap themselves up in a white sheet and await further instructions?"

"No, it was much better than that! They brought along some retired colonel – you know, one of the ones they fix up in these cushy jobs so they can go on making money. Well, he chose to enlighten us about the neutron bomb. A neutron, he told us, is such a small particle that it can go through the tiniest crack. Then he delivered the standard denunciation of 'capitalist aggressors' – word for word out of the papers – and followed up with a real gem: Soviet scientists, he said, have already developed a defence against the neutron bomb."

"What? Come on, tell me!"

"Well, we were all just as interested. See if you can guess what he said."

"I give up straight away! On my back, all four paws in the air!"

"For your information, this method of defence consists of a secret plastic compound, which comes in strips fifteen millimetres thick. If you line the inside of a tank with this plastic, he told us, not a single neutron will be able to get through."

"I love it! The old boy sounds like a fun person to know!"

"I couldn't resist asking him: maybe this plastic is made out of neutron material? Yes, he said, dead serious, that's what it's made from. Well, you can imagine how everyone roared with laughter, and started to calculate how much the tank would weigh."

"So they played him up well and truly?"

"You'd think so, but the fact of the matter is that he had no idea that he was being laughed at. And anyway, we deserve some kind of compensation if we, as engineers, are expected to listen to this kind of mumbo-jumbo. By the way, am I going to get a cup of tea in this house tonight, or not?"

But all jokes apart, at this time we were faced with the decision of how we would continue our lives. It was the end of 1979, and the authorities were tightening the screws. A new wave of arrests swept through dissident ranks. We both realised that if we wanted to preserve our integrity and self-respect, we would soon have to start acting openly. Which would lead to the camps. There was no other path for an honest person to follow. But maybe we should try to emigrate? Admittedly, the chances are almost non-existent, but shouldn't we give it a try? It's time we were starting a family, but what right do we have to bring children into an abnormal atmosphere of KGB surveillance, arrests, and constant moving from house to house? Risking our own necks is one thing, but risking our children?

"Let's apply for exit visas!" decided Igor.

"Us? Apply for exit visas to Israel? By what right?"

"Damn it, I know it's cheating, but just about everyone who leaves is joining what you could call purely fictitious relatives. They write down the first thing that comes into their heads on those application forms! You know yourself that there's no other way! As far as our sage legislators are concerned, it's either that way, or not at all. And what will change if we end up in the camps? I won't have you in a labour camp, and that's that! And if we leave, at least our children will be born in a free country."

"They won't let us leave. You'll see."

"At least, my conscience will be clear that I did all I could. You're my responsibility, after all. And even if we're stuck here, it doesn't mean that we'll just sit back meekly in silence. But we have to give it a try . . ."

So we did try this avenue, doubtful as it was both practically and ethically. We lodged applications on the basis of a false invitation. We're ashamed of ourselves for having done so, but we did it. Relations with parents became very strained: our intention to emigrate came to them as a bolt from the blue. Emigrate? Where? Why can't we be content to live like everyone else? And why should the choices narrow down either to emigrating or to becoming open dissidents? Why on earth are we consciously heading for trouble?

The Kiev visa office (OVIR) did not even accept our applications for consideration. So we sent them off by registered post to the

Presidium of the Supreme Soviet. Shortly afterwards, we received a summons to present ourselves to the Kiev militia. No reason for the summons was stated. We went. Just in case, we were accompanied by Andrei, a friend, who would be a witness if this summons were a provocation.

We were received by several people sitting around a table in plain clothes. Andrei was not admitted, just Igor and me.

"Return the summons forms you received!"

"Who are you?"

"A committee."

"Please explain what kind of committee, and tell us your names."

"We'll ask the questions around here!"

"In that case, you'll have to manage without our answers."

"Why have you applied to emigrate? Whose idea was it? Why don't you want to stay here? Who talked you into this application?"

"We won't answer."

"Well, you're not going anywhere! Don't even dream about it!"

"What is your authority to say so?"

"That's none of your business. You're free – for the time being."

We walked home through the falling snow. Free? It's a nice word. So let's conduct ourselves like free people.

At the beginning of 1980, the Presidium of the Supreme Soviet consigned Sakharov to internal exile without charges or trial. The newspaper *Izvestiya* claimed that this had been done in response to numerous requests from Soviet citizens, in response to the will of the people. But who was left to protest? Just about all the members of the unofficial Helsinki Monitoring Groups were under arrest, and only a handful of dissidents were still at large, under imminent threat of arrest, too. So, we reasoned, our time had come. We sat down and drafted our first letter in defence of human rights: "The people are bound to pay for the crimes of their rulers. But this does not mean that the government has the right to commit crimes in the name of the people."

We are not going to let the authorities smear our names with their dirt. We protest, both of us. Here are our names and address. Of course, we were not the only ones to protest against Sakharov's exile to Gorky. But we joined their ranks, and took pride in it. We knew by that time that there is no demarcation line between silent abstention and silent participation: there are times when both these positions are dishonourable.

Chapter Twenty-three

We had always liked going on long walks, so now we tramp around snow-covered Kiev, discussing how we should live now that we had decided to 'come out into the open'. Well, we'll just carry on as before, renting accommodation here and there for a month or two at a time. No moves have been made so far to kick Igor out of work, so all's fine. When they do sack him, we'll think of something. There are plenty of engineers, physicists and mathematicians who have lost their jobs courtesy of the KGB and who now earn their living as stokers in boiler-rooms, as lift-attendants or navvies. The dissident fraternity is not a cosseted one. We knew about many of them, others were still unknown. But if people much older than we, like Vladimir Greshuni for instance, manage to make a living as a stoker, thereby avoiding criminal charges of 'parasitism' (an unavoidable fate for anyone unemployed in the Soviet Union), then surely we, who are young and strong, will cope?

"Have you noticed," I remarked to Igor, "that there is a disproportionate number of technically minded people among the dissidents?"

"It figures, doesn't it? Just think: they've all been taught to think logically from their youth. Any engineer must be able to assess the accuracy of data, to weigh all factors and think in numerical terms. At the same time, they feed us nonsense about the 'great progress' we're supposedly making, backed up by statistics based on the principle: 'one, two, lots . . .' Remember my 'political information' presentation about housing construction?"

"Of course! So they're not keen to have you speak again?"

"They'd rather choke, I think!"

'Political information' is a ubiquitous group activity in the Soviet Union. It takes place in working hours, so there's no way of getting out of it. Everyone has to take a turn at speaking on a set theme: read out a newspaper article, and then express personal endorsement and enthusiasm. So Igor's turn came in due course in his new job. He tried to wriggle out of it for as long as he could, but finally had to do his duty, because everyone else in his section had done their piece, and nobody would agree to have another go just to get someone else off the hook. Inevitable or not, though, it's still unpleasant to be forced into taking part in spreading lies. Still, as one of Igor's colleagues put it, "it's easier to go away and clean your teeth later, than to contend with all the troubles a refusal to do your bit would mean. Especially when you have a wife and two kids to support."

The subject allotted to Igor was 'The achievements of the Party and government in the sphere of housing construction in Kiev.' How's that, then? The article he was given to read from the paper *Evening Kiev* contained a Party report on this theme, and stated proudly that one million square metres of new housing is erected per annum. Igor took this figure and proceeded to divide it by the number of people living in Kiev: the demonstrable result was less than half a square metre of living space per head. In other words, to get the statutory 13.6 square metres of housing space per capita (without which there is no hope of arranging an 'apartment exchange' with other cities) a citizen of Kiev must wait twenty-seven years. A degree of Party 'achievement' hardly deserving of applause! All Igor's colleagues roared with laughter while he made this presentation, and flocked to congratulate him later on in the corridor: "Good for you! That'll teach them!"

Not surprisingly, that was the last time he was approached to conduct a 'political information' session.

We laughed, too, as we recalled this episode, then indulged in a brief snowball fight before going home. What a wonderful word that is – home. Our current domicile is ours for three weeks: the owner, an old lady, has had to go into hospital, and her daughter, an acquaintance of ours, offered to let us live there rent-free just to keep an eye on the place. The flat is absolutely luxurious by comparison with some of the places we had lived in: a room and a kitchen on the sixteenth floor of a high-rise apartment block on Batyyeva Street. The view out of the window is reminiscent of an old black and white etching of some ancient town plan: everything is spread out below, whereas at the level of the apartment windows there is only the sky and slowly drifting snowflakes. It is warm and cosy inside, and the kettle is on the boil. The opportunity to use this flat came just at the right moment, because we had had to move out of our previous rented quarters ahead of the agreed time, just before New Year. The landlady's boyfriend came to visit, and they didn't want any outsiders underfoot. To make things even more difficult, Igor was down with a severe attack of the flu which was raging through Kiev that winter, and was running a very high temperature. What on earth was I to do? I got him up and dressed, for all that he could barely stand on his feet, packed a bag with all our belongings, and out we went into the snow. As Igor was in no state to think clearly, it was up to me to decide the next step. Even though we had resolved not to move in with his parents, this was an emergency. We'd go there tonight, I thought, and decide what to do in the morning.

Igor's mother answered the door: "Children! Igor, what's wrong with you?"

"Auntie Larisa, he should get into bed straight away – he's got a really vicious attack of the flu. We'll only stay for tonight."

"Heavens, you can stay permanently! You know there's a room you could have!"

It was impossible to convince her that if we were to move in permanently, Igor's father would have trouble at work: in his position sharing family quarters with dissidents was not recommended. In fact, the whole family would suffer, not just him. But Igor's mother is adamant that her son and daughter-in-law are not doing anything bad, so there's no reason for anyone to persecute them. She waves aside any talk of possible house-searches and arrests as fantasies: after all, we're no longer living in Stalin's days. There is a great deal she does not know, and this is not the time for me to launch into explanations about who is being thrown into prisons and psychiatric hospitals, for what reason and for how long. Just my poetry and our first (but not last) joint protest is pretext enough for the authorities, but she will never believe that.

"Where should we put him?" I ask.

"Here, in the small room. Wait a moment, let me put down a sheet. Igor, dearest, can you hear me?"

"Mum, everything's all right! I've got the flu, that's all. Don't come near me, or you'll catch it, too."

"No, I won't, we've all had it already. Come on, lie down and I'll make you a nice, hot cup of tea. Ira, what about you? How are you?"

"I'm okay so far. Auntie Larisa, I've got to dash off to the station. We weren't expecting to be kicked out, and invited Lena down for New Year. She'll be arriving on the train from Leningrad in an hour's time."

Auntie Larisa pulls a face. For some inexplicable reason, she doesn't like Lena. However, she is a generous soul, and says that I must, of course, bring Lena here.

We saw in the New Year at Igor's parents' place: Igor on one divan-bed, Lena and I sharing another. After due consideration, we decided that the invalid could have a glass of champagne: "To a happy New Year!"

The following morning the three of us piled into a taxi I'd ordered, and set off to the Mishins' without so much as a warning telephone call, because they had no phone. It's a wonderful thing that in our country you can always turn up at your friends' homes without warning, even when you're homeless or sick. You'll be taken in without a moment's hesitation. We had tried never to abuse this practice, but this was an emergency, so we felt it was permissible. Lena would stay with an aunt she had in Kiev: she understands the situation, and there's no fear of offence. She'd only stop off at the Mishins' for a moment to say hello.

"Maria Viktorovna, we're here to land in your laps!"

"Happy New Year, my dears! Why didn't you show up yesterday? I thought we'd agreed that you'd be spending New Year's Eve with us?"

"Igor's got the flu. I'll explain everything later. I think I've caught it, too, so keep away from us, or we'll infect you."

"Right, we'll put you into Masha's room in a jiffy, and she'll move in with us."

Maria Viktorovna is the mother of a Kiev dissident who is close to us in age. Her husband, Mikhail Ivanovich, was unable to remain silent when Soviet tanks crushed the 'Prague spring' of 1968. So, when a meeting was held at his place of work at which everyone had to vote 'in support of the policy of the Party', he voted against. Of course, that was the end of his career, but at least he had a clear conscience. Neither of them made any open protests after that, but they are interested in the same books as we are, like the same songs, and their house is always open to all and sundry. They are so proud of their home, too. For more than twenty years they had lived in one room with their daughter Masha and an ailing grandfather, but now they have a co-operative flat, consisting of three whole rooms, a kitchen, and even a separate bathroom! There's room to spare, even somewhere to put up sick friends.

"Lena, I've heard a great deal about you. Come on in, I'll put the kettle on. Let's go to the kitchen."

Oh, those kitchens in city apartments! What words can I find to sing your praises? In these kitchens, over a cup of tea, all concerns and pains are discussed, simple sandwiches sit in the middle of the table, in these kitchens a stranger quickly loses all traces of shyness as he is pressed into service to grind up precious coffee-beans in an old mill, or finds himself helping with the washing-up. It is in such kitchens that the future of Russia is discussed, arguments rage on literary themes, *samizdat* changes hands. At a glance, these kitchens are all very similar: housing designs are largely standard. At the same time, they are all different because each one captures the individual imprint of its owners and the indefinable aura of past and future inhabitants, people of varying destinies, coming in from the rain and snow, and leaving much later than they'd intended, back into the wet darkness.

So let's brew up a pot of tea or coffee with whatever there is in the cupboards we already know well. That is how we felt then, and if we erred a few times due to our youth and inexperience, basically we were still right.

We spent a week at the Mishins', getting over the flu and reading. And then we had the unexpectedly lucky break of the old lady's flat for three weeks.

> On Batyev hill –
> There our house stood.
> As on black silver
> In white silver
> Three concrete walls,
> A strip of glass . . .
> Three weeks of quiet,
> Light and warmth.
> Nothing to lose –
> And the keys in our hands:
> Having swallowed January
> To take a new breath!

When the flu passed, we couldn't help laughing as we looked with sunken eyes at our wan, thin reflections in the mirror. A further touch of pathos was added by the holes in the elbows of Igor's old sweater. We really were a sight to behold! I set about darning the sweater artistically with coloured thread: if you can't hide it, flaunt it! Who's to say that this is not the latest in contemporary design? Igor's sick-leave was over; it was back to work the next day. I still had another three days of freedom: my students were on winter holidays, and I categorically refused to ruin their vacations with tutorials. They'd catch up later. In the meantime, I set about doing a whole lot of household tasks, like washing and ironing. The normal female desire to build a nest – be it in a crowded train compartment, or a hotel or a tent – is something I feel in my bones, inherited through many generations.

> We turned all the locks,
> We brought in bread.
> On the table the manuscripts
> Piled like snow.
> And when it was time to say goodbye –

> The misfortune did not matter!
> Now it was not hard for us
> To go into nowhere.

But at the moment, we still have this flat for two weeks, and the immediate future is as bright and cloudless as it can be at the age of twenty-six.

"Irka, I'm being sent on a business trip to Georgia for three days. How will you get by without me?"

"I promise I'll be good! I'll only cross the streets on a green light, and be extra careful travelling to and from my lessons!"

"Maybe you'll change the times? I don't like the thought of you wandering around after dark."

"Are you crazy? How much money do you think we have to throw around? Just because you won't be there to meet me after my last lesson doesn't necessarily mean that I'll get my throat cut! Nonsense! Nobody's ever hurt me yet."

"What about that guy who knocked you over in Odessa!"

"But I told you, he turned out to be a lunatic – and a violent one at that! You know perfectly well that I can hold my own against any ordinary thugs! Moreover, they'll all take their hat off to you if you answer them back with a bit of wit. In any case, one look at my clothes is enough to convince anybody that trying to snatch my bag isn't worth the trouble. What's more important – I hope you'll bring back some mandarins from Georgia?"

"You can bank on it. This is just when they're in season."

Although I promised not to meet him at the airport, I couldn't resist doing so. He went off in the middle of a thaw, but it's snowing again now. I set off with his fur hat, stroking it as it lies on my lap as I would a kitten. It's late, and there is nothing to see out of the bus windows apart from points of light here and there. It has been a whole three and a half days since we last saw each other.

Terrible! People crowd off Igor's flight, but there's no sign of him. Ah, at last! Here he comes, loaded down like a beast of burden.

"Irka! Oh, it's great that you came!"

"You're not cross?"

"Absolutely furious! Is everything all right?"

"Yes. And with you?"

" Couldn't be better. I've made contact with some marvellous guys. Right in the airport, practically the moment I arrived. You know what Georgians are like: 'Come over to my house, I'll introduce you to my mother!'"

"And work-wise?"

"That's okay, too. Come on, let's get on that bus. I've brought you something . . ."

"Mandarins?"

"Not only that! You wouldn't believe how much stuff I was given – I feel like a pack-mule!"

"In that case, put your hat on, Eeyore!"

At home we spread out a veritable feast: Georgian wine, marvellously fragrant fruits, and some kind of exotic mixture of nuts and raisins.

"Igor, let's declare New Year's Eve tonight!"

"And what about a tree?"

"Look over here!" I switch off the kitchen light, and lead him over to the window. The frost has drawn a definite Christmas tree on the glass, complete with tiny lights made by refracted light from far-off windows. They say that there is no such thing as perfect happiness. How wrong they are.

"Irka, did you write anything while I was away?"

"Of course! Did you think I just sat around twiddling my thumbs?"

"Read it to me?"

We shall bring in a Christmas tree with you – a gauche little shy mite,
And with fright it will shake you as you hold it aloft in your hands.
Long familiar to me, Christmas fear that a child understands –
A fire that is glazed, and the frost, so one can't get a word out!
On its timid small paw an amberstone ring I will lay,
And instead of a toy I will hang on a paper-chain quickly,
And then you will ruffle your palm through its summit so prickly,
And, courteous your bow, "Happy January", you will say.

"Anything else?"

"You can read them for yourself, there's a whole pile."

"Bring it here!"

I do so, and the January 1980 morning finds us sitting over a heap of papers, surrounded by mandarin peel. It is cold, and the light outside is white and sharp. He has to go to work, I'm giving lessons from three o'clock in the afternoon. We'll see each other again at ten o'clock in the evening.

"Bye!"

"Bye."

I walk to the door with him, and quietly make the sign of the cross in the direction of his retreating back. It's snowing, and his tracks are rapidly obscured. And now they're gone completely.

Chapter Twenty-four

Dissent is sometimes just a first step, and at other times it is merely cocking a snook behind a closed door. In the latter instance the KGB is not unduly concerned: that kind of dissent is practised by the whole country, KGB personnel included. What Soviet citizen in his right mind could possibly believe for a moment that he has been graciously endowed with freedom by the beloved Party? Everyone knows that whatever the Party may endow one with, it won't be with freedom. Least of all the rank-and-file citizen. Actually, our 'servants of the people' are more interested than anyone else in the privileges of rank and power: to hell with freedom and similar romantic considerations, they have had a taste of the perks of office, they want more, and will stop at nothing to get it. In fact, you can manage very nicely if you mouth the requisite official lies and applaud at the right moment; as for thoughts – you can think what you like, so long as you don't voice it. The battle for minds was lost by the government long ago; the war they are waging now is to ensure silence.

But the exchange of thoughts and ideas is not silence, is it? The state considers that uncontrolled information must not be disseminated either at home or abroad. If you read uncensored work, then you have to be prepared to pay the price of imprisonment. If you are not prepared, then they'll reduce you to begging for mercy. And the commitments the authorities may demand from you in return will be determined by them, without any reference to you. The same applies if you write clandestinely. It is even worse if you publish or disseminate such work: this is interpreted as a clear case of 'aiming to undermine and destabilise Soviet power': this is the sole motivation acknowledged by the KGB. So Valeri Senderov was quite right when he declared that he was not a 'dissident thinker' but a 'dissident doer'. Everyone who does not conceal that his views diverge from the official line is a 'dissident doer'. Such were the unofficial Helsinki Monitoring Groups which set out to check how the Soviet authorities were complying with the human rights commitments they were bound by international documents to observe within the USSR. Such was the *samizdat* publication *Chronicle of Current Events*, which published factual information about the situation in the country, ranging from economic problems to protests and persecution of dissidents. Such were *samizdat* journals, from the feminists' *Maria* through to the *Information Bulletin*. Such is the unofficial Russian Social Fund for Aid to Political Prisoners and their Families (commonly referred to just as 'the Fund') established by Solzhenitsyn – thoughts are thoughts, but everyday needs remain, and the families of those paying the penalty for incurring the state's wrath must eat: the children of political prisoners get just as hungry as any other children. Such are the lone activists, who spend hours poring over manuscripts after a full day at work. Such are the readers of these manuscripts, as are those who collect and store audio tapes.

Inevitably, the KGB will track them all down: the only question is whether they will be collared sooner or later. At that time, Sergei Khodorovich, one of the administrators of the Fund, was still free. It was only a year later that he was to have his ribs broken by the KGB when beaten under interrogation. Nevertheless, he gave nothing away. But Valeri Repin, who administered the Fund in Leningrad, was detained under investigation for two years and blackmailed by KGB threats of the death penalty into giving evidence against several people who were subsequently imprisoned.

The psychiatrist Anatoli Koryagin had not yet been arrested, either. He carried out examinations of those in danger of arrest, so that there would be evidence of their sound mental health should the authorities decide to throw them into psychiatric institutions for alleged insanity. Nor was Tanya Osipova, my future friend and fellow-prisoner, yet under arrest for her activities as a member of the unofficial Helsinki Monitoring Group. However, Tatyana Velikanova, who was to become my mentor in camp, and who, in my view, typifies human dignity and kindness, was already incarcerated in the KGB Lefortovo prison, without the right of visits from relatives or correspondence. Alexander Podrabinek, who monitored Soviet punitive medicine, was already under arrest, too. There was still some time to go before the arrest of Father Dmitri Dudko, a free-thinking Moscow priest, so popular among young Orthodox Christians: alas, he could not take the pressure, and made a shameful public recantation on Soviet television, to be followed by years of genuine repentance for having 'broken'. The spiritual father of so many surrendered, thereby betraying everyone who sought the path to Christ through him.

It is easy to condemn those who break under pressure, but we do not do so. What right have we to judge? Nobody has broken our fingers during interrogation, the way they did with the Ukrainian poet Vasyl Stus, nor have we been blackmailed by our illness the way Geli Snegirev was. We can only look searchingly into ourselves, and wonder: shall we be able to cope, come what may? Without the support of international fame (which we don't have – we're provincials, and do not know anyone who has influential contacts with the West), and knowing that the Ukrainian KGB (notoriously the fiercest in the whole of the USSR) would be pitiless, would we be able to stand firm if faced with the prospect of dying in obscurity, without the hope that our death would change anything, but just for the sake of our conscience? Who knows? Why did Stus hold out, and Snegirev break? Why was our future friend Valeri Senderov able to emerge from a lengthy sentence in the camps with his honour intact, whereas his closest associate in organising an unofficial free public university, lost his nerve and betrayed everyone he could? But we already have examples before us of those who did withstand: a long list of names to figure on the pages of the as yet unwritten history of our country.

It's easier for us, we're a new generation of dissidents, following a trail already blazed by others. We already know that it's possible to write books in camps and in prisons, if you memorise each paragraph. We know that we would receive covert assistance from many people, from soldiers on escort duty to Moscow professors.

The West? We tend to think of it more as a safe deposit for the preservation of our persecuted culture: you pass a manuscript to the West, it will be published, and then find its way back in the form of a nice, compact book. It's easier to type copies off such books (proper print is easier on the eye), they're easy to hide and carry with you. Bibles come into our country from the West, too: small volumes in vinyl covers, printed on thin rice paper . . . Apart from that, the West means *glasnost*. The Soviet government doesn't like bad publicity abroad, and pays much more heed to foreign public opinion than it does to the opinion of its own citizens. So the more the West knows about our problems, the better. People in the West are free, nobody can hurl them into prison for organising a protest demonstration near the Soviet embassy or for writing a letter of protest for publication in a newspaper.

So this is the frame of mind in which Igor and I consider what our next steps should be. We have no intention of joining any organisations or groups: not because of any danger (it's more dangerous to be obscure loners, in fact), but because we intend to act in accordance with our own consciences and nobody else's. We don't want anyone telling us what to do, nor do we want to order anybody else around.

As our hearts prompt us, so shall we act, and co-operate with those whom we come to trust after looking at them eye to eye. Fear is an ordinary human emotion: the important thing is whether you control your fear, or whether it controls you. It's easier for Igor. The many years of pain he suffered because of his feet have conditioned him to endure any pain at all without batting an eyelid. He can genuinely doze off in a dentist's chair – a Soviet dentist, who uses no pain-killers and is not burdened by such considerations as the possible agony of his patient . . . It's harder for me. Pain, as such, is not too terrible a prospect: it had been drummed into me from childhood that it's shameful to show that you're suffering, and a positive disgrace to cry from pain. My parents were openly proud of the fact that at the age of six, I 'was not scared' of such things as injections, blood, or having stitches after a few unfortunate falls. But what about my claustrophobia? Nobody at home knew that I suffered from it. As cowardice of any kind was to be deplored, I used to descend briskly into the Kiev catacombs, then later into the crypts of the Kiev Monastery of the Caves, even though inside I felt that I would faint from terror at any moment. The dark ceilings and walls seem to press against your shoulder-blades, you can't breathe, a yell of fear trembles on your lips, and you know that if you succumb to it those walls will trap you forever. My claustrophobia had been growing, and I did not even realise the extent of it myself: all I knew was that I became increasingly reluctant to enter basements or small rooms. However, there was always the option of going outside, and when the sky is above you and the sea somewhere close by, the irrational discomfort melts away, and seems as nonsensical as a figment of delirium.

It was Igor who brought the matter into the open, albeit quite by chance, in our very first apartment. He accidentally latched the door of the bathroom when I was inside. That was enough to set me off, and I almost broke down the door by hurling myself at it bodily. Igor, shaken, rushed over to let me out.

"Dearest, what on earth are you doing?"

"I can't bear to be closed in! It terrifies me! I'm even scared of being in a lift, or travelling on the underground! I just never told anyone about it . . ."

"That's silly. Everybody has some fear or other. For instance, I'm afraid of heights."

"You – afraid?"

"Yes. Even now. Balconies, cliffs, that kind of thing. So let's see if we can't overcome these fears. We'll start training ourselves out of them gradually."

To articulate one's fears is already half the battle won; after that, all you have to do is face the fear methodically, a second at a time. You watch the small hand travel around the face of the clock, and know that every second is another tiny victory for you. It was due to this that later, the first time I found myself in a solitary cell, or in a transport van for ferrying prisoners (you can neither sit nor stand normally in these vans), I was perfectly calm. In fact, I gloried in my freedom from the old fear, recalling with gratitude how much time and patience Igor expended on working with me. We went into lifts, into the underground, into telephone booths and basements.

"Are you all right?" he would ask.

"Not too bad. But not brilliant, either."

"Tell me the moment you start to feel bad."

Having no doubt that his hand would guide me out into the light under any circumstances, I discovered new abilities within myself, and this worked when the need arose.

We also have to consider what to do with my poems. What were their chances of surviving numerous house-searches or arrests? We have no way of putting them into the 'safe' of the West. It takes years to build up contacts which make such things possible, and how much time do we have? It was only much later that we realised that this was one problem we need not have worried about: my poetry was circulating much more widely than we thought. But then, in the summer of 1980, we resolved that no matter what, the poems must be saved. Perhaps they would be the only thing left of us in the world.

Preparations for the Moscow Olympic Games were in full swing: arrests escalated in all the 'Olympic' cities, Muscovites were being forced to sign undertakings to get out of the capital for the summer, or at least send their children away. Huge numbers of foreigners were expected in Moscow and Leningrad, and independent contacts between them and the locals did not enter into the plans of the authorities. Their aim was to reduce the number of 'chance people' in the two major cities. Those who were to stay, or even be brought in, were service personnel for the Games, sales and transport staff, and hordes of informers from the organisation which had tried once upon a time to recruit me. There were also, of course, the athletes, the media and the militia. Tickets to Moscow and Leningrad could only be obtained with written evidence that the journey was necessitated by one's job; all private cars were liable to be stopped at any time and searched by the militia. The gaols were bursting at the seams. This was a cautionary measure for the duration of the Olympics.

Yet this was where the free contacts were to be found, and we decided to get to Moscow by hook or by crook, carrying three collections of my poems. Lara had married some time ago, and her surname was now Meyerovich. Unfortunately, I must withhold details of how we managed to reach Moscow and who helped us, as the same power which ordered the setting up of checkpoints on the roads then still holds sway now, and I don't want to make it a present of this information. Our plans were quite simple: we would walk around Moscow, looking into the faces of the 'guests of the capital'. Should we come across a likely candidate, who we were certain was not a KGB officer disguised as a foreigner, we would appeal to that person to take my poetry out to the West: after all, foreigners are free people. Lara walked about twenty paces behind us, my manuscripts in her bag. In the case of our being arrested, she would melt away into the crowd, just an innocent passer-by. If we found someone suitable, we would give her an agreed signal to approach. We would have to speak English, even though our knowledge of it is so poor. After all, it's not too difficult to learn a couple of necessary sentences off by heart: "Please, take out these manuscripts! You can't save us, but you can save these poems! Eventually, they'll return to Russia. Please, help us!"

Unlike us, Lara does speak English, but she's already running considerable risks on our behalf, and we cannot ask her to act as an interpreter to boot.

We wander around the spruced-up summer streets of Moscow, looking for a likely foreigner. Now there's someone who's definitely an American: a middle-aged man in shorts, with a photographer's identity tag on his shirt. We go up to him. He fairly exudes the aura of a citizen of a different world. There is nobody shadowing him: we have become adept at spotting these shifty, insignificant-looking personages. What luck! The free citizen of a free foreign country shies away from us, unconcealed horror on his face: "No! I have nothing to do with literature! I'm a photographer!"

He went on muttering excuses, but we walked off immediately. Why should we cause him any unpleasantness? The heavy, surveillance-permeated air of the Olympic capital pressed down like a lead weight, recalling such depressing reasoning as, "I'm only an employee of such and such a paper, what will happen to my career if I fall foul of the Soviet authorities? Is this what I was sent here for? I'm only a photographer, so don't bother me with unrelated problems!"

He was the first foreigner with whom we had contact, but there was something oh, so familiar in his terrified gaze! Whatever the reason, it was the standard, paralysing fear of the mysterious prohibitions of a mysterious regime, which results in self-censorship, and 'minding one's own business'. Many years later we were to encounter an American professor who began to tell us that Russians are slaves by nature, that such is their mentality. We didn't bother to argue with him, just exchanged a resigned smile: he wasn't worth the argument.

Of course, we had enough sense not to start thinking that this American photographer was typical of all Americans. We became great friends later with Bob Gillette, the correspondent of the *Los Angeles Times*; there were many others whom we would have trusted implicitly in the most difficult of circumstances. But from that time on we knew for sure that the division between those who are free, and those who are not, lies in the heart, it is not determined by geographical boundaries. You can distinguish someone who is free from a coward in any country by looking into their eyes, just as you can distinguish those who value human dignity from slaves, no matter what it is that enslaves them. It is easy to feel free when nobody beats you for it. But what would you do, my friend, if you were to be arrested? After how many sessions of interrogation would you break? Luckily, in every nation, under any regime, there are those who cannot be broken. They are the linch-pin of freedom in happier countries than ours. And in them lies the hope for the future freedom of those who are in the same miserable circumstances as we are now.

We spent two days walking around half-empty Olympic Moscow, conducting an experiment: we wanted to see whether we could find at least one foreigner who would take my manuscripts with the same ease as young Russians, who would come in out of the wind or snow, and go off again into the unknown. We did not find a single such person. I suppose that is nothing to be wondered at, really: we have our problems, they have theirs, and, in any case, why should they put themselves out to help 'these Soviets'? I was absolutely astounded to learn, after my release, that thousands of people in many countries had campaigned for my freedom, stood for hours in all weathers conducting demonstrations outside Soviet embassies and signed numerous petitions in my defence. If only all life's surprises could be like that! We have so many friends all over the world now: it must be our fortunate destiny not to lose faith in humanity as we grow older, but, on the contrary, to see that faith increase. It shows that our young, as yet unknown free citizens in an unfree country are not as alone as they may think in this strange, contradictory world.

Chapter Twenty-five

Igor was lucky enough to find a new job as a Project Engineer, Grade I. This really was a blessing, because it was clear that he would have to quit his old job soon. As we felt ashamed of our earlier attempt to emigrate under false pretence, we wrote several months later to the Presidium of the Supreme Soviet, affirming everyone's right to freedom of emigration from their own country. This right is clearly stipulated in paragraph two of article twelve of the International Convention on Civil and Political Rights, a convention ratified by the Soviet Union. We have no relatives abroad, nor do we intend to go to Israel. Nevertheless, we are determined to emigrate. Of course, we knew that this was virtually impossible. Still, it was more honourable than our first attempt: we were not cheating, but demanding our rights.

Naturally, the only tangible results were problems for Igor at work, and in the OVIR: "Take back your application!"

"Why? And, in any case, what is it doing here? It wasn't addressed to you!"

"Take it back, or it goes straight into the wastepaper basket!"

"That's up to you . . ."

But by that time we thought less and less about emigration: after all, why should this be considered the only way of gaining freedom? Why should we have fewer claims on the land of our birth than those in power? And what would happen if everybody who refuses to bend the knee to the regime emigrates? Or what if everybody were to refuse to obey all these humiliating demands, and start behaving like decent people living in their own country? This last option seemed increasingly attractive to us as time went by. In speaking of 'everybody' I use the word with reference to Kant's concept of categorical imperatives. It was not our place to make such demands on other people. Nor was it our right. But we could certainly ask it of ourselves. Yes, we felt sorry for ourselves, so young and so much in love; yes, we grieved for our future children . . . But there were plenty of other people in the same situation. If we had been told at that stage that we could leave without further ado, we would have packed our bags with very mixed feelings: people still change a lot at that age. So our problem was – which way do we proceed? As we didn't acknowledge the right of 'social milieu' to change our personalities, we made increasing demands upon ourselves. Evening sessions of soul-searching became a dual exercise.

Yet suddenly, Igor gets this new job! We suspect that his father has had a hand in it, exerting some backstairs influence. He does not approve of our intention to emigrate, considers dissident activity a load of rubbish, and has told us so in no uncertain terms. But he loves Igor, and, knowing his son's fierce pride and sense of honour, obviously decided to lend a discreet hand: he has plenty of connections.

Igor plunged into his new work with a will, and by the time he was finally kicked out, had managed to take out three patents for his inventions. Years later, after so many turbulent events, and after we had been stripped of Soviet citizenship, a medal arrived at his mother's address, hailing him as a 'Distinguished Inventor of the USSR'. The bureaucratic machine moves at a snail's pace, and there is no communication between its many departments: someone, somewhere, had assessed the economic benefits of Igor's inventions, and the medal was issued without reference to the KGB. So it duly arrived at Igor's mother's home, and she phoned us in London to tell us about it, her voice a mixture of laughter and indignation.

But now, in the autumn of 1980, we are at the railway station: Igor is off to work, and I'm making use of my students' holidays to travel up to Moscow for a few days, with a bundle of new poems and several human rights documents, just to make sure that they are safely out of the way should something unpleasant happen to either of us. There are no ordinary tickets left, so we have to buy a more expensive one for a compartment. Still, it's an ill wind that blows no good, and I shall at least travel in relative comfort, without having to perform contortions under a sheet to undress for the night.

"Now, you behave sensibly, Irka!"

"I'll be as sensible as sensible can be! Promise!"

"I'll still worry."

"Don't be ridiculous. This is just a quick hop there and back."

He stands on the platform, waiting for the train to move off: one of those strange station partings, when everything's been said, and we merely look at each other through the window.

So far there is only one other person in the compartment with me: a neatly dressed woman in late middle age. She has already unfolded a newspaper and started reading.

"Those villains are at it again in Afghanistan! Just think – they're shooting at our boys!"

I'm sorry for our boys, too: they've been thrown needlessly into that slaughterhouse at the age of eighteen, without being asked, or told the reason why. Shoot, or be shot yourself in front of the whole platoon! And if the friend who had the bunk next to yours was killed yesterday, they will urge you to seek revenge today. But German boys just like these were killed in our territory, when they marched in to enforce decisions made by others. Only occasionally were they pitied when their dead bodies were found face-down in the mud: "Look at him! Almost a kid! Must be straight from his mother's apron-strings! What the hell brought him here . . . see, all rigged out in uniform, too!"

I make an effort to get on my companion's wavelength: "But what are our boys doing there in the first place? You can't seriously believe that they were sent there to render fraternal assistance?"

"Of course not, we're not children. Though I must say, you look so young . . . But we have to bear in mind that if we hadn't gone into Afghanistan, the Americans would be there before you could blink!"

"And you believe that?"

"My dear girl, of course the papers can't say so in as many words. But I have had considerable experience of life, and you can believe me when I say that when our tanks rolled into Czechoslovakia in 1968, there were American planes circling above! It's a struggle between superpowers, without any room for sentiment! Of course, the Afghans don't give a damn about politics, they're only savages. But they should feel grateful that someone is looking after their interests. We need access to the Indian Ocean!"

"What for?"

"For control, of course. You must understand that it is a question of us, or them! Don't you care about the interests of your own people?"

I could only regret the fact that this woman had obviously never had the opportunity to read some of the Third Reich propaganda which she was unconsciously echoing almost word for word. Territories inhabited by savages, the global interests of one's people . . . I had not read such tenets in the original, either, but I had heard about them second-hand. And a great pity, that it was at second-hand: I think they should be compulsory reading in schools, so that children can be taught: this is what they planned, and this was the result in practice. Read them, children, and learn how history punishes those who seek world domination: how their arrogant schemes fail, how flawed is their vision of 'us' and 'them', where 'we' are always superior, our ideas are right, and therefore we should be the ones to wield power.

As a matter of fact, my travelling companion has little time for ideas, dismissing them as 'something for fools'. As far as she is concerned, the whole world is divided into two parts – 'us', and everybody else. And 'our' people – even if they should be the scum of the earth – are invariably better than strangers, who, naturally, think of nothing else but how to seize the moment to subjugate us.

"Do you think, my dear, that I don't know life? My father was arrested in 1937, so you can imagine what my early life was like! We had our share of grief! But we still managed to beat the Germans, and we'll beat everybody else, too, only with fewer casualties, because we'll strike first!"

"What about 'global peace'?"

She smiled condescendingly: "As soon as we put everything to rights, then there'll be peace. Then we'll live happily! Just think how much money we give to Cuba . . . But later these expenses will no longer be necessary, and our situation will be much easier, too, once there's nobody left to fight against! Do you imagine that I don't understand what's going on now? Of course I do, but it's only a temporary measure, while there's resistance."

"And you think . . ."

"Think! Of course I think, don't doubt that! This is the faith of my entire life, and it's not for you youngsters to teach us! We spilled our blood for it!"

"You fought in the war?"

"Well, not personally. But I worked fourteen hours a day at a factory bench as a girl. I stopped menstruating for two years then . . . I suffered from anaemia – we all did! We lost our blood differently at that time . . . But our generation . . ."

Is there any sense in arguing with her? She's already worked herself into a state, and is fumbling around in her handbag for some tablets. Her generation is now either barely making ends meet on a miniscule pension, or has attained the ranks of Party bosses, or died. We are the ones who have to reap the rewards of their endeavours . . . However, General Pyotr Grigorenko belonged to that generation, too, and the Ukrainian poet and Helsinki monitor Mykola Rudenko, serving a sentence in a hard labour camp. Young people tend to be merciless, but for the sake of such exceptions I do not press my companion, and hold back the withering comments on the tip of my tongue. Not because I am afraid that she will inform on me (that kind don't) but because she has popped a tablet into her mouth, because her legs are a mass of blue varicose veins . . . O, Lord, forgive us all and have mercy!

Lara is waiting for me at the station in Moscow, accompanied by her husband, Sasha. I had only met him fleetingly that summer, so he is still a closed book to me. He is obviously a very well educated man, and an interesting conversationalist. He is also well-mannered and kindly. But, judging by the look on Lara's face, there is someone else I must meet.

"Irka, you must be dying for an ice-cream!"

"How ever did you guess? What's on offer?"

"Strawberry, with whipped cream!"

"Wow! Talk about the Moscow bourgeoisie . . . !"

"You said it! . . . I've invited Valeri Senderov to join us, he's been an avid reader of yours for ages."

"Who?"

"You'll see for yourself. It's high time you met him."

Somewhat awkwardly, we sit around a table: Valeri (popularly known as 'Lera'), Boris Kanevsky, Lara, Sasha and I. Boris and I are doing most of the talking, the usual social exchange of jokes. Lera's grey eyes merely observe. But from time to time, he quotes snippets out of my poems, both aptly and inaptly, something I find totally confusing. Finally, we have a brief conversation on the stairs: "Ira, never be silly enough to repeat your attempts during the Olympic Games. Give me all your poetry. And anything else you might have written."

I guess that this is not just for circulation in *samizdat*, but also for the West. However, I ask no questions. This is a man of patent decency, and I trust him immediately. I later learned from Lara that he had been baptised that very day. That explains why he said so little. I like that: neophytes can often be tiresomely persistent in trying to impose onto others the truths they have just discovered. Which only shows that they are not yet firm in their faith, and are trying to compensate for it by external zeal.

Lera is not one of them: in fact, he is not a person to flaunt his emotions at all. It doesn't look as though he has any sense of self-preservation, either. Soon he was to meet Igor, and I felt yet again that I was being protected. As a poet? As a woman? I don't know, but again and again I found myself being edged away from the complex mechanics of clandestine *samizdat*: "You write! Write whatever you want! As for the rest – that's not your concern!"

"Listen, wrapping poets in cotton wool is unheard of in Russia!"

At this point, Igor would usually intervene with a final word:

"Woman! Obey thy husband! You married me, didn't you? Well, then!"

Lera would give a satisfied snigger, and they would go off to discuss matters into which I was not admitted.

The following winter, when the dark clouds began to gather over Solidarity in Poland and our troops lined its borders, I rebelled: it must have been my Polish genes.

"If they bring in the tanks the way they did in Czechoslovakia, Igor, whether you like it or not I'm going to stage a demonstration in Red Square!"

Igor knows that in 1863 my great-great-grandfather took part in the uprising for independence, and that this brought him Siberian exile, tuberculosis and death. For the family it meant the move to Odessa: poor, but without loss of spirit. He knows about the '*pan**
locomotive driver' who steered goods trains to Odessa in a white dress-shirt, and the Polish terms of endearment with which I occasionally address this stubborn, wilful husband of mine, drawing them out of some hidden recesses of memory.

"Irka, if that's the case, we'll go together. We'll probably last about thirty seconds, a minute at best before they bundle us away."

"Igor . . ."

"Do you think my conscience is any different from yours? How many weeks was it after the invasion of Afghanistan that we finally got around to writing a protest? I still squirm when I think about it! But let's phone Lera and tell him, so that at least it will become known that there was a protest action."

Lera reacts calmly: "Let me know when, and under what slogan. You won't be alone."

So it seems that there are Poles in Moscow! But of course there must be: it's a huge city. And their consciences must be just as uneasy as our 'foreign' ones.

There was no occasion to head for Red Square: the Polish communists managed without the assistance of Soviet tanks. They had recourse to internal measures, violating all previously reached agreements. Solidarity went underground. Igor and I, who read everything we could lay our hands on, found an Australian communist newspaper on sale at Kiev railway station. As Australia is a very distant country, and the newspaper was in English, there were no restrictions on its sale. It was from this paper, after sweating over dictionaries, that we

* Polish courtesy title.

learned that Solidarity had a membership of eleven million! The greater part of the Polish work-force . . .

And now there's martial law, telephone connections between the coast and the interior have been cut, arrests . . . No, no, our troops had no part in this, at least not openly. Poland has its own communists, who are hanging on to power as best they can, resorting to flooded pits and armed patrols in the streets.

Taking note of all this, I ask Lera: "When are you going to introduce me to those Poles?"

"Which Poles?"

"The ones who were going to come with us to Red Square."

"I was going to go with you. Just me."

"You?!"

"Of course. Why are you staring at me like that?"

"But you've already got so many things to do! The *Bulletin*, the university, and heaven knows what else!"

"I'm a Russian officer."

And that was that, quite enough to satisfy his high notions of honour and duty. All – well, just about all – graduates of Soviet institutes of higher education are classed as officers of the reserve: there are military faculties, and military camps and similar other levels of military training of which I know little. My Igor, despite his feet, is a reserve lieutenant. He never discussed this with me, but when he was first arrested and an MVD* sergeant, removing his belt, remarked: "How's that, for a 'political'? Sporting an officer's belt, no less!", Igor answered coldly: "I *am* an officer. Any objections, sergeant?"

The warder-militiaman did not voice any.

Ministerstvo Vnutrenykh Del: Ministry of Internal Affairs.

Chapter Twenty-six

Today, Igor wakes up looking depressed. I don't ask any questions, but start brewing a pot of tea: a man should be given something to eat and drink, jollied along, and then all will be explained without prompting.

This spring we are living in Igor's mother's flat. His parents have separated, and his father now lives in a one-room institute apartment. His mother had been inviting us to move in with her for some time, but we were renting an apartment which had turned up out of the blue. Actually, if we had thought about it, we would have realised that there was nothing surprising in the sudden availability of this accommodation. The Komsomol organiser at Igor's place of work had asked him (although Igor was not a member of the Komsomol) whether it was true that he and I were looking for a place to rent. When Igor said that we were, the organiser gave him a telephone number which, according to him, belonged to someone who was seeking lodgers. At that time, Igor had neither the time nor the inclination to ask where the organiser had heard this, nor who the prospective landlord was. Beggars can't be choosers: we had changed apartments nine times in two years, and were frantically hunting for yet another. So we phoned, and reached agreement very easily: fifty roubles a month, so that the apartment would be occupied until such time as the owner's daughter reached marriageable age. Well, stranger things have happened . . .

The first alarm signals came from our friends from Odessa, the Zhuravitskys, when they came to visit us.

"Do you remember that Leningrad artist we suggested you contact?" they asked, naming the man in question.

"No . . . why, what's the matter?"

"Remember, we said that Ira was bound to find his work interesting, and that you really ought to get in touch with him next time you go to Leningrad?"

"Oh, yes, so you did . . . The thing is, we were so busy, we didn't get around to contacting him."

"And you didn't telephone him even once?"

"No. Why?"

"Well, he was summoned by the KGB, who wanted to know how he met you, and what he knows about you. Of course, he didn't have a clue, but he remembered Igor's surname being mentioned, and told us about it."

Aha! The penny dropped. We always kept the pad with dissidents' telephone numbers and addresses well hidden, but the little green notebook with ordinary 'social' contacts was always left in the open whenever we went away for a day or two, because its contents were harmless. It must have been from this book that the name and address of this unknown Leningrad artist had been fished out. In other words, we were under surveillance, and the apartment's owner had been acting under KGB instructions.

We began to keep our eyes open, and noticed that both our landlord and his wife were rather shifty characters, who never looked us in the eye even when they called to collect the rent. However, feelings aside, it became quite clear that somebody was going through our papers when we were out: we verified that by the old method of 'a speck of dust'. The denouement came that autumn. The landlord's wife dropped in and showed an unnecessary interest in our plans for the following day. Once she had established that we planned to be out, she left. Our suspicions were well and truly aroused, so I changed my plans and stayed in the next day, latching the door for good measure. Sure enough, a key was inserted into the lock, and someone started trying to get in. Igor was at work. Of course, whoever it was couldn't open the door because it was latched from the inside, and I lost no time in phoning the militia to report that someone was trying to break into my apartment. A very polite militiaman arrived after the would-be intruder gave up trying and went away.

"Someone tried to enter? Well, it happens. A lot of apartments here in the Belichi have been burgled. Pity we didn't catch them at it. If it happens again, don't hesitate to call us immediately!"

I could well imagine what it would be like if the militia arrived and caught a KGB operative red-handed! These two services loathe each other, but the militia is subordinate to the KGB, so any chance they get to score a point off the KGB is seized with alacrity.

That evening, our landlord came rushing around: "Did you call the militia?"

"Yes, someone tried to force an entry."

"Rubbish! Nobody could have tried to break in! Apart from yourselves, only my wife and I have keys to this apartment!"

"So it was one of you?"

"It's our apartment, and we can come in whenever we like!"

"Your wife was here only yesterday. Why should she come around when nobody is supposed to be at home?"

"That's my business! This place is mine!"

"With the right to enter and search?"

"If you don't like it, you can get out!"

"You'll have the keys tomorrow, and we expect to get our money back: remember, we pay you rent a month in advance. Incidentally, how did you find out that we called the militia?"

Suddenly, he became exceedingly conciliatory: "Come, come, let's not be hasty! Why should you want to move? Don't you like this apartment? Neither you nor I need any trouble, do we? That's the only reason why I upbraided you a little. We can get along quietly and peacefully . . ."

His face, his restless hands, his earnest persuasions are all certain evidence that he is working for 'them', just as we had suspected for several months now. It was imperative that we get out, but where could we go? Maybe we ought to take up Igor's mother's offer, and move in with her and Igor's sister for a while, just until we find something else?

"My dear ones! At last! There's a divan in Oleg's study. No, not a word out of either of you, you silly pups. There's a room that's yours in this house, you know that! Igor, love, I need new shelves in the food cupboard . . . Oh, and some of the tiles in the bathroom have worked loose – Ira, you're the family specialist in such matters: would you . . . ?"

So we remained, and saw in the New Year with a somewhat expanded family: Igor's sister Lyalya has borne a second daughter, Tatyana, and she and her husband were spending more time here than at his parents' place. While Lyalya was in hospital giving birth, we redecorated the whole apartment. With the assistance of Lyalya's older daughter, Anna, we drew murals on the freshly-painted kitchen and nursery walls. The three-year-old Anna would point her little finger, and issue instructions: draw monkeys on the doors, Mumi the troll on the wall, and a 'kandalaka' on the ceiling. We never did manage to determine just what a 'kandalaka' was, but I drew something with big eyes and lots of legs, and the little one seemed satisfied with my interpretation. When, oh when would we be able to have our own little ones, who would live happily in a kind and gentle kingdom of fairy-tales?

The icicles melted off the roof-guttering, I managed to master the art of typing (on a typewriter acquired by chance: I didn't dare touch the electric one belonging to Igor's father in case I broke it), Igor built the extra shelving in the food cupboard, patented yet another invention at work, and compiled a careful index of all my poems in chronological order, frequently accusing me of treating my work with undue carelessness. So far he'd had no trouble at work, and our financial situation was quite good: we were both earning, and it was only as a matter of form that Igor's mother occasionally asked us whether she ought to buy a few more bookshelves. Kind and always on the move, she was untiring in her efforts to ensure that everything in the home was as it should be, that everyone was comfortable and happy.

It is the merry month of May, and I have what my grandmother used to call 'rabbits in my head'.

"Igor! Smile at me!"

"Irka, let's go out and look for lilies of the valley!"

"What a brilliant idea! Are you always such a genius?"

"Only every second day."

The outskirts of the city where we live are only about twenty minutes' walk from some woods. There's a veritable carpet of lilies of the valley under the trees; it's a pity to step on them, and we tread with care.

"Igor, look! A squirrel!"

"You're imagining things. Oh, no, I can see it, too."

"Look at the cute ears and tail on it!"

"You people from Odessa! Haven't you seen a squirrel before? Here, take a look at this: isn't he a beauty?"

He holds a May beetle in the palm of his hand, and he really is a fine specimen, although clearly annoyed, and his body reflects all the colours of the rainbow. After he has told us exactly what he thinks of us, he unfolds his wings and flies off about his business.

"Have you read that, from the point of view of aerodynamics, May beetles can't fly? Their wing span is too small . . ."

"Yes, I have . . . but they fly, for all that! It's because they can't read. And as for those who can – take that!"

I throw an old pine-cone at him, and we fool around, trampling last year's pine needles and future wild strawberry plants.

"Irka, hold on a moment! Look at that!"

He points to what must be the most beautiful lily of the valley in the whole forest: its leaves are delicately curved, just as though it were posing for a painting of a still life. We bend over it, our hair tangling.

"Hasn't it got the most marvellous smell?"

"We simply can't pick him. Let's leave him here – he's too important to touch. Maybe he's the founder of a dynasty?"

"A grandfather and a great-grandfather, for sure. And anyone who dares touch him will be cu-ur-ur-sed! And he'll set the wood-troll on to them!"

"Oooh, I'm scared! Here, catch this!"

Drunk with the scents of the forest, we wend our way back with handfuls of less imposing specimens of lilies of the valley.

"Irka, how did you like it yesterday at X's place?" We never name names aloud as a matter of course, even perfectly innocent ones. Under any roof, they may be noted by the KGB – that organisation is not mean when it comes to spending money on listening devices. Of course, nobody will hear us in the woods, but conditioned reflexes do their job.

"You mean that out-of-town genius they've got visiting them? I thought he was just a primitive demagogue. And aggressive, to boot. He seems to suffer a constant need for self-affirmation, and if you still need that after the age of forty, there's not much hope for you, is there? He can't even argue properly; he's not interested in establishing the truth, only in proving his own superiority. Did you notice the way he changed his basic theses as he went along?"

"And how! Yet they treat him as though he were the Pope, or something – infallible, no matter what nonsense he comes out with."

"Well, they are old friends . . . You and I were still knee-high to a grasshopper when they were busily recording Galich's songs. 'Let us be partial to our friends . . .'"

"You didn't think the atmosphere there was a bit chilly? And that line he kept pushing that one should always doubt, because if you don't doubt something or other, you are 'thinking ideologically'?"

"Well, that was when you said that doubt is a necessary component of searching for something, and not the ultimate aim. And that perpetual doubt is like continual chewing without swallowing. Nobody argued with that, did they?"

"No, but that doesn't mean they agreed. Just think, what if they really are serious about this doubting business: that means spending your life just doubting, and not reaching any decisions, because you're not sure that they're right . . . Which means that you are prepared to let others decide for you what's good and what's bad, what's honest, and what's dishonest . . . And you'll be left to vacillate and try to justify both sides, because you don't want to be guilty of 'ideological thinking'."

"If you pursue that line of argument, then you could say that Jesus

Christ thought in ideological terms. He, more than anyone, defined things clearly."

"Well, it would not be fair to bring Christ into a discussion with an atheist. You can't transfer the argument on to home ground . . ."

"So that's why you brought up Judas?"

"That's something more readily understood by a lot of our 'great thinkers'. No, really, what did Judas do, in today's terms? Identified a Personage already known to half of Jerusalem. He didn't even have to bear false witness at Christ's trial – they managed without him. And the crucifixion. He didn't even need to lie: all he had to do was to confirm 'operational information' personally. A sort of witness. But he has become the symbol of treachery forever, and he did the right thing by hanging himself: it was the least he could do, when he realised the enormity of what he had done. Yet can you imagine how many people, having blurred the lines of demarcation, have found justification for themselves, and live happily, without a care? And they blurred that borderline through specious reasoning and demagogy!"

"You're setting yourself up as a judge and jury?"

"I'm not the Nuremberg trials, nor am I setting myself up as God. But judgement doesn't mean just condemnation: for your information, it can also lead to justification! If I can't judge, then I can't justify anyone – even an informer!"

"Well, don't! The very thought! Look, you have a man with all sorts of good and bad features, and you have his specific deeds."

"But without judging a person – and I agree that it is for God to judge – can't I condemn such actions as betrayal? Or should I succumb to doubts whether it is good or bad? And thereby not consider it a shameful act should I perform it myself? Try to justify myself? . . ."

"What are you on about? Why bring yourself into it?"

"I'm not, heaven knows that's one thing I've never done – betray anyone. But what if these people we were with last night really think like that? Remember, they once said that they have a 'tame informer' who comes to visit them from time to time?"

"Yes, but they warned us when he was there!"

"But they haven't stopped him from coming around all these years! He's also 'a friend from their young days'. And this 'friend' uses their unspoken consent to watch and take note of who comes and when, while they sit around ooh-ing and ah-ing because he can recite Tsvetayeva's 'Camp of Swans'."

"But everybody has their weaknesses . . ."

"Weaknesses – or Judas' reasoning?"

"Come on, have you forgotten how much they've helped us? What do you value more – idle talk over a cup of tea, or deeds? By their deeds, they're our friends, right?"

"Right. You know, I seem to have gone off at a tangent. They say there's a disease called 'stupidity with side-effects' – well, I must have just had a touch of it. It's just that I didn't feel right after yesterday."

"Lofty considerations are neither here nor there, in this instance, surely you realise that? *She* always wants to be an authority in the eyes of younger people, and now her guru has appeared on the scene, and everyone got a bit carried away. As a matter of fact, her husband kept his mouth shut throughout. Do you think they have sessions of soul-searching?"

"I haven't a clue."

"Well, for your information, I had a heart-to-heart with her not long ago. She understands perfectly what we're about. After all, we don't make any attempt at secrecy. So I asked her, maybe it would be better for them if we were to stop coming around? Maybe it's dangerous for their son to visit us – he's a student, after all!"

"And what did she say?"

"You know her just as well as I do. What do you think?"

"Thrust out her lower lip and said that nobody in their house stoops to self-censorship. And told you off for even raising such matters."

"Yes, she did. What's more, she said they would be terribly offended if we stop coming to their house. Mind you, I think their 'infallible genius' would be only too happy never to see either of us again. So whom should we listen to, our old friends, or the old friend of our old friends?"

"All right, all right! Irka, you've made your point, never mind putting the boot in! See – I surrender!"

He drops to the ground, scattering lilies of the valley all over the place, I fling myself down to 'rescue' him, and a swarm of pleasantly surprised ants hurries forward to explore our sleeves.

We were not to know that it was he, and not I, who was right. I did not yet have a feel for such matters, and tended to have blind faith in anyone who had done something good or kind in their life.

Chapter Twenty-seven

It's 8 a.m., which means that Igor has been travelling to work this past half-hour, and I am standing in the queue for milk. We have both hated queues since childhood, but there are two small children in the house, an old lady and five working adults, so milk must be obtained. As I only start giving lessons in the afternoon, I'm the logical candidate to go out and queue. With luck, I need only go every second day, but yesterday I couldn't get as much milk as we needed. A quick glance shows that there are some sixty people in the queue before me. Eight large, condensation-covered drums have already been delivered. All being well, they won't run out before it's my turn. It's essential to get there at least forty minutes before the salesgirls start issuing the milk.

At last, they've begun doling out! Those at the back of the line are worried that supplies will be exhausted before their turn comes, the ones at the front are smugly secure: all they have to worry about is that nobody should try to jump the queue. Ha! Up comes an elderly man, and pokes those crowding around the counter with a little grey book. Another follows hard on his heels. A murmur of discontent begins to rise: "They may be war veterans, but this is a bit much! They could at least take their portion after every five of us! We're human, too!"

The salesgirl puts them back in their place: "Citizens! Haven't you read the directive? War veterans are to be served ahead of anybody else! So stop bitching! We obey the law around here! Give me your container, citizen!"

Several voices join in approvingly: "That's right! They spilled their blood for us during the war, so why should they have to stand around in queues now?"

The directive mentioned by the salesgirl is the first attempt by the authorities to poke their noses into the so-far independent instance of home-grown democracy: the law of the queue. Over the generations, this unwritten law has become increasingly intricate. It includes the writing of numbers on the palm of one's hand, or lists, hastily compiled on sheets of paper, it includes tough young 'volunteers' who ensure that nobody pushes in out of turn, and is also expressed in the form of public opinion: "Come on, lads, let this old lady through! Go on, Gran, don't be frightened! The younger ones can wait a bit longer!"

By this same unwritten law, pregnant women are given precedence, as are those carrying small children (but not those whose babies are in prams – they can wait, just like everybody else), invalids and people who are visibly old. The majority of war veterans fell into this category anyway: the privations of the war years made them age physically well before their time. But the directive according special privileges to them has now been published, and one can't, in all conscience, dispute it: it is true that these people fought for us. However, abuses of these privileges began very quickly, as is always the case when bureaucracy becomes a substitute for conscience: all of a sudden, a host of people aged forty or younger became proprietors of the coveted little grey books. Who? Why? Ah, it appears that military achievements in Afghanistan also qualify one for privileged status. A new annoyance is added to the business of queuing for a railway ticket: there are 'war veterans' who buy tickets out of turn, and then sell them there and then to people at the back of the queue at a profit of three roubles. Transaction completed, they promptly go back to the ticket office, brandishing their little grey book, and buy another ticket for resale. A few deals later, they have enough to buy a bottle of what they fancy. And who can blame them? Their pension doesn't stretch very far: that is one war veterans' benefit that the state is in no hurry to augment.

'Uncle' Sanya, our neighbour, spends hours queuing, even though we know that he was last wounded in the war when the Soviet troops were closing in on Berlin.

"Uncle Sanya," Igor asked once, "don't you have a veterans' book?"

"I didn't even bother picking it up."

"But why?"

"Look here, my lad, I fought the fascists! Not my own people, in order to gain privileges! I don't look all that ancient yet, and when I do – people will let me through without any book. You don't think that all those who have those blasted little books fought at the front, do you? I met up with one of them not so long ago: he spent the whole war comfortably in the rear, pushing a pen, even though he's younger than I am. Spent his time stealing boots, the bastard! And now he barges through everywhere, waving a little grey book. As for me – I'll stand, and take my turn. And I'll go on doing so, while I've got the strength. So which one of us do you respect more – me, or him?"

"You, of course."

"Well, see that you go on doing so! Those who really fought deserve respect. I was putting my life on the line for you on the first Ukrainian front even before you were a glint in your old man's eye. I fought for people, not toilet paper! Go on, it's your turn to be served!"

"After you, Uncle Sanya!"

"No talking in the ranks, son! That's an order!"

"Uncle Sanya, are you trying to insult me?"

"Touchy, eh? Well, all right, then. This way it's better than by flashing privilege books around."

They swopped places, and, on this occasion, there were enough of the precious rolls of toilet paper left for them both. But from that time on, we no longer just nodded in passing to Uncle Sanya, but stopped to offer our respects properly. And he would grin into his moustache, and harrumph in a pleased manner: "Greetings, youngsters!"

I had been standing in line, lost in thought, and in the meantime a drama was unfolding near the head of the queue between an elderly war veteran and a woman from further back.

Her hair is completely grey, his is salt-and-pepper. By the time their altercation caught my attention, they were in full cry.

"Aren't you ashamed of yourself?" demanded the woman. "Look at you – you're younger than I am!"

"You just keep a civil tongue in your head, d'you hear? It's my right! I went through the war, while you sat around at home!"

"You should have gone through what I had to face! By the look of you, you haven't done too badly for yourself, what with extra concessions here and there! My man was killed near Korsun, and me pregnant at the time! So now your grandchildren get milk, and ours have to go without? Just because you survived, and he didn't?!" She spat disgustedly to reinforce her point.

The young salesgirl is clearly upset: "Citizeness, don't make trouble! A directive is a directive!"

A stout young fellow, one of the 'volunteers beside the counter' chips in: "Let me see your book, citizen!"

"By all means! Even though it's none of your business, young fellow! I don't know what things are coming to! But I've nothing to hide."

"Vitali Ivanovich Surzhak. Everybody know now who's short of milk? Say thank you to this gallant defender of ours!"

"How dare you, you insolent pup?"

"Pipe down, there's not enough for me, either! So less of this 'insolent pup' business, if you don't mind! You've nothing to hide? Well, the people have a right to know who their benefactors are. You've been thanked, haven't you? So take your three litres, nobody'll interfere. And you, lady, come on up here and get yours, too. Any objections, folks?"

Nobody objects: the grey-haired woman is already in tears, and everyone feels at a loss. Vitali Ivanovich, muttering about the ingratitude of today's youth, ambles off carrying a full billycan of milk in one hand, and the lid in the other. The woman, sobbing fitfully, extends her container with shaking hands. It's a complex thing, justice. The 'volunteer' goes off, too: what's the point in hanging around when it's clear that the milk is about to run out? The queue begins to disperse: there's a rumour that there's a shop on the Second Proseka selling milk today, maybe it's worth trying there. The years of hunger are behind us, after all: if you really apply yourself, you can usually manage to get some of what you need. In any case, what can you do? Kiev is now ranked in the 'third category' for food supply, and we're even worse off, because we live far from the city centre.

I finally bring back some milk, and a new joke: "Question: What is the most popular sport in the Soviet Union after the Olympic Games? Answer: Conjuring food out of thin air." As well as this, I also bring back a new rumour that's sweeping the city: if you are too free with your comments in a queue, you will find yourself whisked to the nearest militia precinct to be read a lecture, after which you are deprived of your residence permit. They just draw a line through the stamp, and that's that.

Igor is a bit sceptical about this: "I heard that a good six months ago, but I don't know of any case where this has actually been done. That's just the 'rumour department' at work."

I tend to agree: everybody knows that there is a special department of the KGB which specialises in setting such rumours abroad, and this is an important, integral part of propagating fear: after all, even 'they' can't write such things in the papers. For instance, there was this rumour that hordes of recent *émigrés* applied *en masse* to return to Odessa, and fell to the ground, kissing the Potemkin steps the moment they arrived: I laughed myself into stitches over that one, knowing the location of the Potemkin steps, and how far they are from the customs hall through which any 'returnees' would have to pass before setting foot on their native soil. Then there was the one about how best to frustrate KGB efforts at covert monitoring of one's home through the telephone: it was said that the thing to do was to half-dial, and insert a pencil in the finger-holes so that the dial could not return to its neutral position: it's hard to imagine a better way of alerting the telephone exchange to the probability that something 'unsanctioned' is being discussed at that address. All this is done on the assumption that people don't know how to check the validity of this or that piece of information. Just for the heck of it, we once deliberately traced one such rumour all the way back to its source, who turned out to be a pathetic creature, a known KGB informer, who flatly refused to disclose who had told *him* that particular bit of 'news'.

We applied ourselves conscientiously to learning all we could about the methods employed by the KGB, and how to combat them. In fact, the formula for countering them is quite simple: don't believe them, don't fear them, don't ask them for anything. If they summon you for questioning – don't answer; if they put you away – keep your mouth shut; and while you're still at liberty – try to accomplish as much as possible. If by some chance you manage to get your hands on some smoked sausage or a can of condensed milk – give it to those who organise the passing of food into the camps or psychiatric hospitals. If you have some *samizdat* – make sure that as many people as possible get to read it. *Samizdat* that is not worth the paper it's written on drops out of circulation very quickly: why should anyone risk years of imprisonment for reading rubbish? Because of this, *samizdat* is the most prestigious 'publisher' in the world for any author. And the most dangerous. The trials of Sinyavsky and Daniel are in the past; these days *samizdat* authors are persecuted more discreetly, behind closed doors. But the train wheels turn, taking the unsubmissive ones away 'for years, for long, long years', as they say in the song.

Fedorchuk, the chairman of the Ukrainian KGB, noted with satisfaction at a banquet on the 'Day of the Chekist' that over the past year, such and such a number of dissidents was packed off to camps and psychiatric institutions, and that more than half were sentenced on criminal charges so as not to attract the attention of the Western press. There were more than a thousand KGB officials and their wives at this banquet, so, of course, his words got out. Fedorchuk reigns supreme in the Ukraine. In other republics, his equivalents are also not letting any grass grow under their feet: who'll make the best career? Fedorchuk proved to be the most diligent, however. Soon afterward he was promoted to the post of chairman of the KGB for the whole of the USSR, even though later he was demoted to Minister of Internal Affairs. But it was his signature which graced the notorious labour camp Rules of Internal Order: about the issue of hot food only every second day in punishment cells, about the number of socks a prisoner might have, about punishment by deprivation of parcels and meetings with relatives, about censorship of mail ... Later still, Fedorchuk was 'devoured' in a power struggle by his own colleagues, and he disappeared into obscurity after yet another Party conference. The rank ingratitude! The poor man had bent over backwards to excel, going right back to the war, when he supervised mass executions by firing squads in Western Ukraine. Yet, despite all that . . . !

The multitude of methods devised by the KGB is truly awe-inspiring. We could not help being impressed by the sheer creativity its minions displayed. Things like bugging apartments and surveillance are mere trifles, simple daily routine, you might say. How much more effective it is to have KGB officers following you around quite openly, and pressuring you psychologically by repeatedly uttering threats such as, "We'll break your arms and legs, you bastard, see if we don't!"

Occasionally, these threats are put into practice. Beating people up in the streets is very popular among the Ukrainian KGB. They make no concessions to sex, as is evidenced by the assaults suffered by Lydia Ruban, the wife of a long-term political prisoner, or dissident activist Olya Matusevich. Mind you, the Moscow KGB does its best to keep up: they have beaten up people like Vladimir Bukovsky, Sergei Khodorovich, Nina Lisovskaya, and many, many others.

Another popular method is known colloquially as 'a woman with a cake'.

There was the case of one Feldman, who protested strenuously about being refused an exit visa. So it came about that when he was returning home late one night – at 2 a.m., to be precise – a woman approached him in the bus shelter, and dropped a box she was carrying right at his feet. Straight after that, she began to yell at the top of her voice: "Help! I'm being attacked!"

And lo and behold, two hulking men emerged from behind some bushes, grabbed Feldman and twisted his arms behind his back. Right on cue, a militia car drew up, and before you knew it, the 'smart-arse refusenik' found himself on trial on charges of 'hooliganism'. Luckily for Feldman, his defence lawyer proved to be an exception to the rule, and carried out a cross-examination of the 'victim' which has become a legend by now.

"Why wasn't there a cord around the box in which you were carrying your cake?"

No answer.

"Where did you buy the cake?"

"In the Slavutich shop."

"But it was a 'Kiev Torte', manufactured by the Karl Marx factory. Did you transfer it to another box?"

"No, I was coming straight from the shop."

"At two o'clock in the morning? All right, let's say for the present that you were."

The lawyer sent off an official enquiry to the 'Slavutich', asking whether they sold cakes manufactured by the Karl Marx factory. It turned out that they didn't, but got their entire stock from the local bakery.

"Why are you lying?" demanded the lawyer.

The 'victim' burst into tears and admitted that she had been forced to do so. By whom? She refused to say, just went on crying. Fine. The lawyer then turned his attention to the two men who had so miraculously emerged from the shrubbery.

"Where are you from?"

"The Ministry of Internal Affairs school."

"Where do you live?"

"In the school's students' quarters."

"That's on the right bank of the Dnieper. What were you doing on the left bank at two o'clock in the morning?"

"We'd been to a friend's birthday party."

"What's this friend's name?"

They gave a name, and the lawyer demanded that this person be called as a witness. When he came and showed his passport, Feldman's lawyer pounced: "His birthday is in two months' time. Why are you lying?"

Uproar! The scheme fell through! But it would be naïve to expect that Feldman was cleared of the charges for lack of acceptable evidence. No, they simply sentenced him to three years instead of the expected five, and packed him off to a labour camp.

'Democracy in full swing' was the grim joke that went around Kiev in connection with this trial. By that time nobody found it surprising that one of the 'Ukrainian nationalists' had allegedly managed to rape a woman in two minutes (in front of witnesses) in a bus shelter in temperatures around minus 20°C. Slava Zubko, a refusenik, was accused of secreting a pistol in his refrigerator, and of keeping drugs on a bookshelf. This latter case, admittedly, called for some groundwork by the KGB: Slava was summoned to the militia, and his mother to the residents' committee of their house. They were kept there, without any explanation, for hours, and allowed to go only late that evening. Both returned home tired and depressed, and didn't think to search their apartment before going to bed. The next morning the doorbell rang: house-search! Those who carried out the search did not even bother going through the motions of looking for anything, but went straight to the refrigerator and the bookshelf: they were in a hurry.

"Right, what's this?"

"It was all obviously planted there by you."

"Yes, that's what they all say! Come on, get dressed and come with us! Witnesses! – Sign the protocol!"

So Slava was put away. I encountered his mother later, outside the prison. In those days it was customary to go to the prison gates when someone was due for release after being detained for fifteen days, so that there would be witnesses if the KGB tried to stage some kind of new provocation against that person. Slava's small, grey-haired mother was there to meet someone else's son: her own had been sentenced to years, not a mere fifteen days . . .

It's even easier for the KGB to bring trumped-up charges of theft from work. They did that to Petro Ruban. Or to accuse someone of forgery, as they did with Yanenko in connection with a document inviting him to take part in a university session.

"Aha!" they said, "you forged this paper in order to secure extra leave from work, didn't you? That's fraud!"

The fact that the dean's secretary testified at the trial that she had personally written out and sent the invitation in question, made not one iota of difference. The train wheels keep turning, repeating their message: "To the camp, to the camp, for long years, for long years . . ."

Petro Ruban remained unbroken, Leonid Korsunsky didn't. Neither did Kuvakin, nor Volokhonsky, nor many others. One would give way before the threat of death, another succumb to blackmail, yet another sell out for better conditions for himself in the camp. Former inmates of Soviet labour camps knew without doubt that the one who was given the duty of cutting up bread was to be avoided. This was a task assigned to thieves or to those who were doing something on instructions from the camp administration.

If you recant at your trial, there is one thing you will never be able to forgive in connection with your shame: no, it won't be the KGB – you will find hundreds of excuses for yourself and for them. You will never forgive those who didn't break, those who turned out to be stronger than you. And those you will hate to your dying day: because they remained 'clean'. And all your anger and humiliation will be channelled towards blackening them, so that everyone will be in the same boat. In the meantime, the comrades from the KGB will stand back, rubbing their hands with glee: that's right, boys, let them have it! Get them! Attack! At the same time, Western observers will only shrug uncomprehendingly: how is it that yesterday's dissidents are always at each others' throats? Oh, these Russians! But there are also those who broke, but who blame nobody but themselves, there are those who remain in the shadows, lending unobtrusive, but sterling assistance to those who elect to act in the open. There are more and more names of those who refused to surrender their freedom, and this brings us hope. Their memory is a bright one, but, alas, all too often – posthumous.

Chapter Twenty-eight

"Irka, let's go to the Botanical Gardens!"

"The new, or the old?"

"The new ones, and take a look at the Dnieper. Down the bottom there, where the Gardens end, there's a lovely spot: it's really wild, and so overgrown that you can barely force your way through. Nobody goes there. And you know what's there?"

"What?"

"No, I'm not going to tell you!"

"What if I die from curiosity on the way?"

"I'll keep a finger on your pulse. Come on, get dressed!"

To be able just to get up and go is the most important human quality after elementary decency.

I don't need persuading, and here we are, on a bank high above the river: the pre-autumnal beauty of the Gardens stretches behind us, down below is the Kiev Monastery of the Caves (the monks were expelled, but the holiness of the site remains), in front of us is the Dnieper, and beyond that – the left bank and the horizon.

"When I was small, I always used to wish that I could take off and fly from here. Irka! Why are you so quiet? Do you feel a poem coming on?"

"I'm praying."

He falls silent, too. What do we pray about? I don't know. Neither of us knows how to pray with words – well, not properly. Thank You, Lord, for the Dnieper, for these high banks, thank You that we are here under Your skies, and together, and happy. And for all that has been, and is yet to come. Amen.

The promised surprise turns out to be an old nut tree, which has been split by lightning. It's outside the boundary of the Gardens, so that means we are free to take some of its pieces.

"See? Somebody has already sawn off some bits. The sculptors must have got to hear about it."

"Don't tell me you've got your eye on that stump? It wouldn't fit through our door. And, anyway, you'd need a truck to shift it."

"No, but look – there are some smaller branches here, and smaller stumps: can you imagine how they'll look in cross-section? Remember I told you how I wanted to make a figure of a monk on a cliff? It will be my best creation!"

We return home laden and covered in scratches. We are dying to cut up and survey our loot.

"We'll need a circular saw for this. I know someone who'll lend me one. I've got a whole eight days' compensatory time due to me at work, I'll take it and make a start tomorrow."

"Perhaps it would be better to add those days to your annual leave?"

"That's still ages away. I'll work up some more comp. time by then: it's not bad, being the goose that lays golden eggs! They treat me with kid gloves in that place, all the calculating work depends on me. And there's a whole horde of would-be co-authors for various projects. The only nuisance is that the Party organiser is making up to me; he wants to be an inventor, too."

"What's it this time?"

"Helium purifiers. I'll explain the whole idea to you when we get home: it's a beauty! Anyway, to hell with him, let him hang around: he's absolutely useless workwise, but the invention will have to be dragged through the whole bureaucratic process, and that's right up his street: especially if he has a vested interest in it."

But Igor's compensatory time did not materialise. The next day at work he was summoned to the office of the head engineer. Another man was in the office with him.

"How do you do, Igor Olegovich?" said the stranger, extending a hand. "My name's Anatoli Vasilyevich."

"How do you do?"

A handshake can say a great deal about a person, and Igor is immediately wary: this is not a typically open male hand.

"I dropped around here to give you a lift. That saves everyone a lot of inconvenience. We need to have a talk. But not here."

"Where, then?"

"At 33 Vladimirskaya Street. Perhaps you've heard the address?"

"Most definitely! In that case, please show me the summons, and also your identity card."

"What a stickler you are for formalities, Igor Olegovich!"

"I am not a member of the KGB, and unless you have a summons, there is no reason why I should accompany you."

Igor copies the data from the proffered identity card: KGB Major Avilov, and his name and patronymic are as he said. He produces a summons: everything is in order.

"I'll be back in a moment."

"Where do you think you're going?"

"You don't have an arrest warrant, so I have the right to make a phone call home."

Not surprisingly, the telephone is engaged, but that's not Igor's main concern: there's a whole file of my poems in his bag, he'd promised to give them to a friend to read. Igor quickly makes arrangements for the safety of the file, and returns to the office.

"Telephone engaged, Igor Olegovich?"

"How knowledgeable you are!"

A black Volga stands outside, in traditional KGB fashion. They really love to play for effect, these lads, especially with novices. Igor has never yet been summoned to the KGB, so in their eyes he's a greenhorn. Well, comrades, let's see how well you manage . . .

The office into which Igor is ushered looks very ordinary: portraits of Lenin and Brezhnev on the wall, standard office furniture. The interrogation begins very mildly.

"You probably know why you've been asked to come here?"

"I'm sure you will explain it all to me."

"I've heard that you and your wife are intending to emigrate?"

Heavens, it's taken them this long? It's odd, really: so much time has passed, and we haven't even lodged any new applications. Obviously, there's more to this than meets the eye: so they didn't let us leave, so what? Lots of people are refused exit visas, and Slavs don't even qualify. With the possible exception of those who enjoy world fame. So why should the KGB be interested? Admittedly, our application was not worded in quite the usual way: human rights are not a popular issue in official quarters. No, they must have got wind that emigration is not our chief concern at the moment.

"I have no intention of discussing my personal plans with you."

"This is a state matter, Igor Olegovich. You have been involved in classified work."

Igor laughed: "Come now, you must have my personal dossier from the first section. All the projects I've worked on are listed there, and not a single one of them has rated classified status."

"Do you remember being sent on assignment to the Prometheus factory?"

"Of course. That was in connection with the production of bimetallic slabs. There was no secrecy attached to that. You know, I'm allergic to classified work. I've never signed any kind of undertakings for your lot in my life."

"In that case, let's take a look at what others have signed, seeing you brought up the subject of your personal dossier. Well, now: from the university we have information that you have Ukrainian nationalist leanings. You have praised Western technology in private conversations, and criticised the Party. Furthermore, you've made very prejudicial observations about Afghanistan. Ah, here's one from the Prometheus works, too – we sent them a query. It says here that while it's true that you didn't have access to classified information, you could have found out about it if you'd wanted to."

"About what?"

"Surely you can guess! Submarines."

"As a matter of fact, I hadn't guessed. It's interesting, though. Incidentally, who are the signatories to all these snippets you've regaled me with?"

"Come now, you're expecting too much . . . ! However, let's get back to the subject: tell me, what on earth would you do in the West? It's dog eat dog there! Where would you find a job like the one you've got here? You're a specialist, and that means – if you'll excuse my plain speaking! – that you're good for nothing!"

"I'm afraid I don't follow your logic. If that's the case, why is any intention of mine to emigrate a state concern?"

"Igor Olegovich, have you ever studied article fifty-six of the Criminal Code of the Ukrainian republic? Treason is an offence punishable by imprisonment from ten to fifteen years, or by execution by firing squad. I suggest that you give it some thought."

"I am perfectly conversant with that article. Studying Soviet laws is a hobby of mine. However, what is the relevance in this instance?"

"Why, because we can invoke it at any moment – against you, personally."

"How? Am I a spy?"

"Through article seventeen, since you are so well-versed in the law."

Igor roared with laughter: "By intent? Oh, that's marvellous!"

Avilov became visibly angry: stage effects designed to intimidate disintegrate in the face of unfeigned mirth.

"You're not in a circus here, Igor Olegovich! Yes, by intent! And don't worry, we'll find witnesses who'll testify that you intend to sell our country's secrets to the West: various details about the fittings on our submarines, for instance."

"What kind of fittings? Taps? Waste-disposal units?"

"Never mind what kind!"

"Well, I suggest that you determine first what it is I'm supposed to want to sell, otherwise your case doesn't sound very convincing."

"On top of that, there's anti-Soviet agitation and propaganda. What do you say to that?"

"That's quite a radical drop in the level of possible punishment, isn't it? From the threat of a bullet, to a maximum of seven years' imprisonment?"

"Citizen Geraschenko, jokes are out of place around here. Sign this to attest that you have been officially warned."

"Listen, what kind of a fool do you take me for? First you produce a stack of anonymous reports, then you threaten me with a firing squad, after that you go on about intent to commit a crime . . . And you want me to sign an attestation to all that nonsense? Have I violated any Soviet laws to this day?"

"No. Not yet."

"In that case – goodbye."

"I haven't signed a release chit for you yet. Follow me! You refused to be reasonable with me, so let's see how you get along with someone else."

He shepherds Igor down a long corridor, walking behind and clicking his fingers, the way gaolers do when escorting prisoners. Igor finds the whole scenario frankly amusing: it's so cheap and predictable.

"What interesting sounds you're making! Just as described in the *Gulag Archipelago*. How do you do it?"

"Just keep walking!" grunts Avilov, but the finger-clicking stops: why bother, if it doesn't produce the desired effect?

They enter another office. Here, the portraits on the walls are of Lenin and Dzerzhinsky, the founder of the first forerunner of the KGB, the CHEKA. An elderly man in plain clothes sits behind a desk.

"Good day to you, Igor Olegovich. I'm Vasili Vasilyevich Poskrebyshev. It's time we met. I hear you're contemplating leaving the country. Now, I can understand the Jews going, but you? You're one of our lads! We should be working hand in hand! You showed so much early promise, you're a first-rate specialist. Maybe you feel that your present job doesn't offer you enough scope? Well, you've enough published work to rate a dissertation, and another job can be found easily enough."

"I'm sorry, Vasili Vasilyevich, but there seems to be some kind of contradiction here: a few minutes ago Major Avilov was saying that I'm good for nothing, and now here you are calling me an excellent specialist. So which of these two versions shall we consider valid?"

Avilov began to edge towards the door, but the other tapped a finger on the table, and the major froze in his tracks. Oho! Just how high up the ladder is this Poskrebyshev?

In the meantime, Poskrebyshev continues to shower Igor with compliments, hints at a brilliant career, repeats the business about working hand in hand and shoulder to shoulder, wonders afresh at the 'strange idea' of emigration. At this point, if you agree to give up ideas of emigrating, Poskrebyshev will immediately begin to organise his version of 'working shoulder to shoulder'. And your acquiescence will not be perceived as a strength, but as a weakness to be exploited: give the KGB a finger, and they'll take not just your whole arm, but your head as well. Igor knows this full well, so he states his position clearly: "On the basis of international agreements, every citizen enjoys the right to leave his own country."

"There you go again about rights," remarked Poskrebyshev reproachfully. "Very well, sign this paper indicating that you have been cautioned."

"I'll do no such thing. There's not a word in the Criminal Procedural Code about any obligation to sign cautions of any kind."

And so they parted. At the last moment, Major Avilov did an astonishing thing: when he escorted Igor out of the building, he extended a hand, just as though nothing had happened.

"No," said Igor. "I'll not shake hands with you!"

"But why, Igor Olegovich? We began our acquaintance with a handshake!"

"I didn't know who you were then."

Truly, these KGB men are a race apart! I wonder if they try to shake hands with people before putting them in front of a firing squad?

At home I'm awaiting Igor with some interesting news: I've received a summons to report to the KGB.

"Oh, so they're going to have a go at you, too? I'm just back from seeing them."

He tells me about everything that happened.

"So they're trying the old carrot-and-stick method?"

"Looks like it. Well, we'll see what they try to stick onto you. Attempted rape, maybe? Still, every cloud has a silver lining: here I am at home, and it's only three o'clock in the afternoon. I didn't even have to ask for time off!"

That very day, we sawed up the wood we had brought back from the Botanical Gardens: the sections turned out even better than we'd hoped for: beautiful, intricate rings and whorls, ranging in colour from almost black through to pale yellow.

The song Avilov sang to me next day was quite different: not a word about emigration, nor about treason. He read out no anonymous denunciations, and he did not take me along to Poskrebyshev. In fact, he began by complimenting me on my appearance, a compliment entirely due to the embroidery done by my mother-in-law on my outfit: she's a true expert of the art. Not to be outdone, I complimented

Avilov on the colour of his tie, after which he got down to business.

"You write poetry, Irina Borisovna, and other things besides. Like totally unnecessary declarations, for example. And the people with whom you associate are, frankly speaking, very suspicious characters: that includes foreign journalists, and our own social misfits. I suggest you stop all this tomfoolery! That applies equally to you and your husband!"

"And what, precisely, do you want me to stop?"

"You know perfectly well what I mean. All this anti-Soviet activity. Otherwise, you'll have to pay a heavy penalty."

"You must excuse my thick-headedness: what's criminal in my activities? My poetry, or my declarations on issues of human rights, or my choice of friends? Does the law specify with whom one may or may not associate?"

"Irina Borisovna, you are a woman of intellect. I'm talking to you about serious matters, and you're throwing laws at me. We can invoke laws too, if need be. Sign this, please, to attest that you've been cautioned in connection with Article Sixty-two of the Ukrainian Criminal Code – anti-Soviet agitation and propaganda."

Of course, I refused, but this time Avilov kept a tight grip on his temper, having learned a lesson from his encounter with Igor. As we parted, he gallantly held the door open for me, voiced a few more pleasantries, and gladdened me with the news that he was now our minder, and we were bound to have further similarly cosy meetings in the future.

Developments followed swiftly: a trade union meeting was called in Igor's department at work, with only one item on the agenda: to condemn Geraschenko's intention to emigrate as an act unworthy of a Soviet citizen. And to condemn the said Geraschenko and his behaviour, too. Actually, Igor was offered the opportunity to speak, and he utilised it to say that at meetings at work he was prepared to account for his professional performance, and nothing else. Did anyone have any questions about his work?

"No, no questions about your work. Who persuaded you to apply to emigrate? Your wife?"

"I've already told you, I have no intention of discussing my personal affairs here. In any case, why do you think that everyone is so easily led? I ask you again: do I owe the trade union anything? Have I violated work discipline? Do I do my work satisfactorily? As for anything else – that's my private business."

The resolution to 'condemn' Igor was passed, with three abstentions. Later, people came up to him in the corridors, patted him on the shoulder: "Igor, pal, I hope you understand . . ."

Igor did, and took no offence. But he felt sorry for them, and sick about the whole situation.

He didn't eat much in those days, and his mother became worried: "Darling, you'll waste away! Just look at you already – skin and bones! I don't know how Irka can tolerate you like that! Ira, you tell him . . . !"

The three who abstained from the vote to condemn Igor were summoned individually by the department head, who tried to cajole or threaten them into adding their names to those who had voted 'for'. One finally gave in, but the other two, Boris and Peter, remained firm.

"We were idiots not to vote against the motion," they said to Igor later. "The hassle would have been the same, and now we feel ashamed to look you in the face because we merely abstained . . ."

Oh, these half-measures! The state system will not accept them: you have to make a clear choice either way. Try to be neutral, and you will be considered just as much an enemy, but a cunning one. Psychologically, it's very hard to go against an entire system: you always feel alone, and that if the system decides to make mincemeat out of you there'll be nobody to help. Igor reassured Boris and Peter as best he could: had they not proved themselves to be braver than all the others?

Igor's dismissal from work came as no surprise: he had earlier been summoned to the Presidium of the Ukrainian Academy of Sciences, where senior administrator Tsymko, without beating about the bush, said to him: "Resign!"

"No way!"

"Then we'll fire you in such a way that you'll never get another job!"

"Do you have any legal grounds to do so?"

"We don't need laws to deal with the likes of you!"

An unscheduled review of Igor's work was hastily carried out. There was not a single engineer–thermal physicist in the committee, but there was the works Party organiser, the Komsomol organiser and the head of the personnel department. After a session lasting ten minutes this committee pronounced him professionally inadequate, and on 3rd November (his birthday, as it happens) they fired him.

We had been expecting this. We had Tsymko's personal assurance, as well as those of the KGB, that neither of us need hope to get even a janitor's job. Some friends in Leningrad had already instructed us on how to avoid making ourselves liable for prosecution under the 'parasitism' article of the Criminal Code. Their advice was to file an official declaration with the regional fiscal department to the effect that you work from home as a self-employed typist (which was perfectly true in this case, only money didn't enter into it). Not a single tax inspector would believe for a moment that someone would officially claim to be a typist and be willing to pay taxes if there was no income. Their main concern would be to establish who gives you work, and how much undeclared income you've salted away. Well, they would have a long and exhausting search in this instance!

However, the tax must be paid, and some kind of income must be assured in order to buy the occasional piece of clothing, and to pay for transport.

"Igor, I've got two more potential students."

"Over my dead body! You're already flat out, rushing back and forth like a scalded cat! I'm the man, I'll earn the money!"

Our hobby – Soviet law – proved unexpectedly useful. The law forbids the sale of amateur handicrafts out of certain materials (there is a long list, including just about everything except wood, non-precious stones and rope). There was also a list of proscribed precious stones, but it did not include agates or amber. Excellent! How would you fancy a ring made out of dark wood, with an agate? Or a pendant made out of juniper wood, studded with amber? Metal chains are not necessary, because macramé is all the rage. Crosses carved out of cypress wood, wall decorations of various kinds . . . Our first client with a taste for the original sent along others, and we soon had a steady stream of women wanting our wares. We would let them take their own pick of polished stones, and every item we made was a one-off, because we designed each piece individually. Rings, of course, were made to measure. Our clients were particularly impressed that Igor didn't use any kind of device to gauge the diameter of their finger, but determined it by touch. They were not to know that as an adolescent he worked among leading toolmakers, who used to amuse themselves by seeing who could most exactly estimate the diameter of a rod by feel or by sight.

We did have problems with electric tools, but Igor managed to borrow or exchange what we needed, stone polishers and diamond cutters. Officially, these could only be bought by members of the Union of Artists.

Igor's mother and sister bewailed the sale of every single item we produced: "It's so beautiful . . . !"

"Well, I don't produce junk! Come on, Mama, which one do you want? The one with agate, or the one with amber?"

"I've already got an amber one. No, son, you sell them, you pamper us too much!"

"Women should be pampered! Come on, Mum, spare me the business of having to make decisions for New Year: choose an agate for yourself, and also something for Lyalya and Irka. But we won't tell them about it yet . . ."

Chapter Twenty-nine

"Children, are you spending New Year's Eve with us?"

"We're not sure yet. Probably yes, but we'll have to go up to Moscow some time in December."

"What for?"

"Mum, you know you promised not to ask any questions!"

"All right, all right, I won't say another word! Are you both going?"

"Yes."

"You'll give me a heart-attack with all these goings-on, you'll see! But then it will be too late! You're driving me half out of my mind as it is! What are you up to now?"

"Now, Mum . . ."

Igor puts his arms around her, rocking her back and forth like a baby: "Let's fry up some pork scratchings, shall we? And you promised to show us that new piece of embroidery – we were going to knock up a copy of a new pattern for you . . ."

"Don't think you can put me off by changing the subject! Pork scratchings and embroidery patterns my foot! Just wait until you have children of your own, then you'll see what it's like!"

We submit meekly to all her strictures, knowing that the storm never lasts long. When she's letting off steam it's better not to argue. Occasionally we do argue, but that's due to our youthful lack of restraint, which we were to regret later. Mama is actively kind, never hesitating to step forward and help in cases of real need.

When Igor's sister went into hospital to have her second baby, we used the time to decide what colours to buy for redecorating the apartment, but Mama spent long hours at the maternity hospital. On the second day she came home, bringing an unknown woman with her.

"Children! Set up a camp bed in Gran's and my room!"

She settled her exhausted guest down to sleep, and then told us the whole story. Mama saw the woman standing outside the hospital and crying. She would not have been herself if she had not immediately tried to find out what was the matter. It turned out that the woman lived somewhere near Ternopol, with her daughter and forester son-in-law. The daughter was doing a correspondence course at an institute in Kiev. She was pregnant, and when the doctors estimated the date of the baby's birth, they added on three weeks. This is a common practice in the polyclinics, because it cuts down the amount of paid leave women take off before childbirth: by law, they should be released from work on paid maternity leave two months before the birth, but this way is more profitable for the state. So the doctors have their instructions, but this family, living out in the backwoods, did not know, and took the doctors at their word. They estimated that the daughter still had time to travel to Kiev and sit for exams, thereby not losing a year of study. The mother accompanied her just in case, and thank goodness that she did. The daughter's first contractions began when they arrived at the bus depot in Kiev. The mother took her daughter to the nearest maternity clinic, but found herself with nowhere to go. All the hotels were full, so was the Collective Farmers' hostel, and if you tried to sleep at the bus station, they chased you away. And she, poor soul, had sore feet, and was worried about her daughter, and was dead tired. No wonder she was in tears!

"There's no question about it!" declared Mama. "We have room to put her up!"

Lyalya was still waiting to give birth, but our unexpected guest's daughter, Natalia, was discharged very quickly, nursing a three-day-old daughter. But what was to be done? They could hardly undertake the bus journey to Ternopol with a newborn baby!

"She must come here, of course," decided Mama. "Let them both catch their breath a bit: we've got enough room!"

She hastily rigged up another camp-bed, which she sent Igor to borrow from one of the neighbours.

"We'll put the baby here, see – we've already made up a crib for her! And we'll get hold of some nappies, don't worry!"

A taxi delivers Natalia and a tiny, red, crumpled being. The little being's eyes won't open: the lids are stuck to each other with a layer of pus. Her tiny buttocks are covered with angry suppurations. My God, how do they tend new-born babies in that place?! Natalia is very weak and we put her to bed straight away. What were they thinking of, discharging her in such a state? By the evening, Natalia is running a fever, and the baby screams incessantly. We don't know what to do, Natalia's mother is weeping, and ours is issuing orders: "Igor! Call an ambulance straight away!"

Help arrives, mother and baby are examined.

"The mother has puerperal fever. Blood poisoning. Did she have to have stitches?"

"Yes, it's her first baby."

"It's hard to say what's wrong with the baby's eyes, but she must be taken immediately to the Protection of Mothers and Children Hospital. The mother will have to go to another hospital, we'll arrange it straight away. Why on earth were they discharged? Your home address?"

"Actually, they're from the Ternopol region . . ."

"Ah, they're from out of town! That's why they were discharged so quickly from the hospital – to keep the mortality statistics down! It's easier to chuck people out into the street than to treat them. They're not registered in Kiev, so everything can be swept under the carpet."

"Mortality?! Doctor, are they going to die?" cries Natalia's mother, beside herself with terror.

"I'm not God, so I can't say. But we'll get them into hospital right away. Come on, calm down. Let me fill in the forms, don't grab my hand all the time! What's the infant's name?"

"We haven't picked one yet."

"Well, just give me any name! I must fill in these forms!"

Natalia is unconscious, her mother is in hysterics, and Igor and I stand there like stuffed dummies.

"Lesya!" says Igor's mother, taking the plunge. And so she was recorded as Lesya. The doctor ushers Natalia's weeping mother into the next room, and continues with the necessary questions: "Is this your apartment?"

"Yes."

"Dictate the exact address, please. Are you a relative?"

"No."

"Well, how come these people are here?"

"We took them in from the street."

"Just like that? What if she'd died here, who would have been responsible? Have you any idea how much trouble you'd have landed yourself in? Are you mad?"

"So what – should I have left her to die in the street?"

Mama flares up easily, but right now her tone is icy, and so are her eyes. The ambulance staff lapse into uneasy silence: they were borne by mothers, too.

"Stretcher! Let's go!"

The news at first was not encouraging. When Natalia's mother went to the hospital where the baby was being treated, she received unwelcome information: "The first twenty-four hours we fed the baby with milk from a donor. We might be able to manage for another twenty-four, but after that, you'll have to bring us milk from the mother."

"That's impossible! She was in a fever, and the milk stopped!"

"Well, there's nothing we can do about that. We can't risk putting the baby on powdered milk, she's too weak. You'll just have to get some from somewhere. You must realise, your grand-daughter isn't the only baby here. What do you expect us to do? Milk each other? We just don't have enough milk for your baby, and that's that!"

Luckily, Lyalya was back home by now with a healthy baby, and had plenty of milk. She would express it into a jar, and Mama would proudly proclaim that "all the women in our family never had any trouble feeding their babies". Natalia's mother would take this milk to the hospital where the baby was, and then travel to the other hospital to see her daughter, right on the other side of town. Lyalya willingly 'milked herself', noting wryly that she had enough milk for three, let alone two babies.

"The Lord will remember your good deed, daughter!" opined Mama happily. "Remember, you donated some of your milk for little Maksim, when Anna was born, and now you're helping with Lesya. They're your 'milk children'. All the others are healthy, and this little one will pull through with your milk, you'll see!"

And Lesya and Natalia did both pull through. We saw them off home, and shortly afterwards received a letter from Natalia's mother:

Dear Larisa Ivanovna! I'm so sorry not to have written sooner, but my Natalia had to go into hospital again: they didn't finish the treatment properly in Kiev. But now all's well. Please come to see us as soon as you get a chance: you are like a close relative to us now. We decided to christen the baby Lesya, just as you called her. She is already able to smile and say "Goo!" She's lovely, and her eyes are ever so blue . . .

That's our Mama. By the time we set off for Moscow, she is no longer cross.

"Let's sit down for a moment before your journey," she says quietly. "And now – God go with you!" We found out later that she had already worked out why we were going to Moscow: 10th December is Human Rights Day, and it has become an unwritten tradition for dissidents and sympathisers to gather around the statue of Pushkin on this day after work, bare their heads and observe five minutes' silence. Five minutes of silence to symbolise the lack of human rights in our country. It's also in memory of those who perished in the camps, and those who are there now, and those who must endure daily humiliations perpetrated by the 'comrade superiors', who demand daily lies and enforced applause.

The participants in this demonstration are usually seized by the militia, thrown into vans, driven out of the city, beaten up and left in the snow. Occasionally they will arrest some people, or take them down to the militia precinct, where they are bullied and threatened before being released. Anything can happen, and this year our place is there, too: the ranks of Muscovites capable of going to the square for this silent public demonstration have thinned.

We stay at Lera Senderov's place. He casts a meaningful look at Igor: oh, Lord, they're 'protecting' me again! No, really, this is too much! My dear ones, it's quite enough for me that when you notice how I sometimes seem to drift off in the middle of a conversation, you tactfully leave me alone, knowing that poems start to appear in my head without any warning: in the metro, on a train, during a walk, you shove a piece of paper and a pencil into my hands, then take a copy of the completed original and brew me a cup of tea, as I sit there tired and drained. You surround me with the gentle circle of silence among friends. As if there were some kind of conspiracy! And maybe you have conspired to that effect? However, there are limits to everything!

Lera seems unable to understand the reasons for my rebellion: "For your information, ladies and gentlemen, I have no intention of going to the Pushkin monument. This time there is going to be so much scum there, including informers and snotty-nosed youngsters with inferiority complexes. You know, the kind who hover on the fringes of the dissident movement? Really, do you want to join them? Haven't you got anything better to do?"

"We're from the provinces, Lera, and we don't know anything about your Moscow castes and cliques. Nor do we want to. We only know that the idea is a clean and honest one. As for who thinks what of whom – well, these are Moscow concerns, and none of our business."

"You may be right, at that. If it's a matter of conscience, it's not for me to try to dissuade you. Are you willing to take an observer along?"

"We've got Bob Gillette, an American journalist, coming along as an observer. To take a look at how even a peaceful, silent demonstration is treated in our country. He's got his camera at the ready. We've agreed that he'll follow us, and just watch what happens, without interfering."

We exchange smiles with Bob at the metro station: he's got good eyes, this man. From here, we go down into the underpass, and he'll follow about twenty paces behind us. As soon as we emerge from the underpass, we are surrounded by plain clothes KGB.

"Get around behind!"

"Stand still, don't move!"

Oh, like that, is it? I raise my voice and yell loudly enough to be heard right around the square: "Help! Robbery!"

A militiaman comes haring over: "Quiet, quiet! It's all right, we're hunting for a criminal. We'll sort things out in a moment, but stop shouting!"

"Where's your arrest warrant?"

"Don't worry, you'll get your warrant! That is, I mean – we'll sort everything out right now."

They've cornered Bob, too, but he has his *Los Angeles Times* press card, and they decide against tangling with a foreigner. We, on the other hand, are propelled into a militia bus. It's already full: everyone was grabbed as they approached the square.

The man right next to us introduces himself: "Rossiysky."

Sounds like a pseudonym: it's a bit too pat and symbolic. We name ourselves.

"Don't think I've heard your names before."

"We're from Kiev."

"Ah, that explains it . . . they'll take us round to a militia station now, give us a talking-to and let us go. I've been through all this before."

"If they let you go, but detain us . . ."

"Don't worry, they'll release everybody. I know how they work! Just a nice little jaunt . . ."

"Still, could you take down a phone number and call it should anything happen . . . ?"

"Sure. What's the number?"

Rossiysky did not make any phone call on our behalf, even though the Muscovites were released, and the ones from out of town were detained 'for clarification of circumstances'. My first body search. What a revolting feeling it is to have a woman in militia uniform running her hands all over you! Igor was put into a preliminary detention cell, and I went into a general cell facing the duty officer's desk.

A major of some kind appeared on the scene: "Why did you come to Moscow? Where are you staying?"

"I should like to know under what charges I am being held here."

He smiles sweetly: "A woman had her earrings stolen at that station."

"And you're accusing me of that theft?"

"Not yet. But we might. So, are you going to answer my questions?"

"No."

"Well, take a seat on that stool. Maybe you'll change your mind by morning."

My throat is parched, but there's no sense in asking for a drink: you won't get anything for free around here. An hour passes. Two hours. They bring in a drunk, then an obvious prostitute, then a man who looks as though he's been around, and knows it all. He casts a knowing eye over the assembled company, and addresses me: "What are you here for?"

"For your rights."

"What rights?"

"You're human, aren't you? That means you have rights. Even though that's probably not the reason you're here."

"Our rights are a quick punch in the face. Are you a 'political'?"

"I suppose so."

"Oh, well . . . That means they won't release you tomorrow. Look, girlie, you're not pulling my leg, are you?"

"Hardly."

"So tell me in more detail."

"I went to take part in a demonstration."

"Good God! I tell you, kid, forget about that kind of stuff! Listen to me – I've been in the camps – not for your kind of activity, true, but I know what the camps are like. And the transports, with their trained Alsatians. What would you do in those hell-holes? You're young and fresh . . . Really, stay out of it!"

"But tell me, aren't you sick of the 'quick punch in the face' way?"

"Don't tell me you've decided to defend me?"

"You, too . . ."

"Some champion! A little sparrow like you . . . Tell me, someone, why do I always feel sorry for the ones like this?"

He is dragged off to be searched, and doesn't reappear.

In the morning officials in plain clothes come round, and resume questioning me.

"Tell me the charges against me."

"All right, all right, you'll be told."

They clear off, and Igor is brought out from the detention cell. We clasp hands.

"Hey! That's forbidden!"

"By whom?"

"Go and get in the car!"

"Where are you taking us?"

"You'll find out when you get there."

Apart from the driver, there's a cadaverous-looking captain of the militia in the car.

"In yesterday's demo, were you?"

"Yes."

"Well, don't worry, kids. They don't give more than fifteen days in the place I'm taking you to."

He smiled at us over his shoulder. I give you my word, he sympathises with us! His work is dealing with burglaries, thieves and drunks. He has to obey the KGB, but, like most militiamen, he does so with clenched teeth. Now his pride has been injured: some weedy KGB lieutenant is ordering him, a captain, around, and involving him in political affairs. He doesn't know why he has to take us to court, but he doesn't ask any questions: he understands that the most important thing for us now is to be able to hold hands and look at each other.

He escorts us into the court one at a time: first Igor, then me. There is a plaque on the door with the name of some 'people's judge' on it. Igor comes out.

"What happened?"

"Ten days!"

It's my turn to go in.

"Surname?"

"What about yours?" (I saw it on the plaque, but the formalities ought to be observed.)

"I ask the questions around here! And don't step on that carpet: your boots are dirty!"

"Alas, they don't offer you the chance of cleaning up in the militia station."

"Ten days! That'll teach you to push your rights!"

"Kindly give me the document with the verdict on it."

"You'll get it at the detention centre. Warder! Take her away!"

Not only Igor, but the militia captain looks at me questioningly.

"Ten days, to teach me how to push my rights," I tell them with a smile.

Our captain does a very strange thing. He leads us out into an annexe in the corridor, tells us to sit down, and walks off towards the door. He turns his back, and throws a curt order over his shoulder: "Stay here for ten minutes or so, until the car comes round."

We know perfectly well that the car is already waiting outside. Thank you, captain! We kiss, while he stands in the doorway, his back to us, hiding us from any chance passers-by. Ten minutes can be so long, and so fleeting!

"Come on, champions of rights!"

In the car he informs us that I am to be taken to the Butyrskaya Prison, where there is a section for those detained for short periods, and Igor to the men's section in Lianozovo.

"Petya! Drive around for a bit!"

The driver circles around wintry Moscow streets: this is to give us a few more minutes together. How handsome you are at this moment, my love, how warm your hands feel against my icy face! Here we are at the Butyrskaya Prison.

"Wait here."

The captain goes off for a long time. I have no idea to whom he is talking, and about what. Finally, he comes back.

"Don't say goodbye to each other," he warns us. "That's bad luck. Well, come on, little 'political'."

I am received very politely: "You can keep your bag with you, but you have to surrender your watch. Of course, this is no holiday resort ... Have you any other valuables with you? Money? Right, that's fourteen roubles and fifty kopecks: they'll be returned to you when you are released. We shan't be forcing you to work. If you have any trouble in the cell, bang on the wall. Most of the inmates here are hooligans, so you can imagine ..."

I am taken to a cell. Heads are raised from the bunks to look me over. Hooligans, eh? Big deal! People are what they are, and if I don't earn their respect, then I won't be worth it.

"Hello!"

"Hi. How many days?"

"Ten."

"See, Galka? She's got ten days and isn't howling her head off! All you got is seven, and you can't stop bawling!"

"But I got them for nothing!"

"What about you, stranger? What they get you for? What's your name?"

"Ira. They got me for taking part in a demonstration."

"Wha-a-at? You mean to say you got into a fight with the cops?"

"No, what for? It's a long story. We wanted to mark Human Rights Day."

"You a 'political', are you?"

"I suppose you could say that."

"Never mind beating about the bush: was it the MVD that took you, or the KGB?"

"The KGB."

"That means you're a 'political', all right. How about that, girls? So what – will they give you a long sentence once you've done your ten days here?"

"I don't know."

"They're not likely to let you go, you know. You know what they're like: they'll use the ten days you're in here to build up a case against you, put you on trial, and then shunt you off to the camps."

"I know. It happens."

"Well, Irisha, don't lose heart. Everything'll be all right. Here, why are you standing? Hop on to the bunks!"

In the meantime, the captain is taking Igor to Lianozovo. Now that I am no longer there, he sets out to satisfy his curiosity. It's a long journey, and there's plenty of time for a man-to-man talk. Who says that there are no tactful militiamen?

Chapter Thirty

We are nineteen in the cell, and when we all lie down on the plank bunks there's barely room to move. Galka, who's been around, laughs: "This is nothing! They had thirty-two of us in here during the Olympics, and forty in the cell next door!"

Galka is obviously from the world of petty criminals, and has seen the inside of a prison more than once. She recounts cheerfully why she is here this time: "I was drunk, see, and this cop latched on to me. So I ripped off one of his shoulder-flashes!"

My neighbour on one side is an old woman with a completely different story to tell: her neighbours in a communal flat have had an eye on her room for a long time, but she has not obliged them by dying. So they bribed the head of the area militia to trump up a case against her, alleging that she caused a disturbance by being drunk and disorderly. A couple of convictions like that, and you find yourself deprived of your Moscow residence permit.

"But Gran, are you sure you didn't . . . ?" asks Nyura, from a corner.

Galka comes to the old woman's defence: "Shame on you! Just look at her: can you imagine what'd happen to her if she downed even a hundred grams of vodka! *Then* her neighbours would get her room, no mistake, yes, and even put up a candle for the repose of her soul!"

Natasha the prostitute also weighs in with a word of support: "Really, Nyura, what are you talking about? The old girl wouldn't stand up to a puff of wind, anyone can see that! Not like you, you red-faced chunk!"

"Look at yourself, you bitch!"

I feel that it's time to intervene: "Girls, what would you like to hear about today?"

This works like a charm: hearing stories is the only entertainment available, and a story about adventures and doomed love is far more interesting than starting a brawl.

"Irisha, go on about the Count of Monte Cristo!"

"Where did we stop yesterday?"

"Where he gets into the coffin instead of that old geezer!"

"Oh, yes. Well, it was a dark and stormy night . . ."

I carry on with the retelling of the story until I am too tired to go on, and then we all settle down for the night, wrapping our jackets and coats around us – depending on who was wearing what at the time of arrest. Bedclothes are not issued here. The light is not switched off and beats down unmercifully. Igor! I'll come to you in my dreams tonight!

"Rise and shine!"

"Olya, it's your turn to take out the slop-bucket!"

This uncovered bucket which serves as a toilet is yet another of the little pleasures of prison life. There are no proper lavatory facilities in the cell. We are all marched out to the toilet in the morning. After that we eat our skilly, my fellow-prisoners are lined up, searched, and taken off to work. I am returned to the cell and locked up.

"Keep your chin up, Irisha!"

A young woman in militia uniform comes into the cell, which is searched every day in case somebody has hidden something away. They pointedly ignore my bag, so all the 'forbidden' things are stored there: a needle and thread, a razor-blade, scraps of paper and the cartridge of a ball-point pen. The duty militiawoman pokes around under the bunks, peers into the ventilator cavity – and emerges, triumphant, with a 'trophy': a plastic bag containing three compacts of face-powder.

This is a daily game for both sides. The women from my cell are taken to work in the 'Freedom' factory, which manufactures cosmetics in a joint venture with a French firm. My cell-mates are forced to work there, and get no pay. So they steal whatever they can: face creams, lipstick, powder . . . Well, I can understand about the face creams: after all, they're in for about two weeks, and you have to do something about your skin during that time – they're women, after all – but what about the rest of the stuff? And in such quantities? The matter was explained to me on my second day in the cell.

"Look at it this way: for being imprisoned, you're fined a rouble a day. So that's fifteen roubles down the drain straight away. In the meantime, you don't earn anything – for me, that's minus fifty roubles. You forfeit any bonus payments and 'thirteenth salary' at the end of the year, because they notify your place of work about your being here in the can. Count all that up, and you see how much clear profit 'they' make, the bastards?! Our food costs them thirty-two kopecks per head a day. The rest goes to the state, and they don't even pay us for the work they make us do."

"But where does face-powder come into it?"

"Because it retails at seven and a half roubles, plus two roubles for a refill. On top of that, it's a luxury item – 'Gemey', after all! If you manage to swipe enough, you can sell it later, and the time in prison will pay for itself!"

"Or they'll put you away for theft?"

"Not on your life! Even if they find it, d'you think these female cops'll be stupid enough to institute proceedings, or return the stuff to the factory? Use your loaf! They're all on temporary permits here, they haven't got permanent residence permits for Moscow. That's the only reason they take this job, to get one! And their pay's rock bottom, so it's worth their while to flog anything they find in their hostel."

Now I understand how it is that the overseers somehow don't find about half of the stolen property during body searches, even though all the prisoners are searched when they leave the factory, and the cell is searched, too. If all the stolen goods are found, then the prisoners will simply stop stealing, and the militiawomen can say goodbye to free face-creams and eyeshadow.

I am the only one who's not searched, because I don't have to work. Moreover, they know that I'm a 'political', and wouldn't stoop to concealing stolen property. Nor do I. But anything else is safely deposited in my bag to avoid detection during searches of the cell. How could we have drained a boil which made 'Auntie' Lida's life a misery for three days if we hadn't had a razor-blade? Admittedly, we had to use stolen perfume as a disinfectant afterwards . . .

They have a very simple way of discouraging any requests for medical assistance. You don't feel well? Off to the infirmary, if you please! The only hitch is that the time you have to spend in prison is increased by the number of days you are away in the infirmary. Sick leave is not included in 'administrative' sentences. We're due for release just before New Year, so who wants to spend New Year's Eve under lock and key? So Auntie Lida went off to work, moaning and groaning with pain because of her boil; so did Valya, coughing violently and running a high temperature.

The duty militiawoman, pocketing the powder compacts, expresses an interest in my situation: "How are you finding it? These lags aren't giving you a hard time, are they?"

"Not at all!"

The cell accepted me on the very first evening, after I passed an unexpected test: "See here, if you're a 'political', try pushing one of our rights!"

"Concerning what?"

"Why, those who are placed in confinement for a short period like ours are supposed to receive sanitary treatment on the first day."

"What's that?"

"A shower. They do have one here. Did they take you there?"

"No."

"They didn't take any of us, either. We're filthy as pigs, we have to sleep in our clothes, and we can't even rinse our knickers."

"So why have you been keeping quiet?"

"Ha! You tangle with them, they can easily bung a few more days on to your sentence. For arguing with the administration."

"I see. All right."

I bang on the door. To be able to wash and rinse one's knickers, I figure, must be considered a basic human right, even though it is not mentioned, *per se*, in the 'third basket' of the Helsinki Agreements. Pity!

"Who's that knocking?"

"Ratushinskaya."

"What do you want?"

"You've forgotten about the sanitary treatment."

"You'll have it in a moment."

"The whole cell?"

"Don't you think you're going a bit too far?"

"Rules are rules. Why, is there someone in the shower? What difference does it make to you whether one has a shower, or everybody?"

"I'll ask my boss."

To my surprise, we were all taken out for a shower, without any protests from the administration. I decided that this was the result of the lengthy consultation the militia captain had had with someone when he brought me here. But there turned out to be another reason why they treated me with kid gloves: shortly before that, Tatyana Osipova had been held here for a while, and they tried to 'teach her how to go around demanding rights'. They added another fifteen days on to her sentence on the very first day for refusing to do forced labour. She went on a protest hunger strike, and they force-fed her by pouring some kind of gunge down her nose. The story got out, though, and was published in the Western press. It took them a long time to forget the trouble they had because of that 'political' – they were used to a different class of prisoner. I only heard about this a year and a half later, in the labour camp, and I couldn't help laughing.

"So it was thanks to your achievements that I caught pneumonia?"

"What do you mean?"

"Now I understand why they didn't make me work! For your information, the heating in the cells is provided by people, and when everyone's taken off to work – why heat the cells? And in the evenings, when the cells are crowded, enough body-heat is generated to make it unnecessary for the heating to be switched on, too. Half our energy goes into producing body-heat! And I would be alone in that cell all day, blue with cold. It was three weeks before I recovered!"

"Ira, surely you would have refused to work? It's forced labour!"

"Tanya, I would have – but voluntarily. I wanted to know everything, including what went on at the 'Freedom' factory. It's ironic, isn't it, that there should be slave labour in a factory named 'Freedom'?"

We argued about this for a little while longer, and reached the conclusion that each one of us was right in her own way: as a Helsinki Monitor, she had to protest against forced labour, as a poet I could do this work voluntarily, see what went on with my own eyes, and keep a mental record of it in order to make the facts public later. There was no reason for disagreement on principle: at that time we were both taking part in a strike in the labour camp.

But back in the prison, after a shower (using, I must admit, stolen shampoo), my clean and pink-checked fellow-prisoners declared me to be 'a real political' and treated me with great respect. If the way to a man's heart is through his stomach, then in the case of a woman, it is through hot water and a bar of soap!

Yesterday the girls brought back some news: "Irisha, there are blokes from Lianozovo working at the factory, too. We asked around, and they told us that one of them is a tall fellow with a beard, also a 'political'. Maybe that's your man?"

"Probably."

"Well, write him a note. Mashka got a ball-point cartridge from the free workers at the factory. We'll pass it along to him. There's enough paper. But don't make the note too big, or they'll find it when they do the body search."

What should I write? "I'm alive, I'm well" (a white lie, that), "I love you. Courage, beloved! I pray for you. Look after yourself. Your 'I'." I rolled the note into a thin twist, and handed it over. In the evening, they started making victory signs to me from the door – mission accomplished!

Igor was not made to work every day, and that particular day he had been left behind in the prison. In the evening, when the other men were brought back to the cell, they tossed Igor a cigarette:

"Here, Whiskers, have a smoke!"

Short-term detainees are forbidden to smoke: this is yet another form of punishment which I, as a non-smoker, did not feel at that time. Igor, however, was experiencing the 'swollen ears' withdrawal symptom so well-known to all prisoners. The men who went to work at the factory relied on the generosity of the free workforce for cigarettes. They had managed to smuggle out a whole filter-tipped cigarette for Igor in the seam of someone's jacket.

"Now, stop carrying on like a reluctant virgin! We went to a lot of trouble to get this for you."

"No, really, boys, let's pass it around!"

"Forget it, Whiskers! It's yours. You being cooped up here all day by yourself, like a dog on a chain."

Lighting a cigarette off a light-bulb is easy when you know how. But just at this moment, the sergeant on duty peered into the cell: "Smoking, eh?"

"Yes."

"Out you come, then!"

The usual punishment for those caught smoking is to clean the toilets. But for some reason, the sergeant steers Igor into an annexe in the corridor.

"Look here, I know petty criminals when I see them! That's not the reason you're here. Is it true that you're a 'political'? Tell me about it!"

Igor begins to talk about human rights, about dissidents, about the reason he is here.

"What's politics got to do with that?"

"As far as I'm concerned – nothing. There are different political systems under which people live like human beings. It's our government that sees political motives behind everything."

"You reckon we don't live like human beings?"

"Well, why did you, a strong, normal fellow, become a prison warder? For the right to live in a city, for a Moscow residence permit? If we had freedom, you'd live wherever you wanted, and have a job in a factory, or something. Do you like your work here?"

"Not particularly."

"You spend a third of your life here, in prison. Do you call that being free? Is it something you chose freely?"

"But what will you get if you start demanding your rights? They'll just squash you, and that will be all."

"So what's better – to die honestly, or be an accomplice to a crime? Should the Germans have remained silent at the time of Auschwitz?"

"Well, we're not Germans."

"No, we have our own concentration camps. You've just said

yourself, that if you start pushing, they'll squash you. This is our great shame, and an even greater shame if nobody raises their voice against it."

"What about your wife – was she taken, too? Hey, go ahead and smoke if you want to!"

He pulls out a cigarette, which Igor accepts just as readily as the one from the prisoners.

"Yes, they did. She's in the Butyrskaya Prison. For the same reason."

"D'you miss her?"

"Look, let's not go into that!"

The sergeant obligingly changes the subject, and they continue to talk for a long time about the state of affairs in our country, and the life we lead. Finally, the sergeant takes off his cap, and carefully pulls out a thin roll of paper, which he hands to Igor without a word. How did he get my note? Did he find it on someone during a search, or did someone give it to him in the hope of averting any danger of an extension of his sentence? To this day, neither of us knows. Igor read the note. Twice. A message from a prison to a prison, from a wife to a husband. What do we know of values, until we are imprisoned?

The sergeant waited to let Igor get his fill of reading, then struck a match and held it out silently. Just as silently Igor thrust the note into the small flame. Both understood that this had to be done.

The reputation of a 'political' can sometimes lead to the most surprising things. Igor was to learn this on his second day of confinement.

"Hey, Geraschenko! Out!"

He was hustled out of the cell, and hastily told that a black student had just been brought in for seven days. He had had too much to drink in some restaurant, and got into a fight with the militia. On orders from 'higher up' he had been put into a separate cell, and now he was demanding something, but nobody could understand what he wanted, because he couldn't speak Russian.

"You're educated, you must know foreign languages. Maybe you can make out what the hell he wants. We've never had one of these here before; who knows how they're supposed to be treated?"

Dredging up the remnants of basic English from his university days, Igor managed to ask the dark-skinned prisoner what he wanted.

"A cup of coffee!"

Igor burst out laughing when he realised the nature of the request, as did the warders, once it was relayed to them. What a joker! A cup of coffee costs more than the entire daily ration of a prisoner! A cup of coffee – in prison! Explaining this to the foreigner was beyond Igor's powers: even if he'd had sufficient vocabulary, he wouldn't have been able to say a word for laughing. The poor fellow would realise in time that his request was impossible. Back in his own cell, he recounted the story, and everyone collapsed with mirth. They laughed so loudly and so long, that the men in the neighbouring cell began to bang on the wall, demanding to be let in on the joke. When they heard, they fell about laughing, too. In their turn, they passed the story along to their neighbours, and a wave of hilarity swept around the entire block.

The student, actually, turned out to have an ear for languages: everybody was taken to the lavatory in the morning at the same time, and with Igor's help, this black student asked the other prisoners what he ought to say to the prison staff when he was released.

And seven days later, immediately prior to release, he yelled out in almost unaccented Russian: "Hey, you! Goat! It's time to let me out!" ('Goat' is common prison and camp slang for someone who plays the submissive role in a homosexual encounter.) The vengeful prisoners had estimated that when the black student's release time came around, the most hated warder of all would be on duty. They reasoned that if a nickname like that were to be given to this warder by such an 'exotic' prisoner, it would stick forever, and pass from one 'generation' of prisoners to the next. I wouldn't be at all surprised if right now, in Lianozovo, some cell-full of prisoners exchanges conspiratorial winks and sings out: "Hey, you! Go-o-a-t!"

And the hapless warder, branded so seven years ago, rattles his keys in impotent rage and shouts: "Who said that?"

Only to be answered by gales of laughter and the suggestion: "Find out for yourself, Goat!"

The 'Freedom' factory was not the only place Igor and his fellow-prisoners were taken to work; occasionally they would go to the Babayev confectionery works. Short-term prisoners were used to plug production gaps all over Moscow. The goods produced at these works were destined for export, and the citizens of the free world buying delicious Russian sweets were not to know that they were produced with the aid of slave labour. Nor did their governments know. Or did they not want to know? Igor wrote an article about this: 'Administrative arrest: combating hooliganism, or an economic necessity?' It was published in a *samizdat* journal. Igor carefully estimated how much income the state derives from every short-term detainee and gave examples of the reasons invoked to imprison people in this way: in most cases, it is on trumped-up charges, on the principle that 'it won't kill him/her to work for fifteen days'. Actually, I was later charged with writing this particular article, and it's mentioned in my sentence, even though it was clearly signed by Igor. I was never taken to the confectionery works, so I could hardly have written about it. The reasoning of the KGB was transparent in this instance: they figured that on this point, at least, I would break my silence and protest, thereby furnishing them with an accusation against my own husband, even though this would be merely an affirmation of an unconcealed truth. What a cheap gambit! No way was I going to assist them in their despicable little games! So all I did was smile, and say nothing: I can only be proud that such an article should be attributed to me. It is so well written! It contains so many staggering facts! And what about the mathematical calculations? – they're brilliant! This kind of thing is beyond us poets – we're more into emotion . . .

Sasha Meyerovich, known to us until now only as Lara's husband, heard from Lera Senderov that we had not come back from the demonstration. Together, they deduced where Igor and I could be.

The inmates of Lianozovo Prison were brought out to be transported to work at 8 a.m. Igor says that he would never have believed, had he not seen with his own eyes, how they used to force twenty-seven men into the nine cubic metre interior of a Black Maria. Sasha was waiting for Igor at the place of work with a thermos of coffee, a warm sweater and some aspirins. Igor found a moment to slip over to him. Both were in a hurry.

"How much did they give you?"

"Ten days."

All they had time for was to pass the goods from hand to hand, and exchange a quick glance. We had gained one more friend.

Lera waited for me outside the Butyrskaya Prison, but in vain, seeing I was not included in the work parties.

When my ten days expired, the duty warder barked an order: "Ratushinskaya! Mop down the corridor!"

This was the traditional prison farewell gesture: to wash the floor in the corridor before being released. I said goodbye to my cell-mates, and after hugs and kisses were exchanged, went out into the echoing walkway. There was no further word about washing the floor, even though I would have done it gladly: if I had my way, I would have scrubbed out that entire institution in the ten days I was there, to lessen the stink and make it more bearable for the prisoners. It is much more humiliating to have to tolerate filth than to clean it up. But the warder steers me towards the reception office, whispering conspiratorially: "There's some bearded chap there who's been wait-ing for you for an hour!"

Igor? No, it can't be, he must still be in Lianozovo. We would be released simultaneously, and it's a good hour of travelling between there and here. Very correctly, they return my watch, the pendant I had been wearing (Igor's work) and my money.

"Minus ten roubles! Here's the remainder."

During the half-hour remaining before I am officially due for release, they bombard me with questions, wanting to know why we both landed in prison. Only now do I find out that the official charge was that Igor and I had been using foul language beside Pushkin's statue! However, they would not let me have the paper with the judge's verdict on it: it transpired that it was forbidden for them to do so. But the prison personnel want to know the real reason, so I tell them exactly what happened, just the way I explained it to my cell-mates. Their questions, as a matter of fact, are almost identical, as is their genuine surprise: but that's terrible! they exclaim. Of course, what I say is true, but if we carry on like that, we'll be squashed! What could I say to them? Of course it's terrible, of course we'll be squashed. But at least they'll not own our souls. However, this is all heavy stuff, and I don't have the time for it now: that 'someone with a beard' is probably frozen stiff, and it's time they let me go. The uniform-clad militiawomen see me off with the same words I heard in the cell: "Good luck, Irisha! See you don't return here!"

The snow crunches under my boots – free and clean. Well, if they've decided to put me away for a long time, this is when they'll make their move. I already know that there have been numerous cases when they pull in someone for a short-term detention, and then, just as he's on his way home, they grab him again, and hustle him off to the KGB prison. It is almost unbearable to get a whiff of freedom, and then have it snatched away from you. The KGB knows this, and plays on it: they have enough psychologists to counsel them. Well, then? Who's going to pounce on a new one?

A form detaches itself from a tree, and heads straight towards me through a snowdrift: "Irka! Are you all right?"

"Lera!"

I had completely forgotten that he has a beard, too.

"So what's happening in the world? I've become a complete savage . . ."

He understands: no radio, no newspapers – not even Soviet ones – from which one can, with a degree of practice and insight, extract at least some information. Lera hurriedly begins to fill me in, and now we're aboard a trolley-bus, then at Lera's place, where his mother is waiting to greet me: "Irochka! How are you? Would you like to take a bath?"

"Thanks, but I'll wait until Igor gets here. He will come here, won't he?"

Lera and I sit there for one and a half hours, waiting. We drink strong tea, and talk in fits and starts. All our nerves are attuned to hearing the doorbell when it rings. At last! We rush to the door. There he is – thin, his beard long and untidy, eyes sunken.

"Igor!"

"Little girl!"

Forgetting the presence of the others, we throw ourselves into each other's arms.

"Lunatics!" sighs Lera's mother. "Into the shower, both of you! Ira – the white towel's for you, the blue one's for Igor!"

Chapter Thirty-one

New Year. We are celebrating with the family. Our little nieces, having had their fill of presents and romping around the Christmas tree, are in bed, and now it's time for the adults to enjoy themselves. Do we know that this is our last such celebration? Perhaps not, but we sense that it could be one of the last few. Mama has already spoken her mind about our Moscow escapades – Lera phoned and told her – but she has forgiven us by now.

"Ira, why are you coughing like that?"

"It's nothing, Aunt Larisa, it'll pass."

Before we returned to Kiev, we had time for a quick meeting with Bob Gillette near the Puppet Theatre. A number of men wearing identical hats hovered visibly nearby, but Bob remained undaunted, and interviewed us both. His last question was whether either of us had been beaten up.

"No."

And it's a fact that nobody lifted a finger against us. There was cold, hunger, dirt, and the uncertainty whether we would be put away for a longer time to contend with, but we were not physically mistreated. On the contrary . . . but how does one describe that 'on the contrary'? We would not wish to risk causing unpleasantness for the militia captain, the sergeant in Lianozovo, the women warders who didn't look into my bag . . . We know full well that if there had been orders to beat us, then they would have done so. Or force-feed us, or strip us naked for body searches. But there were no such orders, and all these people, within the limits of their situations, treated us as well as they could without risking repercussions. I can talk about this now, because so much time has gone by, and nobody will be able to establish who was on duty when and where, and who it was who helped us surreptitiously. Belatedly, I would like to ask: how is it for you, young men and women who have donned uniform for the sake of a Moscow residence permit, but who try to keep your conscience clear? Will you be able to shed that uniform one day, and not wake at night from dreams filled with the sound of Auntie Lida's sobs? But if you do wake up to the memory of those sounds of weeping from behind a locked iron door, I hope you weather your insomnia, and then never, never again . . . The saying 'one beaten person is worth two unbeaten ones' is true only of those who are beaten by their nocturnal 'ego'. It's painful, more painful than anything, but it is useful. God grant that you retain at least that.

"Children, it's ten o'clock!"

We put on our best outfits – a shirt and a blouse exquisitely embroidered by Mama, and go to pay our respects to the neighbours: "Happy New Year!"

"The best of luck!"

Igor and I have decided that the time has come to start a family. We already know what pressure is brought to bear on pregnant dissident women, from interrogations a few hours before delivery, to false recommendations that the pregnancy be terminated because it is allegedly 'abnormal'. For this reason we have decided that our baby will be delivered at home, when the time comes, with Igor acting as midwife. Living with Igor's family any longer would be criminally irresponsible on our part: we have chosen our own path, but it is not the path chosen either by Igor's mother, or his sister and brother-in-law, or old Granny. And especially not by our tiny nieces, sleeping peacefully under their monkey-decorated ceiling. Finding alternative accommodation is virtually impossible: we are under constant KGB surveillance, and potential landlords would not want to see us again after the first visit from the comrades in plain clothes.

To exchange a four-room apartment is a well-nigh impossible task for the average Soviet citizen. It will be a pity, too, because Mama is really attached to this place. But there is no other way out, and Mama agrees, on the condition that we do all the work involved. She does not fully understand yet how vital this is, and she doesn't want to believe it. She does after the first KGB house-search.

In the meantime, having seen in the New Year in the family circle, we make tracks for Marik's place. He has serious problems, too, albeit completely different from ours. They all stem from his communal-flat neighbour. He's an alcoholic and a drug addict, but he is one of the 'golden youth' elite, so he gets off unpunished, no matter what he does. His father was the surgeon who was entrusted with performing a prostate operation on the head of the Lukyanov Prison! When sober, he's quite a pleasant fellow, but when 'under the influence', he metamorphoses into a killer – quite literally. He threw his mistress out of a fourth-storey window: she was killed, but he got off scot-free because influence was brought to bear, and the matter was hushed up. When he got drunk, he had a habit of coming out into the kitchen brandishing an axe, and accusing Marik of being an informer. He would then start enumerating all his drug deals (of which Marik knew nothing), and threatening to kill him 'so you won't squeal on me!' On one occasion he tried to chop down the door to the room in which Marik lived with his wife Nina and two children. From their shared youth Igor knew that Marik was a good fighter, but in those days you only had to look out for yourself: now Marik has the responsibility of a family. And you can never tell with a drunk: it can happen that something that would lay a sober person out cold will barely affect a drunk. Igor once had the unenviable task of trying to pacify a man who had drunk himself beyond all reason at his own birthday party, and started to attack his wife. Igor tried to fell him to the floor before he could cause any serious harm. So Igor employed the classical manoeuvre of a kick into the solar plexus: this was no time to be choosy. Normally, a blow like that would make anyone collapse to the ground, but in this case it had no effect whatsoever. Igor repeated the blow: still nothing! The drunk remained on his feet. And again! Igor says it was like a nightmare: three times he kicked the man in the solar plexus, exactly as it should be done, on the requisite spot, with no result. The drunk stubbornly remained on his feet against all laws of nature, and moved threateningly towards Igor. There was only one thing left to do, and Igor tried it.

"Come on, Tolya," he said jovially, "Let's have another drink!"

The suggestion found instant favour, and a glass of vodka later, Tolya was peacefully put to bed. The following morning, he expressed great surprise about the huge purple bruises under his ribs, and when Igor told him, could barely believe it: "You mean I tried to beat up Mashka?"

"You went for her with a knife, you cretin!"

"And you did this?"

"Well, how else was I supposed to stop you, drunk as you were? You might have killed her!"

"Oh, Igor, pal, thanks a million! Er – is Mashka really mad at me?"

"That's something you can sort out between yourselves now!"

Mashka, however, had already forgiven her chastened spouse, and handed him a glass of cucumber brine for his hangover: "Here, you fool! Drink this and pull yourself together!"

This had happened five years earlier, but it was firmly fixed in Igor's memory. I had not had such turbulent experiences, and the very thought of it made my blood run cold.

We had decided to spend a bit of time at Marik's, who had already been driven to the point of keeping a sabre he'd acquired somewhere stashed under the bed. Nina, poor soul, couldn't sleep at night, and the children had been packed off to stay with friends for a while, out of harm's way. But living like this for any length of time was, of course, impossible. At least, Igor and Marik between them ought to be able to subdue one man, no matter what state he was in. Actually it never came to that, and several weeks later the neighbour vanished. Either he had stolen something while drunk, or he'd done something that not even one of the 'golden youth' could get away with, for it appeared that he had been arrested. Marik and Nina realised that this was only a temporary respite, but it was welcome for all that, and meant that the children could be brought back for a while.

It was May 1982, and we had finally managed to find a suitable apartment for exchange: three rooms for the family, and one room for Igor and myself. All that remained was to complete the formalities, and then, several months later – our own keys, our independence, and we could start a family. Everything seemed to be working out. A family of friends was off to the Baltic coast on vacation, and gave us the use of their apartment for that time. Of course, the apartment was bugged, we were still shadowed, and kept under surveillance from the house next door: the window from which this was done was pointed out to us. The wife in this particular family, a mathematician by profession, was famed in Kiev dissident circles for her knowledge of the law, and the excellent amateur legal advice she could give. The authorities are not keen on knowledge of written laws: they prefer to act according to unwritten (and frequently contradictory) ones. They did not relish having the illegality of their actions pointed out to them and publicised. The audacity of it! Yet there was not much they could do: this woman's knowledge of the law would have been the envy of any lawyer. Yet the authorities have all these various codes of laws: criminal code, civil code, criminal procedural code and the like, which are virtually impossible for the average citizen to buy. How, then, does that wretched woman know so much? They had tried to intimidate her by attempting to put her away in a mental hospital, to threaten her personally, to try to blackmail her with threats against her children. We knew all this, and that the apartment was bugged and watched. Just as ours was, by now. In any case, the owners of the apartment did not stand to lose anything by letting us live there in their absence. Nor did we, naturally. As for our relatives – it was only to their advantage if we got out of the way for a bit. So we waved our friends goodbye, and moved in. We had another stroke of luck in that we found work – privately, of course – doing wallpapering. To tell the truth, we had done this only once, when we helped our friends, the Mishins, redecorate their apartment. Still we were cockily sure that we would be able to make a good job of anything we tackled: you don't need to be a genius to perform manual tasks. Composing a symphony, now – that we wouldn't have been game to try!

Our daring debut was a success: the wallpaper went on smoothly, the pattern matched, the corners (they were the hardest) were flush, and we earned a whole thirty roubles for just one day's work. We certainly would have become swollen-headed had it not been for the fulsome praise heaped on us by the owner of the apartment: it dissolved any inclination to praise ourselves. In fact, compliments always affected both of us adversely, thanks to the efforts of our parents when we were children.

Generally speaking, this was a happy time: I was finding it easy to write, we were young and healthy, we had friends in different cities, and we had learned to maintain contacts that couldn't be traced. The green Kiev summer rustled around us, we would stuff our pockets with sweets and roam around our favourite places, sometimes with Marik, and sometimes alone. From time to time we would notice that we were being followed, and carry out 'ditching manoeuvres' just for the heck of it, even though the comrades might as well have known that we were only off to Sennaya Street to buy a broom. Even so, it did not do to get out of practice; who knows when the ability to slip a tail might prove vital?

After the noisy case of Kislik (a small, short-sighted man who was accused of beating up a large, athletic young woman at a bus-stop), the KGB was obviously keeping tabs on all six people who had signed a protest on Kislik's behalf. Moreover, Igor and I had managed to get into the courtroom among a group of Komsomol 'chair-fillers' and compile a report on the proceedings. Kislik's family was too terrified to do anything, so someone else had to. The comrades in plain clothes realised too late what had happened, and were mightily put out. Our minder Avilov must have got it in the neck, and therefore issued orders to step up surveillance of us.

In our spare time, Igor taught me some basic karate – just in case. If I was lazy about practising, he would cite Engels: 'No knowledge is useless.' That summer he spoiled me more than usual, exhibiting a rare inventiveness. I only had to give the slightest indication that I wanted something, and you could be sure that he would take it much more seriously than I. Luckily, my tastes were not expensive, or I fear he would have started devising means of manufacturing artificial diamonds in the home. However, when I once mentioned how much

I liked the current fashion for sandals on a wooden sole, he was all enthusiasm: "You'll have a pair better than anyone else's!"

And off he went to his tools. The resulting sandals really were better than anyone else's: beautifully shaped to the foot, exactly the right size, with leather straps and what we both called 'bits and pieces'. Pity I didn't get to wear them for long.

On 22nd June we were awakened by the doorbell. There was nothing unusual in that: we had a constant procession of friends coming and going, students travelling between towns with *samizdat*, or people who had despaired of obtaining justice from the authorities coming for advice and comfort. Igor hastily pulled on his jeans and went to open the door.

"Irka! House-search!"

His voice was perfectly calm, only slightly louder than usual. I had barely time to pull on a dressing-gown, when a whole gaggle burst into the room: an investigator, the search-team, a couple of wall-eyed 'witnesses', and an elderly woman. They started with the usual boring official demand that we "voluntarily surrender all anti-Soviet literature".

This is an old trick, but it's usually good for catching frightened novices: the house is going to be turned upside-down anyway, the *samizdat* will be found, but if you give it up yourself, they promise that this will be a mitigating circumstance. And some do, in fact, pull out materials from under mattresses, out of sacks of potatoes, or some other fairly obvious hiding-place, and hand them over with shaking hands. Anything that might interest the KGB. In the emotion of the moment, they don't stop to ask themselves why the KGB needs the 'voluntary surrender' of such documents. Are they too lazy to look for themselves? No, of course not, and look they will: under the same mattress, in the same sack of potatoes. What they need is to be able to enter in their report that such-and-such voluntarily surrendered anti-Soviet documents – for instance, a manuscript by so-and-so. The next thing is for you to sign this report, thereby helping to establish the KGB's claim that the documents in question really are anti-Soviet. To them, anything they don't like is 'anti-Soviet', but the novice, mesmerised by their terminology and the word 'voluntary', sets his signature, without realising that it will be used against the author later, if he is not already dead or out of the country. And that's the way it will appear in his or her sentence later: on the evidence of citizens such-and-such (the ones who surrendered the *samizdat*, and signed, that is, not the KGB!), the following anti-Soviet literature . . . If the author proves to be beyond the reach of the KGB, this formula will be used in the sentence handed down to 'Citizen such-and-such'.

What are the 'soviets'? By definition, they constitute a parliament, freely elected by the people. What, you're against democracy?! Of course, this word is used generally without any thought for either democracy or free elections. Everyone knows that they are replaced by the dictatorship of the Communist Party of the Soviet Union, and not even the whole of that Party, but an intra-party 'Mafia' which battles for power within the Kremlin. The General Secretary of the Party is, in fact, the leader of the country, and may, if he wishes, become the chairman of the Presidium of the Supreme Soviet without any popular elections: the population is informed of that fact in the papers once he has emerged at the top of the heap of his opponents. On the other hand, he may not wish for the Presidium post at all: now *there's* a problem for the erudite – who were the Soviet heads of state under Stalin?

The party Mafia appropriated the term 'Soviet power' long ago, and has managed to drum it into your head so thoroughly that you did not even notice this card-sharper's trick. And anyway, why should you bother your head with every bit of legalistic nonsense? Communists, soviets, isn't it all one and the same thing? What is more important, names or reality, and meaning is given to words by those who transform them into deeds . . . The mythical adjective is accompanied by a perfectly unambiguous and sharp-toothed noun: power. And it is this power which takes you by the scruff of the neck during a house-search and demands that you qualify as 'anti-Soviet' some typewritten pages which are, in fact, merely incompatible with the totalitarian machine. As well as being anti-Soviet, the *samizdat* in question is also described as 'slanderous' – that goes without saying. This gives the KGB a ready-made formula for proffering political charges of slandering our beloved democracy. Down with the enemies of the people! How many have already been victimised, and how many have signed their names . . . And now it's your turn: be careful, don't antagonise the citizen investigator! This is your last chance to ensure that someone else, and not you, will be imprisoned!

All this was so basic and standard, that we were genuinely bored while the investigator ploughed through his routine about anti-Soviet materials. He wasn't what you could call gripped by fervour, either, because he wasn't really expecting anything from us. But rules are rules. Once the formalities were over, the search of the premises began.

"We demand that you search only in our presence, or who knows what you might plant? And why are the witnesses poking around in our things? Are they members of your team, by any chance?"

"But it'll be faster this way!"

"Never mind about that. We've got plenty of time."

We are not at all perturbed. Naturally, there is *samizdat* in the house: two books of ours – one by Solzhenitsyn, and another one by the philosopher Ivan Ilyin – let alone all the books belonging to the owners of the apartment. However, there is no chance that they will find what they really came for – our contacts: names, addresses, correspondence, telephone numbers . . . It's a shame about the books, but only we will be charged for these, not our hosts. They begin to compile a list of a sackful of confiscated literature.

"Which ones are yours?"

Nice try, but it doesn't work: if we say that only those two are ours, that will be pointing a finger at our absent hosts with regard to the rest. Not directly, but giving information about them, nonetheless. Try again!

"We have no intention of assisting you in any way!"

Suddenly the elderly woman, who had been silent until now, bursts out angrily: "You good-for-nothings! It's all your fault that my daughter's home is being searched! Bastards! You've egged her on, and now you'll lead to her destruction!"

Oh, heavens! Why didn't we guess? This is our friend's mother, Sergeyeva, who has become notorious! Neither her daughter nor her son-in-law has allowed her to cross their threshold for years! We had never seen her, but we certainly knew about her. You get such cases where the mother works hand-in-glove with the KGB, and the daughter is a dissident. This Sergeyeva lent active assistance when Lyalya, her daughter, was being forcibly dragged out to an ambulance waiting to take her to a psychiatric institution, and she tore her daughter's clinging children away from her. Her own grandchildren, from her own daughter. On another occasion she wrote a request on the basis of which the KGB placed Lyalya on the national 'wanted' list (Lyalya, in the meantime, was being hidden by friends, to avoid forced incarceration into a psychiatric hospital): Sergeyeva appealed to the KGB to 'find and return' her daughter. Touching, isn't it? The KGB is not searching for Lyalya to arrest her, but to restore an ailing, thirty-four-year-old child to her distraught mother. In the meantime, the dissident psychiatrist Anatoli Koryagin carried out a thorough examination of Lyalya, and publicised the fact that this woman was completely sane. Voices were raised in the West in Lyalya's defence, too, so she managed to avoid forced hospitalisation.

Now, though, Koryagin is himself in a hard labour camp, and Lyalya and her family are safely in the Baltic states (something the KGB doesn't know). Sergeyeva, however, is here, and advances on me as though preparing to go for my throat. The KGB often have recourse to her services in staging provocations. This time, though, she doesn't go as far as assault, probably deterred by Igor's presence.

"Is this woman a member of your team?"

"While the legitimate tenant is absent," we are informed with a saccharine smile, "her mother has right of entry."

"Does she also have the right of physical assault?"

"Well, that hasn't occurred yet, has it?"

"Make sure it doesn't, then. You brought her here, so you're responsible for her actions."

A curt order is flung at Sergeyeva to sit down and not interfere. She consoles herself by directing a constant stream of the most vile abuse imaginable at us: women can be much more accomplished at foul language than men. We are unmoved by her insults, nor do we care a jot about the rest of them. To make any kind of a response would be tantamount to getting down on all fours and barking at a dog that is barking at you.

The search is over. The witnesses sign the protocol.

"Get dressed, gather up your things, and come with us!"

"Where's your arrest warrant?"

"We don't have a warrant yet. But you have no right to be in this apartment. Hand over the keys to the mother."

Poor Lyalya!

We are escorted out into the street with our rucksacks. We realise that there is no guarantee that a search will not be conducted at our registered place of abode, and that it is better that we be there to prevent such an eventuality from catching the family unprepared. So we hurry there, and quickly tell Mama what has happened. Do you think she was frightened, or reproached us? You don't know that woman!

Chapter Thirty-two

We look hurriedly through all the secret hiding places Igor has made. Letters, address books, anything that may give the KGB ammunition against anyone else must be destroyed at once. There is no time to get anything out of the house, which is almost certainly under surveillance, anyway. It is far too risky to leave all this stuff in the hiding places, even though they are so cunningly constructed. We don't remove my poetry, a prose book I have begun, and assorted articles on different themes: it's a pity to destroy them. Maybe they won't be found after all, and even if they are – they can only be attributed to us, not someone else.

The doorbell rings.

"Hurry, Irka! I'll delay them!"

There are sounds of raised voices from the hallway, I can make out Igor's and Mama's . . . but that's not my concern at the moment. I use a metal ruler to stir burning papers in two enamel basins and a bucket: not a single scrap must remain legible! The names and phone numbers of my students? Burn them too! These youngsters have nothing to do with dissident activity, but neither did the Leningrad artist . . . The little green address book with 'social' contacts in it? Into the fire with it! Ilyusha's letters, too: I don't remember, off-hand, which of his friends he mentioned in them and which of them are still in Odessa, so the letters must be destroyed. The KGB shall not learn a single name in this house: they can take the two of us, but that's all.

I can't bring myself to burn any of the forbidden books, though. There were times when Bibles were confiscated in house-searches. But does that mean that I should burn the Bible? No: it's their fault, their sin, and I won't be party to it. I cram as many books as I can into the secret hiding places, but the ones that don't fit will have to stay on the shelves. Their authors are all beyond the reach of the KGB.

Well, where are they? It's thirty-two minutes since they rang the doorbell. Finally, someone knocks on our door: "Open up!"

A uniformed militiaman stands on the threshold. The militia?

That's strange. Beside him is a man in plain clothes, who introduces himself: "I am the leader of a Ministry of Internal Affairs operations group. I will ensure that everything is carried out in accordance with the law."

He looks at the basins and bucket and smirks, while the KGB men accompanying him let out yells of dismay. The room reeks of burnt paper, and they plunge their hands into the ashes in the hope of rescuing at least something.

"How dare you?!" they demand furiously.

"This is my room, and I'll do whatever I want in it!"

"Just you wait! You'll be sorry! This amounts to resisting a house-search!"

"A house-search? Well, why didn't you say so at once, and show me your search-warrant?"

"You'll get a warrant, don't worry!"

It seems that I missed a great many interesting things while I was engaged in pyrotechnics. When Igor opened the door, the whole lot of them streamed into the hallway: "House-search!"

"Where's your warrant?"

"You'll get it later! We're from the KGB!"

"None of this 'later' business! How do I know that you are who you claim to be? For all I know, you could be thieves! And none of you is in uniform!"

"We have identity cards!"

"And I have the right to privacy in my own home, unless there are legitimate reasons for that privacy to be invaded."

He stood squarely in the middle of the hall, taking up a karate stance: "Not a step further! Or I'll beat the hell out of you!"

Naturally, if they'd all rushed him at once, he wouldn't have stood a chance against them: 'operatives' are taught karate, too. But who will go first? The great tall fellow blocking the hall-way clearly intends to carry out his threat. And their jaws are their own, not KGB property. Of course, a grateful government would, no doubt, pay for false teeth, but there would be a lot of pain and suffering before that. They hesitated visibly, and, as the saying goes, he who hesitates is lost.

Igor seized the initiative: "Mama! Call the militia! This may be an attempt to rob us! Lyalya! Call all the neighbours!"

Igor's sister bounded out onto the balcony, yelling at the top of her voice: "Help! Thieves! Everybody – come and witness! Call the militia!"

A crowd of curious onlookers gathered immediately outside the house, and all the KGB men could do was seethe in impotent fury:

publicity like this is a knife to their hearts. In no time at all, a militia operative group came charging round, armed with pistols and ready to do battle.

"What's going on?"

"These men are trying to force their way into our house."

"We're here to conduct a house-search! We're KGB!"

"They don't have a warrant! Please sort them out, officer!"

A few more precious minutes went by while they established their credentials to the militia. The head of the militia group was opposed to condoning a house-search without a warrant, and took his time about letting the KGB men any further into the apartment. Finally, the senior KGB man took the militiaman by the elbow and steered him out onto the landing for a word or two in confidence. The landing was crowded with all our neighbours, all agog with curiosity. The confidential word had to take place a fair way off, and the militiaman came back looking sour: "The search can proceed."

"Is this on the authority of the militia?"

"Yes."

Igor relaxed from his combat stance, and gestured invitingly: "In that case – all right! However, may I ask you to remain here and see to it that everything is carried out according to the law?"

In the meantime, the KGB operative group was trying to disperse the neighbours: "Comrades! Go back about your business!"

But Igor stuck his oar in here, too: "Why should they go away? You need witnesses, don't you? All your lot burst in here like a band of robbers, and are clearly on your payroll. By law, if I refuse to accept them as witnesses, you'll have to replace them with someone from among our neighbours. That's right, isn't it, comrade militia group leader?"

The militiaman affirmed that this was indeed right. The whole situation was beginning to strike him as amusing. He had set off to what he thought would be a shootout with thieving desperadoes, and instead he found a long-haired intellectual standing in a karate stance and holding a KGB group at bay! No doubt he could already imagine how all his colleagues back at the station would enjoy the story when he recounted it to them, and had nothing against staying to see the end of the performance. Some more time was spent on substituting other witnesses for the 'disqualified' KGB ones, by which time the unmistakable smell of burning papers was wafting through the apartment, and the militia group was having a hard time keeping straight faces.

At this point, the phone rang. It is forbidden to answer the phone during a house-search (so that nobody will find out that it's going on), but Igor and I were the ones under surveillance, so there was nothing to stop Mama from picking up the receiver.

"Our house is being searched!" she announced immediately.

Someone seized the phone from her hand: "What do you think you're doing! It's forbidden!"

"Really! Then why didn't you say so? How am I supposed to know?" countered Mama, in a voice of injured innocence.

Actually, this was quite genuine. She really didn't have any prior experience of such happenings.

In any case, the word was out: and words like 'house-search' travel very fast. While the KGB operatives were still searching, all our friends were busily telephoning the news around, even to Moscow and Leningrad. This was very important, because house-searches are usually conducted in series, within a twenty-four-hour period as a rule, and the sooner people know they're on, the more chance there is to prepare for them.

The infuriated KGB men turned the apartment upside-down, but what they wanted was no longer there, so they raked in everything, *samizdat* or not, including my school exercise books with my childhood poems, lesson timetables, diagrams for geometry problems, our adolescent diaries and heaven knows what else. However, they also got the poetry I had written that summer, and the index Igor had compiled of my work ... Actually, these were only copies, and they were welcome to them: the originals remained safe in the undiscovered hiding-places.

Suddenly, into the middle of all this came Igor's father. He had moved out, as I noted earlier, but had retained residence registration. It turned out that he had been going about his business in the Presidium of the Ukrainian Academy of Sciences, when he noticed what was obviously a KGB man hanging around him. Guessing that something was wrong, he rushed home.

"What on earth is going on here?" he demanded. Having listened to a jumble of explanations, he enquired, in the voice of one used to command: "Who gave you permission to conduct this search? This is my apartment!"

"You'll have the warrant within twenty-four hours," said the senior KGB operative, his tone changing from peremptory to conciliatory, just in case.

"Very well. I'll stay here until you finish. There are books of mine here, too."

"We aren't after your books!"

"I should hope not."

Having finished in our room, they moved to the corridor, and started turning out the cupboards. Igor's mother watched, slowly beginning to boil: "Who taught you to wipe dirty hands against a clean wall? Why should I have to repaint the place after you've gone?"

"You wouldn't have to, if you kept the place clean!"

"Wha-a-at? Are you saying that my house is dirty?! Did I tell you to ferret through the rubbish-bin with your bare hands? Oleg – you tell them!"

"Calm down, Larisa! As for you, citizens, I hope you intend to behave in a civilised manner. I have no intention of interfering in your legal pursuits, but I would ask you to be sure that you don't overstep the bounds of your authority!"

Visibly subdued, the 'citizens' were much more careful when they started searching Mama's and Gran's room. They did so only as a matter of form, anyway, because they were not stupid enough to think we'd hide anything there. All was peaceful and quiet until they got to Gran's bed. Despite her eighty-nine years, Gran was the undisputed boss, and never let anyone touch her bed: she used to make it herself, plump up the pillows and quilt the way she wanted them, and anyone foolish enough to interfere would get very short shrift. This was her own, private, untouchable sphere of independence. And here was some KGB sprig trying to touch her bed with his filthy hands!

Oh, how she exploded! Tiny, stooped, and clucking with outrage, she flew in front of him, chin thrust out belligerently: "Keep away!"

"But I have to search . . . !"

"Search? *My* bed?! I taught good-for-nothings like you in school for forty years! Get away from my bed, do you hear me? Or I'll make the sign of the cross at you, you devil!"

And she raised her dry little arm to carry out her threat. Either the KGB man feared the sign of the cross or he was unmanned by Gran's boiling anger, but he retreated obediently. Gran's bed was the only spot in the apartment to remain unsearched, not even the quilt got ruffled.

While they were going through the children's toys under Lyalya's eagle eye, I entertained the witnesses and the militiamen (who were quite frankly enjoying themselves) with readings of selected passages from the Criminal Procedural Code. At last the KGB group returned: "Where's the typewriter?"

"What typewriter?"

"Your typewriter. The one you used."

"Look for it."

"Who'd you give it to?"

"A house-search is one thing, an interrogation is another. Have you decided to combine the two?"

My typewriter wasn't in the house, as it happened, so they made do with confiscating my father-in-law's electric one. He threw me a very pointed glance, but didn't say a word about it, either then or later. It was not his way to waste time on regrets about material things.

"Right, we're through. Witnesses, sign the protocol! In the meantime, we'll formulate charges against you for resisting a house-search. It's been some time since you saw the inside of a prison for a few weeks, isn't it?"

They telephone somewhere for a car to be sent round, but our neighbours intervene unexpectedly: "We have the right to note down our observations concerning the search before signing the protocol."

"What observations?"

"Why, it says in the Criminal Procedural Code . . . Ira, read that bit again, will you?"

I rejoice inwardly: that was time well spent, indeed! Oh, but it's useful to know the laws of the land! While the KGB grit their teeth, the witnesses record that there was no resistance offered to the search from the moment the militia confirmed its legitimacy. As for before that – well, nobody is obliged to let perfect strangers into their home unchallenged unless they can furnish some sort of authority.

"Damn it, we should have started a fight!" burst out the head of the KGB operatives, unable to suppress his dismay at this turn of events.

"Perhaps you'd like to start one now?" asked Igor with chilling politeness. It's amazing how similar his intonations are to his father's, at times. The KGB group went off, promising retribution. The militiamen went off a little earlier, clapping Igor on the shoulder as they left: "Well, lad . . . !"

We could hear their laughter floating back from the hallway. Igor's father leaves, too. He's far from pleased with the situation, but doesn't utter so much as a word of reproach: it's neither the time nor the place for recriminations. Igor's mother sighs with relief: "Well, now! Shall we have a cup of tea?"

Marik came racing around to tell us that searches were carried out at a number of other addresses in Kiev. His place wasn't touched, but (he names the people involved) had unwelcome visitors, just like ours. Attempts to phone Lera in Moscow failed – looks as though he's had his phone cut off. Marik went off to Moscow the same day. He came back looking drawn and grim: "There was a wave of searches and arrests in Moscow. They've taken Lera, Volodya Gershuni, Kanevsky, and two youngsters."

"And nobody thought to let us know?!"

"I've already had a row with the Muscovites about that. With Tanya and Lena. They thought that you'd know because it was broadcast on Western radio; you know the old joke: 'If you want the Russian news, BBC's the one to choose!'"

"Did you have any trouble?"

"No, they only detained me once in the street, took my passport, read out the details over a walkie-talkie, and then let me go. You can't call that trouble."

"So . . ."

Oh, how terrible, how excruciatingly painful it is when a friend is arrested! How it spurs you on to do even more, before your turn comes! Take my word for it, it becomes much easier once you're imprisoned.

Chapter Thirty-three

A hurried tape-recording of our protest about the latest punitive campaign and of my most recent poems was despatched to Moscow. The next number of the *Information Bulletin* came out, but without Lera's participation. Nobody was arrested in Kiev as yet, but all those whose homes had been searched were dragged in for questioning. For some reason, we were the only ones who weren't. We saw all the others, of course, and it seemed as though everyone had stood up to interrogation very well. Sleepless nights and feverish activity lessened our pain somewhat. Life had to go on, breakfast had to be gulped down, money had to be earned . . . Somehow, all these mundane details – from which our arrested friends were now divorced – made us feel ashamed, even though we understood the wisdom of Ecclesiastes that 'there is a time to scatter stones, and a time to gather stones'.

Our time had not yet come. And if truth be told, what had we done for freedom that could compare with even a fraction of what the others had achieved? *Samizdat*? Writing articles? Protests? No, we had not managed to do much, and we had only started doing anything at all a short time ago. Not like Volodya Gershuni, who was arrested on charges of anti-Soviet agitation and propaganda (it was article fifty-eight in those days) before either Igor or I had been born. How many times had he been arrested since then, too? But even during one of his terms of enforced psychiatric incarceration he managed to write a documentary work and smuggle it out. Or take Lera – just his work on *Intellectual Genocide* is a masterpiece anyone could envy. To say nothing of all his other achievements. The Muscovites told us that he rarely sleeps for more than five hours a night, and can even do without that, if necessary.

My poetry? High-flown words are only of value where they are backed up by the author's actions. That was how I felt at the age of twenty-eight.

So life went on, and our daily existence can't have differed much from that of our fellow-citizens. What does anyone in our society acquire with the passage of years apart from a family and friends? Useful connections. The state wages an unrelenting war against 'privateers', but they are the only ones who make it possible to get by. It is not the fault of the doctor in the local clinic if he can only allow you twenty minutes of his time, or spend a set number of state kopecks on you: nor is he to be blamed for not giving you a prescription for some medicine which is in short supply, and he has to guess rather than make a proper diagnosis. Nor does the dentist who drills your teeth with a blunt drill do so with malice aforethought. What can they do? Of course, they have 'channels' through which they can obtain the necessary equipment and medicine – but this costs money! Of course, you are willing to pay! But if he doesn't know you, how can he risk treating you as a private patient? Not so long ago, the authorities decided to pull medical practitioners into line, carried out a number of cautionary trials, after which doctors and dentists became too terrified to accept so much as an apple from an unknown patient, in case that were interpreted as accepting a bribe in breach of the law.

Private tailors, typists, hairdressers and similar practitioners of the 'shadow economy' wouldn't dream of carrying out some kind of service for a client who did not come to them with a recommendation from a mutual friend or business acquaintance.

If you are what our radio hails as 'an ordinary Soviet citizen' and have no access to special shops for the privileged (about which the radio is reticent), you will have learned from childhood that you must fend for yourself, expect nothing from the state, and only hope that the authorities will leave you alone. You will hail 'private' cars when there are no taxis around, buy food from shadow-economy suppliers when the shelves in the state-owned shops are empty, pay whatever is the unofficial 'service charge' to plumbers, electricians and other vital tradesmen. You, too, will be of use to someone, and people will call upon you for assistance: "Help me out, mate!"

And so you do, depending on what your area of expertise happens to be: mend shoes, say, obtain some article that's in short supply, lacquer a floor or sew trousers. Or just go to your phone and ring someone you know who may be able to provide what is needed.

Thanks to this system, Igor managed to get his teeth fixed that summer, something he had been putting off for far too long. Olga, a new acquaintance, supplemented her income by treating private patients at home. She had a portable drill, the sounds of which she would drown by playing records while she worked. It happened that she and Igor got talking – first about instruments, then about auto-training, then about life in general. Finally, they got on to the subject of poetry, something which was more important to both of them than just social chit-chat. Igor began reciting from memory, and she guessed the authors unerringly. Then my name cropped up, and it turned out that she had already heard something of mine somewhere.

"You mean to say she's your wife? Igor, would it be possible to get some of her poetry to read? And could you show me a photo of her? Maybe you would introduce us? Does she need any dental work done?"

"And how!"

"Igor, my dear, bring her along!"

Amazing, isn't it, the things that can bring readers and writers together! Olga flatly refused to accept payment.

"I guarantee my work for at least five years," she laughed. "If, God forbid, they put you in a labour camp, at least you won't have to worry about your teeth for a while."

She became one of those who hid the *samizdat* manuscripts of my poems: we had enough brains not to rely on a sole copy hidden in one of our secret nooks at home. Not long afterwards, she issued an ultimatum, in truly dictatorial tones: "Listen, you two! I may only be a dentist, but I do have some general medical knowledge! I find it hard to look at you! When did you last get a decent night's sleep? Are you trying to commit suicide? So this is what I'm going to do: next Saturday, I am placing you under 'house-arrest'. For two days. So you can get yourselves together and not think about anything serious. My father has a house outside the city. You can go there and pick St John's wort. The wild strawberries are just ripening ... No, not a word! I prescribe walks in the forest, plenty of milk and fruit! That's doctor's orders!"

How could she have guessed that those two happy days would be our last chance to rest? How did her intuition prompt the precise recipe for that happiness: the forest, wild strawberries and milk? She ran around the forest paths with us and laughed like a young girl, she taught us to dry St John's wort, and read us a lecture on its healing properties. She argued with Igor over the name of a mushroom we'd found, and joined us in trying to decipher the snort of a hedgehog we'd disturbed.

When we parted, she hugged us both tightly: "Look after yourselves! Heavens, I sound like an absolute Cassandra! All the best!"

I was arrested on my way to work: Igor and I had got a seasonal job, picking apples at a state farm. We were both summoned to the farm office, ostensibly to clear up something about our work record books. We were directed to separate rooms – and the KGB were already waiting for me. The idiots had taken out their guns, too: maybe they wanted to vindicate the cowardice of their colleagues before Igor the time they came to search our apartment?

Investigator Lukyanenko formally presented his arrest warrant: Article Sixty-two of the Ukrainian republican Criminal Code, and Article Seventy of the Criminal Code of the Russian Federation. Both articles, as I already knew, are one and the same charge, just the numbers change from republic to republic. Anti-Soviet agitation and propaganda. The penalty ranges from six months to seven years in the camps: they're bound to go for the maximum. Plus five years of internal exile. That means I shall be forty years old when I finish serving my sentence. If they don't kill me off before that.

"I should like to say goodbye to my husband."

"But of course, Irina Borisovna! Hop into the car, we'll take you across straight away. He's over there in the hut with the rest of your work team – there's a search, you see . . . You should both be present."

For some reason, the bit about the search convinced me. I can only justify my error by saying that this was the first and last time that I believed so much as one word uttered by investigator Lukyanenko. What I *should* have done was open my mouth and yell, at the top of my voice: "Igor! I've been arrested under Article Seventy!"

But I didn't – stupid idiot that I was. You'd think I hadn't read books about such things! It goes without saying that the white 'Volga' we drove off in didn't even slow down near the hut mentioned by Lukyanenko. I offered him my felicitations on the first lie of the investigation process, and thanked him for it: it would not do for me to forget, after all, whom I was dealing with.

Here is number 33 Vladimirskaya Street, here are the echoing prison corridors.

"Sit here for a while!"

A small box of a cell: it contains a leather stool and a barred window. There is a peep-hole in the door, naturally. For some reason, my spirits rise: well, world of zeks – admit a newcomer from the younger generation of dissidents!

A uniformed female KGB ensign enters the cell: a great lump of a woman with a forbidding expression. She's overdoing it, though – even without that look on her face you wouldn't mistake her for an angel of mercy.

"Take your clothes off!" she orders, and adds, with undisguised gloating triumph: "All of them!"

Oh, my, isn't she the scary one, then? This particular practice is one I knew of well in advance, and how to react to it, too – with total indifference. Standing naked in front of creatures like this is just like standing naked in front of a cockroach, be they male or female. After searching through my clothes, she turns around and looks me over unhurriedly. There's someone shuffling around outside, too, peering through the peep-hole.

"So how do you like my figure?" I ask blithely.

"Get dressed!" she snaps, immediately losing all interest in those parts of my body untouched by suntan. Well, that's better. What now?

The next item on the agenda is a visit to the investigator's office. I am marched there to the accompaniment of the time-honoured practice of finger-clicking behind my back. It's a very specific and unmistakable click-click-click. Every click makes me straighten my back a little more: let the prison know that a 'political' is being brought through. By courtesy of the KGB scum I am no longer a weak woman: in my present calling one must be strong and proud. Others have managed, and I will, too. It will be an honour to be like them!

Investigator Lukyanenko beams cheerily below a portrait of Dzerzhinsky: "Well, Irina Borisovna, we'll just get you to sign a few papers, and off you'll go, back to your apple-picking!"

Good Lord, but they're primitive! Do they really expect me to believe that they'll release someone arrested under Article Seventy just like that? The whole of the Ukrainian Procuracy would commit mass suicide if anyone arrested on political charges were to be set free after a mere two hours in detention!

"I will not sign any papers of any kind."

Mistake number two! Naturally one should not sign anything, but why did I go and blurt that out straight away? It would have been much better to find out first what inducement they were going to offer in exchange for my 'release'. What would they have asked me to sign? I would willingly do fifteen days in camp prison right now if I could get a glimpse of those papers.

Lukyanenko lost some of his sparkle: "Well, Irina Borisovna, you'll have plenty of time to think that over. Is there anything you would like to know, or request?"

"No."

At least I got that right. It has been rightly said: "Don't believe them, don't fear them, don't ask them for anything." And it's pointless indulging your curiosity, because all you'll hear from them will be lies. He picked up the phone, and issued an order to have me removed.

Click-click-click. The corridor is covered with red carpet: not for comfort, as I have already found out, but to enable the warders to approach cell doors soundlessly. And here's my cell. The ensign fiddles the key in the lock. The cell contains two bunks. A pair of frightened dark eyes stares at me from one of them.

"Hello! My name's Ira."

"Mine's Lida. Have you been here long?"

"About three hours. And you?"

"Two weeks now. And alone all the time . . ."

Her eyes fill with tears. The story she relates to me sounds absurd. She had been working in the food-distribution bureau in Simferopol and came to Kiev on assignment from work. She was suddenly arrested, and now 'they' were formulating a case against her on foreign currency charges. Crimes involving foreign currency are also within the KGB's jurisdiction. It is a criminal offence to possess any kind of currency other than Soviet. I see no particular sense in this, and, anyway, where would an ordinary Soviet citizen get hold of foreign currency? It is mainly the criminal world, thieves, who operate with hard currency, and I would like to know of a single area of the food trade where there aren't thieves. Nevertheless, to operate in the foreign currency league involves theft in enormous proportions. I am not particularly interested in Lida's degree of culpability: it may be that she has been framed in order to protect somebody higher up, but maybe she's involved up to her neck, and is lying to me because she knows that all the cells are wired for sound. There is one thing I know full well: political prisoners do not get chance cell-mates. If there are two or three others sharing your cell, you can take time to try to determine which one is the informer, but when you get only one companion, then the matter is as clear as crystal from the word go.

"What are you charged with?"

"A political article."

"Oo-o-h!"

She lapses into frightened silence. Either she's a first-rate actress, or some poor creature who's only just been recruited after being bullied, browbeaten and threatened with imprisonment. It's time to change the subject.

"Ah, I see you have three books here! Are they yours?"

"They're from the library. You can take any one you want to read."

I examine the cell in detail. A shelf on the wall, two stools. The bunks are pretty awful: vertical and horizontal steel strips about one and a half inches wide, but interwoven with gaps twice the width of my palm between them: that means the mattress will disappear into them. The floor is superb, though – wooden boards. The present occupants of this building had their headquarters here before the war, too, and during the occupation it was used by the Gestapo. I wonder whether it was our lot or the Germans who put down those floorboards? As was to be expected, there is no washbasin. A plastic slop-bucket stands in the corner in lieu of a lavatory. One must give credit where credit is due, though – there's a lid to cover the bucket. A paper on the wall lists all the rules and regulations of the prison. One must be quiet, obey orders ... no point in reading all this: I know it well enough. Meetings and correspondence are permitted only at the discretion of the investigator: that means I needn't hope for either privilege. The items you may have with you are a toothbrush, a change of underwear and two pairs of socks. Those under investigation may have paper and a pencil, those who have already been sentenced may also have a ball-point pen. Spectacles and artificial limbs must be surrendered to the guards every night. I wonder if that applies to false teeth?

"Lida, do you have false teeth?"

"What? No ..."

The poor girl is obviously beyond joking. They really have reduced her to a quaking mess in two weeks! What will happen to her later?

Women may also have a quantity of cotton wool with them, and a lipstick. Though what use is a lipstick when there are no mirrors in prison? It will have to remain one of those mysteries of the Ukrainian KGB. I must confess to a residual curiosity, though. When I was in Lefortovo prison in Moscow, the prison rules were the same as the Kiev ones, word for word, with the exception of the lipstick: Moscow prisoners were denied this beauty aid.

One may also send complaints to the Procuracy of the Ukrainian Republic ... I needn't bother reading this bit, either: I've never heard of the Procuracy intervening on behalf of someone held under investigation. However, what am I going to clean my teeth with tonight? They brought me here just as I was when they arrested me: in a track suit, and a pair of rubber boots. They took away my anorak, because it closed with a metallic zip, and those are not allowed.

Never mind, I'll manage somehow. It's even rather funny to start my life as a zek without any possessions at all, with empty hands. Material possessions weaken us. Let's take a look at the books. Fazil Iskander? M-m-m, not bad ... and what's this tattered thing, with no beginning and no end? It bears a stamp in the middle, stating: 'Prisoners who deface books will be denied the right to use the library. KGB Isolator of the Ukrainian Soviet Socialist Republic.'

I am distracted from Iskander's delightful childhood reminiscences by the clang of the serving hatch in the door: "Take your food!"

Pearl barley soup and bread. Lida feels obliged to issue a hurried warning: "Eat it, or they'll force-feed you!"

"How do you know?"

Her eyes are full of tears again. I don't think I've ever seen anyone so depressed in my entire life. For the present, I don't need any persuasion to eat: it was some two weeks later that I began to experience an inexplicable nausea, and seemed to taste something added to my food. After that they began to stand over me and threaten me with force-feeding. I stubbornly ate only what I could and as much as I could: mainly rusks out of the parcel sent from 'outside'. They ranted for a while, but gave up in favour of other pastimes. The nausea disappeared as soon as I was sent off to camp: I still don't know for sure what caused it.

"Give us your kettle!"

They fill it with boiling water. Lida offers me a caramel – she's already had a parcel from home.

"Thanks."

"You're welcome."

More banging and clanging. This time they open the door: "Bring out your slop-bucket!"

The lavatory consists of two holes in a cement surround. There's a tap, and, of course, a peep-hole in the door. They remain vigilant while we . . . Ah, to hell with them! There's a peep-hole in the cell door, too, and I may as well accustom myself to the fact that there won't be a moment during the entire period of the investigation when I won't be under their eye, even in what should be completely private moments. Well, they're the ones who should feel ashamed, not I! In any case, they're not people here, they're functionaries, and don't deserve any attention . . . However, this is already the second time that I'm having to remind myself of this, and that's a bad sign: it means that I *am* paying attention to them. Still, it's only my first day. At least I keep my face blank, and there's not much chance that any of these turnkeys are mind-readers. Lida cleans her teeth, but I can only rinse my mouth. I can be glad that they've issued me a towel of sorts, skimpy though it is.

"That's so that you can't hang yourself," Lida informs me. I merely nod. Some cell-mate heaven has sent me! By lights out she's in tears again, and knocks on the cell door. They take her away, come back for her things, and I never see her again. The books remain on the shelf.

The hatch in the door opens again to reveal a jovial, bewhiskered face:

"Lights out! Hand in your writing materials, creams, spectacles."

"I don't have any. Nor any artificial limbs!"

"Put the kettle on that stool."

That's so that they can see it. Lida would probably have said that this was to make sure you didn't slash your wrists with the spout. 'Lights out' should not be taken literally. The small, inadequate lamp illuminates my closed eyelids.

Igor! My love, where are you? Are you under arrest, or not? We didn't even get a chance to say goodbye. But then, didn't that militia captain in Moscow warn us that it was bad luck to say goodbye?

O Lord, Thy will be done – unto me and my beloved. And Lera. And all prisoners of conscience. Amen.

Chapter Thirty-four

When Igor was ushered into a separate room in the farm office, his eye fell immediately on a uniformed militiaman, and an unknown man in plain clothes.

"There has been a complaint against you by Citizen Sysoyeva. She says you entered her house without permission."

"That's nonsense!"

"Maybe. That's what we're here to find out. Come with us."

They went to the small house the work team had rented for the season from pensioner Sysoyeva. The moment they walked in, another five men appeared, conspicuously armed. A KGB search!

Major Buyalsky took the bull by the horns straight away: "Where do you keep the literature?"

"What do you mean?"

"You know perfectly well. If you don't want to show us, we'll find it ourselves."

"Where's my wife?"

"She'll be brought around here in a few minutes."

The white Volga carrying me went on its way to Kiev, and Buyalsky and his men began to turn the house upside-down. The elderly owner was frightened out of her wits at first, but cheered up soon: the search didn't last long. As Igor heard later, she boasted all around the village that the KGB hadn't found her illegal still. I daresay clandestine brewing equipment was the last thing on Buyalsky's mind right then. They then presented Igor with a search-warrant for our Kiev apartment. But of course . . . ! Another pleasant little surprise for the family. This was particularly annoying, as we had completed all the formalities for accommodation exchange, and had been intending to travel up to Kiev the next day to pick up the keys to our independent home. Igor had already built new bookshelves for it out of pine, darkened artistically with a welding torch.

Well, they're not important now, either. Igor was hustled into a minibus, surrounded on all sides, and off they went. Igor knew that there wasn't anything of any importance for them to find in the Kiev apartment, but he was worried sick about me. Asking his travelling companions was clearly useless.

This second search lasted seven and a half hours. The yield was not impressive: a field-diary Igor had kept when he went to Kamchatka, a couple of my recent poems, copies of letters we had sent to the Procuracy, and similar trivia. They did, however, take all my documents, including my passport: that meant that I was definitely under arrest.

"The search is over. We shall now make a list of materials confiscated."

They begin to compile the list, clearly playing for time and awaiting instructions whether to arrest Igor or not. At this point Igor did what may seem a very strange thing: while they were fiddling around with the list, he lay down on the divan, and went to sleep, right before their eyes. He didn't do this in order to create an impression (although it did), but because he knew that if they received orders to arrest him, it would be a long time before he got another chance to sleep. Some time later he was awakened by Buyalsky: "Sign the list of confiscated materials!"

"Are you going to confiscate me, too?"

"Not yet."

The telephone had been disconnected, of course, so Igor hurried to find a taxi and set off to some friends of ours, to use their phone. They were already waiting: "We've been trying to get in touch with you since this morning, but nobody was answering the phone, even though we know your grandmother's always at home. Marik's had a house-search, too, he phoned and told us."

"They've taken Ira. I don't know the details."

They quickly phoned around to all the people who should be informed, and went straight off to Marik's place. Nobody spent time on useless exclamations: that could come later; now it was time to act.

The search at Marik's had not been without its amusing moments. About a year earlier, a mutual friend decided to throw out the complete works of Stalin, which had been gathering dust on his bookshelves since the 1950s. Marik was moved to protest: "You must be joking! That's got to be a bibliographical rarity by now! You'll throw them out over my dead body! If you don't want them – give them to me!"

"You're welcome – so long as you make all the arrangements for moving these 'bricks' from here to your own place."

Avilov – the one who was so fond of shaking hands – was in charge of the search at Marik's. When he got to the 'bricks,' he didn't even take them down off the shelf, but ran a hand lovingly over their spines: "How do you manage to correlate the two? Involvement with *samizdat* – and these? I really can't make you out! And to think you were a 'Young Dzerzhinovite' at school, too . . ."

The searchers' main interest was Marik's photo laboratory: he had equipment of very high professional standard at home. What worried Marik was that he had the fifth, sixth and seventh volumes of the *Gulag Archipelago* right there, on undeveloped films. And the KGB would find them any minute now. Sure enough: "What about these reels? What's on them?"

Marik didn't bat an eyelid: "That's unexposed film. See for yourselves – there's nothing on it."

And right before their eyes, he opened them all up, while they were still working out the difference between an unexposed film and an unused one. None at all, O ye intellectual giants: daylight affects them equally! However, Marik felt it prudent not to explain this detail to them.

Later they took him off for interrogation, and he was the first one to hear under which article I had been arrested. As was to be expected, he refused to give any evidence, and was back home by the time Igor arrived.

"Article Seventy!"

Marik didn't have a phone, but they managed to phone Ilyusha from somewhere else that very night: actually, it was already daytime in St Louis.

The following day it emerged that there had been searches at the homes of a number of other people, including the friends about whom Igor and I had argued when we'd gone picking lilies of the valley. Igor and his sister visited them, and that's when they heard about it.

"Why didn't you let anyone know?"

"The search took eleven hours, and we could hardly stand on our feet by the time they left."

Igor, who'd been keeping himself going with black coffee after a sleepless night, merely nodded: "Well – it happens!"

They also knew that I'd been arrested: they had been informed of this before the search of their home commenced. And now they both began, interrupting each other in their haste, to recount how they had managed to secrete this and that at the last moment, and hoodwink the KGB!

In the midst of this, Igor heard his sister's dispirited voice: "Igor – take a look at this . . ."

She was holding the protocol of the search, where it stated, in black and white, that the lady of the house had voluntarily surrendered anti-Soviet documents received from me – that is, a collection of my poems 'and other materials'.

Igor's sister, who knew just as well as the couple in question exactly what this meant, could only shake her head in wonder: "How could you . . . ?"

"We thought that they might call off the search then."

Furthermore, it emerged that they had already been questioned about me earlier, and they had answered. True, they hadn't told everything they knew. In fact, they seemed very proud of themselves for 'diddling' the investigator: all they'd told him about was discussions held in their house over a cup of tea – nothing else. But how much can be discussed over a cup of tea by people who have known each other for years? Heavens, even paid-up informers don't need to go beyond telling their KGB masters what was discussed over cups of tea: I daresay some of them also omit certain things, out of magnanimity.

Igor and his sister exchanged an understanding look. There was no point in trying to explain anything: these were adults, who should be able to see matters for themselves. Piles of *samizdat* were confiscated from them – didn't they know the meaning of political trials?

Igor and his sister did, however, try to explain once again, but the reaction was hostile: "What's all the fuss about? We only told the truth, and not the whole truth, at that! We had to say *something*!"

"Why?"

"Well, when you're asked politely, you can't behave like a boor. Now if the investigator had started shouting, or being rude, that would have been a different matter."

So the 'anti-Soviet materials in poetic form, voluntarily surrendered by citizen such-and-such' were included in my indictment. Six months later I was allowed to acquaint myself with the materials of the investigation, and read the protocols of their interrogation. Yes, they were very thorough in giving details of conversations which took place in their kitchen . . . It looked as though these old friends would be the main witnesses for the prosecution at my trial. What a nightmare! I knew these people – decent people, who had never been informers!

However, the outcome was different from what might have been expected; it's a strange thing, the human heart, and occasionally it acts in a most unpredictable way.

While Lukyanenko was working on me, the other three investigators on the case were slaving away with my friends and relatives. It gives me great pleasure to record that they didn't find their work at all easy. The only 'easy' subjects were the two people I have just mentioned, and Boris Kanevsky, who recanted officially under investigation, and whose sad case is sufficiently well known for me not to labour the point any further. He gave evidence against anybody and everybody.

The others stuck to their guns. Obviously, Igor and Marik responded with flat refusals to give evidence of any kind. And if they were to be charged with obstructing the course of justice? Go ahead – charge us! Igor's mother, a rather unpredictable lady, started off by bursting into tears in the investigator's office: her nerves let her down. The investigator was delighted by such a promising start: they like to see people crying.

Investigator Usaty leaned forward, and crooned sympathetically: "Come now, don't cry, we'll have everything sorted out in no time at all! Maybe she's not as guilty as she seems. You can help her by giving honest answers. I'll tell you what, let's you and I have a nice cup of tea, and a civilised chat . . ."

Stifling a sob, Igor's mother reached into her handbag, and handed him a note which read:

> I have known Irochka since the day she was born, and have always treated her like a daughter. Her arrest is a terrible blow to me, and I simply cannot discuss it with strangers. I am aware of the content of Article One Hundred and Seventy-nine of the Ukrainian Criminal Code concerning penalties for refusal to give evidence. Larisa Geraschenko.

The flabbergasted investigator leapt as if stung: "I will not accept this paper from you!"

"Then to what address should I post it?" asked Auntie Larisa, wiping away a tear.

The investigator took the paper, and ordered her out of his office. Without protest, he accepted a similar missive from Igor's sister. She didn't cry, though, and he didn't offer her a cup of tea. Nor did they have any joy with my parents.

Lyalya Varvak, the specialist on Soviet law, enacted 'a refusal to give evidence, with a break for lunch', which is a legend of dissident folklore by now. She was questioned by Buyalsky, and I'm sure it took a long time for him to recover from this session.

"What do you know about Ratushinskaya's criminal activities?" he asked invitingly.

"And what is the substance of the charge?"

"Anti-Soviet agitation and propaganda. Article . . ."

"I know the number of the article. But that is a description of an offence, not a concrete occurrence. I would like to know for what, specifically, she's going to be tried. For what actions?"

"That's none of your business. It will be determined by the investigation."

"No, you're mistaken. It *is* my business. By law, all I'm obliged to talk about is that which has direct bearing on a committed crime. For instance, if you were to ask me whether Ratushinskaya went to the market frequently, I would only need to reply if that had any connection with the case in question. Otherwise, I need not say a word."

"Don't you lecture me! I told you: Article . . ."

"Listen, you can't bring a general charge of murder against someone, even though there is a murder charge on the statute books. You can charge them with the concrete murder of Ivanov or Petrov. For an act, not the disposition of the article."

"What's murder got to do with it?"

"I was just using it as an example, since it seems that you, despite your legal education, need to have such simple things explained."

"You just answer my questions!"

"How can I, if I don't know which questions are germane to the case in point, and which aren't? You have summoned me here as a witness. I'm not obliged to be an informer!"

Oh, it's hard when a witness knows the written law! An informer is just what the investigator is after: he'll decide later on what to use for formulating charges. That's the whole rationale of political arrests: get them first, and then build up a case against them. You can hardly charge someone with using his constitutionally proclaimed rights to freedom of speech and the press!

Buyalsky spent a fruitless four hours with Lyalya, after which she remarked calmly that as she was not under arrest, she had the right to go out for a bite to eat. He had no choice but to accompany her to a café, and then spend an equally fruitless four hours with her after this break. The whole situation became increasingly surreal, and in the end it was the major who 'broke'.

"The creation and dissemination of anti-Soviet materials in poetic form."

"Well, that makes things a bit clearer," said Lyalya approvingly. "And now – I refuse to give any evidence whatsoever. Please make a note of that in your protocol."

The virginal sheet of paper in front of Buyalsky was decorated with that refusal, and the matter was closed. It was Buyalsky's problem how to explain to his bosses on what he'd wasted a full working day. As for Lyalya – she left with a valuable piece of information: I had been arrested for my poetry. This really was very important: it was unlikely that anyone would be admitted into the courtroom, and there was little chance that my sentence would be available for reading: so how, then, could it be established beyond any doubt just what was the especially dangerous crime against the state which led to the imprisonment of criminal Ratushinskaya? Yet now there was this official admission by a KGB major . . .

Naturally, this information had to be publicised, and this was done without any loss of time, citing the hapless Buyalsky as the source. But the fact that Lyalya's method became a legend was something she was to regret later on. There were others who decided that they could pull off the same trick just as well, if not better, than she. They may have been every bit as intelligent as she was, but they lacked the necessary legal knowledge to play cat-and-mouse with the KGB. And, thinking that they were following in Lyalya's footsteps, a number of people in Kiev ended up by supplying the KGB with evidence (not in my case, but in later ones), and only realising it after the event. But what's done is done: and the KGB can play those games, too. Coming up against them is like playing a game of chess: but it's just you against a harmonious team. And for you it's a blitz tournament, but they can take a break any time and confer amongst themselves over their next move. If you're not a supergrass, then it's best not to make even one move in this game, for the trophy is your conscience. You will not notice how ably they will extract something useful out of your words, and it will be no use repining later that they didn't play fair.

Of course they don't play fair. Didn't you know? Oh, how many 'involuntary informers' there were who had overestimated their own intellectual prowess!

Investigator Kobets, in the meantime, had travelled to Moscow and summoned Lara for questioning. Lara came dressed in her most elegant outfit, and with an English detective novel tucked under her arm. That saved her at least an hour's wait, because the KGB like to keep people waiting around in corridors.

"Wait here."

If you don't have something to read, your nerves will start to tense up as time goes by – and that's just what they want. But the moment a book appears in your hands, you can be sure that you won't be kept waiting for more than five minutes. Lara didn't even have to wait as long as that before the investigator flung open his door hospitably, and gestured for her to enter.

"You and I will be seeing a lot of each other!" he informed her.

"I'm not as sure as you seem to be that this will bring you much pleasure," observed Lara, seating herself gracefully, as though she were in a Parisian salon.

"Did Ratushinskaya conduct any anti-Soviet agitation in your presence?"

"Can you be a bit more specific? Just what do you consider to be anti-Soviet agitation?"

"Did she read you any of her poems?"

"It's quite normal to read poetry in our circles. Which particular poems do you have in mind?"

Mindful of his colleague Buyalsky's regrettable experience, Kobets decided almost immediately that it would be better not to tangle with this woman, either. As a result, the protocol of the interrogation was very brief: yes, they know each other, yes, they're friends. As the investigator declined to specify which poems were considered hostile to the state, the witness refused to answer any questions concerning poetry. And so on. ·

Kobets shoved the protocol across the desk at Lara: "Sign here!"

Little did he know that his sufferings were only about to begin.

"There's a grammatical error here, in the second line."

"I'll amend it."

"By law, protocols should contain no amendments, so that nothing can be added to them after they've been signed. I cannot possibly sign this paper."

Cursing under his breath, Kobets sat down to retype the whole page, and Lara pulled out her book.

"You can read after the interrogation's over!"

"The interrogation is over, isn't it? In our circles, it is considered bad form to sit around doing nothing."

Naturally, Lara found another error in the freshly retyped protocol: this time in the tenth line.

"I'm afraid you're going to have to do it again."

"Why couldn't you have pointed out all the errors at once?"

"How on earth was I supposed to know that the staff of the Ukrainian KGB are practically illiterate?"

Oh, but our Lara was good at putting on a show of Moscow snobbery.

Sweating profusely, Kobets laboured on over the protocol, and from time to time his Moscow colleagues would look in, grinning maliciously: they must have eavesdropped on the proceedings from the next room, and were now doing their best to increase the provincial's discomfiture. After that, one can only seriously doubt the accuracy of the old saying, 'one crow will not peck out another crow's eye'. Then again, maybe birds are more merciful than humans. Kobets never did realise his promise of further meetings with Lara: not a single rendezvous did he suggest. They're all like that, the KGB: they'll promise you the earth, and then back off. Don't trust them, fair maidens – they'll only break your hearts!

Chapter Thirty-five

For several days I caught up on sleep in my first solitary cell. This is not as surprising as it may seem: for the past one and a half months Igor and I had been working twelve hours a day, including Sundays. This was a chance to earn a considerable amount of money: our work brigade estimated that we would get around one and a half thousand roubles – give or take a little, depending on the size of the harvest – for two months' work. And we needed the money desperately – after all, we were expecting to move into our own apartment which would have to be furnished from scratch. Even allowing for furniture Igor could make himself, we would still need pots and pans and other household paraphernalia . . . Moreover, we were in dire need of at least some new clothes. It was essential to buy me a winter coat: Kiev isn't Odessa, and the winters are very cold.

It is strange how unpredictable our emotional responses can be: I survived my arrest, investigation and trial much more calmly than I had expected, yet I was terribly upset to learn, when I was already in camp, that the state farm took advantage of the situation and only paid out fifty roubles for the work Igor and I had both done. Was it for this we slaved so that we could barely straighten our backs every evening, and slept like logs during the twenty-minute breaks between 'assaults' on those blasted apple trees? Was it for this that Igor had to endure terrible pains in his feet, lugging sixty-kilogram sacks? However, the last thing he had on his mind after my arrest was entering into conflict with the dishonest management of the state farm.

Solitary confinement certainly made an impression on me, even though it was hardly the kind intended by my investigator: after all, this was the first time I had ever had a room just to myself. No amenities? Big deal! We hadn't had our own bathroom and toilet in Odessa, either, and it didn't kill us. The peep-hole in the door? I made a point of grinning insolently every time this little aperture opened (as it did every few minutes) when I happened to notice it. Smiling is very beneficial, especially in prison: a smiling face encourages positive emotions. If you want to retain control over yourself, start with your face, that's the easiest way. For several months I was to continue to be plagued by worry over Igor's fate. Had he been arrested, or not? That alone was enough to drive one crazy: maybe at that very moment he was being tortured?

But you have to keep a grip on yourself. In the mornings, they take you out for exercise in a cemented box-like yard which is seven of my steps in length and four in width. There is wire mesh stretched across the top of the enclosure. To keep the prisoners from flying away? I wondered sceptically when I first saw it, but later learned that it was there to stop the prisoners from passing anything over the top into the next enclosure. For some reason, a small bench had been firmly set into the concrete in the middle of the yard. It certainly didn't leave much room for movement . . . After a while, I devised a series of exercises to occupy the whole of the hour I spent daily in this tiny yard. Running on the spot, jumping over that ridiculous bench, a whole lot of stretching and bending movements . . . Composing poetry in prison was my essential need, maintaining silence under interrogation was no more than elementary decency, and refraining from shameful, cowardly recantations – the only way to preserve self-respect. So, upon sober reflection, my only distraction was those sessions in the exercise-yard, and I only missed four of them, due to illness, in the seven months I spent in that prison. Recent heavy physical work had toned my muscles nicely. Admittedly, it was tedious having to count a hundred jumps, twenty knee-bends, a hundred jumps again, sixty forward bends, a hundred jumps . . . I had eaten a lot of fresh apples in preceding weeks, I had a young and healthy body, psychologically I was also well-prepared for my current situation, so who could have fared better than I in prison? So if I were to break, and in the calling of a poet, at that, it would be a disgrace beyond words!

When the lack of Igor's presence pressed very badly, I would try to envisage his face, his lips, his hair. I remembered how, during the last twenty-minute break in the orchard when everyone else collapsed in exhaustion, he ran off and brought me back a beautiful *Belle Fleur* apple. This was nothing short of a minor miracle: there was only one tree with these apples on the whole farm, and I knew for sure that every single apple had been picked from it. I recalled how he had held me in his arms, rocking me gently back and forth when I was choking with fever after my spell in the Butyrskaya Prison. I remembered how, when he was six years old, he had said to me: "Ulysses was certainly very clever, but he told too many lies to be a decent man! And why did he shoot Penelope's suitor, who pleaded for mercy?" And how he taught me the auto-training which enables one to overcome pain of any kind. And how he would rid me of a blinding headache after I had spent the whole night poring over drafts of poetry, just by putting his hands on my temples, absorbing my pain into himself, and then shaking it off.

When the cell, the jeers of the warders ("Aren't you ashamed of yourself, lifting up your legs like that? And you call yourself a lady, too! We know that kind of 'exercise'!"), the gratuitous coarseness of the prison governor, and the paucity of the prison library became too much, I could always go to sleep. You were not allowed to cover yourself with your blanket during the day, but it was no longer forbidden to lie down on your bunk in daylight hours – the liberalism of the 1980s! To tune my mind to sleep was child's play, there's nothing easier. At first they didn't even go to the trouble of waking me up: the investigator had decided to let me stew in my own juice for three weeks, and did not summon me for questioning. I could only be sincerely grateful to him for deciding to employ this psychological manoeuvre. One cannot help but recall how the dissident psychiatrist, Anatoli Koryagin, used to go off to sleep when they decided to torture him with sleeplessness under continuous interrogation: he was forced to stay awake, while his interrogators periodically changed shifts. They didn't know the mettle of the man, though. He simply lay down on the floor after a certain period of time had passed and fell fast asleep under the eyes of his torturers. "Get up!" they demanded, but he didn't even hear them. They emptied a bucket of water over him, but all he did was open his eyes for a moment, shake the water off his face, and go straight back to sleep.

They did not try any 'physical methods' with me. I couldn't help wondering whether this would remain so, or whether they were hoping to lull me into a false sense of security. After the death of Snegirev (whom they had driven beyond all limits), and after what he had managed to tell about what went on here before his death, this prison's reputation was very bad indeed. The scandal generated by Snegirev's death may have forced the authorities to pull the reins in a little. Whatever the situation, though, it was clear to me that the best thing for me to do was write poetry. I had no writing materials at this stage, but I still retained my childhood habit of composing poetry in my head. Sitting down and writing seems an unnecessary chore when you're little! I would open the small window of the cell, and pace up and down, measuring my steps to the rhythm of the poem in my head:

We breathed freedom in verses,
Loyal to our friends we remained.

Baptised by the cold waters
Of a God-rejecting land.
And the courts rumbled their sentences,
And the minions fulfilled the decrees:
The sooner to cover with coppers
The crime of upraised eyes.
Whether murdered, or sold by our brothers –
We are leaving our cities back there:
Some for nowhere, for anthologies others –
Does it really matter where?

The food-slot opens, and a voice asks in a whisper: "What's your name?"

"Ratushinskaya!" I answer, as loudly as possible.

"Quiet, quiet! You're supposed to whisper, too!"

But of course. These little refinements have been devised so that people in neighbouring cells won't know that they're not alone here.

"There's nothing about having to whisper in your prison rules!"

"Get your things together and let's go."

I already have some things to gather, because I have received the legally permitted bundle from home: an ardently wished-for toothbrush, underwear, my 'good' slacks, shoes. However, it's impossible to tell whether it was Igor or his mother who put these things together. I knew that the family would try, in some way, to let me know if Igor was free. And they did. Igor's mother had embroidered a curlicued Ukrainian 'I' on my slacks: as they were the pair I kept for special occasions, this was supposed to convey to me the 'good' news that Igor was free. However, the prison administration ordered the embroidery removed before the bundle was passed to me, and they did such a neat job, there were no traces of Mama's stitching left. So I remained in the dark regarding Igor's whereabouts. Well, it would just have to be borne!

I was transferred to a cell where a grey-eyed cell-mate was already installed. Her name was Lyuba Sachenko. I realised immediately that she was a plant, but I did not even begin to guess her calibre. Later, in the camp, I once got talking to Olya Matusevich about our periods of investigation, and Sachenko's name was mentioned in passing. Olya reacted with astonishment: "You mean to say she's still alive?"

"I don't know about that, but she was certainly very much alive in January 1983. Why?"

Olya told me that Lyuba Sachenko was a notorious informer. She came from criminal circles, but proved too much even for the women criminals in the Kharkov zone. Not only did she inform on the other prisoners to the camp authorities, but she was hysterical and aggressive to boot, and was always trying to provoke conflicts. She was one of those 'trusties' ably picked out by the camp administration to have a degree of authority over the other prisoners and assist the warders. In short, she had gone to such lengths in the Kharkov camp, that the women imprisoned there began to plan her murder. This is something that happens only rarely in women's camps, but Sachenko had gone too far. The camp administration heard rumours about the plot to kill Sachenko and transferred her out of harm's way to Odessa. Olya was already imprisoned there, and this was how she got to hear about Sachenko and her exploits. Sachenko's movements were known until September 1982, but after that she seemed to disappear. Everyone assumed that she had died from a perforated ulcer, which is a frequent cause of death among prisoners in the USSR, and Sachenko was still a prisoner for all that she worked for her captors. She was really ill, but that September, anyway, she sat on her bunk and tried a 'soft' approach in her dealings with me.

"Ira, let's call each other 'thou' straight away, shall we? I'm serving my third year, and I've lost the habit of formal address."

I agreed, and that was another of my mistakes. Even though I knew nothing of her background, I did realise that she had been put into this cell for a purpose. So it would have been better to leave that small psychological barrier of formality between us, one she would have had to surmount every time she wanted to say something to me. This would have helped to keep her at arm's length. My courteous agreement, in this instance, was quite unnecessary, because people of Sachenko's ilk see it only as a sign of weakness.

And then the fun began: this Lyuba did not give me a moment's peace. No matter what came up for discussion, it was a foregone conclusion that it would end in stupid accusations and foul-mouthed abuse. After that, she would invariably dissolve into tears: "Don't hold it against me, my nerves are shot to pieces! Let's have a game of draughts!"

I would relent, and sit down at the board. Life was becoming very hard, though. The purpose and intention of the KGB isolator is to undermine the confidence of the prisoner, to make him feel that he is quite insignificant and has nothing to lose. This is done ably by a number of people who follow a carefully devised strategy: the prison governor, the prison doctor (the one who applied her energies to humiliating Snegirev – occasionally it is enough to strip a man of his trousers to break his resistance), the warders, and, of course, the plant in the cell.

Their first plan was to reduce me to tears. Actually, I find it hard to cry at any time, and allowing myself to shed so much as a tear in prison was something I would never countenance.

"Don't pay any attention to me," suggested Lyuba. "Have a good cry! You'll feel easier, believe me! Don't just sit there like a rock! We're all human!"

Stop! Where had I heard that before? Ah, yes, that huge, wavering shadow, which scooped me up when I was five years old, its horrible face moving closer and closer . . . Those frightening 'hu-u-u-mans' of my first childhood trauma!

But now I recall it with a smile, as I respond to Lyuba's urging by informing her that I have no great aptitude for tears, and would prefer to refrain.

"That's a lie!" she fires up immediately. "You're always lying! You were crying only last night! I saw you!"

Of course, it is she who's lying. The last time I cried was over an abandoned kitten, who was obviously begging us to take him in: a tiny ball of grey fluff on an empty landing. We had no permanent abode of our own, so we could not adopt him then and there. But he didn't understand that, as he miaowed pitifully and rubbed against our ankles; he couldn't understand why these big – and seemingly kind – creatures couldn't pick him up and take him home. And I did cry then – I cried for the kitten, I cried because we, too, were homeless and would have to go away, leaving him on that cold and empty landing . . . The only one to see my tears then was Igor. So we went off, leaving the kitten some sausage which we happened to have with us: at least he wouldn't be hungry, and perhaps someone would take him in – someone who had a home . . . We went away, feeling like monstrous traitors. I had not cried since that time, and would not, for many, many years.

That very day, as I sat reading with my back to the door, the food-slot opened and a warder's snout appeared in the aperture: "Are you crying?"

I turned around in amazement, just as Lyuba chimed in: "She cries all the time, she does! The whole cell's getting damp from her tears!"

The next one to exhibit 'concern' was the prison doctor: "The warders say that you cry every night! You really must control yourself! Have you no pride? I'll give you some valerian drops to calm you down."

"I have no need of your tranquillisers. Why don't you give some to the warders, so that they stop hallucinating?"

The investigator got in his tuppence-worth the next day: "There you go, Irina Borisovna, smiling as if nothing's wrong! But the time will come when you'll be in tears, begging me for mercy! I bet you'd like to have a good cry right now, wouldn't you?"

Heavens, how unimaginative can you be? "We have psychologists here!" added prison governor Petrunya meaningfully.

Those psychologists of theirs obviously favoured the assumption that if two people tell you that you're drunk, you will believe them, and stagger away to sleep it off. Or that if you tell someone a hundred times that they're a pig, they'll get down on all fours and start oinking. Well, that may have been their reasoning, but it isn't mine. After that, they latched on to my exercises. Suddenly, Lyuba began to find them annoying, and the warders tried to forbid this or that movement, on the pretext that I could 'break my back', or something similar. Then they started demanding that if I must exercise, then I must keep my coat on throughout. (Actually, it was my sister-in-law's coat, which was included in the bundle I got from home.) Of course, doing exercises in a coat is virtually impossible. The next psychological attack focused on my husband: first Lyuba informed me with relish that she knew for sure from the investigator that Igor had been killed while trying to escape, then she changed the story, maintaining that he was in the Lukyanovskaya Prison, where everybody knows "they torture the men something terrible. You hear screams coming from that prison every night." And much more, all in the same vein. However, by that time I was fairly certain – judging by the contents of parcels from home – that Igor was safe and not under arrest.

It is not worthwhile detailing all the nasty little ploys they practise on you, but there is one more thing which I must mention for the edification of my women readers: the men can skip this paragraph, as it will never affect them. This is something nobody had warned me about, nor had I read about it in any of the 'prison literature' which had come my way – either the authors felt the matter too embarrassing to mention, or I hadn't read the right books. It is quite commonplace for women to find that their periods stop after they are arrested. This is the result of shock, even if the shock is subconscious. If you should have the misfortune to be arrested and this happens to you – don't worry about it. Your body will get back to normal in a few months' time, a year at the most. Under no circumstances mention it to the prison doctor – especially the doctor in the Kiev KGB prison. It will only cause you further unpleasantness, and nobody will explain anything to you. Put your trust in Nature – she knows best.

But the situation in the cell had to be brought to some kind of order. The entire atmosphere in this vermin warren, with its smirking innuendo, was strongly reminiscent of the unimaginable (and seemingly impossible, in real life) atmosphere described in Nabokov's book

Invitation to an Execution. Even though he had never been imprisoned, he managed to convey something of the feel of such situations.

I managed to sort out Lyuba more easily than might have been expected. One day, when she had worked herself up into a frenzy, she threw herself at me, her fingers curling into talons, screaming that she would scratch my eyes out. There was absolutely no point in banging on the door to summon the warders: I knew that the only result of that would be an outburst of satisfied laughter. Ordinary criminals and 'politicals' are placed into the same cell for that very reason: go on, scream your head off, ask the nice warders to come and save you!

I assumed the karate combat stance Igor had taught me. Yes, I was quite prepared to break Lyuba's arm, or, if that were not enough, to bring her crashing to the floor with a well-aimed kick. I knew I could do it, and she must have sensed it, too, because she came to an immediate stop.

"Come on, Ira, don't get me wrong! It's my nerves – they're torn to shreds . . ."

Well, mine aren't, and it's to your own advantage to remember it. For two days I punished her with silence: I simply didn't hear a word she said. This punishment proved more fruitful than I had anticipated. Firstly, she's a plant and is obliged to communicate with me. Secondly, she's an ordinary gutter criminal, and that type is terrified of solitude. She had an almost physiological need to converse with someone. Finally, she was driven into apologising to me formally, and I set out the conditions of our future coexistence: I would talk to her before our exercise period in the morning, and also after the evening meal – providing she behaved herself perfectly. One word of abuse – and the evening game of draughts would be cancelled, one attempt at provoking some kind of conflict – and I would not speak to her at all for as long as I deemed necessary. Any attempts to initiate a discussion about my family would be similarly penalised, as would any questions about my past.

She accepted all these conditions without demur, and even began to suck up to me, which was just as repellent. Of course, every so often she would backslide: "I overheard the warders talking about you. You wouldn't believe the filthy things they said!"

But by this time it was enough to say: "Lyuba, stop!" to shut her up.

I encouraged her good behaviour, but obliquely; for instance, she knew that if I were 'in the mood' in the evenings, I would tell her the story of some book or film from memory. That old faithful, *The Count of Monte Cristo*, for instance. She preferred to listen, because she found reading tedious. I drew some pictures for her, and she was childishly enthralled by them, asking for more and more.

"Draw me a picture of a kitten," she would ask. "You know, one of those fluffy ones, with a big bow around its neck! And then draw me a chicken!"

. I did feel sorry for her: she was ill, her nerves were really in a terrible state and her interests and desires were about as primitive as is possible: yet, nevertheless, even she had an inner yearning to be treated decently . . . She even became rather attached to me, and though I could have been much harder on her, I didn't go to extremes if it wasn't necessary. In the mornings, I would listen patiently while she related her dreams, and then 'interpret' them for her as favourably as possible: her ulcer would be cured, she would be released early, and so on.

We saw in the New Year together quite amicably. We asked the warders for some of the ubiquitous green paint, and, using a bit of cotton wool around the end of a match, I drew a picture of a Christmas tree on a bit of paper torn out of a school exercise book. We used some chewed bread to stick this drawing to the draughts-board which we had propped up against the wall in a corner, ate a few caramels (these could be bought from the prison kiosk out of the ten roubles a month prisoners can receive from home), and she was thrilled by the 'New Year's cards' I had made – pencil drawings of candles, gnomes, snowflakes and suchlike.

At the beginning of January she suffered a bad attack of her ulcer, and they took her away. Not immediately, of course: she writhed around in agony for fourteen hours while the prison administration telephoned to and fro, deciding what to do. They didn't care about her, but they were worried about one of their stool-pigeons falling from its perch. I had started thinking about declaring a hunger strike to force them into taking her away for medical treatment, but it didn't have to come to that. Just before they took her away from the cell, she shoved a packet of biscuits into my hand. Heaven knows how she could have thought about biscuits in the state she was in.

I was transferred to a solitary cell. Upon my word of honour, it was a relief! The prison governor, Petrunya, assured me that I had not been placed in solitary as a penalty. For the first time ever, he assumed a 'humane' demeanour and admitted that he knew I had the right to protest about being alone: it was just that there were no more women in the prison right then, he explained.

"Don't worry," I replied with a smile. "This suits me fine."

Chapter Thirty-six

I nvestigator Lukyanenko also came around gradually to accepting my conditions: I take no part in the investigation, and reply to no questions for the interrogation protocol. I am perfectly happy to study the protocol and any other materials offered to me, but I sign nothing. If Lukyanenko wishes, I will discuss the weather with him, or classical literature, or any number of similarly neutral subjects. I will not, however, talk about myself, my family, my friends or anything at all connected with the case they are putting together against me. Should I think of any other 'off-limits' subjects, I told Lukyanenko, I would let him know.

At first, predictably, he went through the standard routine of warning me that it was up to him to decide whether I would be allowed to write home, and that the sentence I would receive at my trial would largely depend on the outcome of our little sessions. After that he tried flattery and, when that didn't work, he yelled at me. However, when he saw my smile of pure satisfaction at his loss of control, he pulled himself up at once, apologised, and never raised his voice at me again. On one occasion he threatened to have me placed in the punishment cell – a prison within a prison, you could call it. I expressed a very lively interest: "I haven't been there yet! More power to your elbow, captain; give me a chance to find out what it's like in there!"

But he didn't. He was very quick on the uptake at times. As was to be expected, he tried to tell me all sorts of nasty things about Igor and my friends. When that happened, I would not respond at all: if he was going to change the subject from the Ukrainian climate to something on my 'proscribed' list of topics, he could conduct a monologue.

Once, after I had remained stubbornly silent for two hours, he gave up: "No offence meant, Irina Borisovna!"

"It's beyond your powers to offend me, no matter what you say. But if you want me to reply, remember to keep a civil tongue in your head."

After a few months, he would simply run quickly through the list of questions for that day: "Same answers as usual?"

"Yes, of course: 'no reply'."

"You might like to take a glance through the magazines over there in the meantime: there are some interesting ones among them."

So I would read peacefully while he hammered away at his typewriter to produce that day's interrogation protocol: this took him a long time because he was only just learning to type. When he was through, I would read the protocol and point out mistakes and typing errors. As I refused to sign any of the protocols, he did not need to retype them, but could amend the original then and there. As a token of gratitude he would bring me really interesting magazines and journals such as *Novy Mir* (*New World*). There was an advantage in this for him, too, because after we had discussed the latest 'in' publications, he could air opinions about them in his own social circle. He even once asked me to type up the protocol ("After all, you can type properly, and I can't"), but that, I felt, would have been a bit much – you have to draw the line somewhere!

"You don't help me with my work," I told him, "so why should I help you with yours?"

He pricked up his ears at once. "How could I help you?" he asked keenly.

Of course, what followed was perhaps very cruel on my part, but the temptation was too strong to resist.

"Well, I've been racking my brains for two days now to find a proper rhyme for the word 'apples', and don't seem to be getting anywhere."

I then proceeded to explain about proper rhymes and approximate rhymes, and he fell for this old trick hook, line and sinker. I knew perfectly well that there is not a single proper rhyme for the word 'apples' (*yabloki*) in the Russian language, but he didn't. I reproached myself mentally for inflicting this problem on the unsuspecting Lukyanenko – who should know better than I that chasing an elusive rhyme is worse than a nagging tooth? – but . . . !

Lukyanenko promised earnestly that he would give the matter all due attention, and continued with his laborious hunt-and-peck typing up of the protocol. He had a harder time than usual, because his attention was now divided between typing and searching furiously for a proper rhyme for 'apples'.

He never did return to the subject of mutual assistance after that. Moreover, there were fewer and fewer of the obligatory 'ideological motifs' in what he said during interrogation sessions as time went on.

One such excursion, however, is something I shall remember with delight to my dying day.

Although the case against me rested largely on my poetry, the prosecution did not disdain to make use of 'other materials' confiscated during house-searches, something not always to their advantage.

"When did you meet M. Voloshin, and in what circumstances did he give you his poems?" I was asked once.

"No reply."

Only by straining every sinew was I able to pronounce these words without dissolving into incredulous, helpless laughter. But of course! Among the *samizdat* editions of poetry we possessed there was a typewritten copy of Voloshin's *Northeast* (*Severovostok*) and, naturally, the author's name was on the title page. But what could Captain Lukyanenko possibly know about the great Russian poets of the Silver Epoch? Who was there to enlighten him about the poet Maximilian Voloshin, that he had died long before I was born, and that some of his work had been published, albeit very selectively, in the Soviet Union? Actually, *Northeast* did not figure in Soviet editions, until, in line with *glasnost* and *perestroika*, it was finally published in 1988.

Lukyanenko leaned back in his chair, and looked at me with paternal benevolence: "Irina Borisovna, there you go again, refusing to say a word, thinking that you are shielding your friends! You're throwing away your young life for nothing, believe me! You'll regret it later, but by that time it will be too late. It's not as though any of these fine friends of yours are worth the sacrifice, either! They're all much smarter than you: they answered freely, expressed sincere regrets, and now they're free. We're not monsters, after all ... And Voloshin's one of them, walking the streets of Kiev today, free as a bird ..."

I managed to suppress my mirth at this point, too, but I must confess that this cost me more effort than anything else during the entire period under investigation. In my mind's eye there was a fantastic picture of Lukyanenko conducting a spiritualist séance, complete with ouija board and guttering candles, listening to Voloshin (who was a decent enough man in his lifetime), confessing All and expressing sincere regrets fifty years after his demise, in the hope of getting out of a term in Soviet labour camps! I had no intention of saying anything that might lead to the exclusion of such a gem from my indictment: they don't care what charges they bring against me, so it's not my job to iron out any absurdities in their case. And, in fact, that particular 'offence' did figure in my indictment: "possession of a slanderous document, couched in poetic form, by M. Voloshin. One copy, typewritten." If anyone should disbelieve me – I can prove my claim, as the full text of my sentence was smuggled out of the USSR.

Generally speaking, though, Lukyanenko was not too bad, as investigators go. Towards the end he just ploughed ahead with fabricating the case as he'd been ordered, and didn't bother me with any psychological ploys. Naturally, he summoned me regularly for interrogation: he was a conscientious KGB captain, and was soon promoted to the rank of major. The warders, too, got tired of harassing me when they saw that it yielded no results. I continued to remove my coat in the yard, I kept right on with all the exercises I had devised, and in the end they would ask, quite amiably, whether I'd had enough 'jumping around' as they rattled keys and escorted me back to my cell. Only two didn't give up: the female who'd searched me after my arrest (we didn't know the warders' names, so Lyuba and I had dubbed that particular one 'the Rat') and an elderly, fat-faced man for whom we devised a rather less genteel nickname. For a while, he took to waking me up during his night shifts, by rattling the food-slot, and proclaiming: "I can't see your face! Turn around so that I can see your face!"

After a while I realised that the thing to do was 'not to hear' him: pretend I'm fast asleep, and that's that! Go on, you swine, open the door and come into the cell to wake me up! Only then you'll have to write a report, won't you, and when a pile of such reports accumulates, somebody in authority is going to want to know why you, out of all the warders, have taken to going into a woman's solitary cell during the night!

Prison governor Petrunya obviously did not want to aggravate the situation in any way: I suppose solitary confinement *was* forbidden, and he was glad that I hadn't lodged any complaints about it. He was perfectly civil when he came on his rounds, and stopped looking for pretexts to carp. I was even allowed to have an unlimited supply of books from the prison library: in the beginning it was a maximum of five a week, but now they would bring along up to ten. Among the library's meagre stock of some two hundred titles, there were thirteen Polish books by authors like Senkiewicz, Orzeskowa . . . I plunged deep into them: luckily Grandfather had taught me the Polish alphabet, and I was soon reading them quite easily, without having to pause to puzzle over the meaning of this or that word.

The warders also stopped spying on me when I went about my intimate needs: only the Rat retained her former interest in keeping an eye glued to the peephole in the lavatory door. To my surprise and considerable amusement, the warders found a new hobby; according to the moronic prison rules, I could have a pencil, but not a ball-point pen in my cell. The pencil would have to be sharpened from time to time, but prisoners may not have any sharp metal objects to hand. They had even taken the hook off the waistband of my slacks, substituting a plastic button. So I had no choice but to bang on the door quite often, and ask the staff on duty to sharpen my pencil. They did so, but without any great enthusiasm: who likes being bothered with such trifles? That is, until on one occasion, I said, loudly and admiringly: "Thank goodness! At least *one* person in this place knows how to sharpen a pencil properly! So far I've always got the pencil back looking as though the person who'd sharpened it didn't know one end of a penknife from the other!"

And it is true that this was one of those rare occasions when the pencil came back with a decent point on it. After this, the warders all vied with one another to see who could get the pencil sharpened best: I'd get it back with a needle-fine point every time.

I permitted myself the luxury of composing poetry on paper, but in a patchy, abbreviated form, key words which would mean nothing to anyone but me. Of course, I didn't keep any of those bits of paper: the cell was searched periodically, and so was I. But I could make jottings, commit the poem to memory, and then burn the bit of paper. Lyuba smoked, so she had matches. I started, brazenly, to buy matches too, out of my 'kiosk money'. They came in very handy when I began writing a long poem, which I entitled 'Pencil Letter'. I had only one bit of bad luck, when a couple of warders arrived unexpectedly to search the cell, and I didn't have enough time to destroy the piece of paper I'd been working on. From that time onwards I was much more careful. Searching your brains is beyond the warders' abilities. Every morning, I would recite in my head everything I had written, making sure I remembered it. By the end of my period under investigation, I had a full collection of new poems written and memorised: the KGB had lots of time, and that meant that I did, too. To justify the use of paper, I would copy bits and pieces out of the library books, and it was some time before these were confiscated. However, when I was to be transported to camp, these literary extracts were taken away, and when I arrived in camp I received an official notice of confiscation, stating that the material in question was 'ideologically harmful and anti-Soviet': Pushkin, Tyutchev, Lesya Ukrainka . . . Well, why not?

It didn't take long to sort out the prison doctor, either: I realised very quickly that the best thing to do was to avoid her services altogether. Illness comes soon in prison, but you will be accused of malingering, or the ailment will be used against you.

The last straw was the problem of dental treatment: for some reason, everyone's teeth start breaking up in prison, and I was no exception: a piece broke off one of my teeth. I reasoned that the witch of a doctor was hardly likely to set about me with a drill – that was way out of her sphere. As it turned out, a dentist could be called – at the discretion of the investigator on your case! Lukyanenko had not been brought to heel yet, and he tried to blackmail me into answering his questions in return for a visit from the dentist. I laughed in his face, and was therefore very surprised to be summoned out of my cell three weeks later for dental treatment.

I was even more surprised when I saw the number of people waiting for me in the prison infirmary: the warders on duty, the doctor, someone in a KGB uniform . . . The woman dentist who had been called to the prison to attend to me examined my teeth in front of all these spectators.

"Well, this shouldn't hurt. This tooth will have no feeling left in it by now."

"But it was perfectly all right! A bit has chipped off, that's all!"

"Are you the dentist, or am I?"

After that she did a simple and straightforward thing: pulled out the nerve without any kind of local anaesthetic. My audience watched with unconcealed interest, to see how I would react to the dentist's ministrations. I knew that this was to be a test of how I would stand up to physical pain. I tried to 'switch off' the way Igor had taught me. There was really nothing else to do under the circumstances. I managed to endure everything in silence, from start to finish, and didn't try to break away. Luckily, when you have your mouth wide open, your face is distorted anyway. It was too late to stop the 'treatment', in any case: by the time I realised what that fiend was up to, the tooth had been opened up, and would have to be filled – otherwise I was bound to get an infection, and then things would be really grim. In the end, she filled the cavity with something or other, but I retain only a hazy recollection of that stage of the pro-ceedings. Wooden-faced, I managed to walk back to my cell, and collapsed unconscious on to my bunk only after the cell door shut behind me.

After this I had no doubt at all that to ask for medical assistance in this place would be an act of lunacy, no matter what happened. It was all relatively easy for me, with my small problems like the business with the tooth and the occasional cold: but what must it have been like for Snegirev, who developed a tumour here after being force-fed, and it turned out to be cancer? Let those who dare condemn him for signing a recantation in order to be allowed to die in his wife's arms in a hospital – and even then, under the eye of the KGB. They would not have let him out of their clutches alive in any case.

As far as I was concerned, the prison doctor was someone I resolved to avoid like the plague, along with similar 'persons in white coats'. Life followed its course: reading, composing poetry . . . I also amused myself by mentally staging films, thinking through every scene: the colours, the costumes, whether to shoot this or that episode at a distance or in close-up. I began with devising a film of *King Mateusz* by good old Korczak. The works of this wise Warsaw doctor and writer, who perished in the furnaces of Treblinka, were to be my solace more than once in the times ahead.

The most difficult thing was to remember various smells from the outside world. There were only four of them in the prison: chlorine, prison food, urine and the stuff they used to wax the floors. Did you ever realise that cats smell of blackcurrants? This was a discovery I made in childhood, and proved again and again.

I was genuinely sorry when they transferred me from my solitary cell to one with another prisoner. However, she turned out to be quite amiable, and I had no trouble with her whatsoever. Unfortunately, I had to suspend a rule I had made for myself in solitary – to spend the daylight hours on my feet. It doesn't take long to become accustomed to reading as you walk, and I didn't even notice myself turning around automatically after every six paces. That kept my muscles in trim, and meant that I could keep the cell window open, too, because you don't feel the cold when you're on the move. Now I could hardly keep to this routine without driving my cellmate crazy by pacing back and forth in front of her, like a human pendulum.

By this time I knew quite well why it was that the attention of the KGB had been drawn to my insignificant self, and what it was that they were after. I was indebted to my investigator for the information that my poetry was circulating throughout the country much more widely than I had ever anticipated. And indeed, the list of places where my work had been confiscated in house-searches was quite impressive. Even more astounding was the fact that not only my poems, but my photos – heaven knows who printed and disseminated them in such quantities – were also confiscated along with the poetry. Photos were in demand only when 'the original' in question became dangerously popular. Moreover, some of my poetry had been published in the West, and read on the Russian services programmes of some Western radio stations. Jamming or no jamming, someone would be bound to hear. Then there were clandestine tape-recordings. If that sort of thing were not nipped in the bud, there was no telling how far it would go.

Therefore, there were two simple things that the KGB wanted me to do. Firstly, I was to write an official protest to the West, forbidding publication of my poetry: how dare you?! This would have served the dual function of frightening off Western publishers, and convincing them that it was better to have no dealings at all with *samizdat* authors in order to avoid unpleasantness. Secondly, I was to reject my own poetry, and abase myself in profuse apologies. The publication of such a turnabout in the Soviet press would have alienated domestic readers: poets are very highly regarded in Russia, but by the same token the people do not forgive or forget any manifestation of dishonour on their part. Those who had concealed my poems about freedom would have consigned them to the rubbish-bin in disgust. If you swear allegiance to servitude, you have to bear the consequences.

That was why the KGB tried so hard in the beginning, hoping that I would start whining for mercy, and go along with their demands. And that is why they lost interest in me when they saw that I wouldn't. All that remained for them to do now was to throw together a case against me, and pack me off to the camps for as long as possible.

Chapter Thirty-seven

While I was taking it easy in prison with only three aims to fulfil – keep silent under interrogation, write poetry and do exercises – Igor was having a much tougher time.

In the first place, he decided that it was of the utmost importance to preserve all my poetry. That meant that everything that had escaped confiscation would have to be typed, and handed to people who would reproduce it and pass it on. He had never learned how to type, but now he would have to. He waited for two weeks, and then, armed with an ancient typewriter, shook off his KGB tail and set off to a friend's house well outside the city limits. This house would not be bugged, and the clatter of a typewriter would pass unnoticed.

Our friend professed herself delighted to co-operate: "Of course, Igor! Come on in, I'll put the kettle on!"

Unfortunately, her mother had already heard about my arrest in a Radio Liberty broadcast, and, putting two and two together, came storming into the room; "Are you both out of your minds? Do you want to be arrested, too? You'll end up in Siberia at this rate! I warn you – I'm off to the militia straight away!"

While she hurried off to carry out her threat, Igor quickly packed up the typewriter and his papers, and took off into the woods to hide, after saying a rushed goodbye to our friend. She made the sign of the cross over him: "May God keep you! I hope we'll meet again."

Igor kept to the woods for a couple of kilometres, certain that nobody would be able to find him there without tracker dogs: and if an operational group with dogs were to be sent, he would be long gone by the time they picked up his trail. He travelled back to Kiev changing trains several times, left the typewriter in a luggage locker on one of the outlying suburban stations, and went on with a bundle of my poems hidden under his shirt. He knew that the KGB might be waiting for him at our station – and that was the last thing he needed just then – so he went to an 'emergency address' instead. The owner of that apartment had once said to Igor, "I have never had the courage to stick my neck out, but I understand you, and my home is always at your disposal."

"That could place you in danger," warned Igor.

"Never mind that. Come if you need to."

Why did Igor take this man at his word, rather than turning for help to Leonid Korsunsky, who at that time was hailed as a victim of the KGB and was most insistent in offering to help Igor, especially if any documents had to be passed along? (Korsunsky claimed contacts in Moscow.) Several months later, the Soviet press published a penitent article by Korsunsky, in which he expressed regrets about his 'former anti-Soviet activities' and thanked the KGB for showing him the error of his ways and putting him back on the straight and narrow. How many people had he betrayed before that?

But in the house of our 'shadow' friend, all the poetry I had written prior to my arrest was typed twice, six copies each time. After that, every page was photographed in yet another home. Part of it was distributed among our Kiev friends. The remainder had to be despatched to Moscow, the place where all *samizdat* channels meet, then fan out again.

Suddenly, however, Igor turned up three poems which had somehow been omitted from the newly prepared collection: that meant they would have to be typed and reproduced today if they were to be included. As soon as Igor went out into the street, he saw that he was being followed. All attempts to shake off the unwelcome tails proved in vain. He spent the next few hours dodging around the city, but nothing helped: neither rapid changes from one trolley-bus to another, nor diving through alleyways and back yards. Finally he ended up outside Marik's place, and went into a phone booth to check whether his pursuers were still hard on his heels. They were: he saw them halt on the corner and wait for him to make his next move.

Just then Nina, Marik's wife, came out of the house to buy some bread.

"Igor!" she cried, spotting him at once. "What on earth are you doing there? Go on upstairs, I'll be back in a few minutes."

"I'm being tailed."

"Big deal! Go on up, I tell you! You must be frozen stiff!"

Marik greeted Igor enthusiastically: "Hello, you vagabond! So who's a birthday boy tomorrow?"

"Marik, there are a couple of tails outside. I couldn't get away from them."

"Impossible!"

"That's what I thought, but I was wrong. And I *must* get away from them, because . . ."

"Right, we'll show them!" fired up Marik. "Didn't we grow up in this part of town? Come on, let's go!"

They spent the next hour dodging around places where they knew every stick and stone. The surveillance was being conducted with no expense spared. It involved not only 'foot soldiers', but cars as well, two Zhiguli sedans, a minibus and a Volga. That meant public transport was out: the KGB would have no trouble keeping up. The ones who followed on foot did not come too close, maintaining a distance of about a hundred metres. Entering into the spirit of the hunt, Igor and Marik roamed around until dark, and then made a dash for a yard which they knew had five or six different exits: this was their last hope. By breaking into a run unexpectedly, they won a few seconds' start. Once in the yard, they dived under a stairway which, due to some architect's whim, led down to the ground from the first floor. From this hiding-place they saw their pursuers rush into the yard, mill around indecisively for a few minutes, and then split up and head for the various exits. Thank God nobody had spotted them. They spent more than an hour under the staircase, and then crept out carefully to reconnoitre. A car stood at the next crossroads in each direction, but it was already quite dark, so they managed to slip into the next through yard, and work their way out into another street. Success! Now Igor could head for the 'shadow's' apartment in peace: to bring a tail to the door of someone already known to the KGB is bad enough, but to put them on the trail of a contact as yet unknown to them is a positive crime. Friends like this must be cherished, one should never meet them openly, and pretend not to recognise them if there is a chance encounter. There are always more supporters of this kind than those who burn their bridges and emerge into the open: yet those who remain unobtrusive are just as important as those who 'go public'. Without their help, *samizdat* would not last more than a month, for the KGB would round up and hound all known disseminators of clandestine manuscripts. Without them, the Fund helping political prisoners and their families would have been stamped out long ago, instead of continuing its existence until the present day. Their lot is much harder than ours – I know from personal experience that it is much easier to go into prison yourself than to see others being taken. But they must watch their friends disappear, and cannot even write to them, for that would mean instant exposure of the contact. And they torture themselves over it. Our deepest respect to you, who cherish and protect the free written word!

We owe you everything, for without your efforts we would have been different people. There will come a day when a monument shall be erected in our country in honour of your endeavour, and if not we, then our children shall come to lay flowers at its foot. This monument shall be just as tall and proud as any monument to the Unknown Soldier.

Igor and Marik split up before Igor headed for the flat of one of the 'shadows', where the three poems which were the cause of this whole mad chase were duly retyped with the requisite number of copies. Marik had made Igor promise that he would come to stay the night at their place. Igor got there an hour before midnight, this time without any KGB tails, entering the house through a back door. They switched on the light and saw that there were several 'watchers' standing patiently in the forecourt. Igor was certain that he would be arrested, so he scribbled Marik a note that he wanted to see his mother first. Marik nodded, made a rude sign towards the concealed bugging device, and said loudly, "Well, shall we turn in?"

"I suppose so. Good night!"

They switched off the lights, and rustled blankets as though settling down to sleep. Half an hour later, they left the house without a sound through the back door, which was supposed to be sealed. They flagged down a private car moonlighting as a taxi, and went to Igor's mother's home. She was still sitting up and waiting, even though she had switched off the lights. Ten minutes after the kitchen light was switched on, there was a KGB car standing outside. However, they didn't worry too much about that: it's one thing if the KGB seize you in the street, but if they want to take you when you're inside, they need an arrest warrant. If they'd had such a warrant, they would have grabbed Igor while he was still at Marik's.

Igor, his mother and Marik spent that night together. Mama poured them a shot of vodka: "Swallow that down, boys! It'll warm you up a bit!"

They laughed, and raised their glasses in a toast: it was Igor's twenty-ninth birthday.

By morning, there was no sign of the KGB tails: clearly, they were in no hurry to arrest Igor. They needed to know where my poetry was going, and intercept it. As for Igor – the KGB knew well enough that he would continue exactly as before.

For the next two weeks, he went over various plans for getting to Moscow. There was no point in boarding the Moscow-bound train: he'd be taken off that before it even left the station. He decided to go via Odessa: the train for Odessa left Kiev from a peripheral platform, and it was possible to reach it bypassing the station concourse altogether. His main concern was to get out of Kiev unnoticed; after that things would be easier. He hid one photographed collection of my poetry in his breast pocket, and put another seven into a shoulder-bag. He set off for the station with his sister Lyalya and Marik following at a discreet distance. For two days before that he had hidden out in a 'shadow's' apartment. He worked his way round to the last carriage two minutes before the train was due to pull out, but the militia were there, waiting: "Your documents!"

They addressed Igor, so Marik and Lyalya, who had not been spotted, melted immediately into the crowd of people around the train. A moment later Lyalya pushed her way forward, and hurried towards Igor: "Thank you, young man!" she gushed. "So kind of you to help me with my bag!"

She plucked the bag out of his unresisting hand, and moved off calmly towards another carriage. Igor was hustled off to the station's militia room.

"Hands behind your back!"

"I'll see your warrant first!"

"You'll see it, don't worry!"

Through a narrow corridor, and into the militia room occupied by a militiaman behind a desk, flanked by two benches with a number of detainees sitting on them. The door into an adjoining room was open, and Igor could see four occupied iron-barred cells. One of the occupants was lying on the floor, with his arms tied behind his back.

"Frisk him!"

Two militiamen run their hands over Igor, and feel a bulge in his breast pocket.

"What have you got there?"

"Photos. Not firearms. When you show me your warrant to conduct a body search on me, you can have a look at them."

"Smart, aren't you?"

But they leave the photos to Igor. Their job really does entail looking for and confiscating weapons, they don't give a damn about papers of any description. They lead him back to the anteroom and tell him to sit on a bench by himself.

"No talking to this one!"

"Lieutenant, you promised to show me your warrant of arrest."

The lieutenant doesn't respond, but two others in plain clothes offer an explanation instead: "A woman had this case stolen!"

They point obligingly to a suitcase standing on the floor nearby.

"So what? Did I steal it?"

"Why, yes!" came the beaming reply. They looked very pleased with themselves, these weasel-faced KGB minions. Someone in the cells next door started shouting, and the militiamen stamped off to tie up the culprit. A middle-aged man, one of the detainees, could not suppress his indignation as the moans from the neighbouring room became louder: "You treat people like animals!"

One of the KGB weasels came to life: "Do you realise what article of the Criminal Code observations like that come under?!"

"A remark like that doesn't qualify under Article Sixty-two, nor even Article One Hundred and Eighty-seven (two)," interjected Igor. "And don't you forget that I'm a witness! So belt up! And, in any case, that observation was nothing less than the truth."

The weasel shot Igor a look full of hatred, but kept his mouth shut. Soon these two operatives got a phone call from someone, picked up their suitcase, and left. Igor didn't see them again.

Three hours later, Igor turned to the militiaman seated behind the desk: "Captain, isn't it about time you charged me? You don't have the right to detain me any longer unless you do."

The captain raised an eyebrow: "You don't say! Why, I've held people here for up to two days, and nothing happened to me. I must say, it's interesting to meet the intelligentsia every so often!"

He went away somewhere, and then returned for Igor: "Come with me!"

Igor was taken through a door he hadn't noticed. There were two militiamen there, but nobody in plain clothes.

"We can't hold you any longer. Sorry about all this, pal! You understand – it's not our fault. We had orders from you-know-who to take you off the train. Care for a cigarette?"

Igor took the proffered cigarette, and drew a pleasurable lungful of smoke. The wad of poetry nestled cosily against his chest.

"Of course, this is none of our business . . ." began the captain, but one of the others interrupted him, "Say, mate, what about your ticket? You stand to lose your money! Here, give it to me!"

He addressed Igor in the familiar 'thou' form, and apologised immediately for the familiarity. Igor waved a dismissing hand: "That's okay. It's not as though you were KGB . . ."

"Right! Hang on a few minutes!"

He returned with a full cash refund on Igor's ticket.

"Thanks, captain!" said Igor, and meant it.

"We're not detaining you any longer, you know that, but would you mind telling us what all this is about? You must understand our interest! I can't remember such a to-do in all the years I've been working here at the station. Not even when we were after some armed killers. You know there's a nationwide search out for you, don't you? We've all seen your photo. But you're not some crook, are you?"

"Come on, guys, you know who organised all this!"

"Sure, the KGB, but why? Foreign-currency deals? Espionage?"

"If that was it, they'd have arrested me straight away, not staged some stupid farce with an allegedly stolen suitcase!"

"Well, we figured that, but what could we do? Orders, you know . . . Maybe you're a 'political'?"

"My wife has been arrested on a political charge, and now they're breathing down my neck."

"So what did she do?"

"Wrote poetry."

"You're kidding!"

"No, it's the truth."

"So what kind of poetry causes something like this?"

Igor recited my 'Motherland' to them from memory.

"D'you know any more? Go on, we won't rat on you!"

Igor recited some more, whatever came to mind. They listened.

"Is she still alive?"

"I think so. They take parcels for her at the prison."

For some reason, one of the militiamen took off his uniform cap, twisted it around in his hands for a few moments in silence, then put it back on his head.

"God keep you, lad. And good luck to you and your wife in the future!"

Igor's mother, sister and Marik were waiting outside. A week later Igor caught a 4 a.m. bus from Kiev in the direction of Moscow. He didn't buy his ticket at the booking office, but directly from the driver. It took him more than twenty-four hours to reach Moscow, changing trains and keeping an eye out for KGB tails. Finally he arrived at a friend's home in Moscow without any unwelcome pursuers. He phoned our old friend Bob Gillette, and Todd Ledew of Associated Press. Bob was the first to arrive, and interviewed Igor with the help of the lady of the house who knew English. In those days, Bob did not have enough confidence in his knowledge of Russian. Finally, he suggested to Igor that he write his piece with no mention of Igor as the source of the information.

"Come off it, Bob!" protested Igor.

"But you'll be arrested for this."

"Irka's already under arrest. Honestly, Bob, I beg of you: write up

the interview as verbatim as possible, and don't even dream of concealing my name."

"I feel as if I'm holding a gun to the head of someone who's asking
me to pull the trigger!" expostulated Bob unhappily.

"There's no question of shooting," averred Igor. "This is just as it
should be."

"All right. I'll do it."

Igor gave him a collection of my poetry, the one in photograph
form.

"Sign it."

"But I'm not the author!"

"Doesn't matter. She can sign it later."

So Igor wrote, from both of us: "To our friend, Bob Gillette." We
were not to know then that Bob prophesied truly: I really did add my
name to this dedication when we met years later in Washington.
But that evening, Bob shoved the poetry into the waistband of his
underpants, put his press card into his breast-pocket for easy access,
and exchanged a smile with Igor.

Todd came next, but luckily Igor had no further contacts with him
after that meeting. Several months later he was searched by Soviet
customs, who found some written material which he was taking
out into the free world. When questioned, Todd naïvely told his
interrogators everything he knew: who gave him the papers, and to
whom they were to go in Paris. No, no, espionage didn't enter into it:
the information he was carrying contained details of recent arrests,
and was destined for open publication. Not long afterwards, Todd's
revelations were pushed under our friend's nose.

"Well, Elena Vladimirovna?" crowed the KGB. "See what a nice
little case we can make against you?"

And in truth, they did have enough material to build a 'nice little
case' against her, should they so wish, on political charges. It is
immaterial that all the information was correct, and that the persons
it concerned were all soon to be given an 'open trial'. The very fact
that she gave this information to Todd was enough to render her
liable to prosecution for 'disseminating malicious concoctions, slandering the Soviet state and social system'. Still, Todd may not have
known that. She was saved from arrest by an unexpected pregnancy:
in those days our modest authorities did not care for publicity of that
kind, and pregnant women were not imprisoned – not the ones pulled
in for dissident activity, anyway. Not surprisingly, the doctors attending
her counselled abortion, claiming that there were abnormal features
to the pregnancy. But these dirty tricks were common knowledge by

that time. Irina Grivnina, in her time, had also been advised to terminate her pregnancy while she was serving a term of internal exile, and she was not the only one ... The reasoning was that you were more or less obliged to have an abortion, to make it easier for the authorities to imprison you. Naturally, nobody took any notice of such 'good advice', and went on to have beautiful babies while the KGB could only grit its teeth in frustration. It's a pity that Igor and I had put off having a baby for so long, waiting to get a place of our own.

After these two interviews Igor was photographed, and sent me one of the photos in camp. Jadvyga Bieliauskiene, one of my fellow-prisoners, sighed heavily when she saw it: "Heavens! How tired he looks!"

In fact, when that photo was taken, Igor had not slept at all for two nights in a row, and could not stay any longer in the apartment where the interviews took place, either. A young man who knew all the alleyways of Moscow as well as Marik knew the ones in Kiev, volunteered to get Igor away from the neighbourhood unseen. They were on the move for an hour, by which time they were certain that nobody was following them. They said goodbye, and Igor's guide melted away into the dark. Where to now? Igor knew exactly where.

Chapter Thirty-eight

"Lara, I'm calling from a phone booth."

"Get over here – quickly!"

Igor went gladly.

"Lara, this could be dangerous for you. They've put me on the nationwide wanted list."

"Will you stop talking nonsense?"

She hugged him, pulling him into the flat. "When did you last eat?"

"Can't remember. Ages ago."

She began fussing around in the kitchen. Then came a knock on the door.

"Lara, delay them for a few moments, and I'll make my way out by the balcony. Remember – you haven't seen me!"

But it was only the neighbours, so all was well. Igor caught up on some sleep and rest at Lara and Sasha's. They proved themselves to be really true friends. The last collection Igor had of my poems was left with them. Not so long ago we met up with them in Chicago: they had finally managed to get exit visas from the Soviet Union. We spent some time playing with their children, but when the conversation returned to 'adult' subjects, Sasha sighed deeply: "At least you did something, Igor, but I didn't do anything to combat that regime . . . So what right do I have to pronounce any judgements now?"

"You sheltered me in your home when I was being hunted by the KGB. You brought me warm clothes and coffee when I was in Lianozovo Prison: that alone could have led to your arrest. Where would Irina and I be today without your help? I wish everybody 'did nothing' the way you did!"

The four of us were all people of the same kind (I don't mean ethnically). So what can be said of different rights . . .

Feeling light and carefree, Igor travelled back to Kiev. There was no need to worry about being tailed now: they could arrest him and welcome, as far as he was concerned. He'd accomplished what he set out to do; my poetry was safe. "Irka, I've done everything that had to be done", he wrote to me in a letter to the camp. At that time I could only guess at what lay behind that cryptic assurance.

Igor got a job as a night-watchman, because money was running low. This job gave him the opportunity to make pendants for sale. His father offered financial help, but Igor refused. He'd resolved to accept money from his father only as a last resort, and the situation was not yet desperate. There was not much time for rest, though. The 'protest of the thirteen' had already appeared, and was added to my case. This protest did not make any noticeable impression on the Presidium of the Supreme Soviet of the USSR, but it did warm my heart before I went on trial. I memorised the addresses of all those who had signed the protest. Heavens, how lucky we were to have so many good friends! Only a few had not come up to expectation.

Igor occupied himself by trying to devise some means of passing notes into the prison. Once a month, the family could send me a parcel of items chosen from a 'permitted' list. Things like bacon fat, onions, butter, sugar . . . Igor decided to start with the sugar. What if one could insert a note written with ballpoint pen, on special paper, into a cube of sugar, and then cover up the traces? Wasn't that the answer to the problem? Even if I were to throw that piece of sugar into a cup of hot water, the sugar would melt, but the note would remain intact and legible. He made a special hand-press for the purpose, but the sugar cubes it turned out differed slightly in appearance from those bought in the shops. He then made a special drill, which he used on pur-chased cube sugar – and he was in business! Of course, out of every ten cubes, nine would break up, but the note would go into the 'lucky' cube, after which the tiny aperture could be sealed up with a few moistened sugar grains. However, I was unlucky: the day my parcel was brought to the prison, another came from somebody else, and the warders mixed up the two packs of sugar cubes. So I got an ordinary pack, and some foreign-currency dealer got my 'doctored' one. When he found the note addressed to some 'Irka' and not to him, he immediately handed it over to his investigator to curry favour. From that time on, the rules of Kiev prison were amended to read that sugar might be sent to prisoners only in crystal form, not in cubes. The word 'crystal' was underlined twice with a red pen.

Lera Senderov fared somewhat better: Igor managed to conceal a note in a parcel to him using a totally different method, and hidden in other foodstuffs. When Lera's mother was permitted a meeting with him, she was very surprised (not knowing anything about any notes) when her son, who had never shown any interest in food, talked at length about how 'delicious' the stuff in the last parcel had been . . .

He was equally pleased with the second parcel – for the same reason.

"Igor," I asked as I sat down to write this chapter, "what was it, and how did you do it?"

"Better not write about it," he said. "The KGB haven't rumbled that particular method yet." Then he grinned reminiscently. "That was my greatest coup – getting something like that into Lefortovo Prison. You know it would be great fun, one day, to hold a conference of political prisoners from different countries to compare experiences and exchange ideas. I bet that would be fascinating!"

One fine day Lukyanenko informed me that the investigation was over, and I could acquaint myself with all the papers of the case.

"By law I have the right to choose my own lawyer," I told him.

"Irina Borisovna, you're in isolation – how can you possibly choose anyone?"

"Then I authorise my relatives to choose a lawyer on my behalf."

He sighed with exaggerated bitterness: "I've already had a word with your family about that. They don't want to lift a finger to help you. And they've refused to hire a lawyer. Still, don't worry, we've found someone for you: Galina Korychenko, she's very good."

"No, thanks – I won't have any truck with a lawyer selected by the KGB!"

"Well, in that case you can study the papers by yourself, and she'll go through them by herself. Anyway, she's already been appointed to handle your case."

"I shall refuse her services at the trial."

"That's up to you. But then you'll be left without any lawyer at all."

In the meantime, he was lying glibly to Igor, assuring him that the investigation was still under way, and that it was too early to hire a lawyer for me. It is true that by Soviet law the accused cannot see a defence lawyer until the investigation has been completed.

"I'll keep you informed," Lukyanenko promised Igor, but, of course, he did no such thing. The first Igor learned about my trial was when he received a summons to appear in court as a witness – the day after next. What could possibly be done in the space of the one working day remaining?

On the first day of the trial I publicly rejected the services of the KGB-appointed lawyer, explained my reasons, and said that I would conduct my own defence. Judge Zubets smiled sourly: he and Galina Korychenko were a well-practised double act, and had master-minded more than one political trial between them.

"You have no legal training, and we are obliged to furnish you with qualified legal representation. Your refusal is rejected."

"In that case, I won't take any part in these proceedings. But I retain the right to a final word when your trial is finished."

The rest was sheer boredom. Zubets tried to make me answer, while I sat there like a rock, having made my prepared statement. I had my own reasons to be in good spirits that day. In the first place, it was interesting to learn the contents of the interrogation protocols attached to my case. They had really spared no effort to get evidence against me. It seemed as though they had dredged up anyone who had ever known me in Odessa, starting with my sixteen-year-old sister Alya and ending with my university lecturers, my friends from student days, my former work colleagues ... And after all that trouble, the yield was pathetically meagre: one of my former schoolteachers, Rashkovskaya, testified that I had shown marked anti-Soviet tendencies from the eighth grade of school, but she had, alas, been unable to do anything about that because she was only my chemistry teacher ... The remaining Odessites stood firm: is it any wonder that I love my birthplace? Secondly, although the trial was conducted behind closed doors (which meant that none of my friends or family would be present), I had heard my mother-in-law's raised voice from the corridor: "Let me in! My daughter's on trial in there, and everyone's being kept out, even her husband!"

Dearest Mama! From that moment, I have never called her anything but Mother. But her shout told me something else – Igor must be free! It's one thing to guess, but another to know for sure that today, right now, he is standing on the other side of that door, even if I can't see him.

Naturally, while the lengthy indictment was being read out to a courtroom full of KGB 'spectators', I put my time to the best possible use, and wrote a poem:

> And it's turned out to be just boring,
> no more than that. And the cramped space
> Of the box, the enclosures in the stuffy courtroom –
> A cosy, oakwood barrier
> Between me and the judges: so no one will be confused.
> Eye to eye!
> A childish triumph:
> They're coming back! Are they afraid of uproar in court?
> Perhaps my cheerful gaze is too fierce,
> zek-like? Do they think I might get them by the throat even as
>   they sleep?
> But my brigandage has already been overcome

By the pride my forefathers minted:
What have these servile eyes to do with me?

The second day of the trial turned out to be more entertaining: the witnesses for the prosecution were brought in to testify. There were no witnesses for the defence, just as there was no defence. Korychenko didn't say a word throughout the entire proceedings. All in all, though, I daresay her non-interference was the best thing possible.

I was to receive a pleasant surprise when two of the witnesses, a married couple whose interrogation records had led me to expect the worst, put on a magnificent performance. They refused to testify, stating that the real crime was the fact that someone was being tried for writing poetry, and had to stand in the dock without adequate legal defence. They declared that despite their respect for the law they could not consider the present trial legal, and therefore would not testify at it.

The judge, clearly stunned, tried shouting at them and threatening them with reprisals at work, but they stuck to their guns, and I could only watch them with unconcealed admiration. Judge Zubets had only a tiny consolation out of all this: once both witnesses left the courtroom, he pulled himself together and remarked: "Well, Citizen" (he named the husband) "has rejected his earlier testimony, claiming it was obtained under duress, so we can't use it. But his wife didn't say the same thing, so we can still use *her* pre-trial testimony."

True, she had forgotten to say so. But that's not surprising: the poor woman had been positively seething with indignation as she stated her views! As far as I was concerned, this didn't matter, because I would have been given the same sentence with or without her evidence. This couple were now fighting for their own self-respect, so that the KGB would never again try to drag their names into any dirty business. And they achieved their objective. I felt proud and happy for them.

Then, to my unbounded joy, they summoned Igor. We had not seen each other for half a year.

"Hold on, darling, I love you!" he called out from the doorway.

Before they had him ejected from the courtroom, he told the judge exactly what he thought of this trial, and informed him that I had been elected a member of the International Pen Club (something I had not known: what a lovely, unexpected birthday present!) and that he had every right to be in this room, although the only place unoccupied by a member of the KGB is the dock. Where he was quite prepared to go.

Zubets, beside himself with rage, opened his mouth to retort, but then merely made a sign to the guards. They started to hustle Igor out, but before the door closed behind him, we managed to look once more into each other's eyes.

"So how did I look to you?" I ask him now.

"Well, compliments aside, you were terribly thin, your hair was close-cropped, and you were wearing a track suit. And you were totally silent. Why didn't you say something?"

"I wanted to hear what you were saying. You ought to be glad that I was such a dutiful wife, and didn't interrupt when you were in full cry!"

"Who cut your hair so short?"

"Oh, that was a laugh! My fringe grew down over my eyes, practically to the tip of my nose. Mind you, you need the investigator's permission to get your hair cut. So what with one thing and another, they only got around to giving me a haircut right before the trial. Then there was an added problem: I couldn't do it myself, because scissors are classed as a cutting instrument, and prisoners aren't allowed to handle those. Obviously, there's no hairdresser at the prison – the fellow in charge of prison supplies used to cut the men's hair, but he had no idea how to cut a woman's hair. So he did the best he could, cropping me *à la* village idiot. He apologised profusely for his lack of expertise, too, but I don't think it was all that bad! In fact, I'm thinking of getting my hair cut like that again . . ."

"Just you dare!"

The next witness to be called was Marik. How Zubets didn't have a heart-attack is a mystery to me. However, the tablets which were to hand should I collapse in hysterics came in very useful: Judge Zubets took them instead of me.

"What are your relations with the accused?"

"We're friends, a fact of which I am very proud. I refuse to give any further testimony."

"You'll answer for that in court!"

"I'll consider that an honour."

The judge's threat was not an empty one: Marik was taken to court over his refusal to testify at my trial, as were the husband and wife I mentioned earlier. All three were sentenced to six months compulsory labour and assigned workplaces by the court. Marik took this in his stride. He still has the documents setting out his sentence, and calls them his 'proof of decency'.

The married couple, however, were broken by what followed. Disciplinary meetings were convened at their places of work, and they expressed repentance. They asserted that *now* they would testify if need be. And such a likelihood could have arisen very soon: materials concerning Igor had been assigned by the court to a separate file. Trying to justify themselves, these former friends of ours blamed everything on us: according to them, it was *our* fault that they had ended up in such a predicament. They even arranged a meeting with all our mutual friends, pointing out that people like Igor and me should be avoided at all costs, and insisted that everyone ought to ostracise Igor. Our friends retorted that they saw no reason to do anything of the kind, and that was the end of the matter. Igor, who was present at this 'analysis', was astounded: it was the first time he had seen how aggressive those who have been broken can be towards those who are 'clean'.

"It was a disgusting scene," he told me much later. "Actually, *he* tried to say as little as possible, but *she* more than made up for his reticence. I hadn't heard so much dirt for a long time. I was disgusted, but at the same time I couldn't help feeling sorry for them, somehow."

After my release, all those who declared on that occasion that they would stand by Igor came to congratulate me, bearing bouquets of flowers. I had further confirmation from them that all had happened just as Igor had described: yes, that couple had asserted that they would give evidence next time, and regretted their earlier refusal.

A few days later I was told by a third party that this husband and wife wanted to see me – but alone, without Igor. No, let them share a cup of tea with their 'tame informer', not with me. It is up to my readers to decide whether I was too hard-hearted in refusing to meet them.

Chapter Thirty-nine

The next four witnesses offered Judge Zubets a modicum of cheer: four KGB informers who had tried to worm their way into our confidence, but had been rumbled and shown the door. Sadly, one of them was our friend Alyosha Kozdoba's father. Which just goes to show how different two generations can be. When Alyosha came to see me after my release, he asked to see my sentence documents.

"Alyosha, dear, maybe it would be better if you didn't . . ."

"No. I must."

Even his lips went white when he said that "I must". He started to read, then stopped when he got to his father's name: his father had maintained glibly that I had conducted anti-Soviet agitation and propaganda in his presence and slandered the Soviet authorities.

"Irka . . . I knew about this. I knew, but I didn't want to believe it."

"Alyosha, we're friends, nothing can change that. And you have my deepest gratitude for helping Igor – he's told me about that. As for this" – I indicated the document in his hands – "it has nothing to do with you."

"Irka's alive! Thank God, she's alive!" cried Igor at that moment, coming in from the kitchen with a tray of coffee cups. "Come on, people, this is no day for sadness!" and deftly changed the subject.

But there in the courtroom, listening to endless repetitions of the words 'slander', 'conducted anti-Soviet propaganda', 'wrote anti-social poems' and so forth, I did not feel sorry for the people who spoke them: they had chosen their own path, so let them tread it, for the edification of their children and grandchildren!

Of course, the scenario would have been incomplete without a contribution from Lyalya Varvak's mother, Sergeyeva, whom I have already had occasion to mention. This tireless warrior did not even give evidence, as such. Her job was to pour out as much muck as possible concerning Igor. She appealed to the court to sentence him to death by firing squad. Realising that this was an attempt to break my composure (after all, the case being heard was mine, not Igor's), I kept my cool, and jotted down the more outrageous of her statements with great interest. I still regret that these notes were later confiscated. The most harmless of her epithets was that Igor was an 'immoral son-of-a-bitch'; the rest is unprintable. After reading through my notes back in the cell (my cell-mate and I were both impressed by Sergeyeva's fluency and feeling for language), I couldn't help wondering how anyone could extract a word of accusation against me from that tirade. I could have spared myself the mental exertion: accusations against me were written in *post factum*. The KGB knew that Sergeyeva wouldn't object.

The ones for whom I felt really sorry were my seventeen-year-old pupils, the ones I had coached privately for university entrance exams. The authorities managed to run them to earth, too. Poor kids, they were so afraid of losing their hard-won student places! And this was just the threat that Judge Zubets held over their heads, placing his own interpretation on their evasive answers.

"Did Ratushinskaya make derogatory remarks about the Soviet system in your hearing?"

"Anything she said can be heard in every queue in town."

"Do they know at the university that you associated with a state criminal? We'll have to tell them . . ."

The girl breaks down in tears, and Zubets presses on triumphantly: "Did she try to dissuade you from actively joining in Komsomol life? Well, what's the matter with you? Lost your memory? We already know everything! Why don't you say something? You signed this protocol, didn't you? Do you know what the penalties are for giving false evidence?"

"The investigator wrote all that out, and then made me sign it. He said they taped every word . . ."

"So is your answer yes, or no?"

"Yes . . ."

She leaves the courtroom in tears, and doesn't see my understanding and encouraging smile: don't cry, child! It's not the end of the world! They've bullied and driven you into a corner. You're only seventeen years old, after all! And I could see that you didn't want to co-operate with them! So don't reproach yourself: these things happen. Nobody can condemn children for weakness! They will grow up and become strong. I write this now only because I know that she did not see me smiling at her then.

They brought in another two whom I'd coached, but . . . hold on! Where's Kolya? I'd coached him that summer. Igor told me later that

Kolya, for all that he, too, was only seventeen, told the investigator at his first interrogation to go to the devil, and promptly went off and enlisted in the army. I think the dirtiest and most disgusting feature of my trial was this treatment of young kids whose only 'fault' was that I had coached them in maths and physics. While I sat there helplessly feeling sorry for my erstwhile pupils, a whole lot of stirring events had taken place in the corridor outside the courtroom, and Igor was back home, and not behind bars.

When he was ejected from the courtroom, he heard his sister's alarmed cry, "Igor, watch out! Provocation!"

Sergeyeva, followed by two men in plain clothes, was bearing down on Igor along the narrow corridor dividing the courtroom from the witnesses' waiting room. In the meantime, a couple of burly men were dragging Igor's mother and sister away from the end of the corridor: the KGB didn't want any unnecessary witnesses. Guessing their intent, Igor appealed immediately to the militiaman standing on duty by the door, "Sergeant, they're about to frame me for something! Help me!"

"What can I do?"

Sergeyeva's escorts, seeing Igor saying something to the sergeant, slowed down a little, but Sergeyeva didn't realise this, and kept coming at Igor like a ship under full sail. The corridor was a long one, so by the time she was about six metres away from Igor, her attendants had fallen back about the same distance. This was just the moment to act!

Igor sprang forward towards Sergeyeva: "Turn around and put your hands to the wall, or I'll kill you!"

She obeyed immediately. "Go away, I won't do anything!" she gabbled.

Igor walked past Sergeyeva's gaping 'minders', and at the end of the corridor was immediately surrounded by a tight circle of friends, who escorted him out to a waiting car.

"Igor," I asked him later, "would you really have hit her?"

"Well, I wouldn't have killed her, of course, but I wouldn't have minded inflicting a spot of grievous bodily harm! Yes, I know she's a woman, but how many people landed in gaol out of consideration for her sex? How many people turned the other cheek to her, and found themselves imprisoned? You can bet she doesn't suffer any pangs of conscience – because she hasn't got one. People like that are inhuman monsters – that's been proved over and over! Maybe you'd say a word in favour of Ilse Koch, too? That she didn't deserve to die just because she was a woman? Why d'you think Sergeyeva lost her nerve? Because she knew that I meant what I said! As it was, she got off easily, which wouldn't have happened if she'd tried to sink her claws into me: I could have injured her quite badly while shaking her off! The best way to avoid a fight is to be prepared for one. Creatures like Sergeyeva and those bastards from the KGB have a well-developed sense of self-preservation."

"Have you ever hit a female like that?"

"No, I've never laid a finger on one. I tell you, as a rule it doesn't get that far. They are only brave when they're sure that nothing will happen to them . . . As a matter of fact, I've not heard of Sergeyeva trying to provoke any fights since that time. She ought to be grateful to me, the old harridan, for scaring her off any more transgressions of that kind."

The following day my sentence was read out. While they droned out all twenty-one boring pages (having refused me my right to make a final statement), I sat there and thought, for some reason, about the sea. Warm, green, buoyant water. And the little underwater reef my father had shown me when I was nine years old, and he decided that I was a strong enough swimmer to go that far. This tiny reef was his discovery, and nobody knew about it but the two of us: it was far out from the shore, and very small. There was just enough room on it for two to stand and catch their breath, Papa standing waist-deep in the water, and I – up to my neck. He showed me how to find it with the help of landmarks on the shore: that telegraph pole over there must be exactly in line with the edge of that stone wall – see the white mark on it? And that tree has to be aligned with the chimney on that roof over there: then you can put your feet down, and you'll be on the tip of the reef. How proud he was when Uncle Oleg came to visit, and I took him out to the reef all by myself! And found it, too, and didn't run out of breath. See, old friend? You have your ways of teaching your children, and I have mine! Whose will be stronger?

The day I was sentenced, Igor had to shake off yet another KGB tail. He raced up a hillock, coming up against a four-metre-high wall. Scrambling up, he hung for a moment by his hands, and then dropped down on the other side on ice-covered, slippery asphalt. His pursuer, shouting "Stop, thief!" followed, slipped, and remained prone on the ground. Thanks to this stroke of luck Igor managed to reach a friend's place and telephone Moscow, because our phone had been cut off. Although no 'unauthorised persons' were admitted into the courtroom, the verdict was known: seven years of strict regime camps to be followed by five years internal exile, and the sooner this information was made public, the better.

Igor's mother and sister stood outside the court, hoping to catch a glimpse of me when I was taken away. Lyalya shivered violently in a light summer coat: she had sent her winter coat to me in prison. When Igor came home, she thought, she must make him eat something, and then try to persuade him to snatch at least a bit of sleep.

This was a far cry from how our respective fathers had pictured our futures. Conflict with the authorities was the last thing they would have wished for us. Actually, if they, who grew up under Stalin, had had an attack of 'Pavlik Morozov syndrome', the prosecution would have had cause to rejoice. Uncle Oleg, naturally, lost his post as a director of his institute, and his career was effectively finished. My father was an ordinary engineer, so they couldn't demote him, nor did they summon up the resolution to sack him from his job. Igor's mother had already retired, while my mother was demoted to ordinary teacher status from her post as senior teacher. Not one of our parents reproached us, nor was there any reason to justify themselves. Moreover, they did not consider themselves particularly hard done by.

After he'd finished reading out my sentence, Judge Zubets turned to me: "Did you understand everything?"

"Yes."

"Seven plus five!"

Obviously, he was hoping for some kind of reaction, and I was determined not to give him that satisfaction.

"Yes, I understand that. Do you want to add something?"

By the look on his face, he would have gladly added something – like several more years to the sentence! – but, alas, I'd already received the maximum possible.

The KGB 'spectators' filed out of the courtroom, leaving just the prison warders and myself.

"Seven years!" said the Rat, who happened to be on this shift. "Terrible!" Then added, with satisfaction, "No husband's going to wait that long! He'll be filing for divorce soon enough!"

Stupid fool, she was still trying to achieve the desired effect! As though I hadn't spent the last seven months preparing myself just for this verdict! However, I couldn't resist taking a dig at her, too: "It looks as though our husbands have different concepts of decency!"

I regretted my spiteful words as soon as I had uttered them: by the look on her face, I had unwittingly landed her a blow below the belt. I must learn to curb my hasty tongue: there are some blows which should not be dealt to anyone, even creatures like her.

There was a pleasant surprise waiting for me back in the cell. While I was in court, my cell-mate Olya had been busy creaming butter and sugar to make a 'cake' with some biscuits. She remembered that the following day was my birthday – it had cropped up in conversation once. By the time I got back, her culinary masterpiece was ready, and set out on the chess-board with a plastic bag for a tablecloth. She had carefully traced a '29' on top of the cake with biscuit crumbs.

"Olya! You're an absolute marvel! Thank you!"

"Irisha – what did they give you?"

"Exactly what I expected."

"Oh dearie me! Well, don't let it get you down yet – they may commute the sentence."

"Stop trying to make me laugh!"

"Well, good for you for not crying!"

"Why should I cry? Come on, let's enjoy ourselves! Am I allowed to have some of that today, or must I only look at it?"

"Actually, it ought to stand for a bit longer, so that the cream soaks right through the biscuits. However, under the circumstances – what the heck! Let's have ourselves a party! Now, where can we get a bit of thread?"

We pulled a long thread out of one of the prison blankets and, using it like a cheese-wire, cut ourselves a piece of birthday cake each, and set about celebrating.

Olya had been imprisoned for theft, and they had brought her here from the camps when the KGB started a currency-violations case against her former boss: he had been the captain of a ship on which she had worked as a cook. She had been sent for as a witness. She knew nothing whatsoever about the captain's alleged crimes, and was astounded by the fact that she was held in a KGB prison. To this day I do not think she had been put into the same cell with me to be an informer; Petrunya did not want to keep me in solitary confinement during the trial, and her presence in the prison offered a solution. And, in any case, why should an informer go out of her way to organise a treat for me? I don't think I have ever had a more delicious birthday cake than that one, and in the evening she had me in stitches with her stories of life in the world of thieves.

She herself had stolen by chance (few cooks can resist the temptation to purloin supplies), but her husband was a famous professional pickpocket in Kiev, so she knew all the lore of the world of petty criminals. I was particularly tickled by her story about the carpets. As she told it, one day two covered vans pulled up outside the main General Store in Kiev, an hour before it was due to open for business. Some men got out, and draped a number of carpets over one of the vans. There was a price label on every carpet. The prices were very high, but at that time carpets could not be had for love or money; you had to have your name on a waiting list for at least six months. In the next van there were several men with a cash-register, who took the money of those who wanted to buy, and issued receipts with the official stamp of the store on them.

"As soon as the store opens, comrades," they instructed, "take these receipts up to the fourth floor as proof of payment, and pick up your carpets."

There were plenty of people standing around waiting for the store to open: anyone with any sense at all arrives at least an hour before opening time to be at the head of the queue to get short-supply goods before they run out.

The queue surged forward: "Carpets! They're selling carpets!"

The men collecting payment and issuing receipts asked a militiaman standing on the corner to keep the queue in order, and stop the eager customers from stampeding the two vans. He obliged willingly. Forty minutes later, having raked in an enormous amount of money, the two vans drove away, never to be found. When the shop opened and a wave of humanity surged up to the fourth floor, brandishing receipts, it transpired that the store had nothing to do with the commerce which had flourished so briefly and briskly outside. The news of this confidence trick had swept around Kiev at the time, but I had never heard the details.

Having acknowledged the slickness of the operation, I nevertheless asked: "So how many people got robbed, all told?"

"No idea. My man wasn't involved in that caper, it's not his line. I know about it from some friends."

"But it must have been at least two hundred people, if they were there for forty minutes?"

"To hell with them! Nobody spends their last groat on a carpet. The smallest one cost a thousand roubles, no less. So you tell me – have *you* ever had a thousand roubles in your pocket, just like that? Or two? Or three?"

"No."

"But if you'd had, what would you do with them? Buy carpets?"

"No way!"

"So the ones who got fleeced must've been able to spare the cash. Who can buy carpets if they're just on a salary, you tell me, unless they're some high-ranking official bastard? Thieves can't take offence at other thieves!"

"But Olya, do you really believe that what they did was right?"

"Come on, I've had a noseful of that kind of talk! You think you're the first? Well, you just listen to me: thieves aren't the worst people around, not by a long chalk! It's all very well for you to sit talking of rights and wrongs when you grew up with Mummy and Daddy to look out for you. Me – I grew up in an institution. For juvenile offenders. My Ma died when I was thirteen, and I never even knew my Pa because he was killed during the war. And my bastard of a step-father started on me straight away: either I have sex with him, or clear out of the house. The apartment was in his name. So I walked out, without a thing, just the clothes I had on me."

"But the militia could have interfered! There are laws . . ."

"*Laws*! Much I knew about laws when I was thirteen! Or d'you think I had money to hire a lawyer, maybe? All I knew in them days was how to give a Pioneer's salute, and obey my elders . . . We slept in cement pipes, we did: you know those really big pipes? They're like a corridor, with heating pipes running through them. You crawl into one of those, and you can sleep like a top: the wind doesn't get in, it's warm, and nobody can see you. Then I got packed off to the juvenile 'colony' for vagrancy and theft. But how else was I supposed to eat, if I didn't steal? God, the sights I've seen: wouldn't do to talk about them at night. One thing I'll tell you, though: everyone steals. From cooks to the militia – everyone! There wasn't a single staff member in our colony who didn't steal from the food and clothes meant for us kids!"

"Surely not *everyone*, Olya!"

"Well, there may be a few lunatics who don't. Or saints. As far as I'm concerned, that's six of one and half a dozen of the other. But normal folks – well, if you steal from them, they'll steal back. Thieves are more honest than the government, anyway: the government robs the poor people, but the thieves only take from the rich. Now tell me, have you ever had your pocket picked? Even once?"

"No. But, Olya, I wasn't all that poor, either."

"Regular millionaire, eh? Don't make me laugh . . . ! Want another bit of cake? Once you're in camp you can forget about parcels: the first one you'll get is half-way through your sentence, and once a year after that, seeing you'll be on strict regime. So come on, stoke up on some calories now!"

"When did you leave the colony?"

"When I was seventeen. And what did I have to look forward to? They assigned me a job, but that would have meant living in a hostel, and I was sick to death of institution living! It'd just mean getting robbed again, but by different people. So I went to a friend's place – and you should have seen the crowd she was running round with!

You mightn't believe me, but I was real pretty in those days: legs like a ballet dancer, and a figure to turn any guy's head. I guess I would've ended up going from hand to hand, but my bloke spotted me right off. Felt sorry for me at first, me being so young. He didn't lay a hand on me until we got married, and that's the truth. Maybe you're surprised that I love a thief? Why, he was the first person to treat me decently. And he's a good man, even now. He's got TB, so he's had to give up thieving. But you know, he comes to see me at the camp every time I'm allowed a meeting! All the others envy me . . . Hey, Irisha, don't look so down! It's my fault, idiot that I am, talking like this! Come on, let's think about something a bit more cheerful! Now, why're you looking at me like that? We don't have to agree about everything, do we?"

"Will you tell me about life in the colony later?"

"Yes, later. Not now. You've had enough for one day. Listen, let's dance! If you like, I'll teach you to dance 'The Gypsy'. I used to dance really well, once."

It must have been a strange sight that met the warder's eye through the peep-hole: Olya, hand on hip, began to hum a lively tune and trace the figures of the dance in the narrow space between our bunks. We danced past each other, and the food-hatch clanged open.

"Hey, ballerinas! Keep the celebrations a bit quieter, will you?" But he was laughing himself as he said this. He was a harmless one, this good-natured, rotund warder. We called him 'Winnie the Pooh'.

Petrunya saw the remains of our cake when he came on his round the following day. We had left the '29' untouched, keeping that bit till last.

"What's that?" he demanded.

Olya, who was usually scared stiff of all officials, stuck out her chin belligerently: "I made that! It's her birthday today!"

"Hmph! Actually, things like this are against regulations . . ."

But he issued no order to have our cake removed. He stood there for a few moments looking at it, then turned around and went out.

Chapter Forty

G reetings, my dear one! Well, here I am, and the worst is now behind us. Therefore, what you must do immediately is take your passport, some paper and a pen to write an application, and come here as quickly as possible for a meeting with me. Here's the plan:

Take a ticket from Kiev to Potma, with an intermediate stop in Moscow. There you go to the Kazan Station, and make a booking on train No.42 'Moscow-Saransk' as far as Potma. Get off in Potma, cross the railway bridge to station Potma-2, and at 8 a.m. hop on a narrow-gauge train to Barashevo. Once there, go to the Visitors' House and speak to the woman in charge: she will tell you what paperwork to submit. A personal meeting is permissible for one or two visitors, it can last from one hour to three days, and the sooner you get here, the better.

This first part of my letter to Igor, with details of how to get to Barashevo, was dictated to me on my first day in camp by Raya Rudenko. She knew this route like the back of her hand, because her husband Mykola, a poet and a member of the Ukrainian Helsinki Monitoring Group, was arrested first, and sent to the men's zone of this very same camp. You'd be hard put to find anyone who knew the way better than Raya. She was imprisoned later: Mykola continued to write poetry in camp, and Raya used to smuggle it out and circulate it in *samizdat*. In other words, she had done exactly what Igor was doing now, the only difference being that Igor is a strapping, healthy young man, and Raya is very small. I almost wrote 'small and weak', but that would have been incorrect. Physically she was really petite – like a little sparrow. But a sparrow with a will of iron. She had kidney trouble, she suffered from oedemata, she could hardly eat anything out of the meagre camp rations . . . Yet it was she who managed to plant a small, illegal vegetable patch in the camp, masking it with flowers. It was she who could not bear to see a speck of dirt on the rough, bare-board floor of our hut without cleaning it up. It was she who treasured every word written by Mykola in her memory, ensuring that this rich cultural heritage would not be lost while she was alive . . .

On my first day in camp, it was she who explained to me that it was imperative for Igor to come as quickly as possible, before the camp administration could find some pretext to cancel the meeting to which I was entitled. Such cancellations are within the framework of our humane legislation, and the next scheduled meeting would only be in a year's time. At best, we would have a mere six meetings, at worst – none at all. Tatyana Velikanova predicted that the first meeting would be permitted, but that it would also be the last. As usual, she was right. All my new friends in the camp shared my concern whether Igor would be in time, or not. And would he get my letter at all? The camp censor had passed it, but everyone knows that the KGB can intervene to ensure a letter's disappearance *en route*. While I was settling into camp life, Igor and his mother were already half-way between Potma and Barashevo. They did get my letter, and set off at once. It was an impressive stretch of the journey. For all that the distance was only some fifty to sixty kilometres, there were camps stretching on both sides of the railway tracks all the way. Only camps, nothing else! Igor counted at least nineteen from the window of the carriage. You can't mistake a camp for something else – the barbed wire and guard-towers speak for themselves, and stone barracks beside the line.

"Hey laddie, come over here for a 'quickie'!"

Women stand by the windows of the barracks, lifting up their skirts invitingly: the train moves along very slowly, and the inmates of the women's camps are having a bit of fun. That camp behind them, another appears after a short stretch of ground, covered with Mordovian birches. You can see the prisoners in this one being lined up for a head-count. Then more guard-towers, bristling with machine-guns. The guards wear their uniforms, the prisoners theirs. And still more camps, and more again. Not all of them are surrounded by barbed wire, though: some are marked out with the notorious 'Bruno spirals' – thin, prickly wire woven into large loops and laid out instead of a fence: you can see through it, but it's impossible to climb through: it lies in frozen loops up to eight metres high. If you try to crawl through it, you won't make it even half-way before you get hopelessly tangled and half-garotte yourself.

There are zeks in the train, too, 'trusties' who are allowed to leave the camp without being under guard, and who work outside the camp zone. They return every night, and have to wear the standard camp clothes: black overalls, a black cap, and have their identity tags prominently displayed on their chests: these give their surname and the number of the work brigade to which they belong. They stand in the open space at the end of the carriage, and Igor joins them for a smoke and a chat.

"Igor, don't go there!" pleads his mother. "They're criminals – they'll cut you up!"

Most certainly they're criminals: political prisoners are not assigned to unsupervised work outside the camp zone. They have knives, too, with plastic handles. They sell them on the trains as a kind of souvenir of zek craftsmanship. They somehow manage to get this clandestine 'production' of their camp-bound chums out of the zone. Another article of commerce is brightly coloured cigarette-holders. Buy them, free citizens, and the vendor will split his take with the maker. Money isn't permitted in the camps, but there's plenty of it around in the criminal zones. Favours, large or small, are bought from the guards for cash. Everything has its price. For instance, it costs three hundred roubles to disappear into the neighbouring women's zone so that your absence will 'go unnoticed'. And so on.

Naturally, they have no thoughts of knifing Igor, and their talk is quite friendly. They have an unerring eye for visitors: and, anyway, who else would need to travel here for any other purpose? The only passengers are prisoners' relatives, and camp staff: there is no industry in this area, so the inhabitants of all the surrounding towns are in some way dependent on the camps for their livelihood. There's nothing they can do about it – and one must eat.

"Travelling to see your brother, eh lad?"

"No, my wife."

"No one goes to see his wife!"

It's a sad fact that in most cases it is women who travel to the camps – to see their husbands or sons. Few men travel to see wives who have been put away on criminal charges: they usually file for divorce. Why is that so? I don't know. Why does a cow's tail grow downwards? Olya was not indulging in empty bragging – she really was a lucky exception.

"My wife's a political prisoner."

"Ah, that explains it! She must be in Barashevo in that case."

They know that 'politicals' don't desert their imprisoned spouses, so there's no need for further explanations. The talk that takes place is similar to the one at the Kiev railway station's militia quarters. In a significant change from Stalin's time, political prisoners are now respected by guards and other zeks alike. You have to be a really rotten egg to come in for bad treatment from criminal prisoners if you are in 'for politics'. You are seen as a martyr with a halo, someone who has in some way irked the authorities whom everyone hates. You will get covert help on all sides – from young convoy guards, who will secretly post your letters while you are being transported from place to place, to the urban intelligentsia, who will bend over backwards to get typewriter ribbons for retyping and sending out your writings. I was not at all surprised when my own guards passed me a small cross that Igor had carved out of a walrus tusk – and a cross is one of the items absolutely forbidden in the camps! Nor was I surprised that I managed to wear that cross around my neck the whole time I spent in camp, and was still wearing it when I was released. Only a couple of attempts were made to try to get me to part with it, and then I had to go on hunger strikes to ensure that I could keep it. Generally, the officials whose job it was to give me body searches from head to toe preferred 'not to see' my cross.

The Visitors' House consisted of two rooms with eight bunks in each one for the visitors, a small store-room supervised by the female officer in charge, and a 'conference room'. This was for the camp officials who invariably have a preliminary 'chat' with prisoners' visiting relatives. It was in this room that Igor first encountered the infamous Lidia Podust, the officer in charge of our Zone. It was her direct duty to (as she put it) 'make our lives so miserable, we would never want to come back here again'. Igor realised this as soon as he met her. Even now he cannot suppress a shudder of revulsion when he recalls his first meeting with her.

"Fascist pig! A reincarnation of Ilse Koch, that's what she is. She had the gall to make it clear that your treatment would depend on how well she and I got along! How do you like that?! I told her that I wouldn't even punch her in the face, let alone do anything else . . ."

"How come they let us meet?"

"That was before the meeting that they cancelled. Mind you, she wasn't much better the first time I came, either. She kept insisting that I should persuade you to write a clemency plea, and generally do an about-face. On that occasion I gritted my teeth and didn't say anything."

They escort me to my meeting with Igor: guards armed with sub-machine-guns, barking Alsatians, the lot . . . I am steered into a small house, searched once again, and told to sit down. From the next room, I hear Igor's voice: "Where is she?"

"Wait a moment, will you?"

Finally they let him in, and we throw ourselves into each other's arms. I was arrested in September, and it's May now. In all that time we have seen each other only once – in the courtroom. And now we can be together for two whole days in the same room! Of course, the room is bugged through and through, but we don't care about that.

Igor's mother embraces me, tears running down her cheeks: "Daughter dear! Oh, how thin you are ... I'm going to make you something to eat right now – we've brought so much with us, you wouldn't believe ... !"

She hurries out into the little kitchen of the Visitors' House, and starts unpacking something. That is a tactful way of leaving us alone. There is so much we have to say to each other! We hurry into speech, jumping from topic to topic, hands clasped tightly ...

"Igor, I behaved myself as I should have."

"Silly, d'you think anyone expected any different?"

"Do you know who's supposed to have given evidence against me? Maximilian Voloshin!"

"No! You'll have to tell me about it in detail later."

I look at him more closely and see that there's something bothering him, that he's gathering himself together to tell me something ... Then, as though plunging into a dive from a great height: "Irka ... you must know that I love you, only you! But I was unfaithful to you."

"Do I know her?"

He names a name I know well, oh, so well ...

"Is it serious?"

"No. It was purely physical, nothing else. And it won't happen again. I've learnt my lesson. How could I have trusted her ... ? Irka, Irka, this isn't what I should be telling you!"

He is braced for whatever my reaction might be. But he looks me straight in the eye, and I know what this admission has cost him.

"My poor darling!"

I cradle his head to my breast. Yes, seven years is a long time ... No prisoner has the right to demand celibacy from the one who has remained free. This is understood, a *carte blanche* is tacitly offered, and no questions are asked later. But we never lied to each other, or kept secrets. How right he was to tell me! For later, the KGB, smirking meaningfully, decided to 'surprise' me: "You know what your husband's been up to, Irina Borisovna ... ?"

The woman in question was only too glad to noise abroad what had passed between her and Igor. Her aims had nothing to do with the KGB: they were purely personal, and she even wrote blackmailing letters to me in camp – letters which the camp censor let through without a moment's delay, while confiscating everything sent by Igor. Maybe their combined efforts would have succeeded in breaking up our family – who knows? But they failed because of that most painful conversation of our entire lives.

We love each other, we believe each other, and there cannot be even a shadow of falsehood between us. So what could they do with us, if that's the case? Should anyone feel inclined to censure and moralise, I recommend that they try to serve a sentence, and learn a fundamental truth known to all zeks: in many respects, it is much harder for those who remain at liberty than it is for us. For they must live in the real world.

With a feeling of mutual relief, we moved on to talk of other things, what had happened over the past seven months – of course, we bore in mind that the whole house was bugged. We had to make arrangements about maintaining contact in the future, for we could hardly expect the good offices of the camp censor. So we took refuge in our 'Russian-Russian Phrase Book' – that is, by writing notes to each other. Paper and writing materials may not be taken to meetings, that's why all parties are searched so thoroughly before and after the meeting. But Igor wouldn't have been Igor if he hadn't managed to smuggle in a ball-point cartridge. And the numerous packages of food his mother had brought were all wrapped in newspaper, with pristine margins. We really don't value our domestic press as we ought!

Mama is uncertain what to do. She wants to cuddle me, and to hug us both at once, seeing how happy we are, and at the same time she wants to leave us together . . . The officer in charge of this sector of the camp is a Ukrainian, and not a bad fellow, as they go. Impressed by Igor's accentless Ukrainian, he did his best to set us up in comfort: a bed for Igor's mother was placed in the small corridor between our room and the kitchen. And so we spent two days together, knowing that we might never see each other again. Igor already knew the names of all the women in my Zone. But after my enthusiastic accounts of them (I had already had time to become deeply attached to those who greeted me on my arrival in the political Small Zone) he became noticeably more cheerful: it looked as though his Irka was in the best possible company! Of course, I recited all the poetry I had written during the months I was under investigation, and watching his face as I did so, I needed no other audience. Mama could not bear to listen, but would start crying and leave the room. I still don't know why. None of the poems was pathetic in tone; on the contrary, they were quite upbeat.

When the time came to say goodbye, we all realised that this must be done as calmly as possible, with a smile.

"Goodbye, my dear ones!"

"Good luck, Irka! Keep your chin up!"

I was led away, and they were subjected to a search. The KGB didn't spend much time on Igor's mother, but an hour and a half on Igor. Only after that did they feel certain that he wasn't taking out any written materials.

Twenty-four hours after Igor got off the train in Moscow, all the information on what had happened in the Small Zone for the past one and a half years, and all the poetry I had written since I was arrested were typed up in eight copies and delivered to various places. Only after that did Igor collapse on a bed and go to sleep. How did he manage to smuggle all this out? Well, as Leo Tolstoy once wrote: "My dear, there are ways of doing everything." When the KGB had to justify this great 'leak', their version was that Igor is possessed of a phenomenal memory, and was therefore able to memorise forty-two short poems and one very long one in two days. Well, anything is possible . . .

The atmosphere in the Zone was festive, especially as the sector commander had allowed me to keep one hundred and fifty soup stock cubes from my meeting – truly a cause for rejoicing! We had the makings of a feast, and there was a reason to feast: a meeting with loved ones is a very rare treat, the more so for political prisoners. Everyone congratulated me, and assured me that I looked immeasurably better than before.

Soon I got a short letter on half a sheet of paper:

Irka, my beloved, greetings! Mama and I got back without any problems, except that we got very wet on the way, and the joints in my legs started aching from all the damp. Otherwise, everything's fine. Sorry to be writing such a short note, but I don't have the strength to write a longer letter just now . . .

Now, what normal wife would react joyfully to the information that her husband had trouble with the joints in his legs? But when I began a mad waltz around the room and out into the yard, Tanya Osipova and Tatyana Velikanova understood that the real news was that my poetry and the information about the Zone had been taken out safely and were already in circulation. The mention of Igor's old problem with his legs was a signal we'd agreed on earlier.

Some of the letters to and from the camp were confiscated, some disappeared without trace, but some reached the addressees. The authorities soon began to cancel all our meetings with our relatives, with the result that for the next three years Igor and I did not see each other a single time. My fellow-prisoners fared no better. Actually, two of them were widows, and the husbands of four others were themselves prisoners. The KGB raged and 'tightened the screws': we had no intention of obeying their humiliating orders or begging for mercy. The Small Zone would not submit: we conducted ourselves in accordance with the principles we had determined for ourselves. The political Small Zone in Barashevo was like a tiny sovereign state, with a population which did not submit to the authorities when they made demands which we considered demeaning to human dignity: and they made precious few others! In the camp, I shed the last vestiges of the tolerance I had practised in my dealings with the investigator. I was at least willing to discuss the weather with him, but in camp I considered it unacceptable to exchange any words whatsoever with the KGB. It had been investigator Lukyanenko's job to drag me in for interrogation, but the KGB minions in the camp had absolutely no grounds to pester us: our sentences did not stipulate KGB intervention into our lives in the camp. Of course, I was not the only one to stick to this line of conduct, and the KGB had a tough time: how could they carry out ideological work with us?

I was amazed to see that they were genuinely put out: "Do you think I'm inhuman, or what? So you won't even condescend to talk to us, is that it?" Yes, that's it precisely. I won't. Not because I don't think there's any trace of humanity in you: with every passing day I feel more and more that you are to be pitied. I wouldn't exchange the most terrible isolation cell for your fate: even fainting from hunger and lack of sleep, I wouldn't be in your shoes! I can see that you're suffering from some monstrous complex, but I have yet to work out whether it is an inferiority complex which has brought you into the ranks of the KGB, or whether it developed as a result of your job. I understand how necessary it is for you to force or to wheedle – by any means whatsoever – a handshake out of a decent person. That makes you feel much better, but let others indulge you in this way, don't expect it from me. You try to raise yourself in your own esteem by clutching at the straw of someone's fear of you. But if nobody fears you, you're powerless.

Yes, you can kill, ensure a slow death in punishment cells, you can extend a sentence, torture your victims with cold and hunger, refuse medical assistance to the sick . . . You do all this, yet it brings you no relief. Only the subjugation of other people's souls can bring you a measure of satisfaction, but where's the joy in killing someone who is unbroken, and smiles fearlessly into your face instead of licking your boots? And how alarming it must be for you that more and more people refuse to break, and that all your power is beginning to waver on its foundation of fear. For what else have you got? Special shops full of consumer goods? Travel abroad? Long holidays? But should your control of the country collapse, everyone will have all that, and special shops will no longer be necessary. What, then, will be your advantages over ordinary people? Your reputation as criminals?

In fact, there are times when I would really like to talk to you out of sheer curiosity, just because you are human creatures, when all is said and done. Indeed, it would benefit me professionally. But you issue the ultimatum: submit, or we'll do you in! You torture my fellow-prisoners. I'm still young, but how is it for them? So *you* submit, vanquished on your own field with your entire arsenal, by the unarmed! *Then* I'll talk to you.

And in 1986, that's how it did end. But before that, the Small Zone went through punishment cells, walked around with oedemata from malnutrition, went on strike, refused food in protests ... I wrote about all this in detail in my first book, *Grey is the Colour of Hope*, so there is no need to repeat it now. I am sometimes asked how we survived. I don't know ... We tried. Nature must have endowed women with a greater capacity to endure. There were many deaths in the men's political camps, too many to mention. It had happened in our Zone, too, but not while I was there. I knew of these deaths only from the accounts of my fellow-prisoners.

Chapter Forty-one

"Igor, what was it like for you all that time?"

"Well, I worked as a toolmaker, and earned a bit of money on the side by making pendants, crochet hooks and the like ... And there were the on-going hostilities with the KGB – they kept bombarding me with summonses for questioning. And I would feel on the point of going out of my mind when I didn't hear from you."

"I wrote."

"I know. But the letters wouldn't get through. Can you imagine what it was like not to know for two or three months whether you were still alive? Then I had the collections of your poems to keep me busy, and I gathered information about other camps ... I had a lot of contacts by that time. So I didn't sit around doing nothing. I wangled time off work and travelled up to the camp eight times, hoping that they'd let me see you, but every time they told me that you were being punished, and the meeting was cancelled. I must say that your mother was a tower of strength: talk about being lucky in having a mother-in-law like that! She went with me so many times, and didn't get to see you even once. She didn't shed a single tear on the way, and she behaved magnificently at the camp gates, too. They sure breed tough women in your family! Of course, I had a lot of support from all over: you wouldn't believe some of the places from which I received letters – from America to Australia, and heaven knows where else in between. I suppose none of the letters people wrote to you to the camp were ever given to you?"

"Of course not. I had no idea that perfect strangers were writing to me. None of the women in our Zone were given any letters like that."

"Your camp censor must have had to chuck them out by the sackful. Efim Kotlyar phoned me from the States: do you know what he started there?"

Efim, a friend of mine from student days, emigrated to the West from Tashkent at the end of the 1970s. He read about my arrest in a Chicago newspaper, lying on the beach. He lost no time in rousing support from like-minded people and launched an energetic campaign for my release. I daresay there wasn't anyone – from Amnesty International to American senators – who escaped the efforts of Efim and his helpers. Ilyusha also took a hand in the proceedings: he found translators, and my poems had already been published in two languages. Efim and Ilyusha were old friends, the others – English, German, American, Australian – were new ones. Hapless Soviet diplomats had to become accustomed to seeing my face on posters outside their embassies: yet another one to remember! After all, I was not the only Soviet political prisoner with support in the West; there was a lot of campaigning on behalf of those about whom at least some data was to hand. The visual memory of Soviet diplomats was overwhelmed: here's another one for you! You won't travel to the camps to see him or her, so look at their faces from the windows of your embassies! We demand their release!

The majority of political prisoners were not known in the West: dissident sources were not omniscient, and reports of people arrested in places far removed from the big cities might not filter through, for this entailed finding someone to whom to give the information, someone who'd take it to heart: all this is not easy. Lengthy lists of names can become statistics, yet what of those who do not appear on these lists? They will simply perish without a trace in criminal camps and psychiatric hospitals, their names will never be known . . .

I still feel guilty when I think of them. The only difference between them and me is that they didn't happen to write poetry. So they died, and I'm alive . . . Vasyl Stus wrote poetry in camp, but he was unlucky: the KGB found a collection of his poems during a search in the camp. So they killed him. In 'special regime' camp No.36 in Perm. I read a collection of his work, in Ukrainian, in London. And I wept: for I had been rescued, and he had not . . . Yes, one may say that all this was due to circumstances, that it is foolish to reproach myself . . . But wouldn't it have been easier to a Western reader to remember the short surname 'Stus' instead of my tongue-twisting 'Ratushinskaya'?

Once you have been in the camps, you will know no rest for as long as at least one other person languishes in them. This is the harsh penalty extracted by your inner self in the dark watches of the night. And to argue with that self is useless. Those still suffering will people your dreams, as will those who perished. And they look at you sternly and ask: "Well, how are you getting along?" Then the following morning, an interviewer will say to you: "You must be very happy now, right? You're free!"

Igor had over four years more of this kind of 'happy freedom' than I. The KGB played their cards accordingly: "You're not doing too badly, are you? Your wife's having a hard time, though. The camps are not a holiday resort, everyone knows that . . . And your behaviour will determine how long she'll stay there – for less or for longer than her sentence. You know how it is – extending a sentence poses no problems . . . Now if you were to write her a letter, urging her to be a bit more flexible . . . You don't realise in what a bad way she is, and you don't want to do anything to improve her lot!"

"Did you ever write anything that they wanted you to?"

"What do you take me for?!"

"Keep your hair on! I didn't suspect you of anything, I'm just getting all the details straight. You see, in the camp they sidled up to me on a number of occasions, saying that they had a letter from my husband, but as I always refused to take anything from them, they weren't even offering to give it to me . . . D'you remember Artemyev, the 'Zone curator'? He bragged to me that you had shaken hands with him."

"I'd chop my hand off first! Shake hands with that butcher? In fact, I only saw him once. It was the Kiev lot who worked on me. They had this lieutenant-colonel, Sutyagin . . . Now *there* was a sensitive soul for you . . . !"

Sutyagin really was quick to take offence: I encountered him later. He was extremely modest, too: when I was brought to Kiev prison from the camp, he introduced himself as Romanenko, and it was only later that his real name came to light.

He started on Igor in the best 'humane' tradition: "You think we're inhuman, don't you? Do you think only those with a higher technical education can think? Do you think that if someone is a KGB officer that automatically means he's an idiot? For your information, I qualified as a mathematician . . ."

Igor couldn't resist the temptation: "Can you divide a tensor by a vector?"

"Well, I graduated from university a long time ago . . . You forget a lot as the years go by . . ."

"Do you remember the difference between a derivative and a differential?"

"You're just trying to score cheap points, aren't you? Even though I'm doing my best to make things easy for you! Why don't you drop around to my place for a glass of cognac, see for yourself how KGB officers live? I bet you think we all wallow in luxury and short-supply consumer goods from special shops, don't you? Well, the fact of the matter is that our salaries are nothing much, and our work is far from easy . . ."

Igor only snorted derisively: all his workmates at that time, tool-makers and fitters and turners, could not have dreamt of drinking cognac – all that they could get was moonshine vodka. For all that they were supposed to be 'the workers' aristocracy' and on piece wages.

At first they were wary of Igor: as an engineer, he was a suspect 'intellectual' in their eyes. Igor couldn't understand why there was such antagonism between the workers and the higher-level technical personnel. The reason turned out to be quite simple: the workers were interested in earning a decent wage, and their bosses in lowering the rates for items produced. Igor estimated later that they usually managed to push through reductions of some 15 per cent per annum. So if the workers didn't want to earn less, they simply had to produce more to retain their previous salary on the basis of 'increased output'. After all, the bosses had to report successes in order to gain advancement for themselves . . .

Igor had no doubt that he would get along with the men on the shop floor. "If the workmen don't respect you," he says, "it means you're not worth respecting!"

He was already proficient at working with his hands, so it didn't take him long to get the hang of whatever was new. Toolmakers are true craftsmen and very snobbish about their art. Theirs is not some mechanical conveyor-belt job, you have to use your brains! They know better than any foreman who's good or not, and treat that person accordingly. Soon Igor was accepted as one of them. They were willing to forgive him for being an 'intellectual', and to ignore what they considered to be his 'eccentricities'. They even joked about it good-naturedly: "Hey, lad, don't you even know a good, hard swear-word for when something goes wrong?"

Igor bided his time, and at an appropriate moment poured out a masterly lexicon. They listened to him in admiring silence, and then admitted that the lad could, after all, find the right words when he needed to! The fact that he didn't swear often wasn't held against him: who knows, maybe it's not the done thing in educated circles? But he had proved his mettle, and that was the most important thing. So they looked upon him with an indulgent eye, and took him to their bosom completely after a silly incident, in which Igor dazzled them with a knowledge of the law.

Two men got into a fight, right there at the lathe, in working hours. It was not anything serious, just that they were both young and hot-headed. One of them was from Igor's section. Even though they made amends very quickly, the incident snowballed, and it began to look as though both culprits would lose their bonus payments and thirteenth salary. Things looked decidedly grim: getting a punch in the face was child's play by comparison with what their wives would put them through, without laying a finger on them! How could they hope to explain away a shortfall of at least one hundred and fifty roubles (if not more!) in the family budget?

Igor felt sorry for his workmate, and decided to take a hand in the affair. "Do what I tell you," he said to him, "and everything will work itself out."

Those who heard him laughed sceptically: "A fight at work, and he says it will work out all right? Come on, Whiskers, climb down to earth!"

Igor tried for a Sherlock Holmes-like enigmatic smile, and instructed the sufferer: "You've got nothing to lose now, right? So this is what you do: you write an explanatory letter, just as I dictate it to you. They will demand a written explanation from you anyway, so you can have it ready to hand to them. In a few hours' time they'll be begging you to make some changes to the text. If you stand fast and refuse to change so much as one word, I promise you that the whole matter will be hushed up."

That evening, the unlucky combatant came rushing round, eyes starting from his head: "Igor! It all happened just the way you said!"

"You didn't change anything?"

"No! And they finally said that this time they would let me off!"

"'Go forth, my son, and sin no more!'"

After everyone had finished laughing, they demanded an explanation from Igor, which he supplied willingly. The crux of the matter was that Igor's workmate was not qualified to set the automatic lathe beside which the fight had broken out. Special technicians were supposed to be summoned to do that particular job, but the foreman decided not to bother, and told Igor's workmate to do it. This happens all the time: you have to ignore instructions if you don't want lengthy delays on the job. But as that particular lathe was mentioned specifically in the letter of explanation, airing the matter any further would have meant that the bosses stood to be censured and lose *their* bonuses and premiums. And who, in their right mind, would want that?

The second time, Igor was asked for legal counsel by the deputy foreman. This was a much more serious matter. A lathe was being taken somewhere in a truck. The truck turned over on its side: either the driver (who escaped serious injury) had had a drop too much to drink, or the road was in a terrible shape: some of the unmade roads in the Soviet Union have to be seen to be believed. While the driver went off to look for help, the local tractor drivers dismantled the lathe on the premise that some of its parts might come in useful as spares for their machines. By the time the truck driver returned, all that was left was the base of the lathe, and there was no sign of the predators. The Procuracy instituted an investigation: after all, that lathe had cost the state ten thousand roubles, and who was to make up the loss? The easiest thing to do was to pin responsibility on the organisation which was answerable for the transportation of the lathe. Maybe interrogation would shed some light on the whole story.

The first person to be called in for questioning was the deputy foreman, Vasili Ivanovich, so Igor briefed him very thoroughly: "The first thing they'll do is shove article one hundred and seventy-eight of the Code under your nose. Three years imprisonment. They'll tell you that that's for refusing to give evidence. So you tell them straight away that that article concerns the wilful giving of false evidence, and that refusal to give evidence is article one hundred and seventy-nine. It carries a maximum penalty of six months compulsory labour, without loss of liberty. After that, demand to know who is being accused of what, under which article, and what is the substance of the alleged crime. This is information they are obliged to give you by law. I'll be very surprised if they don't leave you alone after that. But just in case, remember to draw a line through any empty spaces in the protocol before you sign it. And another thing: you have the right, by law, to add any remarks you wish to the protocol – just write them in by hand. If the investigator threatens you with anything, write on the protocol that you were subjected to pressure, quote his threats verbatim, and state in writing that you refuse to deal with him."

As soon as the woman investigator heard the words 'substance of the alleged crime' she lost all her enthusiasm for any further delving. "Do you have a relative who's a lawyer?" she asked. "They wouldn't have instructed you like that in the legal consultation bureau."

"No. Just someone I know."

As Igor had predicted, the Procuracy wanted no more to do with Vasili Ivanovich, who went around shining like a well-polished brass door-knocker: "Thanks, lad! I'll stand you a bottle!"

Igor could only laugh: naturally the state legal consultation bureaux don't help people to get out of the clutches of that same state!

From that day forth, everyone on the shop floor knew beyond any doubt that dissidents could be very useful people. Moreover, communists are not popular among the ordinary workers, they're regarded as parasites. The duty rosters and allocations are the job of the bosses, and in the *Spetsenergoavtomatika* (the name of the organisation for which Igor worked, which produced specialised automatic machinery and details) the same task could be paid one hundred and thirty roubles a day more. If you're a Party member, you will get the best jobs, and holiday permits, and a new apartment without having to wait your turn . . . And they'll make you a foreman, even if you are all thumbs. As well as that, if you have a Party meeting, you will get a full day's pay, even though the meeting may last only a few hours, after which you can go home. Nonetheless, such people are universally despised by their workmates as 'cack-handed loafers'.

"But Igor," I asked once, "wasn't there at least one Party member there who could work properly?"

"There was just one: Tolik Daryin. He was a pretty unpleasant character, but he knew his job and did it well. In fact, the attitude towards him was different: he wasn't personally popular, but nobody took the mickey out of him in the way they did with the other Party members. The workers are a sharp-tongued lot. They used to reduce Lenya Pribylsky to hysterics: his father was a secret policeman, so Lenya's what you could call a hereditary communist. He even boasted once, when he'd had a glass too many, that his mother worked in the SMERSH (counter-intelligence) and had hanged someone with her own hands. He once turned up at work sporting a whole array of World War Two medals on his chest, and you should have heard how they ridiculed him, pointing out that he was only fifteen years old when the war ended! And he, stupid idiot, struck a pose and started carrying on about how 'we on the home front produced tanks . . .' Well, that really brought the house down. 'You can do bugger-all now,' all our lads told him, 'so what the hell were you good for when you were a snotty-nosed kid of fifteen?' And they wouldn't let it go at that, but kept on at him to admit where he got those medals: who'd given them to him? Mummy or Daddy? Boy, was he sorry that he'd thought up such a stupid exhibition . . ."

"Yet people join the Party, for all that?"

"It depends. There was a foreman among our toolmakers, a good guy, and well respected. Well, the management got on to him: join the Party, or we'll demote you. After all, they're the ones who do the promoting and the demoting. A foreman's pay is 15 per cent higher, whichever way you look at it, and he had three kids to provide for. So you can't just tell the management to go to hell. Poor fellow, I saw how he agonised over the situation . . ."

"So did he join the Party?"

"I don't know. You'd been released, and I could think of nothing else. And in any case, I quit immediately, remember?"

Yes, Igor really had nothing else on his mind at that time: he was teaching me to walk again. It turned out that after my time in the camps, I couldn't walk even half a kilometre: I would subside, gasping for breath, on the ground . . . My legs had forgotten how to cover any but the shortest distances. And I had a nasty, racking cough.

But his toolmaker friends came around to have a look at me, to see whether I was worth all the agony they had seen 'Whiskers' go through all this time. I served them tea and recited my poems.

While I was still 'inside', Igor managed to visit my former camp-mate Tatyana Velikanova twice in her place of exile. We have been lucky in that we have always liked the same people, and they have liked us both equally well. A photograph of Igor and Tatyana with a background of Kazakhstan steppe arrived at the camp. I had never doubted that they would take to each other immediately, and so it was.

My second collection of camp poems had reached its destination, to the impotent fury of the KGB: how was it possible, when we had not had any meetings, and all our mail was screened? Igor was summoned for questioning yet again (it was his twentieth summons by that time). He laughed, and the KGB began seriously to suspect that there was a telepathic link between us: how else could such detailed information find its way out of the seemingly sealed-off Small Zone, even such details as the temperature in punishment isolation cells? And who was in those cells, who went on strike, who refused food in protest, and why . . . To say nothing of the full texts of the various collective statements we wrote in the camp from time to time.

It looked as though the KGB would have no option other than to imprison all our relatives, but they still nurtured the hope that they would find out how the information was being passed out. As for our relatives, by this time they all knew each other, and had grown as close in their shared sorrow as we did in the camp. Having no blood relatives among Estonians, Latvians or Lithuanians, we nonetheless acquired an extended family embracing all these nationalities. Oh, if we were to go to the Baltic states now, it would be a completely different visit from the one we paid as green youngsters!

And the time will come when we shall be able to make such a journey. To visit Lagle Parek in Estonia, Lidija Doronina-Lasmane in Latvia, Jadvyga Bieliauskiene in Lithuania – my friends from the Barashevo Small Zone. May God grant their peoples freedom! And ours, too.

Chapter Forty-two

November 1985. I'm in the punishment isolation cell again: ice-cold cement walls, 'hot food' (that is, prison skilly) every second day, a skimpy smock on my bare, numbed body . . . I don't really care: this is to be my final hunger-strike. I lie on the floor, with no strength to move. Even the mice have left my cell, because there are no crumbs for them to pick up. So they've finally won, the bastards. How much time have I spent in their punishment cells and internal camp prisons? Added together – more than a year. In some things, the KGB keep their word: and they had promised me that I would not come out alive unless I signed a recantation. It looks as though the time has come to die.

Kind Dr Korczak appears out of the cell wall to visit me, and I am no longer alone. He smiles – not ceremoniously, but warmly, as though he were paying a house-visit. When I was little, he wove wise stories for me. He believed that when I grew up I would understand the adult dimension of them, too. He has not deserted me now, just as he didn't desert his pupils in occupied Warsaw, and later – in the gas chamber.

I hear someone whispering to me, and I recognise the voice: it's my favourite poet, Mandelstam.

> God's name like a gigantic bird
> flew out from my breast.
> Before me thick mist swarms,
> behind me stands an empty cage.

And another voice, this time a woman's:

> I shall eat black grapes with my sweethearts,
> Young wine I shall drink as I go,
> And watch the grey waterfall streaming
> To the moist, flinty bottom below.

I know these lines: Akhmateva was writing how she would meet again
with those who had died before her! She had nobody left in the world
by that time.

> The lion with his fiery mane will meet you there,
> And the wise ox, full of eyes,
> And the proud gold eagle of the skies . . .

Yes, yes, I remember – this was what the Armenian students had
sung, when none of us was more than twenty years old . . . I hear it
again, every note of the guitar, every voice.

Someone's hand glides gently over my head. Is it time? How shall
I answer for my earthly transgressions when the stone ceiling above
me opens up? There are so many people before whom I am at fault,
to whom I did not say the kind words I should have. How right
was Boris Mityashin, who astounded me when I was visiting in his
Leningrad apartment in 1979: the phone rang, he picked up the
receiver and, recognising a friend's voice, said warmly and simply,
"Hello, dear friend!"

He was not much older than I, but he had already served a sentence
in the camps, and he was able to relate to people without fearing to
be thought 'sentimental', something young people usually shy away
from. He knew that he would soon be imprisoned again, and this
time, he might not survive. I did not understand, then, but remembered
it because I found it so surprising.

I am at fault before my family, for not having enough wisdom to
avoid unnecessary conflicts over trifles. Before Igor, for not having
borne him any children. Before my friends: I could have been so
much more tactful and thoughtful in my dealings with them. I realise
now just how much I love them all. But they are far away, and it's too
late either to tell them or write.

The ringing in my ears gets louder, and I am being borne upwards
and to the left. Suddenly, it's warm. Is that it? So easy? So now there
will be only radiance and peace? But Igor – how will it be for him,
alone?

"My dearest love!"

And I return to the cracked floor of cell No.7, which is set aside in
camp ZhKh-385/2 for the 'politicals': they bring us here from Barashevo to serve spells of punishment.

Ase-Maria Nesse, the Norwegian writer, made an impassioned
speech in my defence at a PEN Club meeting in Hungary, but I knew
nothing about that. An American, Henry Holt, had adopted me as a

daughter, and was now demanding to be allowed a meeting with me, although I have never seen him in my life. An Anglican priest, Dick Rogers, existed on prison rations in a specially constructed cell in Britain as part of a campaign for my release, even though I had not yet heard his name. *Emigrés* from the USSR marked my birthday in New York: I was shown a video-recording of this event later, and was deeply touched to hear a girl with a strong English accent reading one of my humorous poems about a cat who knew how to fly . . . Ilyusha and Efim were in constant contact with Igor, and knew everything that happened in the Small Zone up until September 1985.

In the meantime, General Secretary of the Communist Party of the USSR Mikhail Gorbachev states in an interview to the French newspaper *Humanité* that there are no political prisoners in the Soviet Union . . . !

At 6 a.m. Soviet radio plays the national anthem: 'Indestructible union of free republics.' Radios (or any other items) are not allowed in punishment isolation cells, so I don't hear it. Thousands of people are writing to me, but I don't know about it. I want to sleep.

When camp commandant Zuykov came running to see me the next morning, I was amazed by his promises that if I were to stop my hunger-strike, I would be transferred immediately to ordinary prison regime, that I would not be harassed a moment longer, that all Igor's letters would be given back to me – in fact, they would agree to just about anything. I was even more surprised when they began to give me medical treatment: antibiotics, vitamins, blood transfusions . . . I was returned to the Barashevo camp, and the camp nurse, Tanya, continued to wield a syringe: "Honestly, those veins of yours! It's impossible to get at them!"

This, however, has nothing to do with my imprisonment. When I was a student, and then a young teacher, I used to give blood to make ends meet: you get paid twenty-five roubles for 200 grams, an enormous amount of money . . . But after a while my veins 'receded', which happens to frequent donors, and it wasn't the nurse's fault that it would take up to half a dozen jabs before she got it right.

Raya Rudenko had already taken my third collection of camp poems with her into exile, and buried it deep in Altai soil until an opportunity came to pass it along. I can name Raya, because she and her husband are safely in the state of New Jersey in the USA now. Other helpers must remain nameless, for their own sakes: I can only mention them in my prayers.

Igor received an unexpected phone call: "Igor Olegovich? It's

Sutyagin here. One of my colleagues from Mordovia is passing through, and he'd like to meet you and take a parcel from you for Irina."

Igor cursed himself later: "Like a fool, I believed him! Everything I had sent to you and Natasha Lazareva was always returned from the camp marked 'prohibited items'. So I went, without a summons, voluntarily . . . What an idiot!"

There was no talk of any parcel when he got there. KGB man Novikov treated Igor to a discourse on the dreadful state of my health, and offered to take a letter to me from Igor to persuade me to change my attitude.

"You're the only person she'll listen to!" he concluded.

Igor told him to go to hell. A month later, he learned that I had been brought from the camp to Kiev, and was in the new wing of the KGB prison. He got together a parcel, and brought it over: parcels are permitted in prison.

The KGB persevered in their efforts to talk him into writing an appeal for clemency to the authorities on my behalf. He flatly refused to do this, but gave some thought to the possibility of writing a request to have my 'crime' transferred from Article Seventy to Article One Hundred and Ninety (one) of the Criminal Code. The two articles are very similar, but One Hundred and Ninety (one) stipulates that the crime 'was not aimed at undermining and weakening Soviet power' and the maximum term under this article is three years less than the term I received under Article Seventy. On the other hand, a request like that would be tantamount to admitting that I slandered the state: in other words, he would be giving false evidence. Yet should I die (and the KGB spared no effort to imply that that was the almost inevitable outcome), how would he feel for the rest of his life, knowing that he could have written an appeal, and didn't? The KGB has given up hope of getting anything out of me, and admitted this to Igor quite openly.

What should he do? He walked home. Alone, not having seen me for three years, knowing only that I am alive, he wrestled with himself to reach a decision. And the answer seemed to come from somewhere outside himself: Not a line! All will be well. . . . He stopped in wonder, feeling a touch of the Divine Hand on his shoulder. He has felt it before, and experienced no further qualms, because he knew that this was how it would be.

When the KGB tried to pressure our respective mothers, they declared as if with one voice: "That is for our children to decide, not us." As neither Igor nor I showed the slightest inclination to take up the KGB's suggestions, they decided to try another ploy: maybe the sight of me would provide the necessary stimulus? Even though I have had some medical attention, I look absolutely ghastly – grey and emaciated, just as zeks are supposed to look.

Both mothers, in turn, were granted meetings with me. They were superb: strong and smiling.

"No clemency appeals!" I blurted out quickly to both.

This is not the kind of meeting at which you can even exchange a hug: you are divided by a table, and surrounded by KGB personnel.

"No discussions on forbidden subjects!" But the most important thing has already been said, the rest can be read in a mother's eyes: you got the message? Yes . . .

"My little one! Igor's all right." (Oh, I know what that means!) "We've brought you a parcel. Tell me, what do you need?"

"Warm underwear – the more, the better!"

I am thinking ahead, because I am sure that they will send me back to the camp after this attempt to 'turn' me. The quality of underwear is not stipulated in the camp rules, and the uniforms are not designed for warmth. So I need to take back as much as I can. Everyone freezes in the Zone, and Jadvyga Bieliauskiene seems to be succumbing to a return of the tuberculosis she had contracted in the camps in Stalin's time.

"Of course, dear. Whatever you say."

End of meeting, back to the cell. What next?

"Ratushinskaya! Come and see a parcel!"

What?! Since when have prisoners been called to 'see' parcels? Usually, they simply confiscate anything that's not permitted, and give you the rest. Moreover, it's late in the evening, and parcels aren't issued at this time. So what's going on?

Actually, I was taken along to see a television broadcast. The Russian word *peredacha* (transmission) applies equally to a package, and I had assumed that this is what they meant. The programme was an American one, called *Russian Here*, dubbed into Russian. It showed *émigrés* from the Soviet Union complaining of 'excessive freedom' in America, and asking to be allowed to return to the USSR. Maybe the film had been doctored, maybe not – how could I know?

As viewing this programme committed me to nothing, I watched. I've been five years behind bars, and here's someone complaining of too much freedom! They were used to something else . . . Rubbish, it's got to be false! Or maybe it was filmed tendentiously to begin with? However, that's neither here nor there: the KGB is keen for me to see this programme. Why?

Next day I am informed: "Irina Borisovna, the times have changed. We have *glasnost* and *perestroika* . . . We understand that you're not a criminal. The way is open for you to join the Union of Soviet Writers . . ."

Some enticement! Will that make me write better, or what? But it will be interesting to see what conditions they'll put forward.

"So all you want from me is a clemency plea?"

"No, no! We are well aware of your reaction to the words 'appeal' and 'clemency'. You don't have to appeal, and you don't have to recant anything: your poetry will be published without that! It's a new era! The winds of change . . . Nobody will persecute you now for your views! Comrade Gorbachev . . ."

"Can you keep it brief?"

"Irina Borisovna, in March this year all the women in your Zone wrote to the Presidium of the Supreme Soviet . . ."

That's true, there was yet another protest written at that time. We were furious when we heard that Gorbachev claimed that we didn't exist: we weren't in very good nick, but we were still alive! They hadn't done away with everybody . . . So we wrote: "In order that Gorbachev not be proved a liar, return our civil liberties. Along with freedom of conscience, and not in exchange for it!" This document was confiscated for being allegedly anti-Soviet in nature, and we were formally notified in writing (this was the usual practice) that it had been 'destroyed by burning'. We weren't overly concerned, because this protest, just as all our other ones, had left the camp by our secret channels. So what now?

It turned out that all they want is to re-create the text of that protest: you know how it is, the folks in Mordovia had gone a little too far, and destroyed it in a burst of ill-timed zeal . . . But now, if that document could be 'resurrected', it would be enough to secure everyone's release!

"What about the ones still in the Zone? Will their copies be destroyed the same as before?"

"No, no! We're about to release them all! You can write to them yourself, append the text of your protest, and that's it! We realise that you don't trust us . . ."

What is this miraculous metamorphosis? Someone must really have given it to them in the neck! I don't believe in 'socialism with a human face': I've seen enough of that kind of humanism to last me a lifetime. I've seen one-legged cripples being forced to lug buckets of coal in the camp hospital zone. I've seen women prisoners who had children born in captivity screaming with heartbreak when they were taken to other camps and their children had to remain behind. I heard them with my own ears as I sat in cell No. 7. So what explanation can there be for the transformation before my eyes? I wrote to the Small Zone: no clemency pleas! They're preparing to release us anyway. All they are asking us is to repeat the protest we wrote voluntarily at such and such a time. I appended the text, which I knew by heart.

KGB officer Novikov looked sour when he saw the phrase 'no clemency pleas', but had to accept it when I refused to make any changes. Well! Has the world turned upside-down? I know very well what a clemency plea entails: it was explained to me in great detail by KGB General Marchuk. In the first place, you must state your repentance concerning your crimes against the Soviet state. Then you have to admit that the sentence you received was just. In my case, that would have meant rejecting my own poems, and agreeing that I had come by my just deserts for not keeping my rhymes to permitted subjects . . .

In Lagle Parek's case it would have meant that she should cease demanding the publication of the Molotov-Ribbentrop Pact, as a result of which the Soviet Union reached agreement with the Nazis and annexed the Baltic States and Western Ukraine.

Jadvyga Bieliauskiene would have to forgo organising Catholic Sunday schools for children in Lithuania, and Olya Matusevich would have to turn her back on the Ukrainian chapter of the Helsinki Monitors. And so on.

The next point in the plea must be the words 'I appeal for clemency'. Those who dare not demand must plead, and clemency is extended to those who have erred: otherwise, they would have to be exonerated! And that would mean paying them compensation for goodness knows how many years, wouldn't it? Khrushchev had already tried that, and almost bankrupted the Party in the process.

The third point is a promise not to cause the state any more trouble, and avoid 'undesirable' activity. In other words, not to write any more poetry, not to publicise the Soviet pact with the Nazis, not to teach children the basics of the Catholic faith, not to campaign for human rights – depending on the nature of your 'crimes'.

And now, it appears, all this is no longer necessary? It's enough to reaffirm 'along with freedom of conscience, and not in exchange for it'? And then Jadvyga, who had us worried stiff as she lay muttering in fever, will be released? As will the oldest of us, that stubborn Latvian Lidija Doronina-Lasmane, who is serving her third camp sentence?

Well, time will tell . . . This was another of my mistakes: what use that I had demanded that either the whole Zone gets a chance to repeat that statement, or I would refuse? I shouldn't have consented to write so much as a word: let that be a lesson to them not to burn prisoners' protests! Piece it together from the ashes, if you can!

They had been dancing around me like this for some time: maybe I would manage to pull off everyone's release?

I waited another month for the arrival of identical statements from the camp to be forwarded for my scrutiny, and I would not sign the text a second time. Finally, the papers came, and without a word about clemency. I know Lagle's, Lidija's and Jadvyga's handwriting . . . All in order?

Yes, but not quite.

"Irina Borisovna, you must agree that this is a bit tactless. Even when you apply for leave at work, you 'ask' for it, just as you 'ask' to be hired for some job. It's just a formality, after all . . ."

"As far as I'm concerned, it's not a formality: and I have no intention of asking for anything."

One more word out of them, and I'll retreat into silence. You shouldn't hit someone when they're down, but it looks as though they're marshalling themselves for a new onslaught. No, they pull back.

"All right, all right! We're not the ones who decide, it's the government! If it were up to us, we would have disbanded your camp a long time ago, we're not inhuman! But, frankly speaking, the chances of a release in response to wording like this are about one in a hundred . . ."

If that's how they want it – fine. Now that they've managed to persuade me to write at least something, they're bound to try to get me to write something that they need. They'll have another trick up their sleeve, that's for sure. And they have the gall to make extravagant claims about their humanity! The less said about that, the better! It's true that you were borne by mothers, who sang lullabies to you, fed you . . . I'm even prepared to accept that you have normal human characteristics, but not when you are doing your job. Maybe you love your children, maybe you are quite different when you're away from your work . . . But the totalitarian machine which you serve makes your occupation inhuman, and when you are fulfilling your duties you are liars and scoundrels. I don't hate you, rather, I pity you, but I can find no justification for you: you chose your line of work. You sold yourselves for power and plenty, and now you must pay with your souls. It's one thing to forgive what was done to you, but how can you forgive for others, the ones you killed?

So on that note we parted. The next day, I received an unexpected summons: "Ratushinskaya! You have a visitor!"

Chapter Forty-three

They don't tell me who the meeting's with, of course: I pace along the carpeted corridor, wondering what to make of it all. For years they cancelled all my meetings, and now, suddenly, I'm being granted a third one in one month . . . Are they trying to make up for the omissions of the past, or what? I am thunderstruck when I see Igor.

Physical contact is forbidden: you sit on opposite sides of a table. Also present is a young KGB man, whom I have seen before. Out of the lot of them, he's the closest to a normal human being: I had no complaints against him. He's probably new to the service.

Igor came bearing a single rose, a bud of the deepest – almost black – red. So he remembers my tastes . . .

"May I give this to my wife?"

"How many notes have you hidden inside it?"

Igor bowed, as one acknowledging a compliment: admittedly, the question was not an unreasonable one, even though there were no notes in that particular rose. We look at each other across the table. He hasn't changed at all, just his eyes seem sunken. His hands are scratched – well, that goes with his job . . . he's a toolmaker, after all. He smiles, but there are no words. Perhaps we no longer need words? If we were alone, it might be a different matter. But our young 'minder' warns us that he would hate to have to terminate our meeting if we should start exchanging information. As for everything else – well, we don't need speech . . . Why should he hear what we have to say to one another, anyway? It's enough for us just to see each other.

For some reason, I find myself asking aloud about the dog we had bought for Mama when she retired.

"The temper that mutt's got! Especially when you try giving it a bath!"

We fall silent again. Our guardian surprises us by suggesting that we sit next to each other, while he moves over to the corner to smoke a cigarette. He doesn't need to watch us, all he must do is ensure that we don't talk about 'forbidden' matters, and he hopes we'll respect that . . . He turns his back on us, and we clasp hands. We once used to be able to make our pulses beat as one almost immediately. We can do so still. I should think that was the most silent meeting ever to take place in that KGB prison. I don't know how much time passed before the guardian turned to us again: "You have five minutes left."

When will we see each other again? If at all? My period here will be up in a few days' time: I had been shown papers stating the dates. Then it would be back to the camp. They no longer talk about releases, just drone on about the changed times. Apparently they have not changed to the degree of freeing political prisoners. This meeting had a clear aim: what if we should break at the last moment and 'become more flexible', as they term it? We both knew that it was an old KGB method to let a zek get a whiff of freedom half-way through a sentence, and then snatch it away again. That means we should unclasp our hands now.

> No matter that you and I never know
> What fate promises us tomorrow.
> Our task is fearlessness in woe
> And calm if it's farewell forever.
> Look into my eyes, force a smile to your face –
> Let's remember each other this way!
> It's not yet time to release the brakes,
> We've not even crossed the first circle.
> It's not yet time for me to wail,
> On your shoulder, hard with suffering.
> Five minutes, then they'll lead me without fail
> Behind the gates of another parting.
> Jangle keys: they won't wear us down
> With stamps on their homeward passes!
> One day these five cruel minutes will count
> In our favour – as how many centuries?

Write, learn, burn. A familiar process. As for Igor – he would get it somehow along 'channels' from the camp . . .

One normal working day in October, somebody yelled to Igor over the clatter of machinery: "Hey, Whiskers! Someone on the phone for you!"

Igor was surprised: who could be calling him at work? He ran across: "Igor."

"Irka?! Where are you?"

"At home."

"What???"

"I don't understand it myself."

"I'll be right there!"

He leaps forward, but hands catch his shoulders and he is forced down onto a chair:

"What's the matter? You're white as a sheet! Who was it?"

"My wife."

"She's been released?!"

Igor's workmates all knew our story, and were very sympathetic. They're also *au fait* with the latest developments, and someone pushes a cigarette into his hand: "Here, have a smoke and stay put for a few minutes. Otherwise you'll end up under the first car that comes along. Get yourself together, and then go home: we'll fix it with the foreman."

I am sincerely grateful to them for their thoughtfulness, for he would have been run over. But soon he was home, and Mama, laughing and crying, shut the door on us and went off to make coffee.

The warm hands of my beloved, his very own smell . . . but the tiny wrinkles at the corners of his eyes have become deeper . . . he's wearing a jacket I've never seen before – he must have bought it after I was taken away . . . the room is full of instruments, many unfamiliar, I don't even know what they're called . . . tomorrow, I'll have to clean the place out from top to bottom . . . he's grown wild . . . no, I won't do anything tomorrow, I'm going to stay just as I am, in his arms, becoming a part of him that cannot be separated!

"Oh, my love, my love . . . !"

"Irka! My Irka!"

We are both shaking, and, just as in the old days, we huddle together under his jacket. Time stops – not for the four years and however many days that we have been apart, but for all the holidays that we lived through separately: Christmas with its stars and smell of fir-needles, the purple thunderstorms of May, the swellingly joyous proclamations of 'Christ Is Risen!', and the wild grasses of summer, the brisk chills of autumn, and the strange, light powdering of first snow on the ground . . .

Our minds are in turmoil, and we cannot think ahead: not how strange it will be for him to be wakened at night by me groaning in my sleep in a stranger's voice, not what will happen tomorrow, nor how we shall strain to catch a glimpse of our vanished youth, calling to us like an echo of laughter from the heart of a forest: all we will see will be the movement of a branch, brushed by an unseen bird . . .

We try to figure out what had happened.

"What did they do?"

"Called me to an office and told me that I was being released."

"On what basis?"

"A decree of the Presidium of the Supreme Soviet. They said it was a secret decree, so they couldn't give me a copy. The Presidium, it appears, has decided to extend clemency to me."

"What do you mean – clemency?"

"That's what I said to them – how could that be possible without a clemency plea? And they read out that it was on appeal by the Procuracy of the USSR."

"That's weird."

"Weird isn't the word! Of course, I didn't believe them – I thought they were trying out another of their little psychological gambits on me. They once took me from the camp claiming that I was being sent home to be released, but it turned out to be a lie. That was last June. They took me to a prison and started trying to break my will again. So what was I supposed to think this time? Especially as they didn't just shove me outside the gate, but drove me in one of their cars . . . Yet here I am! Still, what the hell do I want with their unasked-for clemency?"

"Don't worry about that now, we'll write to them later, never fear! Did they return your personal documents?"

"Yes, then and there. They gave me an attestation of my release, too. In fact, they were falling over themselves to be charming, and that alone was enough to make me suspect that they were up to no good."

"Yes, they don't like to have someone slip through their fingers – it must have been a wrench. But, you know, I've talked to Larisa Bogoraz in Moscow, and she told me that they hassled her the same way they did me: 'Write a clemency plea for your husband's release!' Maybe they're seriously planning a series of releases? Larisa's Anatoli is on a hunger-strike, demanding the release of all political prisoners."

"Do you think . . ."

"Fat lot they care about hunger-strikes! But I think they'll release a certain number of well-known prisoners without clemency pleas. You know, as proof of *glasnost* and *perestroika* in action."

"Am I so far behind the times?"

"Use your head: if they really wanted to make any radical changes, why did they grant you 'clemency'? By rights they should have released you with profuse apologies, if writing poetry is not a crime under *glasnost*. And all the others. Do you think the political articles have been excised from the Criminal Codes? Lena Meyerovich was dragged in for questioning by the KGB not long ago. And when your name cropped up, the Moscow KGB officer who was interrogating her said straight out that you should be hanged for your poetry!"

"What a marvellous compliment! I wonder if they all think that?"

"Who knows? Remember that young fellow who was present at our meeting in the prison? Well, he said to me later that you were bearing up magnificently. And you could see that he meant it sincerely."

"He's an interesting fellow. I was brought in to him several times. That was when they had a whole group working on me to find some way of bending me to their will . . ."

"What about him?"

"Actually, he was all right. He genuinely wanted to establish what our differences are. Furthermore, he was the only one who tried to convince me that the KGB was right. All the others followed the principle that might is right, so they could do what they wanted with me."

"What were his arguments?"

"In my opinion, he genuinely believes in totalitarianism. He asserted that somebody has to steer the people in the right direction. And that includes deciding which books may or may not be read. You can't do without order, he maintained: you have discipline in schools, and you have it in the army. At least you could have an honest argument with him; and he really argued his points with passion!"

"So what was the outcome of your polemics?"

"What could it be? I told him that the country was not an army barracks, and nobody had elected the KGB to teach the populace. Then he started on about the common good. We argued for six hours: I was quite impressed – at least he had honest convictions, unlike the rest of that lot."

"Yes, you couldn't call him typical. Maybe that's why he understood why you were determined to stand by your beliefs . . ."

"Well, I did my best to explain it to him. Listen, am I going to get a cup of coffee, or not? I'm dying to have a sip of a forbidden beverage! I can't remember when I last had some!"

The taste of coffee turned out to be quite different from the way I remembered it. It was strange to feel the strap of my old watch on my wrist. The second hand scurried round, tapping out the moments, like a chicken trying to find its way out of an eggshell that stubbornly refuses to crack. What's the time? What's the season? An eternity has passed since I came home, but the clock says that it is only five hours. Should I try on those of my clothes which Igor couldn't bring himself to give away because I had made them myself, feeling that it would be like giving away a kitten to a stranger? Should we put on a cassette with our favourite songs? Should we just light a candle and sit together in silence, our arms around each other, watching October sliding down the other side of the window?

A crowd of friends descended, hugging, kissing, laughing: "Come on, we're listening!"

I found myself relating only funny stories: how the camp guards had once conducted a search of our latrine, thinking that we had a radio hidden in it. Or how we trained mice in the punishment cells. I couldn't bring myself to talk of the horrors, they were still fresh in my mind and before my eyes. When I was going through it, I felt as though I were under some kind of anaesthetic: I knew that I had to keep a grip on myself at all costs. Yet now the anaesthetic was beginning to wear off.

The light shines, I am surrounded by flowers and music. Tomorrow my mother and sister will come from Odessa. Igor's father will be over later tonight. He already knows I've been released. At last we'll hug each other . . . Maybe all this is just a dream? Maybe in a moment I'll wake up in a prison cell?

We have already telephoned Ilyusha and Efim.

"Will you finally come, now?"

"We won't emigrate. But we'll try to get an exit visa for a short while to get medical treatment and see our friends. We'll apply for tourist visas: who knows, they may just grant them. On the other hand, who can predict what they'll do? It looks as though they themselves don't quite know what to do with us now. As a matter of fact, it's not long ago that they threatened Igor with arrest."

How many people we must see now! How many countries must we visit?

Igor tells me about Alyona Kojevnikov. She's Russian, but was born in Yugoslavia, grew up and was educated in Australia, and now telephones Igor regularly from London.

"These last three months were the hardest I had to go through. I can't tell you what a great support she was! And her husband's a great guy, too! You should have heard how she tested me out at first – you'd swear she'd been born and raised here! The first time she phoned she didn't have any proof that she was actually talking to me – how could she know my voice? She knew that she could just as easily be talking to someone from the KGB, claiming to be Igor Geraschenko. So she started reciting some of your poetry, and then stumbled to a halt, saying she couldn't remember the next line. So I immediately picked up where she left off, and finished reciting the poem from memory. She tried a few more times – five in all, I think – and then I asked her whether she was satisfied that I was really your husband?

'Yes,' she said, 'If you were KGB, you'd have had to dig around in your archives for those poems . . .' Actually, we're pigs: we haven't phoned her yet, and she's been worrying that I'm going to be arrested . . ."

Riding high on a wave of euphoria, and not thinking about the time difference, we telephoned London. Of course, it was early morning, and we roused Alyona and her husband Kolya from their sleep. As soon as the operator told them that Kiev was on the line, they assumed the worst: "Igor, is that you? You haven't been arrested?"

"Hold on! Irka wants a word!"

We rejoiced like that for a week. Igor made me drink fruit juices, and fussed over me as though I were a baby. We were not even particularly worried when our phone was cut off for a few days after we'd received more than fifty telephone calls from abroad. I had already had time to relate what had happened in our camp in recent times, and the situation of all my former companions. The last time we had sent out information was in May, I was taken away from the camp in June, and now it was October. We were certain that if I had been extricated, the others would be, too. A lot of my readers – people I had never met – came to call, to offer their congratulations and take away new poems. Through common efforts, I was clothed and shod: it is a tradition that when someone is imprisoned, their clothes are distributed to the families of other political prisoners. Let them be of use to good people, the prisoner doesn't need them. When a sentence draws to a close, new things are bought for the prisoner to take into exile. As I was released unexpectedly, there was a whole series of comical problems. I still wear an 'Orenburg shawl' sent to me from Obninsk by people I did not know then. Igor and I were together all the time: we simply couldn't bear to be apart for even an hour.

Then came the terrible news that Anatoli Marchenko had died in Chistopol prison, while the KGB was trying to pressure him and his wife into making an appeal for clemency. He would never have written anything like that, but while the KGB was making up its mind whether to release him anyway, he died. He had spent a total of some twenty years in the camps. The last news we'd had of him was that a year earlier he had been beaten up mercilessly in a prison corridor by some warders. Then he declared a hunger-strike, demanding the release of all political prisoners. After that, there was no news. The authorities wouldn't let him be buried in Moscow: instead, he was interred in Chistopol.

I received phone calls from abroad, asking me to comment on Marchenko's death. "It was murder," I said. "They've been slowly murdering him all these years. They released me, but killed him. While everyone was rejoicing on my behalf . . ."

Over several months, about a hundred people were 'pardoned' without asking for it. Our Zone emptied at last, Lera Senderov was set free, so were Sergei Grigoryants and Anatoli Koryagin . . . The authorities did manage to prise a number of clemency appeals out of some prisoners, and didn't that fill them with glee! Aha, so you broke in the end, eh? We sorrowed for them: what must they have had to endure? God forbid that we should condemn those who were driven to desperation: the fault is not theirs, it rests squarely on the shoulders of the swine who drove them to such straits. What would these minor successes inspire the KGB to try next?

Other prisoners were kept in the camps as bargaining chips for the future, for the occasional 'grand gesture' to assure the world that *glasnost* and *perestroika* were gaining ground. And sure enough, Levko Lukyanenko was 'pardoned' and released a few days before his sentence expired anyway. Mind you, he wasn't allowed to go home, he went into internal exile. However, aren't we, the rulers of the Soviet Union, humane? See for yourselves how much democracy we have now in our country, see how we've changed . . . ? If Western diplomats name a few more names, and do so insistently, why, we'll release a few more prisoners, after a bit of horse-trading! As for those nobody knows about, whose photos aren't displayed at demonstrations outside Soviet embassies, they can stay put. The same goes for the ones who aren't very prominent (in 1988 there were some three hundred prisoners of conscience known to be in the camps): if they die, there won't be too much noise.

I have been free for two years now, and people keep asking me whether I'm happy. They ask Igor that, too, and Anatoli Koryagin. What more do we need to be content?

Epilogue

It is December 1986, and we are sitting in a plane bound from Moscow to London. And there it is – the lights below us stretch as far as the eye can see.

"Irka, London!"

We hold hands, watching the earth rising up to meet us. The plane makes a perfect landing, and the English passengers, travelling home for Christmas, give a round of applause. Now all we have to do is go through customs, and then there's bound to be someone waiting for us.

Our Soviet passports are on us: we had not rejected citizenship. It was only later that we received a phone call from the Soviet embassy: "By decree of the Presidium of the Supreme Soviet you have been stripped of Soviet citizenship . . ."

That was to make us return our passports: government property is government property . . .

We walk down a very long corridor, and see two figures hurrying to meet us: a tall, fair-haired man and a very small woman.

"Is that Dick Rodgers?"

"No, it must be David Astor. And that's Alyona with him!"

We exchange embraces, but talking will have to wait. David, with Alyona translating, takes charge:

"Irina, let me take your arm on one side, and Igor on the other. There's a huge crowd out there. Whatever you do, don't stop, or we'll be swamped. There's a press-conference arranged for tomorrow, but perhaps you'll say a few words now, in the airport's press-centre? After that, we'll whisk you away to get some rest."

Lord, what shall I say? There hadn't been time to think about anything, and now I hear a multitude of voices: "Irina! I-ri-na!"

Cameras flash, microphones are pointed towards me . . .

". . . Ladies and gentlemen! Soon we shall all be celebrating Christmas in the warmth of our homes. But at the same time, the best people of our country will spend their Christmas in camps, prisons and punishment cells. They are prisoners of conscience: let us not forget about them . . ."

Do they understand, despite the fact that I have made every possible grammatical error? The light of projectors dazzles me, I can't make out any faces properly. Yet one should look people in the eye when talking to them. Do they understand me?

Yes, I believe they do.